THE COLDEST MARCH

YALE UNIVERSITY PRESS NEW HAVEN AND LONDON

THE
Coldest March

Scott's Fatal Antarctic Expedition

SUSAN SOLOMON

Pages ii–iii: E. A. Wilson, drawing of a sledging party.
Scott Polar Research Institute, Cambridge.

Designed by Rebecca Gibb. Set in Electra type by Tseng Information Systems, Inc.
Printed in the United States of America

Library of Congress Cataloging-in-Publication Data
Solomon, Susan, 1956–
The coldest march : Scott's fatal Antarctic expedition / Susan Solomon.
p. cm.
Includes bibliographical references (p.).
ISBN 0-300-08967-8 (cloth : alk. paper)
ISBN 978-0-300-09921-8 (pbk : alk. paper)
1. Scott, Robert Falcon, 1868–1912—Journeys—Antarctica.
2. British Antarctic ("Terra Nova") Expedition (1910–1913)
3. Antarctica—Discovery and exploration.   4. South Pole—
Discovery and exploration.   I. Title.
G850 1910 .S4 S65   2001
919.8′9—dc21
00-054996

A catalogue record for this book is available from the British Library.

The paper in this book meets the guidelines for permanence and
durability of the Committee on Production Guidelines for
Book Longevity of the Council on Library Resources.

10 9 8 7 6 5 4

No one in the world would have expected the temperatures and surfaces which we have encountered at this time of the year. . . . It is clear that these circumstances come on very suddenly, and our wreck is certainly due to this sudden advent of severe weather, which does not seem to have any satisfactory cause.

Robert Falcon Scott
Message to Public
March 1912

CONTENTS

MAPS

FIGURES

PREFACE

In November 1911, Captain Robert Falcon Scott led a British team across the snows of Antarctica, striving to be the first to attain the South Pole. After marching and skiing more than nine hundred miles, Scott and four companions reached their goal in January 1912, only to find that a group of five Norwegians headed by Roald Amundsen had been there almost a month earlier. The stuff of Antarctica's most tragic legend was born as Scott and his polar party all perished on their return journey over the Ross Ice Shelf.

Scott led not one but two expeditions to the Antarctic: one on board the ship *Discovery* in 1901–4 and the second on *Terra Nova* in 1910–12. In the years immediately following his fatal *Terra Nova* journey, Scott was revered as an icon of courage, determination, and sacrifice. Several British generations were taught the moving story of his struggle, and he became a pinnacle in a distinguished line of national polar heroes.[1] But as early as the 1920s, some critics began to raise doubts regarding the actions and even the character of Robert Falcon Scott. One of Scott's earliest detractors scorned the "complete absence of genius . . . in the transport arrangements," drawing sarcastic contrast between Amundsen's apparently effortless success with sled dogs and Scott's failure through reliance mainly on horses and human effort. Scott's leadership also became a target for derision, as did the expedition's planning and scientific goals.[2]

One best-selling book created a devastating portrait of Scott and his men not as stoic pioneers but as inept bumblers, and its well-acted serialization in film brought that story to television sets around the world.[3] Once such seeds were sown, Scott's mistakes grew to assume legendary proportions, radically transforming the figures of all of the men of Scott's fatal expedition from heroism and tragedy to folly and even farce. The contrasting views of Scott as remarkable hero and incompetent bungler now vie for the hearts and minds of those who study Antarctic history.[4]

But decades have passed since the most disparaging works were first published. Today's science has provided unforeseen insights into old questions, ranging from the structure of the human gene to the guilt of criminals and the physics of stars. Might modern science shed new light on Scott's fatal trek? I became intrigued by that question over a period of about fourteen years during which I made four trips to the Antarctic on another purpose — to study its ozone layer. I also studied the diaries, books, and papers of Scott and of the men who had been with him. I read them as a humanist and was moved by these remarkable people, in whom I found much to admire. I read them as a scientist and found pieces of the puzzle in the combination of their words with insights from today's science. In this book I have interlaced the men's own stories with contemporary scientific information to paint my view of their lives, their characters, and the reasons why some of them died.

Part of Scott's story inevitably revolves around the weather. The myth of the bumbling Scott casts him in the role of a whiner, a man who collapsed in the face of a normal and perhaps not even very terrible dose of Antarctic wind and frost. For most of the twentieth century, we knew very little about the weather along the remote route where Scott and his men walked. But in the early 1980s scientists positioned several reliable automated weather stations at sites near his path. The machines were placed there not to probe history but to further the science of meteorology and to improve aviation safety for flights to the research station in the heart of the continent at the South Pole. Those instruments now furnish the first detailed insight in seventy years into the weather conditions along Scott's via dolorosa, the 170°E meridian that reaches from the Pole back to Ross Island on the coast of east Antarctica.

The British are long since gone from the places that Scott's men explored. They largely live and work on the opposite side of the vast continent. Americans and New Zealanders are now the stewards of the sector of Antarctica that extends from Scott's base camps to the South Pole deep in the interior.

It is the colonials who are the contemporary caretakers of the historic huts, and it is the colonials who make the weather measurements that provide a new window into what happened to the men who once lived in them. I began peering in through that window with the unscientific preconception that Scott might have made his greatest error in misjudging the conditions of wind and temperature that he would be likely to encounter on the way back from the Pole. I imagined that he and his men might have met their end because they foolishly failed to consider the most basic parameter that dictates every aspect of life and death in the Antarctic: the weather.

But as I examined the data and studied the men's personal diaries, I realized that it was my view and not theirs that was narrow and foolish. I saw to my surprise that Scott and his team had analyzed the meteorology in exquisite detail, in a manner that can only inspire the greatest admiration by scientist and nonscientist alike. In this book, I will not only describe what the weather they met with was like, but I will also show how they painstakingly approached the critical question of what they ought to expect on the journey to the Pole and back. Their story has been told before and with great eloquence, but here I will add the key dimension of the towering challenge of the weather—one with which they insightfully grappled through each and every step of their sojourning. I will show that in the last month of their lives, nature dealt them a crushing blow in the form of conditions that can now be shown to be far colder than normal, and therefore radically different from those they quite sensibly expected to find. In simple terms, Scott and his men did everything right regarding the weather but were exceedingly unlucky. I will make the case that they were killed not primarily by human error but by this unfortunate and unpredictable turn of meteorological events.

In sifting through Scott's legend, I learned about other sciences that opened additional vistas into his life and fate. The disciplines of sea ice dynamics, nutrition, snow physics, materials science, and human physiology are each relevant to Scott's plight. As I discuss the journey of Scott's men, I will show that more than one myth of Scott as a bungler crumbles when examined with insights from these technical disciplines as they are understood today.

Some components of the legend of Scott's gaffes seem to me to stem from misunderstandings of Antarctic conditions. The unique environment of the coldest place on earth can approach that of another planet, and this otherworldly nature changes how some matters should be perceived. In each chapter of this book, the reader will be exposed to that environment through the eyes of a modern visitor to Antarctica. He is an Antarctic "everyman" who is intended to serve as a living guide to the sights, sounds, legends, and above all the ferocious weather of this singular place. The visitor's experiences and perceptions are not mine alone. He is an amalgam composed from many sources, stories, and conversations with Antarcticans. Nearly all of those friends and colleagues are male, and hence so is he. His experiences did not occur precisely as described in all cases, but each incident is a truthful depiction of modern Antarctic life and illustrates its contrasts and its similarities with the staggering struggles of the early explorers.

As I will show, Scott was a man of remarkable strengths and some stunning weaknesses. He did make some key blunders. And he documented many of his errors with surprising frankness. I seek balance in this book, and the honesty that I hope Scott himself would have wanted.

Regardless of history's ultimate verdict on Scott himself, I believe that the stories of Scott's remarkable companions deserve far better than the bleak place often accorded them alongside a legend of the leader's mistakes. A further goal of this book is therefore to paint a portrait of the members of this exceptional team as distinct from that of their leader.

A few points of explanation may help the reader to follow my depiction of the science, the men, and their captain. I have included five maps that illustrate where Scott's expeditions were based and where key treks of exploration were carried out. I have also presented a series of technical figures that relate mainly to meteorology, but have endeavored to incorporate their messages in the text for those disinclined to study such graphs. The data used to construct the meteorological graphs come from the Internet archive at the University of Wisconsin, Madison, and from volumes 1 and 3 of G. C. Simpson's pioneering treatise (see Selected Bibliography), except as noted. In most cases, daily minimum temperatures are provided as a measure of the men's greatest source of misery and to compare the sparse historical data (typically only three daily readings) with the nearly continuous measurements of the automated weather stations. A glossary is provided to explain terms specific to polar exploration. All of the temperatures are given in degrees Fahrenheit for consistency with the units employed by Scott and his men, but the glossary presents the formula for conversion from Celsius to Fahrenheit and includes a handy table that should allow readers to understand the cold in any units they prefer. All distances are given in statute miles, the unit of measure still common in Britain and the United States. Scott and his men employed both statute miles and geographical (or nautical) miles in their writings. (One geographic mile equals 1.15 statute miles.)

Fourteen men left Scott's *Terra Nova* hut on Ross Island bound for the South Pole in late October and early November 1911, driving dogs, ponies, and motor sledges. In this book, I will sketch key aspects of the personal accounts left by six of those explorers (Scott, Edward A. Wilson, Edward R. G. R. Evans, Henry R. Bowers, Apsley Cherry-Garrard, and William Lashly); three of these men turned back and lived while three others went on and perished. Published works will be referenced whenever possible, so that interested readers can probe the record for themselves. To read the words written by all six men is to become immersed not just in their accounts but also in their individual personae. Their human story contains great tragedy, but it also contains a richness and beauty that rivals that of the continent itself.

ACKNOWLEDGMENTS

M any people's assistance was invaluable to this book.
Foremost among those was Dr. Ryan Sanders, my late colleague
and friend, whose spirit lives on in part here among those whose composite
forms the modern visitor.

I am deeply grateful to Stephanie Bendel, Roger Clark, Diane Doe, Don
Stilson, and Joe White, who listened, constructively criticized, and bore with
me week after week in our writers' group. They contributed greatly to the
final product, as did generous colleagues Ted Scambos, Tom Lovejoy, and
Richard Somerville, who carefully and patiently critiqued the entire draft.

Scientific colleagues from many disciplines provided helpful discussions,
data, and suggestions on specific points: Bob Bindschadler, David Bromwich,
Kenneth Carpenter, Kenneth Carslaw, Sam Colbeck, Howard Cattle, Paul
Dalrymple, Jared Diamond, Igor Gamow, Guy Guthridge, Paul Harris, Matt
Lazzara, John Lynch, Bill Neff, Claire Parkinson, Kevin Trenberth, Steve
Warren, George Weidner, and Steve Wood. Memories of Sir G. C. Simpson
shared by colleague Sir John Mason were also very helpful. Special mention
goes to Charles Stearns, who has led the effort of decades that has resulted
in the Antarctic automated weather station data set and has selflessly made
that information available to all. It is one of the great pleasures of a scientific
life to interact with generous experts like these, and without them this book
would not have been possible.

Grateful thanks are due to Beth Sheid and Robert Holmes for contemporary photographs, and to Bill Neff for one map and David Bromwich for contributions to two of the scientific figures.

Expert drafting and wise advice on graphics provided by Maria Neary were invaluable to the production of the technical figures. Satellite data made publicly available on the Internet by the United States Geological Survey and by the National Oceanic and Atmospheric Administration's ocean modeling group are also appreciated, as are technical reports provided by the International Tin Research Institute on the chemical composition and properties of historic cans.

Personnel at the Scott Polar Research Institute helped greatly in providing photographs and access to the extensive archives and library in Cambridge. I am grateful to the director, Keith Richards, and to Robert Headland, William Mills, Shirley Sawtell, and Philippa Smith. I also appreciate similar assistance provided at the Alexander Turnbull Library, National Library of New Zealand, Te Puna Mātauranga o Aotearoa, Wellington, New Zealand, especially by Tim Lovell-Smith and Heather Mathie. Last but by no means least are the library and archives at the United Kingdom Meteorological Office in Bracknell, England, where Alan Heasman and Ian MacGregor were of indispensable and unique assistance.

I am very grateful to the families of the men of the Terra Nova expedition who generously shared their thoughts and memories, especially Dr. Jean Craig (daughter of G. C. Simpson). I also gratefully thank Arthur and Renate Simpson (son and daughter-in-law of G. C. Simpson), David Wilson (grandnephew of E. A. Wilson), and the Honorable Edward Broke Evans (son of E. R. G. R. Evans, later Lord Mountevans). The assistance, insights, and unflagging encouragement of my editor, Jean Thomson Black, were a major boost to this work. Helpful suggestions by Robert Baldock, Dan Heaton, and Manushag Powell of Yale University Press, along with expert design by Rebecca Gibb, are also appreciated.

My husband, Barry Sidwell, provided many insightful comments and suggestions. He expertly set up our home for Internet and networking, and he tolerated innumerable hours when I wasn't in Antarctica but might as well have been.

All errors, oversights, and other shortcomings remain my own.

THE COLDEST MARCH

The Hut at the Bottom of the World

The wood has been sanded to a smooth finish by the relentless blizzards that have pounded against the hut for nearly a century. In the uncommonly dry air the planks have remained firm, and the styling looks strangely contemporary. If not for the surreal desolation of the frozen landscape that surrounds it, this curious structure could be today's vacation retreat. Indeed, it once was a place of sanctuary—a shelter against the brutal cold of the continent at the bottom of the world. But some of the men who struggled against all odds to reach it, forcing themselves to march through raging storms and chilling temperatures, fell just short of its broad verandah. The warmth of life ebbed out of them a scant hundred and sixty miles away in March 1912 as they perished on the ice after completing the remarkable feat of walking more than nine hundred miles from 77°48'S to the South Pole and nearly all the way back. They reached the Pole on January 17, 1912, hoping to be its first visitors. But they arrived only to find that others had been there just a month before.

The hut's fine woods can be traced to its origins in Australia. The building is roughly square, with each face thirty-six feet in length. It was brought here in 1902 but was used little during Scott's first *Discovery* expedition. Captain Scott returned here in 1910 on board *Terra Nova* to begin his struggle to reach the Pole, and the old hut served the men of his second expedition well and frequently during 1911 and 1912.

The hut sits at the end of a small spit of volcanic land. To the west lies

Figure 1. The *Discovery* hut, McMurdo Sound. Painting by E. A. Wilson, April 7, 1911. Scott Polar Research Institute, Cambridge.

the border of the majestic Transantarctic mountain range. The foot of the spit spills into the ocean but is seldom lapped by waves. The Sound is usually white rather than blue, frozen hard and unyielding.

For many decades the hut stood alone in this remotest corner of the world, but today it is dwarfed by dozens of modern and much less graceful buildings. Around it lies the largest contemporary research station in Antarctica—McMurdo, the hub of America's scientific enterprise on the ice. Only three miles away lies the New Zealand station, Scott Base. In the height of Antarctic summer, about a thousand people live in the comfortable dormitories nearby, and even in winter this desolate landscape is now populated by more than one hundred souls.

The visitor enters the hut on a Sunday. The structure and contents have been carefully restored and maintained as an informal museum, a place where the calendar has remained frozen at 1912. Under the vaulted ceiling, stacks of food and supplies stand in neat rows, as they have for many decades. Heavy wooden skis still lean in the corner, and an overwhelming array of canned and bottled foodstuffs lines every wall. The wind rattles the windowpanes, and its reach is bitter on the exposed flesh of a human face. It feels as if the inhabitants have been gone only a few minutes, as if the door could open at any moment to admit a ghostly troupe of Victorian explorers—Scott, Wilson, Bowers. If they returned now, these three Britons would surely be heartsick to learn that they are no longer emblems of tragic heroism but targets of widespread ridicule. Scott in particular is viewed by many who know of Antarctic legends as ineffective, amateurish, and bumbling. It is enough to make a proud man walk out to his death in the snow, and there are those who say that that is exactly what he did in order to avoid facing the world after his failure to reach the Pole first.

As the visitor leaves, he notices a mummified seal carcass on the verandah near the door. All contemporary residents of this land have heard enough of the legend of Scott the bumbler to believe that the men who marched to the Pole surely died of scurvy on the way back, in part because as proper Victorians they spurned the fresh seal meat that would have

Figure 2. The *Discovery* hut, January 2000. Buildings of McMurdo Station, the operational hub of the United States Antarctic Program, are in the background, including the group of four large dormitories where many visitors sleep. Photograph by Beth Sheid.

helped to avoid the dreaded disease. The visitor pauses for a moment, puzzling over the seal and wondering why it was placed there if not to be eaten. Then he shrugs and tells himself that this meat must have been intended as dog food. He locks up the hut, pulls on his hood, leather gloves, and goggles, and walks out into the force of the cold wind, secure in the knowledge that he is a smarter, more careful visitor to this land than those sadly misguided Englishmen.

ONE

Into the Pack

The visitor approaches Antarctica from the air, in the relative comfort of a plane that soars over the shifting ice pack. Viewed from above, the pack is a complex network of interlocking puzzle pieces. A glimpse of a roving pod of killer whales helps to put the size and the danger of the huge blocks of drifting ice in perspective. Most of the pieces are flat and tabular, but here and there the molded contours of immense hilly bergs thrust up from the surface. Nearly a century has passed since Scott and his men sailed south in their tiny wooden ships, the *Discovery* and the *Terra Nova*, inching their way along the leads of dark water that snake through the treacherous maze of the pack.

In summer, Antarctica is a monochromatic world dominated by white ice and black sea. As the plane reaches the continent, the pack is replaced by pristine slopes of high white mountain peaks, and the wind-whipped snow streams off their summits in curving waves. There are no signs of civilization on the landscape, no trees or settlements. The land below is far from the few small stations that dot the continent today. The mountains slowly give way to vast snow fields, smooth rivers of white that remind the visitor of the plight of the men who were the first to trudge along this barren land. They were utterly alone, lacking even radio contact with the living world beyond the ice. Radio had just been invented, and decades would pass before equipment powerful enough to reach civilization would be deployed on a polar expedition. As the explorers walked along an endless plain of snow, the wind enigmatically covered their tracks, leaving the surface as pristine as it had been for millennia and abandoning them to the struggle of finding their way back. The force of the wind sometimes produced sastrugi, wind-blown snow sculptures perhaps a foot in height. But these were only annoyances to the marchers. The real hazards were found where the flowing snow encountered the obstacles of land. There the pressure ridges reared up to form huge escarpments of snow and ice, while underneath lay the blue crevasses that stretch hundreds of feet down, deep into the cold heart of the continent.

As the airplane turns, Ross Island looms up out of the frigid landscape, a free-form statue in ice with three distinct lobes formed by the contours of its shores. Mounts Erebus and Terror jut up above the frozen sea. The glaciers that flow down from their summits render much of the island a maze of crevasses. The research station lies on its western side, across the sheltered Sound from the coast. As the plane circles before landing, the visitor may catch a glimpse of the graceful arc of ice that delineates the Barrier, a formidable shelf of ice and snow that begins just beyond the island and extends far beyond the southern horizon. The Ross Sea forms a vast bay underneath the Barrier, more than a hundred feet beneath the snow surface. The Barrier and the great Beardmore glacier beyond it are a highway to the Pole in the distant south.

For centuries, men wondered whether there might be a great southern land beyond the known coasts of South America and New Zealand. Among the first to sail those waters, pushing his ship deep into the pack in 1841, was Sir James Ross, who "observed that great wall of ice which he named the Great Barrier. At the eastern end of this wall he achieved his highest latitude, 78°11′S., an advance of nearly four degrees on his predecessor." [1]

The Barrier's imposing face is a sheer cliff of snow, reaching nearly two hundred feet in height over much of its vast length of four hundred miles. Today it is no longer the challenge it once was, and it now bears its discoverer's name (Ross Ice Shelf; see map 1). Beneath lies the sea that Ross and other early sailors conquered, but the Barrier stopped them at the bor-

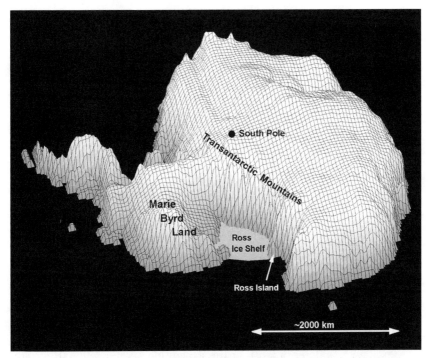

Map 1. Representation of Antarctica and its topography. The vertical scale has been exaggerated to illustrate the steep grades that lead to the interior of the continent. Computer-generated image courtesy of Dr. William Neff.

der to Antarctica's interior. Several expeditions followed Ross to Antarctic waters, prompted in part by the potential for commercial whaling and sealing.[2] Toward the end of the nineteenth century, both poles became a focus of attention in science and exploration—for they were the last remaining untouched corners of the planet. The sea discovered by Ross drew his countrymen back to its icy waters several times in the first few decades of the twentieth century, as the British competed with other nations for priority in Antarctic discovery.

In 1893 the president of the Royal Geographical Society, Sir Clements Markham, resolved to organize a British expedition to probe the virtually unknown land beyond the Great Barrier. Such an undertaking required a large capital investment, and Markham led a multiyear effort to secure the necessary funds. A single private gift of the then-staggering sum of £25,000 was among the donations collected. This brought the total close to £92,000, equivalent to more than three million dollars today.[3] About £44,000 were expended for the design and purchase of a new ship, the *Discovery*, which would bear the expedition to Antarctica's shore.[4]

Robert Falcon Scott was born near Plymouth in 1868, the eldest son among four sisters and two brothers whose father had owned and sold a small brewery. "Con" followed the traditions of his family in pursuing a military career. His father had been the youngest of five brothers and the only son who led a wholly civilian life.[5]

Scott was a midshipman when he first met Markham, who was visiting a cousin who happened to be the commodore of the training squadron in which young Scott served in 1887. Twelve years later Scott was a first lieutenant on leave in London. He wrote of a day when he walked down Buckingham Palace Road and "espied Sir Clements on the opposite pavement, and naturally crossed, and as naturally turned and accompanied him to his house." Through this chance encounter, Scott said that he "learned for the first time that there was such a thing as a prospective Antarctic expedition; two days later [he] wrote applying to command it."[6]

Markham was determined that the expedition should follow the traditional mode that characterized British exploration in the nineteenth century, namely, "to afford opportunities for young naval officers to acquire valuable experiences and to perform deeds of derring doe." Markham sought a very particular sort of man to command the endeavor that he had brought to fruition, writing that "the fatal mistake, in selecting Commanders for former polar expeditions, has been to seek for experience instead of youth. Both cannot be united, and youth is absolutely essential. Elderly men are not accessible to new ideas, and have not the energy and capacity necessary to meet emergencies. . . . The inexperience and haste in decision of young leaders are disadvantages which sometimes accompany their youthful energy, but they alone have the qualities which ensure success. . . . New ideas, novel situations meet with cordial welcome when young men are at the helm." Along with youth and inexperience, Markham wanted a leader with a "scientific turn of mind," for he was resolved that exploration, particularly polar exploration, must embrace dual goals of geographic and technical discovery.[7]

Scott was appointed leader of the expedition in June 1900 and took extended leave from his naval obligations (then at the rank of commander) for the purpose. He was acutely aware that he amply met Markham's criteria of youth and inexperience, writing frankly that "I may as well confess at once that I had no predilection for Polar exploration."[8]

Thus began Scott's journey to the coldest place on Earth. Scott's writings frequently reflect relentless doubts of his own abilities to meet the challenges of the task before him, along with a high regard and appreciation for the men who served under him. On the *Discovery* expedition, he chose two sailors to accompany him on a historic trek past the mountains west of Ross Island onto the high plateau, seamen "Taff" Evans and William Lashly, both of whom later played major roles in Scott's last expedition. He described those men in his account of November 22, 1903: "I have little wonder when I remember the splendid qualities and physique of the two men who remained with me. . . . Evans was a man of Herculean strength. . . . He had been a gymnastic instructor in the Navy, and had always been an easy winner in all our sports which involved tests of strength. . . . Lashly . . . had one of the largest chest measurements in the ship. He had been a teetotaller and non-smoker all his life, and was never in anything but the hardest condition." Following this praise of his companions, Scott not only expressed concern about his own merits but wondered whether he deserved an equal share of the food: "My own weight . . . fell so far short of the others that I felt I really did not deserve such a large food allowance, though I continued to take my full share." Scott was clearly not a confident officer who met the tasks of command with assurance, even admitting, "I had set my mind on obtaining a naval crew. I felt sure that their sense of discipline would be an immense acquisition, and I had grave doubts as to my own ability to deal with any other class of men."[9]

Apsley Cherry-Garrard, at age 24 one of the youngest members of Scott's fatal *Terra Nova* expedition, described his leader as a man of extraordinary personal charm: "an attractive personality, with strong likes and dislikes, he excelled in making his followers his friends by a few words of sympathy or praise: I have never known anybody, man or woman, who could be so attractive when he chose."[10]

A window into Scott's personality and style of human interactions is furnished in turn by his enthusiastic description of Cherry-Garrard: "Cherry-

Garrard has won all hearts; he shows himself ready for any sort of hard work and is always to the front when the toughest jobs are on hand. He is the most unselfish, kind-hearted fellow, and will be of the greatest use to the expedition."[11]

Scott was admired by many of his men not only for his personal charm but also for his physical stamina in the daily toil of marching and skiing across the Antarctic (referred to as sledging, after the wooden sledge, a sled on which supplies were carried; see glossary). Cherry-Garrard, for example, wrote that "sledging he went harder than any man of whom I have ever heard."[12]

Scott's account of his *Discovery* expedition hints at the problems the inexperienced commander was to face in his polar travels and in subsequent analysis of those voyages by a curious world. He is often remarkably honest about damning events that bear on his leadership, as in his description of preparations for the departure of an exploratory party on March 4, 1902: "I am bound to confess that the sledges when packed presented an appearance of which we should afterwards have been wholly ashamed, and much the same might be said of the clothing worn by the sledgers. But at this time our ignorance was deplorable; we did not know how much or in what proportions would be required as regards the food, how to use our cookers, how to put up our tents, or even how to put on our clothes. Not a single article of the outfit had been tested, and amid the general ignorance that prevailed the lack of system was painfully apparent in everything."[13] More surprising than the problems encountered is Scott's frank description of them in a document meant for public consumption. The writings reveal an honest and complex man, a leader who dwelled relatively little on precautions and much on testing as he went along.

Scott devoted the year from June 1900 to June 1901 to a frenzy of preparation for a three-year polar absence, noting that "few people can realize what an extraordinary variety of articles is required on such an expedition as ours, where a ship and its crew are to be banished from all sources of supply for a lengthened period." The firm of Colman's donated nine tons of flour and a quantity of mustard, Cadbury gave 3,500 pounds of cocoa and chocolate, and Burberry contributed windproof clothing.[14]

In October 1900 Scott took pleasure and guidance from meeting the great

Norwegian explorer Fridtjof Nansen, who was a leading figure in the race to conquer the high Arctic. He did not reach the Pole but set a farthest-north record by sledging to near 86° in April of 1894.[15] Scott and Sir Clements Markham traveled together to Norway and "gathered a great many practical suggestions from Dr. Nansen." From Norway they went to Berlin to meet the leader of a planned German expedition. In both encounters Scott felt that he was "met with the greatest kindness and consideration," and he apparently enjoyed becoming part of the small, elite corps of international polar explorers.[16]

On June 3, 1901, *Discovery* was brought from Dundee to the London Docks Company, and on the last day of July 1901 the ship wended its way down the Thames to begin its southern voyage. The wooden vessel was of the "old English whaler type, designed to sail the high seas and push forcefully through the looser ice-packs."[17] *Discovery* had two coal-fired boilers that delivered about five hundred horsepower to assist in pushing through the pack in calm winds. The bow was reinforced by "a network of solid oak stiffeners [of] a strength which almost amounted to solidity . . . cunningly scarfed to provide the equivalent of a solid block." The crew's average age was twenty-five, and the ladies of New Zealand jokingly dubbed the young men in their oak ship the "babes in the wood."[18]

The strength of the bow allowed *Discovery* not only to push aside the ice pack but also to do modest penetrations, even though the ship was not an icebreaker (fig. 3). Scott wrote:

Many a time on charging a large ice-floe the stem of the ship glided upwards until the bows were raised two or three feet, then the weight of the ship acting downwards would crack the floe beneath . . . and the ship would gradually forge ahead to meet the next obstruction. This is the principle on which the ice is broken by all . . . ice-breakers. . . . I have often been asked why . . . ice-breakers are not employed for such expeditions as ours. It is because the ice-breaker is built of steel, and except when breaking very thin ice, is in constant need of repair; nothing but a wooden structure has the elasticity and strength to grapple with thick Polar ice without injury.[19]

Figure 3. *Discovery* finds a way through the pack ice. Painting by E. A. Wilson. Scott Polar Research Institute, Cambridge.

The destination of the expedition was the sea discovered by Ross, for here "it was certain that a high latitude could be reached, and that the work of the expedition could be conducted in the heart of the Antarctic area. Geography saw in this region a prospect of the reproduction of those sledging journeys which had done so much to complete the mapping of the Far North; meteorology grasped at a high latitude for the fixed observation of climatic conditions; magnetism found in the Ross Sea that area which most nearly approached the magnetic pole; geology was attracted by the unknown mountainous country which fringed its shores."[20] In this and many other passages in his writings, Scott reveals an abiding interest in both exploration and science. Cherry-Garrard noted that "Scott, no specialist in any one branch, had a most genuine love of science. . . . He showed not only a mind which was receptive and keen to learn, but a knowledge which was quick to offer valuable suggestions. . . . In pure and applied science, it is doubtful whether this side of an expedition in high northern or southern latitudes has ever been more fortunate in their leader."[21] Dr. George "Sunny Jim" Simpson, the meteorologist of the *Terra Nova* expedition, echoed this view in describing Scott as a man whose "interest in every scientific problem with which the expedition was concerned was intense and I do not think that I have ever met a man who had the true scientific spirit so utterly unalloyed."[22] Science was one of Scott's greatest strengths, and he won the high intellectual respect of the technical experts under his command.

As *Discovery* sailed south, Scott remarked on the beauty of the samples of sea creatures revealed in the microscope, noted the changing character of the vast southern ocean's phytoplankton, and eagerly anticipated an end to the pack ice.[23] *Discovery* traversed the pack in less than a week, entering the shifting ice on January 5, 1902, and reaching open water to the south on January 11.[24] Scott's diary entry of January 21 provides a sense of the utterly unknown world that the ship probed:

> We had a rather curious and exciting adventure. Owing to some inexplicable wounds found on the bodies of seals, it had been suggested that a land mammal might exist in these regions, though hitherto unseen by man. Most of us were incredulous of this theory, but on that

night we suddenly came on a floe covered with soft snow which bore
the impress of footprints wide apart and bearing every appearance
of having been made by a large land animal. The excitement was
great and observers with cameras were soon over the side and breath-
lessly examining this strange spoor; but alas! it was soon detected that
the impress was that of a webbed foot, and gradually we came to the
conclusion that the footprints were those of a large giant petrel, and
that their distance apart was due to the fact that they had been made
when the bird, half-flying and half-walking, had been lazily rising on
the wing.[25]

As the ship cruised along the edge of the Great Barrier, Scott gained the
first inklings of the staggering challenge that its climate would pose to his attempts to explore it. He noticed that "during the night the wind came off the
barrier, and the temperature fell to 10°; shortly after, it again came from the
sea and the temperature rose to 25°. . . . We began to wonder what that great

Figure 4. Water-worn caves in the face of the Great Ice Barrier, latitude 78°18′S, longitude
177°04′E. Drawing by E. A. Wilson, January 24, 1902. Scott Polar Research Institute,
Cambridge.

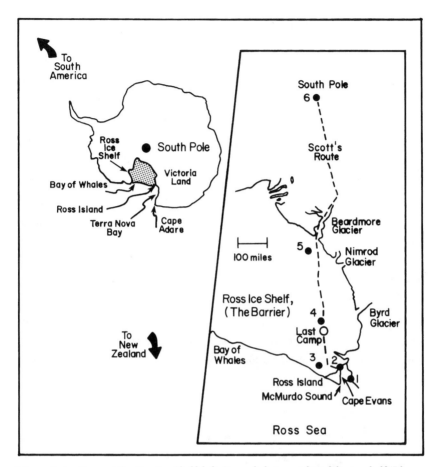

Map 2. Antarctica and the Ross Ice Shelf, left. Expanded view, right, of the ice shelf ("the Barrier"), showing Ross Island, Scott's route for his 1911–12 trek, and the contemporary weather stations that now lie along his path. (Station 2 is a manned system at New Zealand's Scott Base research station, while the other stations are automated). Note that the detail map is oriented with south at top.

snow plain would be like in winter if it produced this great fall in the warmer summer air."[26] With this expression of scientific curiosity, Scott began to ponder the question that would define the last stages of a battle for his life about a decade later (see map 2).

On January 30 the *Discovery* crew sailed past the Bay of Whales to find solid ground to the east. They were able to identify rock patches, and they called the new territory Edward VII Land after the king. On February 4 Scott personally took in the first airborne view of the Antarctic in a pioneering hydrogen-filled-balloon ascent over this just-discovered land (fig. 5). After the fact it was revealed that "had anyone used the valve . . . it would not have closed properly and nothing could have prevented the whole show from dropping to earth like a stone."[27]

After this risky interlude of exploration and technical experiment, Scott changed course for Victoria Land on the western side of the Barrier. By February 8 the ship had sailed into McMurdo Sound west of Ross Island, and "as we eagerly scanned the coast of the mainland our hopes rose high that we should find some sheltered nook in this far south region in which the *Discovery* might safely brave the rigours of the coming winter and remain securely embedded whilst our sledge-parties, already beyond the limits of the known, strove to solve the mysteries of the vast new world which would then lie on every side."[28]

The Australian-made hut was erected on the shore of Ross Island in the beginning of February 1902 as a shelter for sledging parties. The spit of land on which it rested became known as Hut Point Peninsula (map 3). The original expedition plan called for *Discovery* to turn north before winter began,

Figure 5. The launch of a hydrogen-filled balloon over Antarctica in 1902. Photographer unknown. Number 70370, Alexander Turnbull Library, Wellington, New Zealand.

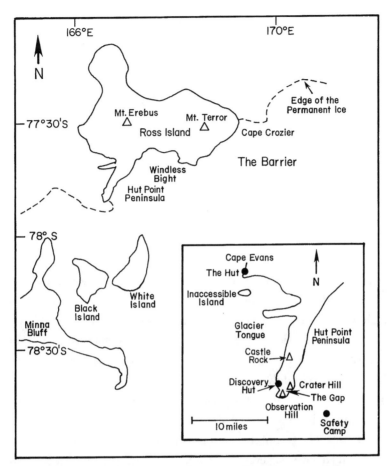

166°E 170°E

N

Edge of the
Permanent Ice

—77°30'S

Mt. Erebus
Mt. Terror
Ross Island

Cape Crozier

The Barrier

Windless
Bight

Hut Point
Peninsula

— 78° S

Cape Evans

The Hut

N

White
Island

Inaccessible
Island

Black
Island

Glacier
Tongue

Hut Point
Peninsula

Minna
Bluff

Castle
Rock

—78°30'S

Discovery
Hut

Crater Hill
The Gap

Observation
Hill

10 miles

Safety
Camp

Map 3. Ross Island and its environs as they were in the early 1900s, with an expanded view of Hut Point Peninsula in the inset. Note the location of the *Discovery* hut near the tip of the peninsula. The United States' McMurdo Station now surrounds the *Discovery* hut (see fig. 2), and New Zealand's Scott Base is through the gap on the edge of the Barrier.

but Scott decided to allow the ship to freeze in so that the crew could live on board the vessel for the duration of the expedition, confident that at McMurdo Sound he had found a safe and sheltered harbor.[29] This proved correct, and *Discovery* remained frozen in the embrace of the thick ice of the Sound just off Hut Point Peninsula for the next two years.

Of Dogs and Men

Antarctic weather has many faces. The first-time visitor who arrives at McMurdo in late winter enters a frigid world shaded in twilight even at high noon. When the plane lands and the door swings open, the icy air hits his cheek like a slap. The temperature at this coastal site often plunges to minus forty degrees Fahrenheit, occasionally as low as minus sixty. The visitor notices how oddly rigid his blue jeans become in this cold—even the smallest amount of perspiration freezes hard within the fibers of clothing that crackles as he moves. Cold air tears at his lungs, and his nose becomes curiously stiff. The bite of the wind is painful, and the visitor quickly learns the necessity of covering every inch of his skin before opening a door. But after only a few weeks he starts to get used to conditions he once would have considered unbearable. The warmer days begin to feel strangely comfortable, and when the temperature reaches $-10\,°F$, he feels as if a heat wave had begun.

As the season advances, the veil of darkness is slowly lifted. One day the red orb of the sun emerges, just above the frozen sea. He will always remember the moment when the sun returned, because he missed it keenly in the days of unending gray and black. Within a few short weeks, the sun's rays transform both the weather and the colors of his world. The frozen sea brightens to vibrant blue and white, and the surrounding landscape becomes a dazzling vista of majestic snow-covered peaks. Mirages shimmer on McMurdo Sound. As the visitor looks out across the icy surface of the frozen water, for an instant he sees the ghostly form of a sailing ship. But then he turns his head slightly, and the sails disappear.

McMurdo begins to feel like part of planet Earth again when summer arrives, and the inhabitants no longer dress as if they were living in the cold of deep space. By midsummer the temperatures at sea level soar to plus twenty or more in the basking warmth of continuous sunshine, and the visitor dons shorts in the traditional display of the hardiness of Antarctic veterans. His bare legs are exposed only for a few minutes as he walks around the station. If he gets cold, it's easy enough to run inside a nearby building. But he's still proud of his toughness, and he struts like a peacock for a moment or two.

It is only on the stark plateau near 10,000 feet elevation in the interior of the continent that Antarctic weather takes on its most hostile form, with daily temperatures often dipping below −20°F even in summer.

Shortly after their arrival at McMurdo Sound, the men of *Discovery* began to explore the frozen world around the ship (fig. 6). A preliminary sledging trip to White Island brought back the news that local travel was a challenge: "They had crossed ridges and hummocks and crevasses. . . . Our travellers shook their heads over the bright prospect of a smooth highway, in visions of which many had indulged up to this time." For the rest of February and into early March, the men set up huts for meteorological and magnetic observations, practiced skiing, sent out another small exploratory sledging party, and even used a windmill to generate electric light on board ship.[1]

On March 11, 1902, tragedy struck. A sledging party encountered a blizzard while returning to the ship. Blizzards in the dry climate at the bottom of the world are seldom associated with the fall of new wet snow as they are in most other locations. An Antarctic blizzard is a period of strong winds sufficient to whip existing snow up off the surface and change the landscape to a formless wall of swirling white powder—a world in which it would be difficult if not impossible to find one's way. Instead of waiting out the storm in their tents, the inexperienced group decided to attempt to reach the vessel. Scott's remarks show a surprising lack of preparation for this contingency:

Figure 6. *Discovery* frozen into the ice at the edge of McMurdo Sound. Photographer unknown. Number 132528, Alexander Turnbull Library, Wellington, New Zealand.

"It was impossible for us to have known fully the serious nature of such an act and the utter confusion which must ensue. It was an experience which had to be bought."[2] For one man, the experience was obtained at the highest possible price.

The sledgers attempted to find their way through the blinding, windblown drift along a steep, snow-covered surface. Several men wore soft fur boots that provided no traction underfoot. Scott's account of the incident conveys the helplessness of the group to prevent the tragedy:

> As they proceeded they found the slope growing steeper and the dif-
> ficulty of foothold increased, especially for Vince, who was wearing
> fur boots. . . . Their leader suddenly saw the precipice beneath his
> feet, and far below, through the wreathing snow, the sea. Another
> step would have taken him over the edge; he sprang back with a cry
> of warning, and those behind him, hearing it, dug their heels instinc-
> tively into the slippery surface, and with one exception all succeeded
> in stopping. . . . Before his horror-stricken companions had time to
> think, poor Vince, unable to check himself with his soft fur boots had
> shot from amongst them, flashed past the leader, and disappeared.[3]

A cross was erected within sight of the hut, in memory of seaman George T. Vince. It still stands there, in honor of the first man to die in the Antarctic under Scott's command.

As the *Discovery* crew explored the region around them, they began to observe key aspects of the local meteorology. Scott wrote: "We realised for the first time what a difference there might be in the weather conditions of places within easy reach of the ship. It was not only in the matter of temperatures . . . but also in the force and direction of the wind."[4] It was already becoming clear that the regions they hoped to explore would display widely varying weather, and that experience would be needed to forecast what might be found on any journey.

As the men practiced sledging and took their first tentative steps at exploration, they found the dogs to be a special challenge. Scott described the struggle to handle their animals in March of 1902: "The dogs entirely refused to work. . . . The best of them only exerted a pull of about 50 lbs, and this with very dispirited and downcast mien; the rest hung disconsolately back on the traces and had to be half led, half dragged over the frozen surface."[5] Roald Amundsen encountered similar problems with his canines on arrival in Antarctica in 1911. Amundsen wrote: "The dogs had spent half a year in lying about and eating and drinking (on the ship) and had got the impression that they would never have anything else to do. . . . When at last we succeeded, with another dose of the whip, in making them understand that we really asked them to work, instead of doing as they were told they flew at each other in a furious scrimmage."[6]

But Scott's difficulties went deeper than a temporary loss of canine work habits. Part of the problem was attempting to employ both men and dogs pulling together on the same sledge, a strategy never used by Inuit or Siberian trainers. A more serious difficulty was the animals' diet, for as time went on Scott learned that the dried fish brought as dog food caused illness. Scott wrote: "I had intended to take ordinary dog-biscuits for our animals, but in an evil moment I was persuaded by one who had had great experience in dog-driving to take fish. Fish has been used continually in the north for feeding dogs, and the particular article which we ordered was the Norwegian stock-fish such as is split, dried and exported from that country in great quantities. . . . It was this very fish that poisoned our poor animals. . . . On looking back now one sees the great probability of its suffering deterioration on passage through the Tropics."[7] Other Antarctic explorers brought dried fish across the equator for dog food without problems, so Scott's difficulties must have involved more than the climate alone. Scott's negative experiences with dogs on his *Discovery* expedition surely influenced his later decision to make limited use of them on his 1911–12 attempt to reach the Pole, a choice that would dominate his legacy as a polar explorer.

Scott realized that a group of men who intend to drive dogs to their limit and kill and eat them in the process "is invested with a capacity for work which is beyond the emulation of a party of men."[8] Roald Amundsen's rival expedition used dogs for food and for their service in exactly this manner in 1911. Amundsen wrote that "no butcher's shop could have exhibited a finer sight than we showed after flaying and cutting up ten dogs. Great masses of beautiful fresh, red meat. . . . The delicate little cutlets had an absolutely hypnotizing effect."[9] But Scott felt that "this method of using dogs is one which can only be adopted with reluctance. One cannot calmly contemplate the murder of animals which possess such intelligence and individuality . . . and which very possibly one has learnt to regard as friends and companions. On the other hand, it may be pointed out with good reason that to forego the great objects which may be achieved by the sacrifice of dog-life is carrying sentiment to undue length." While recognizing the value of dogs and frankly admitting to his own sentimentality, Scott's final verdict on the use of dogs goes beyond the practical and the sentimental to reveal a highly romantic view of exploration: "In my mind no journey ever made with dogs can approach the height of that fine conception which is realised when a party of men go forth to face hardships, dangers, and difficulties with their own unaided efforts, and by days and weeks of hard physical labour succeed in solving some problem of the great unknown. Surely in this case the conquest is more nobly and splendidly won."[10]

For centuries, polar explorers used wooden sledges to carry food, tents, fuel, and clothing. Much of the time, Scott and his men resorted to "manhauling," in which they placed themselves in harness and pulled the sledges behind them, becoming their own draft animals. They frequently drew two hundred pounds per man.

The exertion of the march and the quality of their Burberry windproof clothing kept the men warm while man-hauling even in the coldest conditions, but speed was of the essence when making camp, in order to gain shelter before the chill became unbearable. Rapid preparation of warm food was also vital, as was removal of footwear and clothing that had become wet with perspiration on the march. Extreme care had to be taken in the placement of any wet articles, particularly boots, which were bound to freeze within a few minutes and which must not be allowed to solidify into a form that would make them difficult to put on again later. The method used to put on a frozen boot was simply to warm it slowly with one's foot, taking care to balance the unfreezing of the article with avoiding frostbite of the human appendage. Fuel could not be spared to generate the needed warmth; it had to be supplied by flesh alone. Repeatedly the sledger had to worm his cold feet into his boots, extract a foot and warm it with his hands when the cold became intolerable, then return the poor foot to its chilling task of penetrating the reluctant boot. The process could take hours, and it became a torture for those who were already suffering from frostbite. Scott described the putting on of frozen fur boots as "a matter of excruciating agony." Similarly painful procedures applied to clothing, to the man-hauling harnesses, and particularly to the sleeping bags, which retained the perspiration and breath vapor of their occupants with stunning efficiency. Most men found the outside air much too cold to breathe at night, so they were forced to sleep with their sleeping bags closed. With every breath they added to the armor plate that made the fur bags a place of agony rather than respite.[11] As one man put it, "a crack left open, or a hole in the skin, lets in cold air like a knife and is enough to keep one awake all night long, forming a cake of ice round the aperture inside the bag."[12]

Cherry-Garrard described a process in which "we got into some strange knots when trying to persuade our limbs into our bags, and suffered terribly from cramp in consequence. . . . First thing on getting out of the sleeping-bags in the morning we stuffed our personal gear into the mouth of the bag before it could freeze: this made a plug which when removed formed a frozen hole for us to push into as a start in the evening."[13] Although it may be difficult to imagine the pain involved in this process, some perspective is gained by noting that Cherry-Garrard's sleeping bag weighed eighteen pounds at the start of a six-week winter journey but forty-five pounds at its end. The added weight was solid ice. Scott summarized the frigid discomfort that robbed the men of their rest: "If refreshing sleep comes at all on a spring sledge journey, it will be in the early morning hours, when the sleeping-bag has thawed down on its occupants."[14] Thus the explorers often started the morning with frozen feet, man-hauled two hundred pounds on the march for eight to twelve hours, and lay that night in an icy pool of sleepless misery.

Only the men's boots and sleeping bags were made of animal skins, for fur clothing would have accumulated even more of the dreaded ice during man-hauling than did the men's windproof cloth outfits. Contemporary studies demonstrate that comfort for those engaged in heavy work under cold conditions depends critically upon preventing sweat from accumulating close to the skin.[15] One modern explorer who man-hauled in Antarctica in 1993 (Ranulph Fiennes) relied upon fabric clothing like that available at the turn of the century. He noted that such material was the only workable choice at the time because the extreme effort of man-hauling led to heavy sweating even at −40°F, requiring the use of a breathable fabric rather than fur.[16]

The primary foods on sledging journeys were pemmican (a mixture of lard and dried beef), biscuit (similar to hardtack), tea or cocoa, sugar, and sometimes frozen seal meat. The warmth of the food and drink was "a moment to be lived for—one of the brief incidents of the day to which we can look forward with real pleasure. The hot food seems to give new life, its grateful warmth appears to run out to every limb, exhaustion vanishes, and gradually that demon within which has gripped so tightly for the past hour or two, is appeased."[17]

Experiments in sledging revealed a number of other lessons, some of which would return to haunt Scott in later years. A particularly significant finding concerned the cans that contained paraffin, the life-giving oil used to cook food and melt water: "The oil was carried in small rectangular tins. . . . Each tin had a small cork bung, which was a decided weakness; paraffin creeps in the most annoying manner, and a good deal of oil was wasted in this way. . . . It was impossible to make these bungs quite tight, however closely they were jammed down, so that in spite of a trifling extra weight a much better fitting would have been a metallic screwed bung. To find on opening a fresh tin of oil that it was only three-parts full was very distressing, and of course meant that the cooker had to be used with still greater care."[18]

It would not be his last experience with this problem. On March 2, 1912, a few weeks before his death, Scott reported grimly that on reaching his supply cache, "We found a shortage of oil; with most rigid economy it can scarce carry us to the next depot."[19]

In September 1902 Scott's men had their first encounter with a formidable enemy that is frequently credited with their death. When his second-in-command returned from a sledging journey, he and the two expedition doctors reported an outbreak of scurvy in the crew.[20] Today we understand scurvy to be a vitamin C deficiency that is readily avoided by eating fresh foods, but at the turn of the century conflicting theories abounded for its cause and prevention. Vitamins had not yet been discovered, and even the great Norwegian explorer Fridtjof Nansen was reported to have argued that the origin of the ailment lay in tainted tinned foods—for example, as a result of improper canning.[21] Several previous polar expeditions had ended in painful death because of this fearsome disease, and the use of lime juice as a preventative had fallen into disrepute in the latter half of the nineteenth century as a result of a series of deaths on British Navy expeditions. Like others of his time, Scott couldn't be sure of the precise cause of scurvy.

Dr. Edward Adrian Wilson was junior surgeon with the 1902 expedition. "Bill" Wilson was born of Quaker stock in Cheltenham in 1872, the second son of a medical practitioner. He followed in his father's footsteps, becoming qualified as a medical doctor. But he was also a talented artist and keenly interested in the natural sciences, particularly ornithology. Wilson's love of nature and science reflected his deep devotion to God and religion, and his art served as its expression: "My little bird-pictures are just visible proofs of my love for them, and attempts to praise God and bring others to love him through his works." Wilson considered becoming a missionary, but was persuaded by his parents to first obtain his medical credentials; shortly thereafter he joined the *Discovery* expedition. He had contracted tuberculosis while working in the impoverished areas of London on his medical training, and he had scarcely recovered from the disease by the time he applied to join the voyage.[22]

Wilson began the habit of keeping a personal journal in his teenage years, a daily regimen that he would maintain until February 27, 1912, a few weeks before his death on the Barrier.[23] His published diaries are less lyrical than

Scott's. They reflect a strong factual and scientific bent and focus largely on the physical world around him. During a sledging journey on November 12, 1902, for example, he noted that "the dogs pulled very well indeed and we had a good going surface, few and small sastrugi, all running southwest. All the forenoon we were in dense whiteness, no sun, nothing visible, and yet nothing falling apparently, except some fine drift. . . . Fine solar halo with an inverted arch of light above it." [24]

Scott and Wilson differed on the matter of religion as well as in writing styles. In a letter to his wife, Wilson wrote: "Only once have we got on religious subjects, but soon I found that his ideas are as settled in one direction as mine are in another, and our only agreement was that we differed." [25]

Wilson gave Scott a report of his medical examination of the sledging party, noting that three of the men had very badly swollen legs. Wilson further described swollen and spongy gums in two members of the party and discoloration in the legs of one. These writings show that Dr. Wilson understood and recognized the symptoms of scurvy and was not reluctant to document them. Scott himself remarked upon the symptoms of scurvy, noting that "the first sign is an inflamed, swollen condition of the gums. . . . Spots appear on the legs and pain is felt in old wounds and bruises; later, from a slight oedema, the legs and then the arms, swell to a great size and become blackened behind the joints." [26]

Scott and his companions not only recognized the signs of the disease but took quick steps to cure it following this first outbreak by "serving out fresh meat regularly and by increasing the allowance of bottled fruits." Here one of the cornerstones of the legend of Scott's misjudgments must be rejected on examination of the writings: it is not true that Scott contracted scurvy through a preference for preserved foodstuffs or a Victorian aversion to eating unfamiliar foods such as seal.[27] From *Discovery*'s first weeks in Antarctica, the crew ate seal frequently, and they consumed more of it when scurvy threatened. Scott described the food eaten in early January: "We had been regularly feeding on seal-meat, and on the whole, even at this time, we found it palatable. . . . It has a distinctive flavor in a similar degree to beef or mutton." With the onset of scurvy Scott increased the consumption of fresh seal from three times weekly to daily. He also ordered that "no tinned meat of any description should be issued." A nearby seal colony was the source for a plentiful supply of the life-giving fresh food. One member of the crew took advantage of the returning sunlight and "our own Antarctic soil" (readily found in summer near Hut Point, where the snow accumulation is typically not great) to grow a crop of mustard and cress under the wardroom skylight. Scott reported on October 15 that "enough cress has been produced for one good feed for all hands."[28]

Scott wondered whether his canned provisions were the cause of his men's ailments, but it should come as no surprise that a man of his scientific leanings correctly concluded, based on observation of improved health following increased consumption of seal, that the solution to the problem of scurvy lay in the "inestimable advantage of fresh food. . . . It seems evident that the whole circle of the Antarctic seas is abundantly provided with animal life. It is not conceivable, therefore, that any party wintering in the Antarctic regions will have great difficulty in providing themselves with fresh food; and, as we have proved, where such conditions exist there need be no fear of the dreaded word 'scurvy.' "[29] This solution served when the party was near the coast, with its many sources of fresh food, but it would prove more difficult to avoid scurvy on the sledging journeys that took them into the interior.

By early summer, the crew had recovered from their encounter with scurvy and were enjoying much warmer temperatures — often above zero °F. A sledging party began to trek southward at the end of October 1902, with the aim of establishing a record for traveling the farthest south (map 4). A supporting team helped bring 2,100 pounds of provisions out past 79°S, and on November 13 a group of fifteen men shared the glory of standing farther south than others ever had. The dogs had started strong on this journey, but by November 18 the animals were weak and listless. The supporting party turned back, but Scott continued south along the Barrier with nineteen dogs and two human companions — Edward A. Wilson, who was to become his closest friend and a key member of the 1911 expedition, and Ernest Shackleton, who began his explorations of the Antarctic as Scott's sledging mate but later became one of his greatest rivals (fig. 7).[30]

Years later, when Scott and Wilson lay dying together in a tent on the Barrier, Scott described his feelings for Wilson in a letter to Wilson's beloved wife, Oriana: "I should like you to know how splendid he was at the end — everlastingly cheerful and ready to sacrifice himself for others. . . . I can do

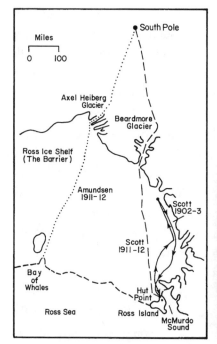

Map 4. The Ross Ice Shelf, left, with the routes of Scott's farthest-south journey in 1902–3, his route to the Pole in 1911–12, and that followed by Amundsen in 1911–12. Note location of McMurdo Sound. Ernest Shackleton pioneered the British route to the Pole in 1908–9, forging the path also taken by Scott up the Beardmore glacier. Right panel shows a modern satellite image of the Antarctic, constructed using advanced very high resolution radiometer (AVHRR) data. Image courtesy of the United States Geological Survey mapping site, available on the Internet (see Selected Bibliography for site address). Note that map is oriented with south at top.

no more to comfort you than to tell you that he died as he lived, a brave, true man—the best of comrades and the staunchest of friends."[31]

As the dogs continued to weaken, the men were forced to pull ever-heavier weights. Scott noted that "our appetites seem to be increasing by leaps and bounds, it is almost alarming." He was beginning to understand the huge strain imposed by the sustained effort of man-hauling, even in the relatively warm conditions they now enjoyed. November 27 was "beautifully bright, clear and warm, the temperature up to +20[°F]."[32] Summer had arrived on the Barrier.

The dogs scarcely pulled and the surface became rough. The three men were forced to relay their loads, going forward with half their burden, then returning for the rest. They were walking three miles to advance one, but they continued to plod on to the south. Wilson's examination of the dogs on December 7 revealed that some of the animals were suffering from dysentery and passing blood. On December 9 the miserable party of men and dogs covered only two miles for the day. Wilson's autopsy of the dog Snatcher revealed that the animal had died of acute peritonitis.[33]

On December 16, after 31 days of relaying, the three men laid a depot just south of 80°. There they placed three weeks' provisions, which Scott reasoned was enough to cover the return journey, pulling far lighter loads. They had marched 380 miles thus far. They continued southward, carrying provisions for four weeks along with their clothing and camping equipment. They began slaughtering some of the weaker dogs to feed those that remained,

Figure 7. From left, Shackleton, Scott, and Wilson before departure for the southernmost sledging journey of the *Discovery* expedition. Note the packed sledges behind, and the explorers' canvas clothing. The flags on the sledges were personal crests typically carried by each officer. Photographer unknown. Number 22334, Alexander Turnbull Library, Wellington, New Zealand.

and on December 16 "poor Vic was sacrificed . . . for the common good." The dogs remained thin but became a little healthier after eating their mates, supporting the view that the dried fish was a key part of their problem. Meanwhile, the men passed "from the hungry to the ravenous."[34] On December 5 Wilson described his dreams of food in vivid terms, writing, "Very hungry always, our allowance being a very bare one. Dreams as a rule of splendid food, ball suppers, sirloins of beef, caldrons full of steaming vegetables. But one spends all one's time shouting at waiters who won't bring one a plate of anything, or else one finds the beef is only ashes when one gets it. . . . One very rarely gets a feed in one's sleep."[35]

In spite of the strain of the journey, Wilson found the energy to make numerous drawings of the spectacular landscape, many of which he later rendered into striking watercolor paintings. Scott described his companion's work with admiration: "Wilson is the most indefatigable person. When it is fine and clear, at the end of our fatiguing days he will spend two or three hours seated in the door of the tent sketching each detail of the splendid mountainous coast-scene to the west. His sketches are most astonishingly accurate; I have tested his proportions by actual angular measurement and found them correct."[36]

On December 20 the dog Grannie collapsed and was carried for a time on the sledge by the men. A few days later she provided the other animals with three days' food. For the men, breakfast on the march consisted of tea and a dry "fry" of pemmican and biscuit in the Primus cooker. Lunch was a small piece of seal meat, half a biscuit, and eight to ten lumps of sugar. Supper, the best meal of the day, consisted of a "hoosh" (stew) of pemmican or seal meat, which was boiled in a central cooker while cocoa was made in the outer one.[37]

Wilson had been monitoring the men's health carefully, reporting in his diary for December 4 that he carried out "a thorough search in all three of us for any trace of scurvy and . . . found not a suspicion in any one of us."[38] But on December 21 Scott reported that Wilson had told him that "Shackleton has decidedly angry-looking gums," and the specter of scurvy rose again.[39] Wilson's diary puts the onset of the scurvy in a rather different light, however, not only in terms of severity but also in the key matters of dates and afflicted parties. It was not until the entry for December 24 that Wilson's diary notes:

"As a result of today's medical examination I told the Captain that both he and Shackleton had suspicious looking gums, though hardly enough to swear to scurvy in them." [40]

Scott decided to increase consumption of seal to combat the problem but to continue pushing south. Scurvy is a disease that can rapidly become debilitating, and the decision to continue was fraught with the risk that someone would become unable to march—which could spell death if the others were not strong enough to carry the patient on the sledge.

Wilson was also suffering from another health problem as he marched south: snow blindness. The darker surfaces of ocean, rock, and vegetation that cover much of the earth absorb a great deal of incoming sunlight, but snow is a highly reflective rather than absorbing surface. The mirror of snow efficiently casts sunlight back into the faces of polar travelers. The human cornea can be sunburned through overexposure, leading to an intense pain not unlike severe sunburn. Wilson frequently endured snow blindness because of his insistence upon sketching despite the risk. He was clear and detailed in his technical descriptions of his ailment, noting, for example, on December 26: "My left eye got so intensely painful and watered so profusely that I could see nothing and could hardly stand the pain. I cocainized it repeatedly." He marched blindfolded and dreamed of the woods of England: "Sometimes I was in beech woods, sometimes in fir woods, sometimes in the Birdlip woods . . . and the swish-swish of the ski was as though one's feet were brushing through dead leaves, or cranberry undergrowth or heather or juicy bluebells. One could almost see and smell them." [41]

Position was approximated by the use of a sledgemeter, a wheel that hung off the back of the sledge and recorded the distance traveled. But this approach gave only a crude measure, and accurate determination of the party's location relied upon a theodolite to measure the exact position of the sun. Travelers to the tropics notice that the sun is high in the sky at noon, and the days are close to twelve hours long regardless of season. Outside the tropics, the sun's elevation—its angle above the horizon—is not as high, and the days are long in summer and short in winter. The cycle reaches an extreme at the Pole. In polar summer the sun ceases to set altogether, and in polar winter it never rises. And at every location on Earth, measurements of solar, stellar, or lunar position above the horizon provide the time-honored technique for precise navigation. Longitude can be deduced by measuring the solar position at noon and at a second known time, so precise timekeeping is essential to any explorer. On December 23 Scott's readings of the theodolite implied a latitude of 81°30'S.

In other latitudes, compasses are a boon to navigation. But they are of limited use in polar regions. The magnetic poles that attract the compass needle do not coincide with the Earth's geographic poles, and compasses therefore no longer provide a simple means of determining direction in very high latitudes. Furthermore, the compass responds feebly as the magnetic field gradients weaken at high latitudes. Cherry-Garrard wrote that "owing to the proximity of the Magnetic Pole the pull of the needle is chiefly downwards. It is forced into a horizontal position by a balancing weight on the N. side, so it is obvious that its direction power is greatly reduced. On the ship, owing to the vibration of the engines and the motors, we were absolutely unable to steer by the compass at all when off the region of the Magnetic Pole."[42]

But compasses were not altogether useless on sledging journeys. The compass variation—the difference of the needle's direction from true south—could be evaluated by using an accurate series of theodolite observations. Knowing the direction of true south along with the variation from it as indicated by the compass, the explorers could use a compass as a valuable aid to keep going in a particular direction during a day's march—even on days of blowing snow or ice fog. But the theodolite was the only exact means of determining position, and sightings on the summer sledging trail could be performed only on those relatively clear days when the sun could be seen.

On Christmas Day the three men treated themselves to a glorious breakfast of biscuit and seal liver fried in bacon and pemmican fat, along with a large spoonful of jam. The dogs walked in slack traces, and the three men pulled the sledges without them. They daydreamed of Christmas in England, and Shackleton produced a plum pudding "the size of a cricket ball." But within a few days the effects of the Christmas feast wore off. Scott recognized that "we had cut ourselves too short in the matter of food, but it was too late to alter arrangements now without curtailing our journey, and we all decided that, sooner than do the latter, we would cheerfully face the pangs that our meagre fare would cost." Scott also wrote that "such a state of affairs is . . .

a false economy, and the additional weight which we should have carried in taking a proper allowance of food would have amply repaid us on this occasion by the maintenance of our full vigour."[43] In spite of this evaluation, he would find himself short of rations again in less than a year.

On December 30 the trio made its southernmost camp at about 82°16′S. This was not as far south as their original hopes. Scott blamed the shortcoming mainly on the failure of the dog team, a judgment that would tragically prejudice his future use of canine transport. But he took comfort in the fact that "we have made a greater advance towards a pole of the Earth than has ever yet been achieved by a sledge party," a notable badge of distinction in exploration.[44]

As the three men turned homeward, they attempted to reach the mountains that could be seen to the west of the Barrier (see map 4), largely for the scientific goal of collecting rock specimens from a record southern position. But as they veered closer to the land, they were thwarted by a maze of dangerous crevasses. A member of Scott's second expedition described crevasses as

death-traps in your path, opened by the pressure of slow-moving ice against the land. Snow covers them and they can be detected only by a slight unevenness. . . . One of the party goes ahead, prodding with a ski-stick. The chief safeguard, however, is the sledge itself, which is twelve feet long and, being some way behind the men hauling it, acts as an anchor to the sledger who goes through the surface. Down he goes with a sickening fall, but the harness holds him and he swings round, helpless but safe, until his companions can get him out. . . . Time after time there comes that hideous fall; the moment's fear that the harness will not hold.[45]

On this day, Wilson wrote, crevasses "were constantly giving way as we crossed them one by one on the rope. We never unroped the whole time, as there were crevasses everywhere and not a sign of some of them, till one of us went in and saw blue depths below to any extent you like."[46] At the edge of the coast they found an insurmountable chasm between themselves and their tantalizing scientific goal. The trio reluctantly gave up their geological

Figure 8. Members of a party on Scott's second expedition experience crevasses. Photograph by T. Griffith Taylor. Scott Polar Research Institute, Cambridge.

aspirations and continued due north on the Barrier, locked in a struggle between their stamina and the hundreds of miles that still lay between them and the ship.

On New Year's Eve, 1902, the three desperate Englishmen scraped a fallen dinner off the waterproof floorcloth of their tent. The summer temperatures were warm, and the sailors took advantage of a strong breeze from the south (southerly), rigging a sail on the sledge to lessen their load. The sledge now sailed effortlessly along, but the sick dogs could barely walk beside it. By January 3 only seven dogs were left of the original nineteen; by January 9 only four remained. January 7, 1903, brought pleasantly warm temperatures, reaching 34 °F at noon, but wet snowfall began the next day, and the surface changed, suddenly gripping at the sledge runners. The party was now fifty miles from the depot with less than a week's provision, and they could barely move the sledge. On January 9 the surface improved, and the men were able to sail along again with the blessed aid of "a good southerly breeze all day." A sighting by theodolite on January 11 revealed their location as ten or twelve miles from the spot where they had depoted the vital provisions that would sustain them for the rest of the journey.[47]

The surface continued to be problematic, and in an effort to improve the glide of the sledges, the men stripped the German silver plating off of the runners. This provided little benefit.[48] The key factor was the temperature, which determines how readily a thin film of liquid water can form as the runners of sledges or skis glide over the snow beneath them. The friction of skis or sled runners on snow provides heat to melt the surface crystals that would otherwise grind on a sliding object, producing instead a self-lubricating effect. Formation of an optimal liquid layer lies at the heart of skiing, and temperature is a critical factor in the delicate balance of forces that makes skiing or pulling a sled either torturous or easy.[49] As Cherry-Garrard concluded years later, "the ideal surface for pulling a sledge on ski was found at a temperature of +16 °F."[50]

Modern scientific studies show why Cherry-Garrard was correct in his observation that both warmer and colder temperatures lead to rougher going. At warm temperatures, too much liquid forms as a slider works its way over the snow, and the excess water grips at the ski. At very cold temperatures the surface crystals remain stubbornly frozen despite the slider's friction, and the crystalline surface is dry and intractably frigid. Modern skiers treat the surfaces of their skis with waxes designed to optimize both glide (for forward motion) and grip (for pushing off) under many weather conditions, but such preparations were in their infancy at the turn of the century.[51] Furthermore, it is vastly more difficult even with contemporary waxes to maintain both glide and grip under variable temperature conditions when pulling a heavy sledge than when skiing unencumbered. One method used by Inuit peoples and by explorers familiar with their practices was to build up a layer of ice on the runners; such an approach is helpful under some weather conditions.[52]

Scott's team frequently struggled with too-warm or too-cold temperatures that made pulling a heavy sledge over the snow a towering challenge.

Scott was beginning to fear that he and his men might have difficulty finding their depot when, on January 13, he spotted it through the theodolite telescope as he took a latitude reading. They reached the depot and treated themselves to a "fat hoosh." Scott concluded that "things stand favourably for us; we have perhaps 130 miles to cover to our next depot, but we have a full three weeks' provisions." Things looked favorable only briefly. The next day Wilson examined the three men and found that all three now had some symptoms of scurvy, with Shackleton's the worst.[53] Rations of seal were increased in an effort to combat the disease. Shackleton began walking beside the sledge rather than pulling. He was coughing and spitting blood, perhaps not only from scurvy but also from bronchial problems.[54] Overcast weather added to the trio's plight, creating a gray, indistinct world in which the party could barely find their way. The sun on which they depended for navigation was veiled by "thick blank whiteness." All they could do was to search for traces of their outbound tracks or try to identify the vague landforms sometimes glimpsed around them. Scott describes the misery of trying to find the correct path in this formless haze: "It is difficult to describe the trying nature of this work; for hours one plods on, ever searching for some more definite sign. Sometimes the eye picks up a shade on the surface or a cloud slightly lighter or darker than its surroundings; these may occur at any angle and have often to be kept in the corner of the eye. Frequently, there comes a minute or two of absolute confusion, when one may be going in any direction. . . . It can scarcely be imagined how tiring this is or how trying to the eyes."[55]

Wilson bemoaned January 18 as a "hopelessly overcast day, with nothing to steer by or fix one's light-dazzled eyes on. After an hour's marching we found the steering so erratic that we camped and waited to see if it would clear. . . . We did three hours and then camped as Shackle was feeling bad. . . . One can see nothing at all, either in the sky or below it, all one uniform brilliant grey light without a break." Remarkably, Wilson's main concern centered not on losing the trail but on the loss of scientific opportunity as they struggled with these conditions. He wrote: "Very depressing this white pall, and very disappointing to be forced to keep going on and on, knowing that we are missing for good our opportunities of sketching and surveying."[56]

The last dog was finally put out of its misery on January 15. Shackleton collapsed on January 18 but was able to march beside the sledge again in the next several days. On January 27 the three desperate men finally sighted their beloved landmarks, Erebus and Terror (see map 3), and on January 28 they reached another depot and renewed their precious supplies of food. On February 3, 1903, they staggered into the McMurdo Sound camp and the haven of the ship, after ninety-three days of a march of more than 960 statute miles. Scott said that he and his companions were "as near spent as three persons can well be. If Shackleton has shown a temporary improvement, we know by experience how little confidence we can place in it, and how near he has been and still is to a total collapse. . . . We have known that our scurvy has been advancing again with rapid strides."[57]

Scott, Wilson, and Shackleton had suffered through scurvy, snow blindness, intractable snow surfaces, crevasses, and the deaths of their sled dogs. But one factor worked very much in their favor on this, their first foray onto the Barrier: benignly warm weather. Daily minimum temperatures recorded by the party averaged +16.5°F, in good agreement with the mean values now measured over more than a decade of modern observations from automated weather stations in this region. But even in a month blessed by such summer warmth, the three men barely survived. Figure 9 provides a glimpse of the far greater challenges they were to face in the future. On a January day about nine years later, Scott reached the South Pole. The Pole's elevation of nearly 10,000 feet leads to daily minimum January temperatures typically not near +20°F, like those experienced on the farthest-south journey of 1902–3, but instead a chilling −20°F. Scott attempted to cross the Barrier on the return from the Pole not in January (as in 1903) but in March, and the figure shows the rapidity with which the warmth of January fades to typical daily minima near −20°F in March on the Barrier at sea level. In short, the weather the group dealt with on the *Discovery* farthest-south trek in 1902–3 was by far the mildest that Scott encountered in his exploration of the Antarctic, a veritable day on the beach by comparison to what the continent held in store for his future and that of the men who marched beside him.

Scott returned to *Discovery* to find that a relief vessel had arrived, the *Morning*. The ship brought the eagerly awaited mail and news of home, as well as a badly needed supply of coal and other provisions. But February drew

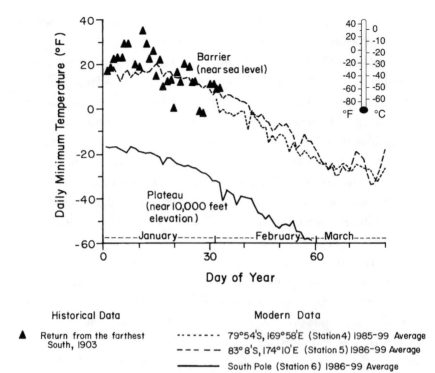

Historical Data

▲ Return from the farthest South, 1903

Modern Data

········· 79°54'S, 169°58'E (Station 4) 1985-99 Average

─ ─ ─ ─ 83° 8'S, 174°10'E (Station 5) 1986-99 Average

───── South Pole (Station 6) 1986-99 Average

Figure 9. Daily minimum temperatures encountered by Scott, Wilson, and Shackleton in 1903, along with contemporary data showing typical conditions for January, February, and March at stations 4, 5, and 6 (see map 2). The colder temperatures at the Pole in summer are largely due to its high elevation, about ten thousand feet above the sea level of the Barrier (see map 1).

to a close with *Discovery* still locked tight in her icy winter home. Some of the crew, Shackleton among them, were sent home with the relief on March 2, 1903, while the rest remained on board *Discovery*, waiting to see whether it would break free by the end of the season. But on March 14 Scott "admitted the certainty of a second winter."[58]

The fall and winter of 1903 were spent in the relative comfort of the ship. Among other diversions, the men engaged in hockey games on what can safely be called the southernmost ice rink in the world, until the failing light forced them to give it up. In the continuous darkness of polar night, the winter temperatures reached as low as −67.7°F at the ship. When sunlight returned in September, Scott led a small party across the Sound to lay a depot in preparation for another long journey.[59]

While Scott prepared for further exploring, Wilson sledged with a small group of men in late September to Cape Crozier, the site of an immense emperor penguin rookery. Wilson's party endured temperatures as low as −62°F as they slogged through the snow toward their goal. The men went to the rookery in hopes of collecting eggs still incubating in late September but were surprised to see that the chicks had already hatched. They were able to collect some abandoned eggs, however, and "Wilson was glad of the opportunity of studying the chicks at a more tender age than they were seen last year."[60] The life cycle of the grand emperor penguins of Cape Crozier became the subject of Wilson's intense professional passion as a naturalist. After the *Discovery* expedition he published a scientific paper expressing great interest in the emperors' "quaint life histories," particularly the chicks' ability to "weather a month of temperatures constantly as low as −40°F."[61]

On October 12, 1903, Scott again left the ship with twelve men (and none of the dogs, which he now deemed undependable). This season, his party would travel together to the high plateau that lay west of the mountains across the Sound, in Victoria Land. A small subgroup would go farther, penetrating the interior of the continent as deeply as possible on the high plateau to the west. They pulled more than two hundred pounds per man on four eleven-foot sledges as they ascended a glacier of ice and snow.[62]

Scott found the landscape "wonderfully beautiful. . . . To describe the wildly beautiful scene that is about us tonight is a task that is far beyond my pen. Away behind us is the gorge by which we have come; but now above and beyond its splendid cliffs we can see rising fold on fold the white snow-clad slopes of Mount Lister," one of the tall peaks in the Transantarctic range.[63]

The party was caught in a blizzard that Scott described as warning them of the need to be less "careless in leaving our things outside the tent. . . . Our sleeping-bags, with socks . . . and other garments, lay scattered about on the ice whilst we were having breakfast when suddenly the wind swept down on us; before we could move everything was skidding away over the surface." But in spite of this warning, caution still appeared to be in short supply, for a few days later another series of strong gusts robbed them of a critical item.

Figure 10. The emperor penguins at Cape Crozier. Drawing by E. A. Wilson. Scott Polar Research Institute, Cambridge.

The book *Hints to Travellers*, which contained the required celestial information needed to find latitude and longitude from theodolite readings, had
blown away.[64] Perhaps remarkably in view of the fact that they now had no
sure means of establishing their position, the party decided to risk becoming
lost and pushed on. By the end of November 13 they reached an elevation of
8,900 feet and attained the polar plateau.

On November 14 Scott outlined a new way to determine the latitude without *Hints to Travellers*. The beautiful Transantarctic Mountains, which had
frequently guided their travels on the farthest-south journey of the previous
year, run largely along a meridian near 160°E. In contrast to the frozen sea
that lay beneath the men when marching on the Barrier, this mountainous
coast range, though largely snow covered, is part of the "land" of Antarctica.
Scott could see the lofty peak of Mount Lister and several other landmarks
known to him, and he determined the party's latitude at that point by measuring his bearings relative to these.

But in continuing west the party would leave the mountains behind and
enter a featureless plateau. Scott wrote:

> The prospect which lay before us of wandering over this great snow
> plain without knowing exactly where we were . . . had naturally been
> much in my thoughts. . . . It occurred to me that we might gather
> some idea of our latitude if I could improvise some method of as-
> certaining the daily change in the sun's declination. With this idea I
> carefully ruled out a sheet of my notebook into squares with the in-
> tention of making a curve of the sun's declination. I found on reflec-
> tion that I had some data . . . for I could calculate the declination for
> certain fixed days, such as the day when the sun had returned to us.
> . . . Other points were given by observations taken at known latitudes
> on the glacier. . . . I plotted all these points on my squared paper, and
> joined them with a freehand curve of which I have some reason to be
> proud, for on my return to the ship I found it was nowhere more than
> 4' in error.[65]

The loss of *Hints to Travellers* only a few short days after noting the hazards
of losing their belongings to the wind is illustrative of Scott's surprising flaws,

but his innovative approach to overcoming the problem also reveals remarkable strengths. The two incidents, one embarrassing and the other impressive, were both described frankly in his book about the expedition.

The party knew that the air would be bitterly cold at the high elevation of the plateau, where summer never really comes. On November 21 Scott recorded temperatures below −30°F all day. On November 22 Scott chose the seamen Evans and Lashly to accompany him onward into the heart of Victoria Land, and the rest of the party turned back. For three more weeks the trio continued to march westward, undergoing what Scott characterized as the "hardest physical work that I have ever experienced." They had to find their way around and over the highest sastrugi they had yet seen; these were formed by the strong winds that were "the plague of our lives. It has cut us to pieces. We all have deep cracks in our nostrils and cheeks. . . . One of Evans' fingers has a deep cut on either side of the nail which might have been made by a heavy slash of the knife." [66]

On November 30 they finished their last westward march. Turning for home, they encountered heavy overcast in which they could barely see the crevasses and sastrugi in their path. The hungry party was running short on food. As conditions worsened, Scott's admiration for his two companions grew. He found both the seamen "undefeatable" and noted with satisfaction that "I learn a great deal about lower-deck life—more than I could hope to have done under ordinary conditions." [67]

The sky cleared and for a few days the three men were able to progress much more easily. In spite of continuing cold and wind they achieved long marches of about ten hours per day. On December 12 it was overcast again, but they caught glimpses of land. On December 13 "Evans had his nose frost-bitten. Evans's nose has always been the first thing to indicate stress of frost-biting weather. For some weeks it has been more or less constantly frost-bitten. . . . When I told him of its fault today, he said in a resigned tone, 'my poor old nose again; well, there, it's chronic.'" [68] Seaman Evans was one of the first members of the party to suffer from severe frostbite when Scott and four companions marched to the South Pole in 1911.

By December 15 the land could be seen all around, but the team were still unsure of their exact location. They had to find the specific glacier they had climbed in order to descend the mountain range in relative safety, but they recognized no landmarks. Luck was with them, in the guise of a potentially disastrous mishap. As they groped their way over the icy surface, roped together and tied to the sledge,

> suddenly Lashly slipped, and in an instant he was sliding downward on his back. . . . I was whipped off my legs and we all three lay sprawling on our backs and flying downward with an ever-increasing velocity. . . . We had ceased to slide smoothly, and were now bounding over a rougher incline, sometimes leaving it for several yards at a time. . . . At length we gave a huge leap into the air and yet we travelled with such velocity that I had not time to think before we came down with tremendous force on a gradual incline of rough, hard, wind-swept snow. . . . In another moment I could thank heaven that no limbs were broken. . . . As soon as I could pull myself together I looked round and now to my astonishment I saw that we were well on towards the entrance of our own glacier; ahead and on other sides of us appeared well-remembered landmarks.

They had descended some three hundred feet, by Scott's estimate. In the distance to the east lay the familiar summit of Mount Erebus.[69]

Though within reach of home, they were not yet out of danger. Evans and Scott fell into a deep crevasse, and Lashly barely managed to keep himself and the sledge from plunging in along with them. But all three emerged from this last brush with death unscathed, and they shortly reached one of their depots, with its life-sustaining supplies of food and fuel. On Christmas Eve, 1903, they arrived home at last. They had been gone eighty-one days and had covered about 1,000 miles.[70]

Scott survived his two major sledging journeys of 1902 and 1903 through great effort and on the slimmest of margins. At every turn he chose a path with limited safety cushions and the greatest risks: in deciding to continue in spite of a possibility of scurvy on the farthest-south journey in 1902, in choosing to march into the heart of the featureless plateau without navigational tools in 1903, and in pushing the boundaries of human endurance with limited food allotments on both journeys—this last after explicitly noting that it was a foolish economy on the first experience. Through wretched experience he learned, or believed that he learned, about sledging, frostbite, leakage of paraffin, and dogs.[71]

The unflattering legend of Scott as a bungler and worse suggests that he was deliberately deceptive in noting scurvy only in Shackleton on December 21, perhaps to vindicate going no farther than 82°16′S. Yet in his diary he graphically admits to specific symptoms of the disease in himself and Wilson as well as Shackleton after they had turned back. For example, Scott wrote on January 14: "I myself have distinctly red gums, and a very slight swelling in the ankles."[72] Wilson's diary offers no clarification on whether Scott's writings were deliberately misleading. But it is evident that Wilson emerged from the voyage with deep admiration for Scott, reflected in his remarks in a letter to Cherry-Garrard years later about joining the second expedition: "I know Scott intimately, as you know. I have known him now for ten years, and I believe in him so firmly that I am often sorry when he lays himself open to misunderstanding. I am sure that you will come to know him and believe in him as I do, and none the less because he is sometimes difficult."[73] Whether Scott lied or simply "laid himself open to misunderstanding" in his description of scurvy on the farthest-south trek of 1903 cannot be established with certainty. That Shackleton was gravely ill seems clear, and he later wrote of being invalided home due to a broken blood vessel in his lungs.[74]

Scott forged deep personal bonds on this first expedition, not only with Wilson but also with the two seaman, Evans and Lashly. All three became key members of his second expedition. Scott and his companions were blessed with a large measure of good fortune, strikingly illustrated in the hair-raising slide into the glacier that unveiled the way home from the high plateau. Scott was to push the boundaries of his fortunes even harder on his next expedition.

THREE

The Return

The visitor leaves Antarctica as he came, on a military airplane. It is nearly summer, but the ice covering McMurdo Sound is still more than five feet thick, and the large jet sits incongruously but safely on the frozen sea. The visitor takes one last look at the beauty of the mountain range across the Sound as he boards. The plane spirits him away over the pack, and in five hours he is nearing New Zealand.

The transition back to the living world stimulates senses that have been dormant for months. As the plane descends, the visitor suddenly becomes aware of the rich smell of damp earth. He hadn't given much thought to the virtual lack of scents in the sterile world of Antarctica, but now the smell of the land penetrates his senses even before touchdown. He stares out the window, captivated by the sight of hills covered in deep, vibrant green. It's a color whose tones he had almost forgotten, and he blinks repeatedly as his eyes adjust to the strange sight. The plane lurches slightly as the wheels touch the runway. The air feels humid and warm, and he removes his coat before stepping outside into the soft breeze that has neither a howling voice nor a vicious bite. The best is yet to come, for his dinner that night will be a fresh garden salad, bursting with the wonderful tastes of tomatoes, cucumbers, and carrots. After three months with no fresh fruit or vegetables, these ordinary foods have been transformed to rare, exquisite delicacies.

Before leaving Christchurch, he visits the Canterbury museum to see the extensive collection of artifacts from Scott's expeditions. The cans of

Huntley and Palmer biscuits look just the same as those he saw in the *Discovery* Hut. But here they are protected behind glass, and the museum guard keeps a watchful eye on the visitor to make sure he doesn't touch the wooden sledge in the corner. Sledges are still used to transport some equipment in Antarctica, but now they are lighter and smaller than this antique. The twelve-foot wooden sledge looks terribly heavy, and the canvas man-hauling harness next to it is enough to make the visitor shudder as he reflects on how it must have felt to drag two hundred pounds across the snow for hundreds of miles.

Next to the sledge is a glass-fronted display case containing a set of pony snowshoes. They are about eight inches in diameter, and round rather than racquet-shaped like those generally used by human travelers. The visitor recalls hearing a tale about these peculiar relics recounted by an Antarctic veteran, who claimed that among Scott's many ridiculous mistakes was completely forgetting to take pony snowshoes on a critical supply-laying journey. As a result, the poor beasts floundered in the deep drifts, and some died. It is just one of many anecdotes in the legend of Scott's errors.

The visitor pauses in front of the exhibit of the men's clothing. The material looks thin, nothing more than basic protection against the wind, with little or no insulation. The visitor sighs, wondering why Scott failed to realize how much warmer the fur clothing favored by Amundsen would have been. But it is the visitor who has failed to understand the enormity of the battle that Scott and his men fought against their own perspiration as they dragged those heavily laden twelve-foot sledges across endless miles. Fur clothing would have become impossibly icy when every day was a grinding march of fifteen miles in the harness, pulling a sledge that sometimes stuck like glue to a frigid snow surface. But imagining how this would have felt is beyond the visitor's understanding, even though he has just returned from a trip to the frozen continent. The visitor rode on a snowmobile during his comfortable stay in the great South, and the sledge that carried his equipment trailed easily behind.

As 1903 drew to a close, it was past time to start for home. Scott was painfully aware that *Discovery* had been frozen in the ice for almost two years, and there was no guarantee that the Sound would break its grip on the ship that summer—as it had not in the previous year. Ten and a half miles north of *Discovery*'s bow, a team of men began sawing the ice in late December. The location of the saw camp was based upon the previous December's ice conditions, following instructions left by Scott, who was still working his way back from the journey to Victoria Land.[1]

Temperatures were warm, about +35°F, but the work was grueling. After two years of sledging, the men felt that "if it had been leg work there would have been no difficulty . . . but the new departure exercised a different set of muscles altogether." Eighteen-foot-long saws were forced down into the ice and raised using ropes attached to a tackle block on a tripod. The ice beneath the men's feet was about seven feet thick, and great efforts yielded only 150 yards of progress per day. This seemed a futile effort, given that twenty miles of ice lay between the ship and open water.[2] There was little choice but to wait and hope that nature would come to their aid. Scott therefore ordered a halt to the proceedings and sent the men back to the ship.

While the others returned, Scott and Wilson went north to "watch the ice edge and see what chance there is of a break-up." As Scott brooded about freeing his ship, Wilson enjoyed the opportunity to study the penguins that they found along this short journey.[3]

On January 5 Wilson and Scott awoke to the surprising sight of two new ships floating near the ice edge in the Sound. The *Morning* and the *Terra Nova* had arrived for their rescue. Scott learned with great dismay that his orders were to abandon his beloved *Discovery* if the icy barrier between the hull and freedom did not break up in the next six weeks. What they needed was a storm, with the strongest possible wind, for wind far more than warmth drives the breakup of polar ice. Scott wrote: "It is a curious irony of fate that makes one pray for a gale in these regions, but at present bad weather seems the only thing that can help us." On January 28 Scott woke in his bunk back on board *Discovery*, "astonished to hear the ship creaking. . . . The whole ice-sheet was swaying very lightly under the action of a long swell." It appeared that they might have a chance to break free.[4]

On February 5 and 6 the men detonated charges set in the ice, trying to assist the swell and forge open a lead to the water. But the swell subsided a few days later, and on February 10 Scott reluctantly began to make plans to abandon ship. The next day, though, a light snow began falling and the breeze picked up. By February 14 a strong wind swept out of the southeast and "a glorious sight met our view. The ice was breaking up right across the strait, and with a rapidity which we had not thought possible. . . . Within an hour or two . . . the open sea would be lapping on the black rocks of Hut Point." Their relief ships assisted by pushing against the ice. After a final explosive charge set just fifteen yards ahead of *Discovery* on February 16, the ship broke free. The weather looked threatening, and Scott gave the order to start the engines for steam. The wind that had been their salvation now began to threaten their survival. The full force of a gale struck on February 17, and the steam power proved no match for the howling wind and strong currents. *Discovery* was pushed hard aground near the island. For hours the ship was battered and tossed in the shallows, pounding against the bottom with terrible force. Scott wrote:

> We took the shore thus at about 11 am, and the hours that followed were the most dreadful I have ever spent. Each moment the ship came down with a sickening thud which shook her from stem to stern, and each thud seemed to show more plainly that, strong as was her build, she could not long survive such awful blows. . . . Towering above us within a stone's throw was the rocky promontory of Hut Point; on its summit and clearly outlined against the sky, stood the cross we had erected to our shipmate [Vince's cross]. I remember thinking how hard it seemed that we had rescued our ship only to be beaten to pieces beneath its shadow.[5]

But luck was with them. Late on February 17, 1904, the wind dropped, and for the first time in two years, they sailed away from the peninsula, with no serious damage inflicted to the ship. Scott wrote: "As we sped along we looked for the last time with almost affectionate regard on the scene which had grown so familiar, on the hills of which we knew every ridge and fold. . . . One wonders what is happening now in that lonely solitude."[6]

On September 10 they reached the coast of England, south of the Isle of Wight. Scott finished his account of his first Antarctic expedition as follows: "To attempt to describe the hearty welcome which we received from our countrymen, and the generous tributes which have been paid to our efforts, would be beyond the scope of this book. . . . For me and for the small band who laboured so faithfully together in the *Discovery*, there has been one cloud to dim the joy of this home-coming . . . the sadness of the day which brought the end of our close companionship and the scattering of those ties which had held us together for so long." [7]

Scientific circles had criticized the planning of the expedition (and in particular the choice of a naval officer rather than a scientist as commander) before the *Discovery* left England.[8] Now the technical findings were critiqued in such places as the prestigious journal *Nature*, where a well-known geologist who had vied with Scott for leadership of the *Discovery* expedition acerbically remarked, "It is disappointing to learn that we cannot expect any additions to the deep-sea fauna of the Southern ocean," and "More than once during the course of the expedition the observations desired were accidentally noticed, but the conditions are not stated with sufficient precision to be of service." [9] These caustic statements may have inspired Scott to devote greater resources and attention to science on his second expedition, an emphasis for which he would be subject to still more derision in years to come, as the dual demands of science and exploration taxed his men and their resources. But along with criticism came acclaim. Scott was promoted to captain and feted as a hero by London society. He made a number of new friends, including the playwright Sir James Barrie (whose most famous work is *Peter Pan*). Scott took a further nine months of special leave to complete his popular book describing the expedition and to conduct a lecture tour that had been promised to the Royal Geographical Society.[10] Through his new circle of acquaintances, he met and fell in love with Kathleen Bruce, an unconventional artist who had studied sculpture in Paris. He returned to his naval duties in summer 1908. In the fall of that year, Miss Bruce and he were married, with Auguste Rodin among those in attendance.[11]

Bill Wilson also lectured on his experiences after returning from the Antarctic, but his speeches focused on his ornithological studies of its unique birds. He reworked his scientific notes for publication by the Natural History Department of the British Museum and exhibited his paintings of Antarctica's wildlife and landscapes. His experiences in Antarctica were opening new and welcome doors to him for a future as a scientist. He confided to his father his private hope that his book on the emperor penguin would become a classic.[12]

In 1905 Wilson took on completely new responsibilities as field observer to the Board of Agriculture's Commission on the Investigation of Grouse Disease, whose goal was to ascertain why Scottish grouse in particular were dying in large numbers. Over the next five years Wilson collected thousands of specimens and personally dissected two thousand grouse, ultimately identifying a minute threadworm as the cause of the fatalities. Wilson's agreement with the Grouse Commission included a commitment to paint color plates to illustrate the report. He also accepted appointments as illustrator for two other books, one on British mammals and another on British birds.[13]

In February 1907 Ernest Shackleton announced a plan to attempt to reach the South Pole. His primary backer was a Scottish industrialist, Sir William Beardmore, for whom Shackleton later named the great glacier that proved to be his gateway to the Pole. Wilson received a letter from Shackleton dated February 12, 1907, containing an entreaty to "dear Billy" to come with him to the south as second in command.[14] A warm friendship had developed between the two men on the *Discovery* expedition, and Wilson's diary often described walks for exercise "with Shackle to the top of Observation Hill."[15] But Wilson refused his friend's offer. He may have already privately promised to return to the Antarctic with Scott. And he also had other commitments about which he was surely becoming passionate, for Wilson wrote to Lord Lovat of the Grouse Commission on February 15, 1907, to inform him, "You may perhaps receive letters asking that I may be liberated from my Grouse work to go on another expedition to the Antarctic. . . . I have refused the offer and am quite prepared to stand by the Grouse. . . . I feel that it would be absurd and unfair to throw up the Grouse Inquiry work just when I have begun to get a grip of it."[16]

Scott considered the area of McMurdo Sound to be his particular territory, for it was he who had explored and documented it through his *Discovery* expedition. Shackleton promised Scott that he would not use the Sound but would instead base his work in the Bay of Whales on the eastern side of the

Barrier if at all possible. This agreement was negotiated by Wilson, who was the mediator in a growing rivalry.[17] But Shackleton later reported that he was unable to find a safe anchorage on the east side of the Barrier, and his base was indeed established in McMurdo Sound, on Cape Royds.[18]

Shackleton and his companions used Manchurian ponies to alleviate the dreaded need for man-hauling. The last pony (named Socks) was lost in a crevasse on the Beardmore glacier. His loss was "a serious matter to us, for we had counted on the meat. . . . For traction purposes he would have been of little further use." Shackleton and his three companions continued on by man-hauling, and in January 1909 they established a new farthest-south claim of 88°23′, roughly one hundred miles short of the South Pole. They turned back and barely survived the return to the coast. They staggered into their base at Cape Royds on February 28, 1909, and reached England that June.[19]

In the following September, Scott opened an office for a new British Antarctic expedition. His only son, Peter Scott, was born the same month.[20] Shortly thereafter, Wilson accepted Scott's offer of a position as head of the expedition's scientific staff. And in November 1909 Scott's rival Shackleton was knighted to honor his remarkable Antarctic trek.[21]

Scott planned to follow Shackleton's promising strategy in relying mainly upon Manchurian ponies. He also took some dogs. And he held out hopes that motor sledges—motorized tractors—might prove to be the technological advance that could conquer the challenge of attainment of the Pole. He wrote:

> Ordinary motor engines have worked well in extremes of heat and cold and under various circumstances where the prospect of failure seemed imminent, moreover in our proposed adaptation we eliminate the most fruitful cause of motor car troubles, the "tyre." . . . Motor traffic in the Antarctic regions is a thoroughly practical conception and one which if successful promises the traveller a range of action unthought of. I cannot but think that the patient and exhaustive process of trial for which we are now preparing will produce a machine as reliable and certain in its action as any motor car in daily use.[22]

In an article in the *Morning Post* on October 12, 1909, Scott's plans were described as

> a series of relays, the question of food transport not being left to any haphazard inspiration of the moment, but being carefully pre-arranged in view of a prolonged sojourn away from the base. . . . Captain Scott seems inclined to place chief reliance on the motor sledges. He has been experimenting on snow slopes in Norway with a motor shod with hardwood runners which are fixed in sections on endless bands in the same manner as in the case of the caterpillar traction engines, which have proved so well adapted for negotiating rough ground, and he has every confidence that this novel plan of locomotion over glacier ice will prove a most important factor in solving the problem of traction, which is in reality the problem of the South Pole.

A complex drama also occurred in 1909 on the stage of north polar exploration, one that would soon extend its reach all the way around the world. In May the American explorer Frederick Cook arrived at the Danish settlement of Upernavik in Greenland, claiming to have reached the North Pole by dogsled in April of the previous year. He was unable to return in 1908 before winter arrived, and he and two Inuit companions survived the northern winter of 1908–9 in a shelter on a remote cape of northern Canada eating mainly musk ox. Cook sailed from Greenland to Lerwick in Scotland, where he sent a cable home to New York announcing his achievement. Cook's claim of being first at the North Pole was the banner headline of the New York *Herald* for September 2, 1909. Cook continued to Copenhagen, where he was celebrated as a hero. In the middle of an elaborate dinner in his honor given by a Copenhagen newspaper on September 6, 1909, the news arrived that Cook's countryman Robert E. Peary had also returned from Greenland, claiming to have reached the North Pole by dogsled with his black assistant Matthew Henson and two Inuit companions in April 1909, about a year later than Cook's claim. In the bitter battle that ensued, each disputed the veracity of the other's story. Not one but two Americans claimed the North

Pole in 1909, and the controversy continues today as to whether either truly achieved it.[23]

Roald Amundsen was one of the most renowned polar explorers of the turn of the century. Together with Cook, Amundsen had wintered on board a ship frozen into the Antarctic ice as a member of a Belgian-led expedition in 1898.[24] In 1905 Amundsen led his own expedition, the first to sail through the Northwest Passage in the Arctic.[25] He had been planning to attempt the grand prize of Arctic exploration—the North Pole—when the news arrived of Cook's and Peary's claims. Amundsen announced a complete change of program. Rather than sledging to the North Pole, he would drift across the North Polar Sea by ship. But the proposed North Polar Sea expedition was only a public cover, hiding a secret plan to be first at the South Pole.[26]

South Pole fever was building to a crescendo in Britain as 1909 drew to a close. The upstart Americans had claimed the North Pole, but Britain held the glory of the most recent records for southernmost exploration, set by Scott in 1903 and Shackleton in 1909. An article in the *Globe* declared that "it would be most unfortunate if any other nation were to reap the final glory of Antarctic exploration. Great Britain has done all the pioneer work, and has already established a sort of claim over the South Polar Continent" (*Globe*, October 13, 1909). The man to fulfill that national claim was obviously Scott, veteran of the 1902–4 expedition.

There were rumors of more than one possible rival. Peary of the United States was thought to be considering an expedition of his own (*Morning Post*, February 4, 1910). Although that expedition never occurred, the Japanese and Germans were indeed preparing to embark for the South.[27]

Because Amundsen had announced his plan to be in the Arctic while the British team would be in the Antarctic, Scott approached him with the suggestion that simultaneous magnetic measurements by the two expeditions might reap benefits in furthering the scientific understanding of the magnetic fields that encircle the Earth from one pole to the other. Scott and Tryggve "Trigger" Gran, a Norwegian who was to be part of his team, tried to contact Amundsen, but to no avail.[28] Presumably Amundsen had no wish to interact with the man who was already his unknowing rival, and he knew full

Figure 11. Captain Scott prepares to depart for Antarctica. Photographer unknown. Scott Polar Research Institute, Cambridge.

well that there was no possibility of acquiring any such bipolar data, because he would not be going to the Arctic.

Donations to finance the expedition came from across the empire. School fund drives raised money for particular items, though the expedition and not the schools carried out the procurement. For example, the money to purchase the sled dog whose name was Suka—the Russian equivalent of Lassie—was donated by the girls' secondary school in Derby, while the pony Snippet was financed by Eton College. Captain Scott's reindeer sleeping bag was the gift of the County School in Cardigan.[29]

Eight thousand men volunteered to go south with Scott.[30] They came from the many corners of Britain's vast empire, and among the scientists chosen were one Canadian physicist and two Australian geologists. The men and officers selected from among these for the shore party were all members of the British military services, while the complement of eight scientific personnel were civilians. In addition to Scott and Wilson, thirty-one men were chosen for the shore party. Among the members of the expedition were five sailors from the *Discovery* days, including Evans and Lashly, with whom Scott had trekked to the high plateau of Victoria Land in 1903.[31]

Lieutenant Edward R. G. R. Evans served as Scott's second in command. He had been a sublieutenant on the *Morning* during her relief of the *Discovery* expedition. He was not related to the seaman of the same last name, though both were of Welsh background. The lieutenant was born in London in 1880 and entered the British Navy in 1895.[32] His highly successful military career ultimately led him to the rank of rear admiral and a barony. He was described by many as boisterous and outgoing, and during the 1911 expedition Cherry-Garrard gave him credit for doing much to "cement together the rough material into a nucleus which was capable of standing without any friction the strains of nearly three years of crowded, isolated, and difficult life."[33] The lieutenant's account of the 1911 expedition was published in 1922 and was dedicated to Lashly and another seaman, Thomas Crean, whom he credited with saving his life on their return journey from 87°34′S.[34]

Scott's old ship the *Discovery* had been sold to the Hudson Bay Company after its service in the Antarctic, and the High Commissioner for Canada declined to release the vessel. The strength of *Discovery*'s bow made the ship well suited for Arctic work, and it was engaged in the lucrative fur trade, bringing supplies to the trappers in Canada and returning to England laden with pelts.[35] For the expedition of 1910, Scott instead acquired the *Terra Nova*, the old Scottish whaler that had participated in their relief in 1904, along with the *Morning*. Like *Discovery*, this ship was equipped with sails and with coal-fired steam engines, but it was old and leaky, and it proved "not economic in the manner of coal consumption."[36] The ship's drawbacks became one of several challenges to the expedition.

Lieutenant Evans was charged mainly with preparing the vessel to sail, while Scott handled the design of the scientific program and the all-important task of fund-raising. The ship was cleaned and painted, and its hull was reinforced. The sails were altered and mended, and after the work was done Lieutenant Evans and his crew were "proud as peacocks of our little ship."[37]

The stores officer came from the Royal India Marine. Lieutenant Henry Bowers became known as "Birdie" during the expedition, in honor of his prominent nose. He was born in Greenock in 1883, the only son of a sea captain from a long line of Scottish seafarers. Following in the family tradition, he became a cadet on board the HMS *Worcester* in 1897 and joined the Royal India Marine in 1905.[38] The national pride in Antarctic exploration is evident in the response from the director of that service when Bowers was asked to join the expedition in 1910: "I am very pleased indeed that a R.I.M. officer should be keen on going and feel it is a great compliment to the Service that you have been appointed."[39]

Bowers began his tenure on the *Terra Nova* expedition inauspiciously, falling nineteen feet down the main hatch on the day he arrived in England from Bombay. He suffered no injury, though, and Lieutenant Evans wrote that "this was only one of his narrow escapes and he proved himself to be about the toughest man amongst us."[40] Bowers was 5 feet, 4 inches and stocky, while Wilson was a slim 5-foot-10. Herbert G. Ponting, the expedition photographer, put the contrast into artistic terms: "Wilson, tall and lean, clean-cut and aquiline of feature, with thews of steel and without an ounce of superfluous flesh on his slim, athletic frame; Bowers short and thick-set, with body and limbs as tough as teak."[41] Bowers was greatly admired on the expedition for his remarkable resistance to cold, for his exceptional stamina, and for being a man who could be counted upon by his mates to do his utmost for the common good. Among others, Scott repeatedly marveled at Bowers, as in this diary entry from the sledging journey to the Pole in 1911: "Very cold wind down glacier increasing. In spite of this, Bowers wrestled with theodolite. He is really wonderful. I have never seen anyone who could go on so long with bare fingers. My own fingers went every few moments."[42]

Scott's second expedition had broader goals in both science and exploration than his first. In addition to the assault on the Pole, he "intended to bring back a rich harvest of scientific results. Certainly no expedition ever left our shores with a more ambitious scientific programme, nor was any enterprise of this description ever undertaken by more enthusiastic and determined personnel."[43]

In his head of scientific staff, Dr. Wilson, Scott had a versatile man who may be best described as one of a now-dying breed of scientist called a naturalist, broadly interested in the science of the world around him in all its forms. He was a careful observer of that world, as evidenced not only by his drawings and paintings of its sights but also by his attention to its sounds:

> There has been a very low temperature all day today, down to −49.5°F at the ship and −53°F at Cape Armitage and the usual hazy mist that comes with it and the cracking of the ice and the rigging are very noticeable in the still dead calm of the moonlight. Another thing we have noticed again today. During the last cold snap down below −40°F I noticed a faint hissing noise, in the cloud of one's breath, a few moments after it had left one's mouth. I mentioned this in the ward-room [officers and scientists], but no one took much notice of it. So this evening when I noticed it again, very strongly, I offered to pay for drinks all round if they came up and couldn't notice it. So the Captain came up first with me on the upper deck and after trying about five minutes at last caught it and then he couldn't drag himself away until his ears began to get frost bitten. The sound is so high-pitched, like a whispered sh-sh-sh, or like the fine crepitations one hears in one's hair when one rolls it between the thumb and finger, or when one combs it with a vulcanite comb on a dry hot night, or perhaps the nearest thing of all, but one which only a doctor will ap-preciate, like the finest crepitations of pneumonia heard through a stethoscope. So quiet and high-pitched is the sound that one's ear is not ready for it and one hears every sound in the rigging except that.[44]

But while interested in many things, Wilson reserved his greatest passion for ornithology. Among his principal objectives on the *Terra Nova* expedition was a winter return to the emperor penguin colony at Cape Crozier to collect eggs in their earliest stages of development. Wilson's view of the expedition's and his own goals are described in a letter to his father in September 1909: "Scott is a man worth working for as a man. . . . We must get to the Pole, but we shall get more too. . . . We want the scientific work to make the bagging of the Pole merely an item in the results."[45]

Wilson was in charge of two navy doctors, whose duties included para-sitology and biological studies, along with a civilian staff of seven. The parasitologist was Dr. Edward "Atch" Atkinson, who played an unexpectedly key role in the expedition when he was forced to assume command after Scott's death. The civilian scientists included three geologists, a biologist, an assistant physicist, an assistant zoologist, and a physicist-meteorologist, Dr. George "Sunny Jim" Simpson.[46] Simpson launched a fund drive in his home town of Derby to raise the donations needed to acquire the expedition's meteorological instruments. Five hundred pounds in all were collected, a generous sum that allowed the purchase of the very finest equipment.[47] Like Lieutenant Evans, George Simpson went on to a distinguished career following the expedition. He became the director of the United Kingdom's Meteorological Office in 1920 and was knighted in 1935.[48]

The assistant zoologist was the young Mr. Apsley Cherry-Garrard. Cherry-Garrard was born in Bedford in 1886, the only son and namesake of Maj.-Gen. Apsley Cherry-Garrard. The Cherry family was of French origin, and had settled in Plumpton in the fifteenth century. The Garrards had been lords of the manor of Lamer since the mid-sixteenth century and had enjoyed considerable prominence; among other distinctions, three of them had served as Lord Mayor of London. When the male line of the Garrards ended without issue, the estate passed to the son of a sister of the family line, and Maj.-Gen. Apsley Cherry became Cherry-Garrard, a man in possession of not one but two substantial estates. His son studied classics and modern history at Oxford. In 1907 the elder Apsley Cherry-Garrard died, and young Cherry-Garrard became the lord of Lamer.[49]

Cherry-Garrard's cousin was Reginald Smith, head of the publishing firm of Smith and Elder and a close friend of Edward Wilson. Cherry-Garrard met Wilson through this cousin in 1907 and decided to volunteer to go along if Wilson and Scott returned to the Antarctic. He wrote to Wilson in late 1909 asking to be part of the expedition but received a polite response stating that no promise could be given and warning that he ought to be prepared for disappointment. In early April 1910 he wrote again, offering a donation of £1,000 and repeating his desire to become an expedition member.[50] As lord of Lamer, Cherry-Garrard was a wealthy man. The sum he donated was more than six times Wilson's annual salary of £150 as field observer for the Grouse Commission.[51]

Cherry-Garrard still was not accepted. He nonetheless asked that his donation stand, whereupon Wilson corresponded on behalf of Scott, asking Cherry-Garrard to come to London for a meeting. Wilson wrote: "That is an action [the donation] which appeals to him, not because of the money for which he cares very little, except impersonally, in so far as it helps the expedition to be a success—but because he knows what to expect of a man who felt it was the right thing to do. . . . Be prepared to submit to be examined medically in the event of your being accepted." Cherry-Garrard was severely nearsighted, and the fogging of his glasses by his own breath and perspiration was to render the Antarctic a severe challenge for him. But his dedication overcame his limitations of vision. By February 1911 Scott wrote from a camp on the Barrier that he found it "difficult to express my satisfaction with Cherry-Garrard. He is always ready for everything . . . always to the front when hard work is to be done . . . and does it all in a genial unostentatious way." Cherry-Garrard was sometimes called the "The Cheery One" by the men of the *Terra Nova* expedition.[52]

By the time he returned from the Antarctic, Cherry-Garrard had slogged through more sledge journeys than any other surviving member of the expedition. One of those journeys was a torturous trip in which he desperately waited at a depot on the Barrier, hoping and praying that Scott, Wilson, Bowers, Lawrence Oates, and seaman Evans would reach him. Oates and Evans were already dead, but Cherry-Garrard couldn't know that as he waited and scanned the horizon. Cherry-Garrard spent the rest of his life anguishing over his decision to turn around when he ran out of food for the dogs, wondering whether he should have gone south across the Barrier to search for his friends by killing some dogs to feed the others, contrary to orders. He returned to England from the Antarctic profoundly changed and tormented by this experience. He is reported to have suffered from depression in his later years—no longer the cheery young man he once was.[53] His memoir of the expedition, *The Worst Journey in the World*, is not only a remarkable first-person recounting of the events of the expedition but also his self-described "catharsis of the writer's conscience."[54]

Another wealthy aristocrat and volunteer for the expedition was Lawrence Oates, captain in the Royal Inniskilling Dragoons. Like Cherry-Garrard, he gave the considerable sum of £1,000 to the expedition's coffers, but there was little question of his being accepted with or without such a generous

Figure 12. Captain Lawrence E. G. Oates of the Inniskilling Dragoons with his charges on board the *Terra Nova*. Photograph by H. Ponting. Scott Album, number 11224, Alexander Turnbull Library, Wellington, New Zealand.

gift. Oates was a highly skilled horseman who was to have charge of the all-important ponies. Lieutenant Evans describes the master of horse as a silent man who "showed himself to advantage in managing the ponies. . . . He was very fond of telling us that a horse and a man could go anywhere."[55] At 5-foot-11, Oates was a relatively big man for his day.[56]

Scott chose several more specialists to join his expedition of 1911. The addition of these men appears to reflect key lessons learned from the *Discovery* expedition regarding the need for expert knowledge in particular areas. The Norwegian ski-runner Gran was "very useful in helping us to learn the new fittings and the use of two sticks."[57] Lieutenant Evans wrote: "The Norwegians use different kinds of paraffin wax and compositions of tar and other ingredients. . . . Gran had brought from Christiania [Oslo] the best of these compositions."[58] Exaggerations in the legend of Scott's missteps suggest that the British didn't employ skis at all. It may well be argued that the men of *Terra Nova* were poor skiers and that not all of them took advantage of Gran's expertise. But they clearly did use skis, and Gran advocated the most up-to-date techniques. He had also brought the best ski waxes, composed of paraffin, similar to those employed today. But many such preparations are best applied before setting out on the trail and require careful melting and hot application of the waxes.[59] In the severe conditions of Antarctic exploration many miles from base camp, there was barely enough fuel for the minimum supplies of the water and food needed to sustain life.[60] Extra fuel for ski waxing would be unthinkable on the march to the Pole.

Another critical specialist was the master of dogs. Cecil Meares was an adventurer who had been involved in fur trading in Siberia, where he had acquired experience in dogsled driving. He had also journeyed into Tibet and the Lolo country between Tibet and China, from which he brought back the body of a slaughtered companion, and had traveled to the far-off lands of China, India, and Burma. In sum, he was "a man of action and a most entertaining messmate."[61]

Meares "had adventure in plenty when selecting the dogs and told us modestly enough of his journeys across Russia and Siberia in search of suitable animals. . . . Meares crossed by Trans-Siberian Railway to Vladivostock, thence . . . round the Sea of Okotsk. . . . Thirty-four fine dogs were collected, all used to hard sledge travelling." Meares also selected two Siberian and seventeen Manchurian ponies in Vladivostock—all white, as Scott believed these to be hardier than those of other colorings. Along with the animals, he acquired two young Russians to help care for the menagerie: a dog driver named Dimitri Gerof and a groom named Anton Omelchenko. Meares and his charges traveled by steamer from Siberia to Lyttelton, New Zealand, where they joined the *Terra Nova*.[62]

Near Lyttelton harbor in the city of Christchurch, Scott obtained the services of a prominent businessman, Joseph J. Kinsey, who served as his agent. This trusted man handled a myriad of logistical matters from New Zealand, the last outpost of the empire that the ship would visit on her outbound voyage and the one from which they had fond hopes of transmitting the news of their success.[63]

At a farewell luncheon for the main party in England, the president of the Royal Geographical Society, Maj. Leonard Darwin, wished the expedition Godspeed and proclaimed that Captain Scott was going to prove once again that "the manhood of our nation is not dead and that the characteristics of our ancestors who won our great Empire still flourish amongst us." [64] With this remarkable charge before them, the men of the *Terra Nova* set sail for the Antarctic on June 1, 1910, with Lieutenant Evans in command. Scott continued struggling to raise funds, planning to take a faster passenger liner to join the ship in Capetown, South Africa.[65]

Bowers wrote to one of his sisters, "Mother and May saw me off. . . . The dear old mother was very upset but held up. Of course she thinks of the danger too much. . . . I think she will be alright once she gets home, the truck-load of coffins on the platform alongside us hardly led to cheerfulness." [66]

The expedition had been put together quickly and funded much less lavishly than *Discovery*. As a result, all personnel were stretched to their limits. The tasks of shoveling coal and pumping out the bilgewater demanded the efforts of seamen, scientists, and officers alike. Wilson described the chore of coal trimming as "a dirty business . . . transferring coal from the main hold, where the bulk of it is stored, into the two bunkers, one on each side of the engine room stokehold. The bunkers hold about 50 tons each and have to be filled periodically, so that coal can be got for feeding the furnaces. . . . We take it in three hourly spells. . . . It is hot work and in 10 minutes one is streaming with sweat and black as Kaffirs." In one stint lasting three and a half hours, Wilson and Bowers shifted seven tons of coal from the hold to the bunkers with the "ship rolling so heavily that we were continually dodging avalanches of coal in the dark." [67]

The pumps were driven mechanically when under steam, but while the vessel was under sail the bilge had to be pumped out by hand. It took the efforts of eight men thirty to forty-five minutes at the pump every four hours to keep it pumped out.[68] Cherry-Garrard described the hand-pumps: "The spout of the pump opened about a foot above the deck, and the plungers were worked by means of two horizontal handles, much as a bucket is wound up on the drum of a cottage well." [69]

As difficult as the work was, it had a great benefit to the expedition in creating an unusual understanding among men of vastly different backgrounds. Lieutenant Evans remarked that "in this fashion officers, seamen and scientific staff cemented a greater friendship and respect for one another." [70] By the time they arrived in South Africa, Wilson noted with satisfaction that "the happy family on the *Terra Nova* is still the happiest crew imaginable. It is marvellous that so many men shoved together at random into a ship in which comfort is almost absent, should have shaken down without a quarrel through the whole voyage."[71]

Wilson had an additional personal task for which he awoke at four on many mornings during the journey despite the extreme exhaustion of contributing to the pumping out of the ship and his many other duties. His commitments to the Grouse Report were not quite finished, and he was determined to send the completed documents and illustrations home from South Africa. He "got a corner prepared in a sort of baggage room cabin where I could stand and write to do some work in quiet. . . . No one has a table to write at and I purposely do all mine standing as I invariably fall asleep at once if I sit down."[72] He managed to win his battle with fatigue and sent the required materials home. Two days before he began the trek to the Pole, on October 29, 1911, he wrote a letter to his friend Reginald Smith in which he said: "I shall be frightfully keen to see if the mail brings me a copy of the Grouse Report!" A ship arrived with mail in February 1912, bearing the requested copy.[73] But Wilson never made it back to receive the document he had so eagerly anticipated. He died on the Barrier in late March.

Special friendships developed between some of the men as the ship sailed south. Bowers wrote to his mother that

Cherry and I went to a place called Hawkes Bay for the day and bathed and gave the dogs a run, we have also been to Muizenberg— the Brighton of South Africa—where you can run for miles and miles on a long beach. . . . Cherry is a very sensible youth and as steady as could be. . . . I fancy he is going to be a barrister . . . [and] pretty nearly a millionaire. Both he and Oates are most unassuming and might be worth nothing for all they show or speak of it. Cherry is very generous to me. . . . [I] fight with him all the time to keep him from paying for everything. Needless to say your son would not sponge off even a millionaire.[74]

In South Africa, the experienced horseman Oates initiated Dr. Atkinson into the pleasures of riding, when the two "rode to the hounds one day at

Wynberg." These two "naturally silent men" became great friends, according to Lieutentant Evans.[75]

Scott came on board the *Terra Nova* in South Africa while Wilson went ahead on a passenger liner from Capetown to Australia. Wilson's charge was to arrange for the Australian geologists to join the expedition in Melbourne and to see the premier of Australia in order to "persuade him that we were a worthy object on which to throw away 5000 pounds of federal money." These funds would be enough to allow for an additional year's work in the Antarctic. The Australians were at first reluctant to contribute, having helped Shackleton only a few years earlier. But after a few days of consideration, the request was granted in the form of £2,500 from the government and £2,500 from a private individual.[76]

While in Melbourne, Scott received a telegram. According to Lieutenant Evans, it read: "Beg leave to inform you proceeding Antarctic — Amundsen." Cherry-Garrard quotes it thus: "Madeira. Am going South — Amundsen." Regardless of the exact words the now-lost telegram contained, the message was terse but clear. Although Scott and his men knew about Amundsen's remarkable feats of exploration in the far north, the import of the telegram was not fully grasped at first. Cherry-Garrard wrote: "Though we did not appreciate it at the time . . . we were up against a very big man." Lieutenant Evans's thoughts turned to practical and logistical questions: "We all knew that Amundsen had no previous Antarctic sledging experience, but no one could deny that to Norwegians ice-work and particularly skiing, was second nature and here lay good food for thought and discussion. Where would the Fram [Amundsen's ship] enter the pack? Where would Amundsen make his base?"[77]

The *Terra Nova* sailed out of Melbourne bound for New Zealand, where "New Zealanders showed us unbounded hospitality; many of us had visited their shores before and stronger ties than those of friendship bound us to this beautiful country."[78]

For Wilson, the journey from Australia to New Zealand was a particular delight. Birds were especially abundant on this leg of the sojourn, and Wilson found daily pleasure in ornithological encounters. He wrote: "My diary becomes rather a record of birds than of other business, but it was a most enjoyable trip." He and his assistant Cherry-Garrard caught and skinned numer-

Figure 13. The deck of the *Terra Nova* after departure from New Zealand. Photograph by H. Ponting. Scott Album, number 11234, Alexander Turnbull Library, Wellington, New Zealand.

ous albatross, petrel, mollymawk, and other specimens for the expedition's growing collection.[79]

They reached Lyttelton harbor on New Zealand's south island on October 29, 1910. There they collected their dogs, ponies, the last few men, and many contributions of mutton and other foodstuffs. *Terra Nova* had already been heavily laden leaving Cardiff, and the vessel departed New Zealand a perilously overweight "floating farmyard," according to Lieutenant Evans. Paraffin and oil drums were stored in the hatch spaces, and three huge wooden crates containing the motor sledges were secured by chains to the deck. The upper deck was packed to bursting with bales of hay, sacks of coal, and cans of gasoline. Dogs were chained to rails and bolts wherever space allowed on the deck. The dogs had to be separated from one another to avoid the savage fights that frequently broke out among these wolflike northern animals. The ponies were better behaved and could be harbored closer together. The best part of the crew space was converted to pony stables.[80] The deck itself was nearly invisible, covered with layer upon layer of cargo.[81]

On December 1, 1910, the *Terra Nova* was just off Campbell Island at 50°44′S. A full-force gale struck with devastating effect. Wilson described

> heavy green seas . . . [which] came on board over the rail, both on the weather side and, still more disastrously, on the lee side as she rolled to leeward wallowing into a trough of the enormous seas, got under the whole of these cases and gradually loosened the ropes and wedges which held them down. . . . Then the whole lot starting moving about and breaking one another up. We had to plunge every now and then into the drowned waist of the ship, seize one of the broken cases and haul the two tins of petrol up onto the poop to save them from being burst. . . . The seas were coming in so heavily that 5 tons of deck cargo of coal in sacks was thrown over the side to facilitate the job of securing the petrol cases again.

The violent tossing of the ship by the waves posed grave dangers to the health of the all-important ponies: "One of the horses went down and was got up on its legs again, then another and another."[82]

Lieutenant Evans's account was substantively the same, although as a sailor he particularly lamented the fact that to "sacrifice coal meant curtailing the Antarctic cruising programme," and he counted the lost coal at double Wilson's estimate of five tons.[83] Scott's diary concurred with Evans's estimate of ten tons.[84] Evans also described

> decks . . . continually swept by the seas and . . . rolling . . . so terrific that the poor dogs were almost hanging by their chains. Meares and Dimitri, helped by the watch, tended them unceasingly, but in spite of their combined efforts one dog was washed overboard after being literally drowned on the upper deck. One pony died. . . . Oates had a most trying time in caring for his charges and rendering what help he could to ameliorate their condition. Those of his shipmates who

saw him in this gale will never forget his strong, brown face illuminated by a hanging lamp as he stood amongst those suffering little
beasts. He was a fine, powerful man, and on occasions he seemed
to be actually lifting the poor little ponies to their feet as the ship
lurched heavily to leeward and a great sea would wash the legs of his
charges from under them. . . . Oates' very strength itself inspired his
animals with confidence. He himself appeared quite unconscious of
any personal suffering, although his hands and feet must have been
absolutely numbed by the cold and wet.[85]

Orders were given to furl the jib sail. Cherry-Garrard wrote that "Bowers
and four others went out on the bowsprit, being buried deep in the enormous seas every time the ship plunged her nose into them with great force. It
was an education to see him lead those men out into that roaring inferno."[86]
Bowers cheerfully described his watch as "eventful" in a letter home to his
sisters and his mother. He also told them that balls of grease formed when
coal dust mixed with the oil from the engines. This ignominious dirt soon
began to plug the pumps and threaten the ship.[87]

Lashly was chief stoker on *Terra Nova*, in the front line of the battle to keep
the engines and pumps going. Wilson wrote of the stoker's struggle: "Lashly,
for instance, spent hours and hours up to his neck in bilge water beneath the
foot plates of the stock hold clearing these balls of oily coal dust away from
the valves which could be reached in no other way. The water gained and
gained until at last it was impossible to reach the valves without getting under
the bilge water entirely and that then became impossible."[88]

As trying as the gale was for Lashly, it was much worse for the dogs. Bowers's letter to his mother described their torment: "The dogs, made fast on
deck, were washed to and fro, chained by the neck, and often submerged for
a considerable time. Though we did everything in our power to get them up
as high as possible, the sea went everywhere. . . . However, of this we cared
little, when the water had crept up to the furnaces and put the fires out, and
we realized for the first time that the ship had met her match and was slowly
filling." With the fires out, the men turned to the hand pumps, but these
were choked with coal balls as well, and the water rose ominously in the hold

while the gale reached force 11 on the twelve-point Beaufort scale, or about seventy miles per hour. Bowers struggled to secure the gasoline cases and "had all the swimming I wanted that day." [89]

At this point they had neither steam nor hand pumps, and the ship was filling fast. They could not open the hatch to get to the pump well in order to clear the blockage because the waves were incessantly breaking over it, and they would surely sink in minutes if the hatch flooded. The men formed a chain at the ladder to the engine room and bailed with buckets in two-hour shifts for the next twenty-four hours, with "Scott himself working with the best of them and staying with the toughest. It was a sight that one could never forget . . . some waist deep on the floor of the engine room, oil and coal dust mixing with the water and making everyone filthy, some men clinging to the iron ladder way and passing full buckets up long after their muscles had ceased to work naturally." [90]

Lieutenant Evans and Bowers had similar views on the crisis. Bowers philosophically wrote in his letter to his mother, "Still, 'risk nothing and do nothing,' if funds could not supply another ship, we simply had to overload the one we had," while Evans reflected that "we could not expect to accomplish our goal without running certain risks." Both men had long experience of the sea. Bowers told his mother that "at our worst strait none of our landsmen who were working so hard knew how serious things were. . . . Had the storm lasted another day, God knows what our state would have been, if we had been above water at all. You cannot imagine how utterly helpless we felt in such a sea with a tiny ship. . . . The great expedition with all its hopes thrown aside for its life. God had shown us the weakness of man's hand and it was enough for the best of us." [91]

The only way to reach the suction well of the hand pump without opening the hatch was to cut through an iron bulkhead, a labor of hammer and chisel that was begun at dawn on December 2 and finished at 10 o'clock at night. [92] When the hole was finally ready, Lieutenant Evans and Bowers squeezed through, leading the effort to clear the pumps. They worked "till after midnight passing up coal balls . . . twenty bucketfuls of this filthy stuff, which meant frequently going head under the unspeakably dirty water." They made a wire grate to protect the pump suction from any recurrence of this terrible hazard, and a relieved crew finally stopped bailing and began the much easier task of hand pumping. By 9:00 A.M. they were able to raise steam again. Two ponies and one dog were dead.[93]

Bowers remarked to his mother: "That Captain Scott's account will be moderate you may be sure. Still, take my word for it, he is one of the best, and behaved up to our best traditions at a time when his own outlook must have been the blackness of darkness."[94]

As the iron bulkhead was being cut and a ray of hope began to dawn, Scott took a moment to write in his journal: "We are not out of the wood, but hope dawns, as indeed it should for me, when I find myself so wonderfully served. Officers and men are singing chanties over their arduous work."[95] His men had begun to show their mettle, and with the likes of Lieutenant Evans, Bowers, Lashly, and Oates under his command, he had many reasons to be optimistic.

As they passed from the living world back to the crystalline continent, the men found its beauty overwhelming. Wilson wrote: "The sunlight at midnight in the pack is perfectly wonderful. One looks out upon endless fields of broken ice, all violet and purple in the low shadows, and all gold and orange and rose-red on the broken edges which catch the light."[96] Lieutenant Evans enjoyed the view from high on the mast as he scanned for the best path through the ice. His description is no less passionate: "Glancing down from the crow's nest the ship throws deep shadows over the ice and, while the sun is just below the southern horizon, the still pools of water show delicate blues and greens that no artist can ever do justice to. It is a scene from fairyland."[97] Cherry-Garrard also waxed artistic: "We have had a marvelous day. The morning watch was cloudy but it gradually cleared until the sky was a brilliant blue, fading on the horizon into green and pink. The floes were pink, floating in a deep blue sea, and all the shadows were mauve."[98] Scott was equally enthusiastic about the icy vista: "The scene was incomparable. The northern sky was gloriously rosy and reflected in the calm sea between the ice, which varied from burnished copper to salmon pink; bergs and packs to the north had a pale greenish hue with deep purple shadows, and the sky shaded to saffron and pale green. We gazed long at these beautiful effects."[99] The accounts reflect far more than mere description of the landscape and its color. The remarkable beauty of the Antarctic not only amazed but also moved the men of the *Terra Nova*. The returning *Discovery* hands may have been uncertain whether they now felt more affection for the white cliffs of Dover or for those of the Barrier. As Wilson wrote: "These days are with one for all time—they are never to be forgotten—and they are to be found nowhere else in the world but at the poles. . . . One only wishes one could bring a glimpse of it away with one with all its unimaginable beauty." [100]

FOUR

The Safety of Supplies

The visitor recognizes many of the faces of his fellow passengers on the flight back to Antarctica. Like him, most of them have been away a year or two but have been drawn back to this inhospitable but beautiful place. The plane skids to a stop on the ice runway, and a short truck ride takes the visitor to the station. The surrounding landscape is even more stunning than he had remembered. He gazes with fondness at the striking contours of the white mountains across the Sound.

Even though he is a veteran now, he must attend the safety orientation session. He nods sagely as Antarctica's special perils are explained. He already knows that one must watch for any trace of whitening of the skin on one's companions, the first sign of frostbite. He is also well aware of the need to walk only where flags have been placed to mark the routes that are free of crevasses. He has been doing some reading of the diaries of Scott's men since he was here last, and he suddenly realizes how easy things now are by comparison—how convenient that the safe places are all carefully marked. There is no need to plunge through uncharted and deadly territory, as Scott and his men did.

He goes to the food storage center when orientation is over, to look up an old friend who works there. The temperature-controlled warehouse is huge, and he walks up and down the empty aisles searching for his buddy. This building is always kept a few degrees below freezing. It feels too warm after the intense chill of the outside air, and he opens the zipper of his heavy parka. Towering shelves surround him on both sides, reaching a height of some fifty feet. On each shelf are neatly stacked cardboard cartons containing a dazzling array of foodstuffs. There are boxes of cereals, salt, sugar, and coffee. The next aisle contains frozen vegetables of every variety he has ever eaten, and some such as okra that he would not gladly eat again. One of the large mechanical cherry pickers used to access the stores in the upper reaches of the warehouse sits idly at the base of a huge column labeled "potatoes, raw."

A fabled accounting error of a bygone year has led to a stunning over-abundance of butter, and he walks past row after row of brown cardboard cartons labeled "butter, pats." There is believed to be enough butter here for at least the next eight years. The rest of the food stores are more modest, but everything far exceeds current needs. The warehouse goods would easily feed the two hundred people currently at the station for two years without resupply. There is, quite simply, plenty of everything, and there will be more coming via ship and plane. He remembers what he has learned about Scott's expedition, and he laughs as he wonders what the efficient Bowers would have thought of such excess.

He finds his friend sorting through boxes of frozen shrimp and lobster. The two men arrange to meet later in the bar. A new shipment of good New Zealand wine has just arrived, his friend tells him. It will be pleasant to catch up with each other over a glass.

He pulls up his parka zipper as he steps outside again. The air temperature is about −25°F, and the wind has a sharp sting. As he passes the edge of the Sound, he notices a pair of seals lounging lazily like big cats at the ice edge. A third animal surfaces at a hole to his left, breaking the slushy water with a splash and a loud snort. Until a few years ago, one or two seals were killed every year, to feed the sled dogs that were used for nostalgic rather than practical reasons. But the last of the dogs is gone. The seals no longer have anything to fear from the human visitors, who bring more than enough lobster, butter, and wine to Antarctica.

The sun is setting now, and the Sound is bathed in rich hues of deep purple and red. The visitor walks over to stand on a spit of land at the ice edge for a while, enjoying the sight of these gloriously unique polar colors. The languid sunsets in the clear dry air here far surpass any others, and he is transfixed by the display. Then the wind picks up and bites at his cheek. He turns and hurries up the hill toward the dormitory that will be his home for the next two months. He will have a private room, complete with a bed and a desk. The temperature inside the dorm will be kept at a comfortable seventy degrees Fahrenheit. But the toilet will be down the hall, and he frowns as he considers this imposition on his customary amenities. He pulls his parka tighter to his neck as he passes the *Discovery* hut. The timeless building looks exactly as it did the last time he was here. It was, he now knows, the home of sixteen men for a month in 1911, and of course it has never had any amenities at all.

A man bundled up in a parka and balaclava walks toward him. He glances over as he passes. Then the other man advises: "You'd better get inside; your cheek is turning white."

As the *Terra Nova* crossed the Antarctic Circle, temperatures dropped and the daily habit of deck bathing with a bucket of seawater quickly lost popularity. Only Bowers "kept going in all weathers."[1] His routine was described by the photographer: "Bowers would cast a bucket over astern, and hauling it aboard full of icy water and slush, would upset it . . . over his nude anatomy. . . . After these acts of self-affliction, Bowers—who normally differed from the rest of his shipmates by the remarkable pinkness of his skin—would exhibit a fiery glow from head to foot."[2]

On Christmas Day, 1910, the men of the *Terra Nova* dined on fresh penguin, roast beef, plum pudding, mince pies, and asparagus. All hands attended the Christmas service led by Captain Scott—no one had to stoke the engines or con the ship, because they were stuck tight in the dense ice pack. Although the sea was not frozen solid, their search for open leads was excruciatingly slow, stymied by thick, encroaching ice that choked their progress. They inched southward by only thirty-one miles in the week around Christmas. The delay caused by the heavy ice conditions was now becoming a bigger threat to their success than the gale had been. Lieutenant Evans expressed his concern as the days ticked by, with "all these dogs and ponies cooped up and losing condition, with the *Terra Nova* eating coal, and sixty hungry men scoffing enormous meals. . . . It was, of course, nobody's fault, but our patience was surely tried."[3]

Terra Nova arduously worked its way through the dense ice pack to more navigable waters between December 9 and 30.[4] Amundsen and his men crossed the pack in only five days, January 2–6, 1911, finding it "so loose that we were able to hold our course and keep up our speed for practically the whole time."[5] Shackleton had cleared it in just two days, January 16–17, 1908.[6]

The contrast of Scott's three long weeks stuck in the pack may be interpreted as evidence of gross miscalculations even in his seamanship. But today's science sheds important light on this part of the legend, for it shows that Scott's troubles stemmed not from poor sailing acumen but from the inexorable physics that drives the sudden seasonal breakup of the ice that forms a wall around the Antarctic each year. *Terra Nova* tried to push her way through the ice blockade prematurely—in early December, rather than January. Scott's own *Discovery* cleared the pack ice in just a week almost nine years earlier—but it did so in January. And we now know from the dispassionate eye of satellite sensing that the sea ice around Antarctica melts remarkably quickly each year in December, as illustrated in figure 14 for the 1999–2000 ice season. There is always a large seasonal change in the ice pack like that which occurred in 1999–2000, though it fluctuates somewhat from one year to another depending upon such factors as variability in the atmospheric winds that blow on its surface, the snow blanket that covers it, and the warmth and saltiness of the ocean currents that flow beneath it.[7] In the space of just a few weeks, the ice in the Ross Sea region around Antarctica changes character from an impenetrable broad wall to a loose thin patchwork each year, something that Scott could not have foreseen but which is easily measured with current instruments. Scott's experiences stuck in the pack foretold the scientific understanding of sea ice that was not grasped until many decades after his death.

Lieutenant Evans made frequent trips to the crow's nest, searching for a route out of the maze. Although he did not explicitly note the early date in the season, he did remark that the ice was far more extensive than he had seen on his previous journeys to the Antarctic, writing that "we were rather unfortunate as regards the pack ice met with, and must have passed through 400

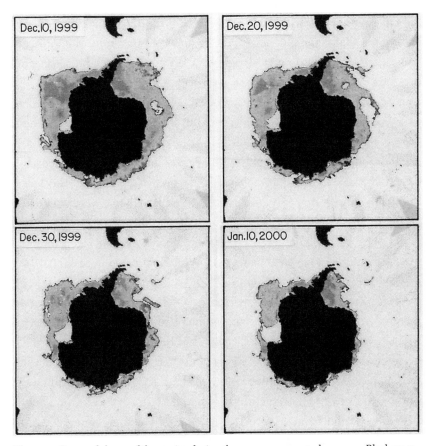

Figure 14. Seasonal decay of the sea ice during the 1999–2000 austral summer. Black areas denote land and ice shelves—permanently frozen regions—while shaded regions show the annually varying ice. Darker shading indicates more densely packed ice; note that the Ross Sea is at left. From advanced very high resolution radiometer (AVHRR) sensor data archived at the Ocean Modeling Branch of the National Center for Environmental Prediction, publicly available on the Internet (see Selected Bibliography for site address).

miles of it from north to south," consistent with the typically broad stretch of thick ice found in the Ross Sea sector in early December.[8] The perceptive Bowers most clearly recognized the explanation for their plight, writing to his sister that "our long spell in the Pack is phenomenal. . . . Of course we have tackled the pack earlier in the season than ever before."[9]

Terra Nova's delay not only consumed critical supplies and taxed the ponies, dogs, and men but also narrowed precious windows of key opportunities that were to come in the next few weeks. The first of these occurred as the expedition selected where to land. Scott, Wilson, and Lieutenant Evans had agreed that Cape Crozier would be an ideal spot from which to base their operations. Wilson was "dreadfully keen on the beach being selected as a base" because of the proximity of Cape Crozier to the vast penguin colony that had been found there on the *Discovery* expedition.[10] The naturalist hoped that study of the "life history of this strangely primitive bird" would be of great value to the expedition's scientific goals.[11] The birds would also provide a convenient source of fresh food. Last and surely most important, Cape Crozier abuts the Barrier directly (see map 3). A base on this beach would not only shorten and simplify the approach to the Pole but would also greatly increase safety, because, as Lieutenant Evans pragmatically noted, starting from here as opposed to elsewhere on Ross Island, "we should be spared the crevasses which radiated from White Island and necessitated a big detour being made to avoid them."[12]

Terra Nova steamed up to the steep face of the Barrier at Cape Crozier. Lieutenant Evans noticed the "tide washing past the cliff faces of the ice; it all looked very white like chalk. . . . Later in the afternoon blue and green shadows were cast over the ice, giving it a softer and much more beautiful appearance." The photographer recorded the scene on film, providing the world with its first motion-picture view of the Barrier. (That historic film is currently distributed in a video entitled 90°S.) The crew lowered a small boat, and Scott, Wilson, and Lieutenant Evans led a foray to evaluate the possibility of a landing. But the swell was too great, and it became clear that the rough seas would not permit safe landing at this most desirable cape. Waiting for the swell to subside was not an option, for the loss of ten tons of coal in the gale and many more in the obstinate pack ice had left them with no choice but to land as best they could, and quickly. They therefore returned to the ship and quickly steamed around to the other side of the island, with which they had become so familiar in 1902–4. But here they only encountered more bad luck. The strait of the Sound was frozen solid to the south of Inaccessible Island, so that there was no possibility of reaching their old *Discovery* base at Hut Point Peninsula. While less well positioned than Cape Crozier, Hut Point does lie close to the Barrier and hence to the route to the Pole (see map 3). Barred now from landing on any haven on the Barrier, they had little choice but to seek out a new and less desirable location. They

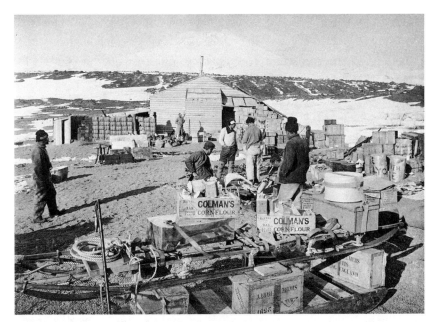

Figure 15. Organizing the supplies on the beach at Cape Evans. The hut is under construction in the background. Photograph by H. Ponting. Scott Album, number 2938, Alexander Turnbull Library, Wellington, New Zealand.

selected a little cape just north of the ice edge at the foot of Mount Erebus. "Captain Scott named it Cape Evans after me, for which I was very grateful," wrote the lieutenant.[13] Overland routes to the south in this area of Ross Island are rendered impassable by extensive crevasses. Fifteen miles of potentially unstable sea ice now lay between this cape and the closest edge of the Barrier near Hut Point. Scott thought that the sea ice was not a great problem, writing that "these bays would remain frozen until late in the season, and . . . when they froze over again the ice would soon become firm."[14] He was to learn that neither of these optimistic suppositions would be realized in 1911.

There was much to be done. A new prefabricated hut had to be assembled on the beach. While it was being erected the men lived on the ship or in tents on shore. The stores had to be unloaded and systematically organized for the planned two-year stay (fig. 15). Three parties were also scheduled to leave the base within a few days: the geological group would go across the Sound to explore the mountains to the west; a second party would go by ship to the virtually untouched land they had found to the east of the Bay of Whales on *Discovery* (Edward VII Land) to establish a second base and begin a year of explorations in that area; and a third party would strike out due south to lay a depot around 80°S (about two hundred miles away), which would serve as a major supply station for next season's assault on the Pole.[15]

A stepwise approach to the polar journey, in which supplies were laid out in depots, was fundamental to their plan. The darkness of winter and the impenetrable shield of pack ice that it spawned dictated arrival no earlier than midsummer, too late to strike out for the Pole in the same year and return safely before the next winter's deep freeze began. Instead, they would lay a depot as far south as they could manage in the first year, putting as many provisions as possible on the trail before them. Then they would have a jump start for the next year's effort. The depot journey of the first year would also help to condition the animals and men to the hardships they would be facing. Amundsen followed a similar approach.[16] Finally, and perhaps most important, the party would gain direct experience of the nature of the Barrier and its weather in the precise season when they expected to be returning across its forbidding expanse after attaining the Pole.

The men of the *Terra Nova* set to work unloading the ship on January 4, 1911. Two of the three motor sledges were put ashore promptly, so that they could immediately be used to haul other supplies. The dogs and ponies were next. After more than five weeks of confinement in their stalls on board the ship, the ponies were quickly "rolling and kicking with joy." The ice underfoot where Scott and his men unloaded was measured to be about three feet thick on January 4, according to Wilson.[17] The dog teams were soon running loads over it between the ship and the shore, a distance of a mile and a half on smooth ice.[18]

Lieutenant Evans described Bowers's supervision of the unloading: "The provision cases came ashore and were stacked in neat little piles under Bowers's direction. This indefatigable little worker now devoted himself entirely to the . . . stores."[19] Meanwhile, Dr. Wilson's knowledge of anatomy was put to the task of killing and flensing seal carcasses, adding to their reserves of food the fresh meat that had helped stave off scurvy during the *Discovery* expedition. He was assisted in this bloody but important work by seaman Evans.[20]

The ponies were inspected by Oates and certified one by one as fit for work. Scott esteemed the skills of his master of horse: "Oates is splendid with them—I do not know what we should do without him."[21] The horses pulled loads of seven hundred to one thousand pounds from the ship to the shore, some much more willingly and efficiently than others. A few were weak, others were "steady workers," some were downright vicious, and one was strong but extremely obstinate. Cherry-Garrard became convinced that this last animal (named Weary Willie) was "a cross between a pig and a mule."[22]

The motor sledges made a promising start. The newest vehicle towed loads of 2,500 pounds over the ice at a speed of about six miles an hour, while an older one pulled a ton.[23]

On the edge of the floe one morning, Scott noticed

> six or seven killer whales. . . . They seemed excited and dived rapidly, almost touching the floe. . . . As we watched they suddenly appeared astern, raising their snouts out of water. I had heard weird stories of these beasts, but had never associated serious danger with them. Close to the water's edge . . . our two Esquimaux dogs were tethered. . . . I did not think of connecting the movement of the whales with this fact, and seeing them so close I shouted [to the photographer]. . . . He seized his camera and ran towards the floe to get a close picture of the beasts which had momentarily disappeared. The next moment the whole floe under him and the dogs heaved up and split into fragments. One could hear the booming noise as the whales rose under the ice and struck it. . . . Whale after whale rose under the ice, setting it rocking fiercely.[24]

Fortunately, neither the photographer nor the dogs fell off the floe into the water, as the whales evidently had hoped. But the whales would continue to patrol the ice edge, seeking further opportunities to hunt the men and animals of the *Terra Nova* expedition.

Lieutenant Evans and Cherry-Garrard both worried about the ice near the ship on the evening of January 7. The lieutenant wrote: "The floe by the *Terra Nova* is very thin and rather doubtful," while Cherry-Garrard recorded that "last night the ice was getting very soft in places, and I was a little doubt-ful about leading ponies over a spot on the route to the hut. . . . It has been thawing very fast the last few days, and has been very hot as Antarctic weather goes." Cherry-Garrard also noted that one of the seamen plunged through the ice up to his neck the next morning. In spite of this frigid warning of the unstable state of the ice, the third and last motor sledge was unloaded a half-hour later. Cherry-Garrard was one of a group of about twenty men who began to pull it away from the softer ice near the ship with a long tow line. Suddenly the machine sank, nearly taking two men along with it to the bottom of the Sound—a depth of about one hundred fathoms.[25]

Lieutenant Evans gamely stuck by his captain in writing about this inci-dent, noting, "It was nobody's fault, as Simpson and Campbell both tested the floe first and found it quite thick." It is worth noting that Evans's book was written after the expedition and was intended expressly to "keep alive the interest of English-speaking people in the story of Scott and his little band of sailor-adventurers, scientific explorers, and companions."[26] In contrast, Wil-son was not a military man but a doctor, scientist, and artist. Although his writings reveal considerable devotion to Scott, Wilson also strove for accurate portrayal of the world around him in his paintings and in his diary. Wilson's private journal was never intended for public reading, and on January 14 he wrote, "We are a very happy lot and so far have had the most unexpected good fortune with but few accidents and hitches, none of which, except possibly the loss of the third motor, could possibly have been foreseen or avoided."[27] The memoir of one of the Australian geologists provides a fuller account of Scott's precise role on this fateful day: "Captain Scott and Lieutenant Camp-bell were testing the ice, and warned me to be especially careful of certain wet patches near them. I got through to the shore without incident, but this unhappily was not the case with the motor sledge, which started off immedi-ately afterwards. . . . The whole of the machine crashed through the ice; and despite the utmost efforts of the hauling party it sank in a hundred fathoms. Thus was lost nearly a thousand pounds' worth of valuable machinery, and since it is made largely of aluminium, it corrodes extremely rapidly."[28]

Scott wrote simply: "I stupidly gave permission for the third motor to be got out this morning."[29] He was in a hurry to unload quickly, and moving the ship to a different location would have consumed not only time but also precious coal reserves. But as the ice beneath the motor sledge gave way, an indelible and frequently cited entry in the legend of Scott as a bumbler was recorded. Less often noted is Scott's brutally honest and self-critical description of the event in a diary that he knew would be subject to widespread scrutiny.

The ship was quickly moved, and the unloading of stores continued in a safer location. Spirits remained high, as Lieutenant Evans noted: "We called the sandy strand . . . Hurrah Beach; the bay to the northward of the winter quarters we christened Happy Bay."[30]

The men lived in tents while the main hut was constructed. At fifty by twenty-five feet, it was considered a palace by the lieutenant and called roomy and warm by Cherry-Garrard.[31] The hut was a wooden structure insulated with quilted seaweed. This palatial home was shared by as many as twenty-five men for months during the winter season in 1911. A bulkhead formed of cases of provisions separated the area where the officers and scientists lived from those of the seamen, for the expedition had imported Victorian views of class and propriety to the bottom of the world. The dogs were tethered on chains and ropes near the hut, while a lean-to stable was built for the ponies on the north wall of the structure, using bales of fodder and tarpaulin roofing. Bowers also constructed a storeroom along the south wall.[32]

Two ice caves were hollowed out in a snowdrift to the lee of a hill next to the hut. One of these conveniently served as a freezer for meat supplies, and the other was used for magnetic measurements. Lieutenant Evans took charge of making these caves, but he was assisted by many others, "even roping in Captain Scott, who did a healthy half-hour's work when he came along our way."[33]

Scott turned his attention to the issue of attainment of the Pole, determined that the prize would be won if not in the coming year then in the one to follow. Based upon discussions with Meares and Oates, he asked Kinsey, his agent in New Zealand, to send down a team of Indian transport mules on the ship next year, "such as were used by the Thibetan Expedition. . . . They did wonderful work . . . at great altitudes and in very low temperatures."[34] He then wrote to Maj. Gen. Douglas Haig, chief of staff in Simla, India, to formally request the animals, explaining:

We are entirely dependent on this transport and should any ponies
fail in the coming winter we shall be handicapped and possibly miss
our goal next season. With ample food it is my intention to make
a second attempt in the following season provided fresh transport
can be brought down; the circumstances making it necessary to plan
to sacrifice the transport animals used in any attempt. . . . I have
thoroughly discussed the situation with Captain Oates, and he has
suggested that mules would be better than ponies for our work and
that trained Indian transport would be ideal. . . . Oates and another
member of my expedition, Mr. Cecil Meares, have both seen the
wonderful work done by mules in northern India, and especially during the expedition to Thibet. . . . We are all very much in earnest
here and feel that it *must* be an Englishman who first gets to the Pole.
Pray help us if you can.[35]

Meanwhile, the first year's effort would depend heavily on the ponies and on
the skills of their handler, Captain Oates.

The shore party moved into their new home on January 18, 1911, but twelve
of them left it on January 24 to begin the journey south to lay the critical
depot of provisions in support of the next spring's march to the Pole. They
had waited in order to give the ponies a chance to regain their health, for the
five-month journey on board a sometimes-heaving ship at sea, followed by
the strenuous work of unloading the vessel, had taken a great deal out of the
animals.[36] Eight pony sledges and two dog sledges dragged a total weight of
more than five thousand pounds southward, with a goal of depoting a ton of
food and fuel at about 80°S.[37] The men and their animals left Cape Evans
in "a state of hurry bordering upon panic," according to Cherry-Garrard, because the sea ice that formed the only viable route between them and the
Barrier was breaking up. Indeed, although they did not realize it at first, the
ice behind them went out the next day.[38] They won this little race with time,
but by a very slender margin.

Scott found an opportunity to write a letter to Lieutenant Evans's wife as
they passed Glacier Tongue on their route south: "I thought you might be
glad to have a note to tell you how fit and well your good man is looking,
his cheery optimism has already helped me in many difficulties and at the

present moment he is bubbling over with joy at the delights of his first sledge trip. . . . I daily grow more grateful to you for sparing him for this venture. . . . With all kind regards and hopes that you will not allow yourself to be worried till your good man comes safely home again . . ."[39] The care and attention to detail often paid by Scott not only to his men's feelings but also to those of their families as evidenced by this letter present a revealing contrast to the apparent lapse of leadership that had led to the loss of the motor sledge a few days earlier.

This poignant letter, along with many others written by the shore party, was entrusted to those who remained on board *Terra Nova*. This ship would not be frozen in for the year, as *Discovery* had been. Because the *Terra Nova* expedition did not have enough funds to charter a relief mission, it was imperative that the ship flee the ice before the winter set in. In addition to these safety concerns, it was also necessary for the vessel to return to New Zealand in order to purchase supplies for the second year.

Dr. Atkinson developed a very sore heel and was left behind with seaman Crean. Together the two men were to go back to the shelter of Hut Point and prepare the *Discovery* hut to become the home for the entire depot party on the return from the Barrier. There the men would wait until the ice froze hard enough to bear them safely back to Cape Evans. The *Discovery* hut had been visited by Shackleton, who had apparently left a window open two years earlier, sometime before he departed Antarctica to return to glory and fame in England. The interior of the hut was now encased in ice and snow, perhaps as a result of this unwelcome intrusion by Scott's rival. Shackleton, however, would later protest that he had carefully closed the window before departing in 1909, suggesting that the wind may have been responsible for the breach.[40] Whatever the source, the doctor and his companion labored hard to clear the hut out before Scott and the others came back. Coincidentally, the parting of the two groups would have been difficult if not for a stroke of good luck a few days before in finding an extra tent and a spare cooker left behind by Shackleton on the Barrier but not yet concealed by snow.[41] Thus at nearly every step the lonely visitors to the Antarctic were influenced by and reminded of the few who had previously left their footsteps on its white plains.

The ponies began the depot journey pulling eight hundred to nine hun-

Figure 16. A camp on the Barrier. Note the snow walls erected to protect the ponies from wind. Photographer unknown. Scott Album, number 11447, Alexander Turnbull Library, Wellington, New Zealand.

dred pounds apiece, progressing well across the hard ice of the Sound. The two dog teams consisted of eleven animals each, and at first they dragged about five hundred pounds "at a snail's pace," according to Scott. As some lameness was noticed in two of the ponies, the loads of both ponies and dogs were reduced. The dogs' performance improved, and on January 29 Scott rated their work as excellent. A day later the party reached a spot well up on the Barrier that they called Safety Camp: they were now clear of the unstable ice of the Sound and relatively safe on the more reliable Barrier (see map 3). But that surface posed a new threat to their progress. The ponies sank deeply into the snow and the going became difficult and slow.[42]

Trudging through the snow was also a trial for the men, for even the skilled Norwegian ski expert Gran found it impossible to use skis while leading a pony. After a morning's march in which he sank heavily into the snow, Gran attempted to ski alongside his pony. But as he approached the animal, the pony started and careered off, perhaps frightened by the swish of the skis, and the men all took to plodding through the snow alongside their beasts from that point on.[43]

A lone set of pony snowshoes had been brought along, and the next day these were placed on the hooves of Gran's pony, Weary Willie. Scott wrote: "The effect was magical. He strolled around as though walking on hard ground in places where he floundered woefully without them." A dog team was immediately sent back to see whether they could reach Cape Evans and retrieve the rest of the pony snowshoes, but to no avail. The ice had gone out south of Hut Point, and nothing but open water now lay between the old *Discovery* hut and the new one at Cape Evans.[44] Scott's optimistic hopes that the ice would hold until "late in the season" were quickly dashed, with devastating impact. Thus the long delay sailing through the pack ice too early in the season, the inability to establish a base at Cape Crozier, and an overoptimistic view of the conditions to be faced after reaching shore at Cape Evans combined to frustrate their efforts at depot laying. These individually small problems built a tower of challenges for the next year's polar trek.

The legend of Scott's gaffes holds that the pony snowshoes were forgotten at the start of the depot journey. But the master of stores was Bowers, whose attention to detail was already evident and was to become legendary in the months to come. The meteorologist Simpson offered the following testimony to Bowers's remarkable qualities: "Bowers was of great help to me in the balloon work. . . . One day I had just released a balloon when I exclaimed to Bowers, 'Damn it all, I have forgotten again to take the number of the instrument.' Bowers replied that it was number 23. I was surprised for I did not know that he knew there was a number stamped on each instrument. When I expressed my surprise I added, 'I suppose you did not notice the number of the instrument which we sent up last week.' 'Yes,' he replied, 'that was number 15.' "[45]

Indeed, one set of pony snowshoes had been carried, proving that forgetfulness was not the problem; eight sets could have been brought as easily as one. Rather, Scott's diary reveals his esteem for the views of his master of horse on this key matter: "Oates hasn't had any faith in these shoes at all, and I thought that even the quietest pony would need to be practised in their use." It seems clear that the lone set was brought only for experimentation, while the rest were left behind out of respect for Oates's expert opinion that they would likely prove useless. This act of faith in his man cost Scott greatly in the all-important matter of the distance that could be gained on the depot journey. Scott wrote: "It is trying to feel that so great a help to our work has been left behind. . . . It is pathetic to see the ponies floundering in the soft patches. . . . They generally try to rush through when they feel themselves sticking. If the patch is small they land snorting and agitated on the harder surface with much effort. And if the patch is extensive they plunge on gamely until exhausted." [46]

The depot party began marching at night in the hope that colder night-time temperatures would improve the surface for the ponies, or at least increase the animals' comfort by allowing their rest period to occur in the relative warmth of the day. But after beginning their first night march, the men realized that the single set of pony snowshoes had indeed been left behind at Safety Camp, presumably by Gran, whose pony had last worn them. The ski-runner's talents were put to good use, as he quickly skied back to retrieve them. [47]

Scott increased the food allowance from the twenty-six ounces per day per man used in 1902–3 to thirty-two ounces per day per man on this journey. He noted with satisfaction that the rations appeared to be sufficient when their loads were being drawn by the animals, writing: "Our food allowance seems to be very ample, and if we go on as at present we shall thrive amazingly." [48] But although the men were well, some of the animals were not. Wilson, who was driving dogs together with Meares, wrote on February 3 of his concern for the dogs, who "are getting 1 pound of dog biscuit each a day. . . . They are all thinning down very much." [49]

On February 4 the party reached a spot they called Corner Camp, as it was here that they turned due south, having cleared the islands and bluffs around Ross Island (map 5). A blizzard descended upon them. Although the air was warm (about 20°F), it was clear that "hell is on the other side of the thin sheet of canvas that protects us." [50] Cherry-Garrard described the spectacular power of his first Antarctic blizzard: "Outside there is raging chaos. . . . Fight your way a few steps away from the tent and it will be gone. Lose your sense of direction and there is nothing to guide you back." [51]

The dogs were comfortable in the holes they dug in the snow, and "the

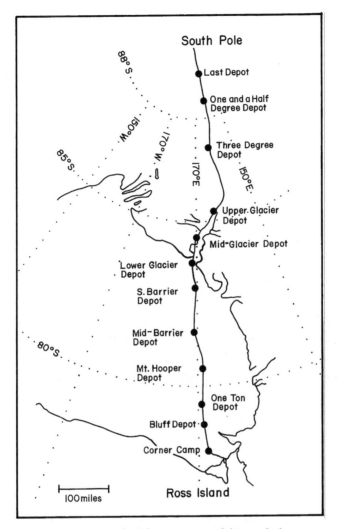

Map 5. Scott's route to the Pole in 1911–12, with his supply depots. Most depots held enough food for about one week for the returning parties. Note that map is oriented with south at top.

only trouble they give is from twisting up their harness into knots by turning round and round every time they get up, before lying down again."[52] Cherry-Garrard commented on two dog half-brothers who "always insisted on sharing one hole and for greater warmth one would lie on the top of the other. At intervals of two hours or so they would fraternally change places."[53]

But the ponies were another matter. Some of them had begun the trip in poor condition. Now they stood outside in a blizzard for three straight days, at the end of which "all look[ed] listless and two or three [were] visibly thinner than before."[54] To make matters worse, the horses had just come through the warm tropics, and, as Oates explained in a letter to his mother: "These poor ponies are having a perfectly wretched time. They have their summer coats on and this wind which is blowing now is bitterly cold for them."[55] The ponies were given more food, and the men began to build snow walls at night to keep the wind, which nearly always blew from the south, off their horses (see fig. 16). Because the dogs went much faster than the ponies, they began to start a few hours later.

The column continued marching south, but the ponies were weakening daily. Oates proposed taking them all as far south as possible, then killing those too weak to return and depoting the meat for provisions for the polar journey. But Scott badly wanted to save as many ponies as possible; whether his motivations were primarily sentimental or practical can be argued. The ponies were essential to the plan of minimizing the dreaded man-hauling in the next season's long march to the Pole, and Scott wrote: "We must save all the ponies to get better value out of them next year." But his thoughts also reflect strong sympathy with the animals, as in the following description of one pony: "The poor thing is a miserable scarecrow and never ought to have been brought."[56] In any case, Lieutenant Evans was sent back with two seamen and the three weakest ponies. The remaining southbound party consisted of five men (Scott, Oates, Bowers, Cherry-Garrard, and Gran) leading ponies, along with two men (Wilson and Meares) driving dogs.

Bowers impressed his captain with his unusual resistance to the weather: "Bowers is wonderful. Throughout the night he has worn no head-gear but a common green felt hat kept on with a chin stay and affording no cover whatever for the ears. His face and ears remain bright red. The rest of us were glad to have thick balaclavas and wind helmets. I have never seen anyone so unaffected by the cold."[57]

The next day the skies cleared and the march continued, but the surface was difficult and the ponies sank "lower than their hocks frequently."[58] Weary Willie could not keep up, and the pony and his leader fell behind. When the dogs caught up with the floundering animal, "the whole team turned into wolves like a wink and made for the horse as it lay in the snow. . . . Gran and Meares both broke their sticks promiscuously on the dogs' heads and the horse kicked and bit at them, and they were at last driven off, but not before the poor beast of a horse had been pretty severely bitten."[59]

A few days later, one of the horses bit through his hobble and ate freely of the men's biscuit. The horse was put on a steel wire, but Wilson noted with concern that the animals' own food didn't seem to satisfy them—they were "dreadfully hungry."[60] The ponies were being fed from bales of compressed fodder but seemed to lose weight alarmingly regardless of the quantities consumed. Cherry-Garrard described the pony food: "Theoretically this fodder was excellent food value, and was made of wheat which was cut green and pressed."[61] The experience confirmed Oates's doubts that the fodder might not meet the ponies' needs. Only though his urging had supplies of hay, oil-cake, bran, and crushed oats also been brought on board the ship, and it was now evident that those stores were invaluable to further progress.[62] Indeed, the dragoon had purchased some of these goods with his personal funds and had smuggled them onto the overloaded ship.[63] Although very few of these critical commodities were available on the depot journey, they would be used more extensively the following year.[64]

Scott's diary for February 16 describes temperatures falling to −21 °F, accompanied by a strong breeze from the southwest. The challenge of the weather finally nipped even the exceptional Bowers. Scott observed that Bowers: "started out as usual in his small felt hat, ears uncovered. Luckily I called a halt after a mile and looked at him. His ears were quite white. Cherry and I nursed them back whilst the patient seemed to feel nothing but intense surprise and disgust at the mere fact of possessing such unruly organs. Oates' nose gave great trouble. I got frost-bitten on the cheek, as also did Cherry-Garrard."[65] In this misery of cold, they built their depot the next day at 79°28.5′S at a spot deep within the Barrier, about 150 miles (130 geographic) from Hut Point.[66] Among the items placed there were seven weeks' worth of full food supplies for one four-man unit, 8.5 gallons of oil (twelve weeks' allotment for a four-man unit), such miscellaneous supplies as extra butter, oats, and dog biscuit, and a minimum thermometer to document the coldest temperature that the coming winter would bring.[67] They named this lonely spot on the Barrier One Ton Camp, but this "camp" or "depot" was

Figure 17. One Ton Camp. Photographer unknown. Scott Album, number 11466, Alexander Turnbull Library, Wellington, New Zealand.

no more than a large cache of stacked wooden boxes, cans, and other miscellaneous supplies, marked by a flag (fig. 17).

Scott reflected on the difficulties that were likely to be faced in the next year, noting that "Oates' nose is always on the point of being frost-bitten. . . . I have been wondering how I shall stick the summit again, this cold spell gives ideas. I think I shall be all right, but one must be prepared for a pretty good doing."[68] Modern medical studies demonstrate that humans do acclimatize to cold conditions. Remarkably, fingers become inured to immersion in ice water, and subjects cease to shiver when placed into frigid all-body chambers.[69] In the coming months, Scott's men slowly adapted to Antarctic conditions, and, like test subjects in contemporary medical experiments, some of them adjusted more readily than others.

The party divided again for the return journey. The horses were taken by Oates, Bowers, and Gran, while Scott and Cherry-Garrard returned with Wilson, Meares, and the dogs. Cherry-Garrard and Wilson took turns running alongside the sledge while the other was carried by their dog team. On February 21 Wilson "knew from the noise and feel under foot that every now and then we were crossing lidded crevasses. . . . This sort of surface continued for a mile or a mile and a half and I was running my team abreast of Meares, but about 100 yds on his right . . . I suddenly saw his whole team disappear, one dog after another, as they ran down a crevasse in the Barrier surface." Cherry-Garrard remained with the team while Wilson assisted Scott and Meares. The men quickly realized that they had been running along rather than over the hidden crevasse, which not surprisingly had given way from the pressure. The lead dog had remained on the surface, along with the sledge and the last pair of dogs in the team, but the animals between them now hung in a "great blue chasm." Two dogs had slipped out of their harness and fallen to a snow ledge below, beneath which was an abyss. The men quickly moved the sledge off the crevasse lid. Meares was then lowered down on an alpine rope, from which he cut the nearest dogs out of their harnesses and hauled them up. The lead dog was beginning to choke from the pressure of his load, so the men secured his harness and freed the animal. One by one, the dogs were pulled out of the crevasse until only the two on the ledge remained.[70] Over the objections of his men, Scott insisted on being lowered down personally to pull the last dogs out. Cherry-Garrard wrote of Scott's technically minded fascination with the crevasse: "While we were getting him up the sixty-odd feet to which we had lowered him he kept muttering—'I wonder why this is running the way it is—you expect to find them at right angles,' and when down in the crevasse he wanted to go off exploring, but we managed to persuade him that the snow ledge upon which he was standing was utterly unsafe."[71]

Following this near-catastrophe, on February 21 the dog party reached Safety Camp, where they met Lieutenant Evans, the two seamen who had accompanied him, and the sole pony survivor of their return trek. The other two animals had perished on the march back despite tender care. The dogs were also exhausted by the depot journey, though they had pulled well. Scott wrote: "The dogs are thin as rakes. . . . Ravenous and very tired. I feel that this should not be, and it is evident that they are underfed." Five tons of dog biscuit had been brought to Antarctica on board the *Terra Nova*, as Meares felt that these enriched biscuits would prove an ideal food. Although some

Figure 18. The *Terra Nova* arrives at the Bay of Whales in 1911. Note the Barrier in the background. Photograph by an unidentified Norwegian photographer on board Amundsen's *Fram*. Number 25505, Alexander Turnbull Library, Wellington, New Zealand.

dogs gained weight on these rations while on board the ship, the depot journey showed that their nutritional needs for the demanding work of sledging could not be met with biscuits alone.[72]

The next day Scott and his band of men marched to Hut Point, expecting to find Dr. Atkinson and his companion, as well as the messages that ought to have been dropped off by the ship on its way out of the Sound. Seeing signs of habitation but no men, they returned to Safety Camp in a state of growing worry and were relieved to find that the others had gone there to meet them. They had passed en route but not seen one another because the parties had taken different paths.

The message the doctor carried from the ship was stunning. When the *Terra Nova* had sailed into the Bay of Whales (see map 2) in order to search for a spot to land the second group of men, who were to explore the land to the east of the Barrier (sometimes called the eastern party), they had encountered Amundsen, his men, and their 100-plus dogs.[73] It may at first seem remarkable that these two tiny groups of human souls literally ran into each other on the vast continent, but examination of the map of the coastline, including its semipermanent ice shelves, reveals the logic behind this encounter. The broad outline of Antarctica had been sketched by sailing expeditions of the nineteenth century. The Ross Sea region and the Barrier were known to provide a coastline that was considerably closer to the Pole than other sectors. The east side of the Barrier offered a closer approach to the Pole if a safe site could be found where the Barrier was not subject to calving and not so high as to make unloading a ship impossible (see satellite image in map 4). Shackleton had also tried to land in the Bay of Whales in 1908, but the sight of large icebergs gave him grave concern for its stability as well as for the safety of his ship; he therefore abandoned this attempt and landed on the known safety of Ross Island instead.[74] The Bay of Whales on the east side of the Barrier and Ross Island to its west were hence likely locations for the two rival expeditions of 1911.

The British and Norwegian explorers warily but politely toured one another's facilities, had breakfast and lunch together, and parted. Etiquette demanded that the men of the *Terra Nova* now abandon their notion of putting a base in this area, and the planned eastern party instead became a northern party. The ship was severely short of coal and had to return to New Zealand without delay. The party therefore had little time to search for a good site for their work; they chose the region near Cape Adare because it had been the location of the first wintering on the Antarctic continent, by Carsten Borchgrevink and his crew in 1899.[75] The northern party endured an ordeal of epic proportions during the *Terra Nova* expedition, spending a second winter marooned not in the relative comfort of the Cape Adare hut but in an ice cave, surviving almost entirely on seal meat.[76]

Although Scott described the encounter with Amundsen as "startling," he also determined that "the proper, as well as the wiser, course for us is to proceed exactly as though this had not happened. To go forward and do our best for the honour of the country without fear or panic. There is no doubt that Amundsen's plan is a very serious menace to ours. He has a shorter distance to the Pole by 60 miles. . . . He can start his journey early in the season—an impossible condition with ponies."[77]

Wilson was far more skeptical of Amundsen's odds for success: "As for Amundsen's prospects of reaching the pole, I don't think they are very good.

. . . I don't think he knows how bad an effect the monotony and the hard travelling surface of the Barrier is to animals. Another mistake he seems to have made is in building his hut on sea ice below the Barrier surface instead of on the Barrier itself. It will be a fortunate thing for him if the whole hut doesn't float out into Ross Sea."[78] Amundsen's analysis of the stability of his camp was quite different: "The inner part of the bay does not consist of floating barrier. . . . The Barrier there rests upon a good solid foundation, probably in the form of small islands, skerries, or shoals."[79]

We now know that the great Norwegian explorer was wrong in his conviction that land lay beneath the Bay of Whales, while the naturalist Wilson was closer to the truth in his analysis. Amunden's camp may have been on the Barrier (not sea ice, as Wilson guessed), but the entire region is unstable, despite the proximity of Roosevelt Island, which lies not underneath Framheim but to its southeast. The Barrier near the Bay of Whales continually flows at an average rate of about a quarter-mile per year, and it is also subject to occasional abrupt calving. Later installations in this area include the U.S. bases of Little America I, II, III, and IV and a glaciological station called Camp Michigan. Remnants of several of these stations that once rested on the edge of the Bay of Whales have been seen on icebergs adrift in the open sea.[80] By good fortune these chunks of the Barrier broke off after the stations had been abandoned rather than during their occupancy. But in 1987 and 2000, for example, massive icebergs more than one hundred miles long calved off of the Barrier in this area, eliminating Amundsen's Bay of Whales entirely as a feature of the coastline.[81] Modern satellite images such as figure 19 demonstrate that the great explorer was lucky rather than prescient, for the sea and not the land lay beneath his camp. If the ice of the Barrier underlying Amundsen's hut had broken off during 1911, as it has on some other occasions, the Norwegian party likely would have survived because the breaking off of a large berg is a slow process. But surely their story would have been profoundly different.

Scott decided that more supplies should be moved south, but the dogs were too exhausted to be of further service. Meares and Wilson remained behind to care for them, feeding the hungry animals their fill of seal meat.[82] On February 24, seven of the men, along with their sole pony, began hauling more material toward the Barrier. They passed the returning main pony

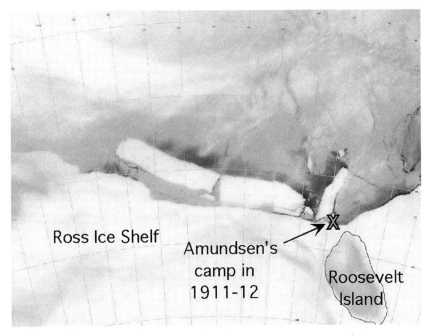

Figure 19. Satellite image of the calving of massive icebergs in May 2000 in the precise area where Amundsen's camp stood in 1911–12. The camp was once at the location of the calving berg marked by the letter X. Roosevelt Island to the southeast of Amundsen's camp is completely snow-covered. The flow of ice around this island plays a key role in the calving of large icebergs to its north, rather than stabilizing it, as Amundsen suggested. Image courtesy of the Antarctic Meteorology Research Center, University of Wisconsin, Madison, and Matthew Lazzara.

party at a distance. On February 25, Oates, Bowers, and Gran arrived at Safety Camp together with the ponies, while the southbound party reached Corner Camp a day later. From here Lieutenant Evans, Dr. Atkinson, and two seamen were instructed to return slowly to safeguard the health of their pony. Scott, Cherry-Garrard, and seaman Crean meanwhile headed back at top speed for Safety Camp, where Scott "found everyone very cold and depressed." The weather had taken another turn for the worse, and it was extracting a severe toll on the hapless ponies.[83]

The entire party left Safety Camp the same day in order to get the animals quickly to the shelter afforded by Hut Point. A large thaw pool had been seen on the sea ice between this area and the hut, and Scott and his companions had a discussion of whether to go via the ice or to take a more difficult overland route via "the Gap" (see map 3). Wilson was "all for the Gap, for I didn't believe that the sea ice would still be safe." He and Meares departed the camp first with their dogs. When they left the safety of the Barrier and passed through to the sea ice, Wilson noticed that the area was "broken up by fine thread-like cracks—evidently quite fresh—and as I ran along by the sledge I paced them and found they occurred regularly at every 30 paces which could only mean that they were caused by a swell. . . . The cracks in the ice we were on were actually working up and down about ½ an inch with the rise and fall of a swell. Knowing that the ice might remain like this with each piece tight against the next only until the tide turned, I knew we must get off it at once. . . . We therefore made for the Gap."[84]

Wilson and Meares picketed the dogs and pitched a tent on solid ground, then went back to the frozen shoreline with a pick and shovel to try to smooth the surface for the ponies that they expected to arrive at any moment. But the two men soon saw that the ponies and their leaders were not coming along right behind them but instead were miles out on the strait, trying to reach Hut Point by the unstable sea ice. Wilson couldn't understand why Scott would do such a thing. Then Wilson saw the men and animals turn around. He assumed that the party had recognized the danger and would camp on the safety of the Barrier. It was only later that he learned that it was the inexperienced Bowers and not Scott who was leading the horse party across the shifting ice.[85]

Scott was not with his men on the fragile surface of the Sound because he had split the party once more. The pony Weary Willie had collapsed as soon as he started, and Scott, Oates, and Gran stayed with the animal, making "desperate efforts to save the poor creature," even giving him a hot oat mash. Despite these ministrations, Weary Willie died that night.[86]

While carrying out this unsuccessful attempt to save the horse, Scott sent Bowers, a man with no prior polar experience, to lead a party of Cherry-Garrard, seaman Crean, and four of the all-important ponies onto an area known to be unstable. This incident is sometimes cited in the legend of Scott's errors of leadership. Less often recounted are the acts of courage of his men, told modestly here in the journal Bowers sent home to be read by his mother and sisters:

Orders were to push on to Hut Point over the sea-ice without delay.
. . . On coming to some shaky ice we headed farther west as there
were always some bad places off the cape. . . . About a mile farther
on I began to have misgivings; the cracks became too frequent to
be pleasant, and although the ice was frozen from five to ten feet
thick, one does not like to see water squelching between them, as we
did later. It spells motion, and motion on sea-ice means breakage. I
shoved on in the hope of getting on better ice round the cape, but
at last came a moving crack, and that decided me to turn back. . . .
We got well into the bay, as far as our exhausted ponies would drag,
before I camped and threw up the walls, fed the beasts and retired to
feed ourselves. . . . It was very dark and I mistook a small bag of curry
powder for the cocoa bag and made cocoa with that, mixed with
sugar; Crean drank his right down before discovering anything was
wrong. It was 2 . . . before we were ready to turn in. I went out and
saw everything quiet; the mist still hung to the west but you could
see a good mile and all was still. The sky was very dark over the Strait
though, the unmistakable sign of open water. I turned in. Two and a
half hours later I awoke, hearing a noise. Both my companions were
snoring. I thought it was that and was on the point of turning in again
having seen that it was only 4:30 when I heard the noise again. I
thought—my pony is at the oats! and went out.

I cannot describe either the scene or my feelings. I must leave
those to your imagination. We were in the middle of a floating pack
of broken-up ice. . . . As far as the eye could see there was nothing
solid; it was all broken up and heaving up and down with the swell.
Long black tongues of water were everywhere. The floe on which
we were had split right under our picketing line and cut [the] poor
[pony] Guts's wall in half. Guts himself had gone, and a dark streak
of water alone showed the place where the ice had opened up under
him. The two sledges securing the other end of the line were on
the next floe and had been pulled right to the edge. . . . I shouted
to Cherry and Crean and rushed out in my socks to save the two
sledges; the two floes were touching farther on and I dragged them

to this place and got them onto our floe. At that moment our own floe split in two but we were all together on one piece. I then got my finnesko [fur boots] on. . . . I have been told that I was quixotic not to leave everything and make for safety. You will understand, however, that I never for one moment considered the abandonment of anything.[87]

Cherry-Garrard thought it was "madness to try and save the ponies and gear when it seemed the only chance at all of saving the men was an immediate rush for the Barrier."[88] Bowers was adamant that he would try, and so his mother would apparently have guessed by knowing him.

Cherry-Garrard and Crean loyally remained with their leader and companion, and the three men began working their way south across the floes, toward the safety of the Barrier. They would wait for the drifting chunks of ice to come near or touch one another, and then they would jump the ponies across. Some floes split one another on impact, while others bounced apart and became unreachable. Progress across this treacherous maze was slow, but the party was edging closer to safety.

Then the killer whales arrived, perhaps attracted by the opportunity to feed on the seals that no longer had the safety of the ice as an escape. They may also have whetted their appetites on poor Guts. The huge black dorsal fins of the whales poked out of the oily water between the ice floes as they searched for more prey. Cherry-Garrard later described the cauldron of the Sound that day: "Killer whales . . . were cruising about in great numbers, snorting and blowing, while occasionally they would in some extraordinary way raise themselves and look about over the ice, resting the fore part of their enormous yellow and black bodies on the edge of the floes. They were undisguisedly interested in us and the ponies, and we felt that if we once got into the water our ends would be swift and bloody."[89]

After six hours of jumping from floe to floe, the men drew close to the Barrier only to find a lane of open water thirty or forty feet wide at its base. It was impossible to take the ponies farther, but an agile man might find an opportune arrangement of shifting floes on which to cross. Bowers reasoned that Cherry-Garrard, given his poor vision, ought to stay on relatively safe ground. He sent Crean to try to find a way through and seek help. Bowers later wrote of the precarious position that he and Cherry-Garrard were in as they stood stoically with the ponies: "It only wanted a zephyr from the south to send us irretrievably out to sea; still there is satisfaction in knowing that one has done one's utmost, and I felt that having been delivered so wonderfully so far, the same Hand would not forsake us." [90]

Meanwhile, Wilson had witnessed the plight of the pony party from the shore with field glasses. Crean succeeded in climbing off the Barrier and reaching Scott, who had already spoken with Wilson and was rushing in their direction. When Scott arrived at the Barrier edge, he immediately ordered Bowers and Cherry-Garrard to climb onto a large iceberg that had gotten stuck in the lane and use it and their sledges as ladders in order to climb out. They did so and were welcomed by a relieved Captain Scott: "I realized the feeling he must have had all day. He had been blaming himself for our deaths, and here we were very much alive. He said: 'My dear chaps, you can't think how glad I am to see you safe.'" [91]

Scott wanted to leave the ponies and equipment, but Bowers insisted upon at least pulling out the cargo. The men got their supplies up onto the Barrier, but the ponies and the two sledges remained below. Oates and Bowers shoveled furiously, desperately trying to build a crude snow road to get the ponies out. But then the ice started moving again. They managed to haul the now-empty sledges up to safe ground but stood helplessly on the Barrier as a faint southeasterly wind widened the crack between them and the animals. The three remaining ponies stood huddled together on their floe as it drifted slowly away, toward the open sea.

The exhausted party of men camped for the night a half-mile in from the Barrier edge. And the next morning after breakfast, the persistent Bowers once again went down to the ice edge, carrying a pair of field glasses. The pony floe had miraculously lodged on a long point of the Barrier to the west. It looked as if there might be a chance of saving the animals. The men immediately raced off to try. But when they reached the animals and began to guide them across, the first pony failed at a jump less strenuous than those he had readily cleared the day before, perhaps because the animals were stiff from standing still for hours. The horse fell into the frigid water. After a fruitless struggle to pull him out, Oates killed the pony with an ice pick to preempt a more painful and tortured death in the jaws of the killer whales. The men

Figure 20. Dr. Wilson and the pony Nobby. This animal was the sole survivor of the breakup of the sea ice in February 1911. Photograph by H. G. Ponting. Scott Album, number 11393, Alexander Turnbull Library, Wellington, New Zealand.

chose a new spot and tried to rush the next pony over the lead. He repeatedly refused. Finally, this horse cleared, and the other followed. There was only one more jump to reach safety. The first horse went over it easily, but just as the second animal approached the edge of the ice, a school of whales surfaced in the lead. The frightened pony swerved in midair and landed in the water. This pony was the one that Bowers had been leading throughout the depot journey, and the man had daily expressed his affection for the animal by giving him three lumps of sugar out of his own ration. The men struggled to pull the horse out while the whales cruised all around them. At any moment, the thin ice could have been shattered by a whale's flukes or head. Finally Oates said, "He's done; we shall never get him up alive." This time it was Bowers who killed his pony with a pickax, to save the animal from being eaten alive by the dreaded whales.[92]

Bowers's courage and determination in extricating his two men, the valuable supplies and sledges, and one lone but important pony from oblivion is a tale that can only astound the modern reader. That he was a man of many remarkable attributes, as impervious to fear as he was to the cold, is apparent. He was also a product of a bygone era. This is nowhere more evident than in an earlier letter to his mother in which he wrote: "Nearly everybody is provided with Shetland things. I am glad you have marked mine, as they are all so much alike." [93] Thus the mother who read the letters describing her son's daring exploits in the gale and on the sea ice had also personalized his clothing.

The men and the rescued pony now crossed to Hut Point via the land route, working their way over steep rocky slopes. From a vantage point on the island, Scott was surprised to see that a large feature known as Glacier Tongue (see map 3) had broken away and drifted out to sea. This massive abutment of ice had been stable since the *Discovery* days, so its fracture underscored the ferocious nature of the swells and blizzards that had swept across the Sound in the past month. Scott began to worry about the safety of the base camp at Cape Evans, for it was located on a low beach. Scott told Bowers that he had no confidence in the motor sledges after seeing their wooden rollers become broken while being unloaded from the ship. His faith in the dogs had been shaken by the starvation they had suffered on the depot journey, and he felt that he had "lost his most solid asset—the best of his pony transport." [94] Scott returned to Hut Point an unhappy man.

The religious Wilson attributed their misfortunes to God's designs, writing that "the whole train of what looked so like a series of petty mistakes and accidents was a beautifully prearranged plan in which each of us took exactly the moves and no others that an Almighty hand intended each of us to take. . . . The whole thing was just a beautiful piece of education on a very impressive scale." [95]

Scott himself lies at the heart of this divine drama. His leadership style had evolved from his first to the second expedition. He had honed his personal touch, and these skills allowed him to knit the majority of the men into a remarkably happy and hardworking group. He worked beside them in such tasks as bailing water on the ship and hollowing out the ice caves on the land. In sharing these and a myriad of other tasks he won respect and loyalty from many. He wrote appreciative letters to the men's families, valuing their efforts and abilities. But perhaps because his esteem of his men was so high and his personal confidence limited, he put the ice novice Bowers in command of a party that would end up very nearly floating out to sea, and he left all but one set of pony snowshoes behind, having been advised by Oates that they might not be practical.

The loss of coal in the gale and the tardy arrival in the Antarctic due to the extensive stretch of early-season pack ice they encountered were two elements in the tale that could scarcely have been anticipated. Because both coal and time were limited as they searched for the location to unload, the crew's haste set a domino effect into motion: because they opted to quickly base their camp at Cape Evans rather than at Cape Crozier or Hut Point, they were left a more difficult and longer route for the depot journey and similarly for the Pole in the coming year. Their problems were further compounded in a striking manner when the ice went out between Cape Evans and Hut Point, for the all-important pony snowshoes that would have made the depot journey far easier on the animals then became unreachable.

As he had on the *Discovery* expedition, Scott pushed his luck—this time with some disastrous results. Lieutenant Evans exhibited a touch of criticism of his captain when he wrote of the near-loss of the dog team in the crevasse: "Scott returned with the dog teams. In order to cut off corners he shaved things rather fine." Although all of the dogs were retrieved from the fall in the crevasse, one of the valuable animals later died from injuries suffered in the event.[96] Things had also been shaved too finely when the third motor sledge was unloaded onto thinning ice, but with the more immediate consequence of a rapid descent to the bottom of McMurdo Sound. One man began to sharply criticize Scott in private. Oates wrote to his mother, "The loss of the horses was Scott's fault entirely."[97]

After Weary Willie died, Scott noted that "these blizzards are terrible for the poor animals. Their coats are not good, but even with the best of coats it is certain they would lose condition if caught in one, and we cannot afford to lose condition at the beginning of a journey. It makes a late start necessary for next year."[98]

A late start also would mean a late finish—or no finish at all.

FIVE

The Start of a "Coreless" Winter

The visitor is late for the evening science lecture. He waited too long for his favorite flavor of ice cream to be brought out at dinner, and now he'll have to hurry across the station to the science building.

He shivers and pulls his parka hood up tightly around his face. Today the sun barely emerged from the mountainous horizon across the Sound, and the temperature now is −35°F. The cold snow is stiff and sandpapery beneath his rubber boots. This means that he can run without risk of slipping, so he picks up the pace and lopes across the surface. The snow squeaks loudly as he races along a slightly sloping grade. It's the very spot where he slipped and fell less than a week ago, on a day when the temperature was about +10°F. But today his boots seem to grip the frigid ground like magnets on metal. He wonders what it would have been like to drag even a lightly loaded sledge across the cold snow of the Barrier in these conditions.

He arrives at the lecture hall just as the presentation begins. The speaker is a veteran Antarctic scientist who has spent more than two decades studying weather and climate. He has dedicated his career to building up a network of automated weather stations scattered around the continent. Many of these lie near Ross Island, but there is one at the South Pole, and a handful at a few remote places between. Their primary purpose is to aid aviation safety around and along the corridors of transport to the manned U.S. stations at the Pole and at McMurdo. The weather station network not only reduces the risks to those who travel and work here but also provides a unique window into the meteorological conditions in the coldest place on Earth.

The speaker and his team of students and postdoctoral associates service each of these instruments on an ongoing basis. The automated devices dutifully collect wind, temperature, pressure, and some humidity data, even in the harshest conditions. The visitor reflects upon the relative ease of obtaining this information now, compared with the remarkable efforts of the men of the Terra Nova expedition. He has read that it was usually Bowers who would stand out in the relentless cold and wind, swinging the sling thermometer three times a day in every variety of weather and meticulously penciling the numbers in his meteorological log book with numbed fingers. Today the machines automatically record temperature and wind every ten minutes around the clock, and the data points are transmitted to the United States immediately by satellite.

A lock of white hair falls over the speaker's forehead. The man brushes it back with fingers that are badly swollen by large frostbite blisters. Perhaps getting this data is not so easy after all.

The speaker has begun his annual circuit to care for the weather stations, and he shows a chart of their positions. He says that things were dicey this year when the plane landed near the instrument on the Barrier at 80°S. The visibility was obscured by low-level blowing snow, and the pilot very nearly dipped a wing in the uneven surface. The man shrugs as he casually describes this brush with disaster, for risk is an everyday occurrence in the Antarctic. Like other scientists, this man is enthralled with Antarctica and the beauty of his data. He deliberately understates the dangers involved in getting them.

The visitor studies the diagram displaying the weather station locations. There is one instrument located just south of the remote place in the midst of the Barrier where Scott and two companions perished on their return from the Pole. There is another machine a few degrees farther south, also near the meridian that served as their route. There is a third at the Pole itself, and a fourth quite close to the place they called Corner Camp, just east of the islands that fringe the edge of the Barrier. The speaker has carefully kept them all running continuously for many years, and there is a touch of pride in his voice as he presents a table showing that there are now

Figure 21. An automated weather station. Wind speed, wind direction, and air temperature sensors are mounted at the top of the ten-foot tower. Some units measure relative humidity and the vertical temperature gradient below the tower. Temperatures are measured with platinum wire resistance thermometers, seen here next to the chain on the left-hand side. Pressure is measured with a quartz transducer. Data are typically obtained every ten minutes and are transmitted in real time to a satellite, from which they are relayed back to a ground station outside Antarctica. The data are archived on the Internet by a research team at the University of Wisconsin, Madison (see Selected Bibliography for site address). Photograph by Rob Holmes.

THE START OF A "CORELESS" WINTER

fifteen to twenty years of continuous data available from these and other locations.

The speaker describes the average annual cycle of temperature observed at each place, noting the special conditions of wind or proximity to the sea that make each area differ. But he emphasizes that they all share the common feature of a "coreless" Antarctic winter, in which temperatures drop rapidly after summer solstice, much more rapidly than at stations in the Arctic. There is hence no central core of deep midwinter cold—it is simply cold all winter long.

The lecture ends and the visitor raises his hand to pose a question. He noticed a station called Bowers on the map, located near the very top of the Beardmore glacier around 85°S. But no data were shown from that location. Where are the data from Bowers? he asks.

The speaker shakes his head. That site was among the most challenging that he has ever encountered. It was in a remote place of intense cold, wind, and drift. The instrument bravely reported data for nine months, then fell silent. It was decided that it would be far too difficult to keep observations going in a spot like that. And so the record of the automated weather station at Bowers is a brief one that mirrors that of its namesake, who perished on the Barrier at the age of twenty-eight.

By March 4, 1911, the men of the depot party were reunited at Hut Point. They converted the hut's verandah into a shelter for the remaining ponies and the dogs. They found fire bricks in a large trash heap left by earlier occupants and were able to construct a brick stove and chimney in which to burn seal blubber for heat and cooking. Even so, wrote Cherry-Garrard, "to say that the hut was cold is a mild expression of reality."[1] Blubber also supplied light, in the form of crude lamps made of metal matchboxes containing a cube of the seal fat embedded in a piece of wax.[2] The blubber smoke blackened the men's skins and deposited a thick layer of grease on their clothing. Although Dr. Atkinson and his companion had managed to clear out most of the snow and ice from the interior, the space between the ceiling and the roof was encased in an immovable chunk of blue ice, which slowly melted in "the most infernal drip-drip." The men protected their sleeping and work areas with an awning that had been left behind from the *Discovery* expedition, and they strategically hung tin cans to catch the worst of the runoff.[3]

They settled in at the hut, anticipating that the ice would freeze in less than three weeks to allow a safe return to the main base at Cape Evans. But Lieutenant Evans recorded that "time after time the sea froze over to a depth of a foot or even more and time and again we made ready to start for Cape Evans to find that on the day of departure the ice had all broken and drifted out of sight."[4] Scott considered attempting an overland journey along the slopes of Mount Erebus. But these routes were "crowded with crevasses," according to Wilson.[5] It was Wilson who convinced an impatient Scott that the overland trip would be too risky and cautioned against venturing out on the unstable young sea ice. As Cherry-Garrard recalled in an introduction to a biography of Wilson, "Several times we prepared to cross the newly frozen ice to Cape Evans, and several times Scott, after a quiet talk with Bill, gave up the idea as too dangerous."[6] There was no choice but to continue to wait for the deep freeze of Antarctic winter to harden the ice.

On March 14 the western geological party—three scientists and seaman Evans—returned from their surveying trip and joined the others at the hut, bringing to sixteen the number of people in the 1,300-square foot, one-room structure.[7] The Australian geologists were particularly appreciated as engaging conversationalists. The days were mostly passed in the welcome arms of sleep, in walking for exercise around the nearby hills, or in hunting seals, cooking meals, conversing, and reading. Women's suffrage was among the controversies of the day that elicited stimulating debates in otherwise quiet times.[8] Little reading material had been taken along on the depot journey, for the pressing need to move as many pounds of man and pony food as possible dictated the lightest possible personal loads. But a motley collection of miscellaneous papers and books had been left behind at the hut by the *Discovery* crew. Among these were dated copies of the *Girls' Own Paper* and the *Family Herald*, and an incomplete copy of a novel called *My Lady Rotha*. Cherry-Garrard wrote of this book that "the excitement was increased by the fact that the end of the book was missing."[9]

Cherry-Garrard described life at Hut Point as a far-south version of Robinson Crusoe. He appeared to enjoy the interlude on the peninsula, noting that "Hut Point has an atmosphere of its own. . . . Partly aesthetic, for the sea and great mountains and the glorious color effects which prevail in spring and autumn would fascinate the least imaginative; partly mysterious, with the Great Barrier knocking at your door, and the smoke of Erebus by day and the curtain of the Aurora by night; partly the associations of the place—the old hut, the old landmarks, so familiar to those who know the history of the *Discovery* expedition." [10] Wilson spent much of his time engaged in sketching and painting, and like Cherry-Garrard, he enjoyed the environment, especially the "glorious color at daybreak." [11]

But Lieutenant Evans was a man who loved the open vistas found at sea, and to him the dark hills surrounding Hut Point were melancholy and foreboding. He described how "night shadows of cruel dark purple added to the natural gloom of hut point and its environments. . . . How sinister and relentless the western mountains looked, how cold and unforgiving the foothills, and how ashy grey the sullen icefoots that girt this sad, frozen land." [12]

On March 16, 1911, Evans led a party of eight men that included Bowers, Oates, and Cherry-Garrard on yet another sledging journey onto the Barrier. The goal was to transport more supplies to Corner Camp by man-hauling, so as not to risk the dogs or ponies. As the men struggled to complete this trip of about one hundred miles, nighttime temperatures plummeted to below −35°F on the edge of the Barrier. The sledges ceased to glide, and pulling became "very heavy. . . . Dragging even light sledges when returning from the depot proved a laborious business." The cold in turn brought the ice, which collected on the inside of the tents and showered down on the men during meals. The merciless condensation also found its way into their sleeping bags, which "made life at night a clammy misery." [13]

The extreme cold became the party's most feared enemy. The cold was generally worse than the wind, for the toil of hauling the sledges often kept the men warm on the march, even in breezy conditions. On March 18 Lieutenant Evans described the wind as strong and the visibility as about ten yards. Yet he and his men continued marching in these semiblizzard conditions, and their concerns centered not on the wind or on what would now be called the wind chill but on the frigid nights. During the agony of a midwinter journey on the Barrier under even colder conditions, Cherry-Garrard later wrote, "In such temperatures the effect of even the lightest airs is blighting, and immediately freezes any exposed part. But we all fitted the bits of wind-proof lined with fur, which we had made in the hut, across our balaclavas in front of our noses and these were of the greatest comfort."[14] Through great care the experienced men could usually protect themselves from the wind, but there was no defense against the cold that robbed them of desperately needed sleep by turning their breath and perspiration into chilling layers of misery in their clothes and sleeping bags. Wind from behind was a particularly cherished help to the march, and a head wind was a manageable problem as long as the temperatures were not too severe. But there was one special combination of cold and wind that could daunt even Bowers: when the breeze blew too strongly in their faces for the exertion of man-hauling to overcome its chill. On his way to the Pole in December 1911, Bowers wrote of days of "absolute agony" and times when "the arms got numbed with the penetrating wind no matter how vigourously they were swung."[15]

Roughly four hundred miles to their east, Amundsen and his men were also hard at work moving material in preparation for their next year's polar journey. On March 3, Amundsen and his team of men and dogs reached a latitude of 81°S, deep on the Barrier. There they encountered temperatures of −49°F. Amundsen wrote: "If one compares the conditions of temperature in the Arctic and Antarctic regions, it will be seen that this temperature is an exceptionally low one. The beginning of March corresponds, of course, to the beginning of September in the northern hemisphere—a time of year when summer still prevails. We were astonished to find this low temperature while summer ought to have lasted, especially when I remembered the moderate temperatures Shackleton had observed on his southern sledge journey." In spite of the harsh conditions, Amundsen's party continued south. Amundsen fed his dogs on dried fish and pemmican rather than biscuit; he and his men depoted 1,234 pounds of dog's pemmican at 81°S and another 1,370 pounds near 82°S before turning north again. But abundant food was not enough to keep the animals healthy in such frigid conditions, and his dogs became "terribly emaciated" as they worked. Eight sled dogs died on Amundsen's depot journey. He returned to his base on March 19, 1911, four days before Lieutenant Evans and his companions returned to Hut Point from their trip to Corner Camp.[16] Both groups had experienced a taste of the Barrier in winter, and it was still only March.

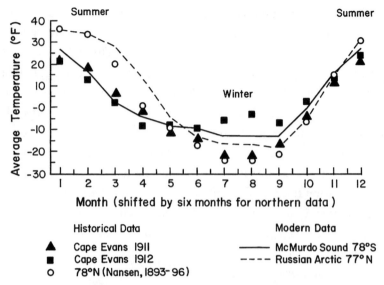

Figure 22. Comparison of the seasonal cycle of temperature in the Antarctic and Arctic, both in ocean and coastal environments, based upon recent data, along with the historical measurements presented in Simpson's 1919 treatise. Nansen's farthest-north expedition provided key meteorological data for the high Arctic at the turn of the century (see Simpson, *Meteorology*, vol. 1). The Northern Hemisphere observations have been shifted by six months in this figure so that temperatures in like seasons can be compared. Note the much cooler summer and far earlier onset of winter in the Antarctic. The long period of low temperatures in Antarctica from April through September, represented by the relatively flat solid line, gave rise to the term *coreless winter.*

    The cruel conditions of Antarctic winter had already been glimpsed before the *Terra Nova* expedition. Scott's *Discovery* expedition had provided full seasonal coverage of the temperatures at McMurdo Sound in 1902–4. These data were given to a noted Austrian meteorologist, Julius Hann, for analysis. Hann pointed out that the observed temperatures in March at Hut Point in 1902–4 were nearly as cold as those found in midwinter (July); this was markedly different from typical data from the Arctic, where the deep cold of winter is restricted to a few months around the solstice. Hann therefore declared the Antarctic winter "kernlos" (German for coreless) in a scientific work published in 1909.[17] Figure 22 illustrates the onset of the cruelly coreless Antarctic winter about two months before that of the Arctic.

Although Amundsen expected to find Antarctic temperatures in March similar to those of the Arctic in September, Scott and his companions knew that they faced a coreless winter like those they had already encountered on *Discovery*. Indeed, in this respect Scott's scientific leanings and his laying of key groundwork in his 1902–4 expedition meant that he was better informed than Amundsen of the weather conditions that were likely to be encountered—a stark contrast to the portrait of Scott as a bumbler whose ignorance is legendary and complete. Amundsen was "astonished" by the temperatures he encountered on the Barrier in March, but Scott's own work had revealed the "coreless" winter years earlier. Nonetheless, Amundsen had surely prepared extremely well, and he was amply armed for conditions far worse than he expected to find. He ventured onto the unknown of the Barrier with more than enough supplies and dogs, so the surprise at the temperatures that he noted in his writings did not substantially impede his progress in exploration. In short, Amundsen included generous safety cushions, while Scott chose narrow margins.

At this point, it may be useful to question whether the temperatures reported by the early Antarctic explorers can be considered accurate. The meteorological results taken by navy men on Scott's first expedition had been a target for severe criticisms from scientific circles, although recent analysis implies that those arguments were unfounded.[18] The inclusion of Simpson, a civilian with excellent credentials, including a doctorate in science and experience in meteorology, shows Scott's determination to avoid such attacks upon his second expedition. In addition to his personal qualifications, Simpson obtained the finest thermometers of the day—thanks to both the generous financial contributions of the people of his native Derbyshire and loans of equipment from such distinguished scientific institutions as the London, Australia, and New Zealand Meteorological Offices. Before sailing, he calibrated not just one but two large thermographs at Kew Observatory in London; these were used as the standards to which the expedition's other thermometers were scaled and checked. Each portable thermometer was also meticulously calibrated at Kew before departure. Temperature and wind data were taken hourly at Cape Evans during the *Terra Nova* expedition, using multiple instruments.[19]

Modern measurements lend important support to the care with which the meteorologists of the *Terra Nova* expedition conducted their work. Two years of data were recorded through great personal efforts by Simpson and his assistant Charles Wright at Cape Evans in 1911–12. The observers often worked around the clock to ensure a continuous data stream. Automated weather stations and recording devices began to make the job far easier on its human attendants many decades later. And the data recorded by the men of the *Terra Nova* expedition compare remarkably well to observations collected by the machines of the late twentieth century, as shown in figure 22, supporting Simpson's calibration.

Simpson's thermometers were mounted on screens near the main base camp to allow free airflow past the instruments. In polar regions, it is particularly critical that temperature be measured in the free airstream rather than in pockets of air that may be warmer or colder than the surroundings. On sledging journeys, temperatures were measured with a sling thermometer twirled vigorously by the observer to avoid the possibility of pooling of cold or warm air around the instrument. Because mercury freezes at temperatures below −38°F, the liquid material in the sledging thermometers was "spirit" (alcohol or toluene). Simpson meticulously cross-calibrated the mercury and spirit thermometers at Cape Evans. He also showed that three different sledging thermometers gave essentially the same result when measurements were taken in close proximity during the trek to the Pole.[20] Platinum wire resistance thermometers have since replaced the sling thermometer that Bowers and others so diligently twirled. The wires are generally accurate over a broad range of temperatures, but Simpson's approach of comparing nearby observations to check for instrumental problems is still employed today.[21]

While the timing of the coreless Antarctic winter was a challenge to science at the turn of the century, the temperatures of Antarctic summer were an even bigger mystery. Scientists pondered the puzzle of why Antarctic summer is so much colder than the corresponding Arctic season, given the symmetric and powerful warming effect of the sun at both poles in their respective summer seasons. It was the insightful Simpson who first solved this conundrum by noting that the highly reflective snow surface—the same surface that plagued Wilson with snow blindness because of his sketching—

cools the Antarctic summer by sending the sun's energy back to space instead of absorbing it. Simpson wrote, "Of the solar energy which falls within the Antarctic Circle, such a large proportion is lost by direct reflection from the snow that the remainder is not sufficient to raise the temperature of the air to the freezing point before the solstice is reached, and the energy commences to decrease." [22] In contrast, the oceans of the north absorb the summer energy provided by the sun and thereby warm more readily. The Antarctic therefore begins and ends its summer at temperatures well below freezing, maintaining a continual reflective mirror of snow and setting the stage for a very cold winter.

Scott's esteem for his meteorologist is reflected in his description of Sunny Jim Simpson: "admirable as a worker, admirable as a scientist, and admirable as a lecturer." [23] Simpson was put in command of Cape Evans when Scott and the polar party left it for the last time in late October 1911. Scott began his parting letter of detailed instructions for such matters as changes that ought to be made to the hut in his absence with the warm words "My Dear Simpson," and he noted that Simpson was "fully aware of my plans and wishes," suggesting that the two talked frequently.[24] On February 18, 1911, during the depot journey, Scott noted in his diary that the minimum temperature was −16 °F when camp was broken; next to this sentence he made a note to himself: "inform Simpson!" [25] This confirms that the two men discussed such key matters as the observations of temperatures on the Barrier.

Simpson's three-volume treatise summarizing the meteorological findings of the expedition was published after many years of painstaking analysis, long after Scott was dead. In completing the preface to his great labor in 1919, Simpson wrote: "Over and over again as point after point was cleared up I have longed to be able to show the result to Captain Scott, for there was hardly a problem of Antarctic meteorology which we had not discussed together. . . . To most of us who have given our lives to science our investigations are frequently tinged with an unscientific desire to increase our scientific reputations, but with him it was the added knowledge alone which gave pleasure." [26] Thus as he penned the preface to the book culminating his efforts of nearly a decade, Simpson described Scott as the truest of scientists, a seeker of understanding and not of status. It is evident that the two men enjoyed sharing their thoughts about meteorology while in Antarctica, and that their relationship was a close one.

Simpson also understood the link between Antarctica's summer cold and its associated coreless winter. Simpson wrote: "At the end of summer, the ice in the north is thinner than at the end of winter, there is some open water, and the surrounding land surfaces are still free from snow, and, therefore have a relatively high temperature. All these effects supply heat, and keep the [Arctic] temperature high, thus when the sun sets for the last time in October [month 4, fig. 22], the temperature in the north is 24.9° higher than when it rose in February." He also wrote of the vastly different autumn conditions in the snow-covered continent of Antarctica, where temperatures simply follow the sun, thus producing the starkly coreless winter, during which temperatures begin to plunge as soon as the sun starts to set.[27]

That rapid drop of temperatures after solstice, which had been sampled during the depot journey (especially by Lieutenant Evans's party during their sleepless nights on the Barrier) is critical to any party attempting to attain the Pole in high summer and return safely in February or March.

Although the *Discovery* expedition had documented the temperatures of McMurdo Sound, little was known of the Barrier temperatures in the coreless winter when Evans led his brave party onto its northern edge in March 1911. Cherry-Garrard participated in that journey and afterward wrote: "It seems that we might have grasped that these temperatures were lower than might have been expected in the middle of March quite near the open sea."[28] But although Cherry-Garrard was surprised by the chill of the air around him, the frequently large differences between temperatures on the coast and those of the Barrier in March of 1911 were anticipated by Simpson. McMurdo Sound enjoys the benefit of proximity to the ocean (albeit a partly frozen one), and Simpson knew that the temperatures in this region would be considerably higher than those of the surrounding Barrier.[29] Recent meteorological analyses show that the complex terrain of Ross Island and its nearby mountain ranges further moderate the climate of the Sound through their blocking effects on cold drainage winds from the continental interior.[30]

Simpson discussed the ups and downs of temperature during the sun-lit and dark portions of a twenty-four-hour day in the Antarctic in his writings, and he considered the difficulty of obtaining accurate averages with at most three daily measurements available on sledging journeys.[31] Lieutenant Evans's account of the March 1911 struggle to reach Corner Camp placed greatest emphasis on the discomforts of the cold nighttime temperatures encountered.[32] On a later sledging trip in intense cold, Cherry-Garrard expressed similar trepidation regarding the nighttime conditions, describing "the long shivering fits following close one after the other all the time we lay in our dreadful sleeping bags." Indeed, the nights were so uncomfortable that Cherry-Garrard found that "the day's march was bliss compared to the night's rest, and both were awful."[33]

The ever-vigilant automatic weather stations now record data every ten minutes around the clock and thereby document the daily minima to high accuracy. On the other hand, the thrice-daily observations obtained at the staggering human cost of standing out in the wind and twirling the thermometer could miss the minima by a few degrees. Comparing the daily minimum of the sling thermometer observations to the modern data therefore provides a conservative measure of the conditions that led to the greatest discomforts suffered by the men of the *Terra Nova* expedition. Scott's men sometimes placed the thermometers under the sledges at night, however, out of reach even of the midnight sun, so that the nightly minimum could more accurately be measured. Simpson noted that cold air could pool at night under the sledges, so such observations might overestimate the nighttime cold by a few degrees.[34] The true daily minimum of the historical data likely ranges between the values from the sling thermometers and the under-sledge measurements.

The minimum temperatures experienced by Scott's depot party as they struggled to keep their ponies going in the deep snow in February 1911 are graphed in figure 23, along with those recorded both with the sling thermometer and with the under-sledge approach during the nights of misery endured by Lieutenant Evans's party in March of the same year. Lieutenant Evans's party shivered through a few nights of temperatures below −30 °F in March but were relieved by the warmth that followed. The automated weather station describes its findings only in mechanical rather than personal terms, but those data tell an average story quite similar to those of Shackleton, Evans, and Scott's depot party.[35] The average daily minima recorded by

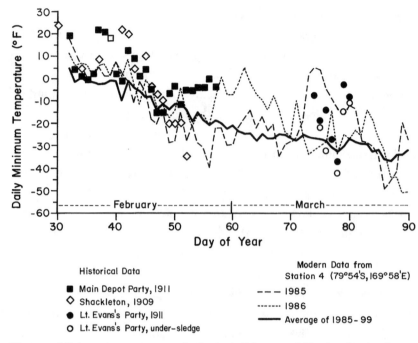

Figure 23. Minimum temperatures on the Barrier in February and March, reflecting the historical data collected by Scott's depot party (February 1911), Shackleton's party returning from its farthest-south trek (February 1909), and Lieutenant Evans's party (March 1911), as well as modern data from the automated weather station at 79°54′S, 169°58′E (station 4, near One Ton Camp; see map 2). The heavy line shows the long-term average from this station, while the dotted and dashed lines illustrate the ups and downs around the average that occurred in two typical years, 1985 and 1986.

the automated weather station at 79°54′S in February and March of the years 1985–99 are close to the data of 1909 and 1911, and the ups and downs for two representative recent years (1985 and 1986) show that temperatures on the Barrier sometimes fall below −30°F for a few days in March. But relief comes quickly in a normal year, for the temperatures typically swing back and forth from such conditions to balmy times near freezing within a few days at that time of year.

Simpson and Scott surely discussed the temperatures and other conditions encountered by the depot party, by Shackleton, and by Lieutenant Evans's group. Together Scott and his meteorologist strove to understand the weather, and if they assumed that the conditions documented by the depot journey and by the lieutenant's party were typical of what could be expected on the Barrier in February and March, then modern data demonstrate that they would have been quite correct. More data would be gathered in the coming months that would help to refine their thinking. And armed with that scientific information, Scott planned his assault on the Pole.

Wilson described Lieutenant Evans's returning party as "glad to get in [to the hut] as their kit was pretty solid with ice."[36] But if the ice on the men's bodies was described as solidly frozen, that on the Sound was still unstable. As April began, Scott and his men continued to wait for the ocean waters to freeze while the coreless winter on the Barrier to the south deepened.

On April 9 the ice went out yet again. Scott was increasingly impatient to return to the main base at Cape Evans because "the thought that the hut may have been damaged by the sea in one of the heavy storms will not be banished," but he also resolved not to risk the all-important ponies on young sea ice.[37] On April 11 a group of nine men led by Scott finally departed Hut Point for the main hut, while the other seven remained behind to care for the dogs and ponies until such time as the ice became safer. Scott tried hard to reach the Cape in one long day's march but was stymied around 10 P.M. by darkness and the onset of a blizzard.

The party camped on the sea ice, a matter of considerable discomfort for Bowers in particular. He resolutely determined to stand guard against any recurrence of his experiences during the return from the depot journey: "You knew that there was only about six or ten inches of precarious ice between you and the black waters beneath. Altogether I decided that I for one would be awake in such an insecure camp." The storm abated a bit the next day, and the party moved to a narrow platform on the terra firma of a tiny island in the Sound, where they waited for two days as the blizzard howled around them. On April 13 the weather finally improved, and they were able to reach the safety and relative sophistication of Cape Evans.[38]

It was Lashly who first spotted a group of men arriving.[39] The photographer Ponting found them nearly unrecognizable at first, due to heavily blackened faces and long beards. According to Bowers, "Ponting's face was a study as he ran up; he failed to recognize any of us and stopped dead with a blank look— as he admitted afterwards, he thought it was the Norwegian expedition for the space of a moment."[40] After a full breakfast that included the luxuries they had longed for, such as hot rolls and milk, the men enjoyed their first baths in eighty days.[41] A flare was fired to reassure those left at Hut Point that all was well, and a fire was used as a return signal. By mid-May the ice had thickened enough to ensure safe passage for the ponies, and the rest of the men and animals made the journey from Hut Point. There were then twenty-five men in the fifty-by-twenty-five-foot main hut at Cape Evans, a domicile Cherry-Garrard compared to the Ritz Hotel.[42] Among the modern conveniences to be found at the main Cape Evans hut was gaslight, provided by an acetylene plant rigged by one of the mechanics who would service the motor sledges. Captain Scott, meteorologist Simpson, photographer Ponting, and parasitologist Atkinson each set up a cramped work space in the hut, and every man had a small cubicle. In September 1911 Simpson laid the first Antarctic telephone line, a bare aluminum wire between Cape Evans and Hut Point, but this pioneering attempt at phone service worked well only in cold weather, and the line broke after a few months of use.[43]

In spite of the close quarters, relations between the men were surprisingly congenial.[44] Cherry-Garrard attributed the harmony to several factors, but paid special tribute to the personal qualities of Wilson and Bowers. Of Wilson, he wrote:

> I cannot do justice to his value. If you knew him you could not like him: you simply had to love him. . . . He never for one moment thought of himself. In this respect also Bowers . . . was most extraordinary. . . . We had many such, officers and seamen, and the success of the expedition was in no small measure due to the general and unselfish way in which personal likes and dislikes, wishes or tastes were ungrudgingly subordinated to the common weal. Wilson . . . set an example of expedition first and the rest nowhere which others followed ungrudgingly: it pulled us through more than one difficulty which might have led to friction.[45]

Scott had a similar view of Wilson's remarkable value to the expedition's morale, writing that "the Chief of the Scientific Staff sets an example which is more potent than any other factor in maintaining that bond of good fellowship which is the marked and beneficent characteristic of our community." [46]

Oates was a man of rather different character, sometimes described by his companions as taciturn, and by Cherry-Garrard as "a cheerful and lovable old pessimist."[47] An Eton-educated aristocrat, Oates spent his teenage years on the family estate at Gestingthorpe Hall but eschewed such trappings as the curtains some men hung around their bunks as "effeminate luxury."[48] The younger Australian Debenham considered Oates a special friend and described him as a man "without the slightest pretension of any sort except to being a gentleman[,] and the casual observer would take him to be the stable-man with unusual good manners." Others were surprised to learn that this unassuming man was a promising dragoon captain, that he had served with distinction in the South African war, and that he was an avid and knowledge-able student of history. Oates was a reserved person who "loathe[d] society" and felt most comfortable with his ponies.[49] And there was a great deal of work to do with those animals, for Scott was depending heavily upon them for the polar journey.

Another of the horses had died from a mysterious illness while Scott was on the sledging trail, and although this animal had a hostile and intractable personality, the unexplained death added to Scott's worries. A dog had also perished, but that creature had been sick for some time and this death was not unexpected. Scott was impressed with the work that had been done in his ab-sence to house all of the valuable animals and improve their condition, a state that he deemed "as justly due to our Russian boys as to my fellow English-men." Lashly and the young Russian groom had finished the construction of a comfortable stable. Scott sadly noted that he "could but sigh again to think of the stalls that must now remain empty," for only ten ponies remained of the original nineteen that had sailed from New Zealand. He found the dogs now looking healthier than when he last saw them, an improvement for which he praised the care provided by the young Russian dog driver Dimitri.[50] Oates also praised his companions, including his Russian assistant, writing in a let-ter to his mother, "The fellows in this expedition are a first rate lot of chaps and I have got on splendidly with them, Anton . . . the Russian boy who has helped me with the ponies has been excellent."[51]

It was clear that the only chance for better work from the sled dogs in the coming struggle was more sustaining food, and more of it. During the winter, about nine hundred pounds of dog's pemmican was therefore made from seal meat.[52] The ponies' health regimen included increased food, oilcake, and exercise, the latter provided by the specific man who was to be each animal's leader on the south polar journey. Upon Bowers's return to Cape Evans with Scott, he immediately chose "the other big Siberian horse that had been a pair with my late lamented—they were the only Siberian ponies, all the rest being [smaller] Manchurians."[53]

After a respite of only three days, the energetic Scott was once again on the sledging trail, this time leading a party of eight men back to Hut Point to bring badly needed supplies and relief to those left behind there. Five of the newcomers changed places with the Hut Point veterans, who then sledged back to Cape Evans on April 21. It was a cold trip, well into the coreless winter, although on the coast rather than on the bleakness of the Barrier. The account of this short journey again underscored the fact that perspiration made the men into their own worst enemies in frigid conditions. Scott set a very brisk pace, and the party "arrived bathed in sweat—our garments were soaked through, and as we took off our wind clothes showers of ice fell on the floor. The accumulation was almost incredible and shows the whole trouble of sledging in cold weather. It would have been very uncomfortable to have camped in the open under such conditions, and assuredly a winter and spring party cannot afford to get so hot if they wish to retain any semblance of comfort."[54]

Cherry-Garrard felt a sense of loss at leaving the old hut behind. When the relief party arrived, he wrote, "We had spent such a happy week, just the seven of us, at the *Discovery* hut that I think, glad as we were to see the men, we would most of us have rather been left undisturbed." When he later reflected on the time spent at the old hut eating seal and living an exceedingly simple existence, this Oxford graduate philosophically mused that the experience had taught him that "the luxuries of civilization satisfy only those wants which they themselves create." But one luxury to which Cherry-Garrard was pleased to return was the more extended library to be found at the Cape Evans hut, and he gladly turned some of his attention to Kipling and other popular novelists.[55]

Wilson and Bowers began a routine of walking together to the nearby meteorological screens to service them and take measurements. Some of these devices were positioned a mile or more from the main hut, in order

Figure 24. Bowers, left, and Wilson take a midwinter meteorological reading near the base at Cape Evans. Photograph by H. Ponting. Scott Album, number 11353, Alexander Turnbull Library, Wellington, New Zealand.

to monitor the local variability of the weather. Bowers and Wilson carried out this task even on winter days of intense wind, total darkness, and drifting snow.[56] As May drew to a close and temperatures at Cape Evans plunged as low as −27°F, Bowers continued his daily regimen of washing himself with snow, which he fetched each morning while still in pajamas. Wilson often joined him in these ablutions, but the others began to bathe less frequently.[57] Cherry-Garrard took some satisfaction in a day when Wilson's resistance to cold was finally overcome by the challenge of the weather: "It was Wilson's pleasant conceit to keep his balaclava rolled up, so that his face was bare, on such occasions, being somewhat proud of the fact that he had not, as yet, been frost-bitten. Imagine our joy when he entered the hut one cold windy evening with two white spots on his cheeks, which he vainly tried to hide behind his dogskin mitts."[58] Now the Antarctic weather had bitten even the resistant Wilson and Bowers.

Lieutenant Evans also braved the cold again, but in his case the reason was the hard work of detailed surveying of the nearby coastline. He was assisted by the Norwegian ski-runner Gran, and the two men spent "much time dancing when nearly sick with cold, our fingers tucked under our arms to recover their feelings. . . . In spite of the cold, the gloom, and the sad whistling wind that heralded the now fast approaching darkness, I felt glad to work with my sextant and sketch-book under the shadow of those fantastic ice-foots hung round with fringes of icicle. . . . Some of the cloud effects at the end of April were too wonderful for mere pen or brush to describe."[59]

A thrice-weekly lecture series was begun. Topics were as broad as the men's own backgrounds and interests. Simpson lectured on meteorology, while Ponting captivated his companions with beautiful slides of time spent in Japan. Bowers reviewed the evolution of sledge foods, and Oates held forth on horse management.[60]

One lecture of considerable interest to the men was given by Dr. Atkinson on the subject of scurvy. He described the symptoms of the disease and the leading theories of the day as to its cause. The navy doctor favored the then-prevalent view that tainted canned goods were the root cause of the disease, with perhaps some effect from damp and cold. He also cited acid intoxication of the blood as being as least a symptom if not the origin of the ailment.[61] We now know that scurvy is caused not by tainted foods but by a deficiency of vitamin C. Unlike many other animals, humans can obtain this compound only from their diet or as a supplement.

Most fresh fruits have a high vitamin C content, and their health benefits in curing scurvy were reported as early as the turn of the fifteenth century. Although drinking lime juice subsequently became a standard practice in the British Navy, the juices commonly distributed around 1900 were far from fresh, and hence had little effect in combating the disease. The problem was due in part to the prevailing methods of preparation and handling, which included evaporation to decrease the volume (a strategy that not only reduced weight and size but also diminished the benefit, because heat destroys the vitamin). Perhaps most tragically, the widespread use of copper vats and tubing probably chemically destroyed some of the precious vitamin C in the juice. In the 1800s several British expeditions of exploration had reported severe and even deadly bouts with scurvy in spite of regular consumption of lime juice, and though British sailors are known far and wide as "limeys," the fruit juice had clearly failed to protect those men in the form in which it was being distributed at the time.[62] This turn of events threw the benefits of fruits as a traditional curative under a shadow of doubt at the turn of the twentieth century. But early explorers had also reported the success of fresh meat in combating scurvy, and in the discussion following the lecture, Wilson espoused his view that fresh meat offered the party's best defense against scurvy.[63] Certainly the benefits of meat had been appreciated by the observant Dr. Wilson on the *Discovery* expedition in 1903.

The advantages of a fresh-meat diet in polar regions are evident in the health of the Inuit people, whose primary foods are meat and fish and who have little or no access to fruit and vegetables over long periods in winter. In 1928 an Arctic explorer named Vilhjalmur Stefansson would personally demonstrate that Europeans could similarly remain in good health for a full year in which nothing but meat was eaten.[64] Although Inuit peoples consume large amounts of meat, they carefully avoid consumption of the livers of certain animals, notably the husky dog and the polar bear. Animal livers are rich in a variety of fat-soluble vitamins, including A, D, and K. Scientific analysis confirms the traditional wisdom of the Inuits: the liver of the Arctic sled dog contains potentially lethal amounts of vitamin A. But the liver of southern seals has a far lower vitamin A content than those of dogs or polar bears, implying little risk of poisoning.[65] And seal liver is a remarkably potent source of life-giving vitamin C. One chemical analysis showed that lightly boiled samples of seal liver contain fourteen to thirty milligrams of vitamin C per one hundred grams. One hundred grams of fresh lime juice contains a similar amount—about thirty mg of vitamin C. Seal flesh is less rich in the vitamin, but yields about 0.5–2.5 mg per hundred grams.[66] Although the men of the *Terra Nova* expedition had no way of knowing of the liver's special benefit to their health, they did know that of all the parts of the seal, it happened to be the one whose taste was most enjoyed by many of them. Nearly every diary contains mention of the pleasures of eating seal liver. It was the backbone of a standard Hut Point breakfast as described by Cherry-Garrard.[67] The senior of the two Australians relished a "grand feed of seal liver seasoned with peas." [68] And in a striking union of empire and exploration, seal liver curry was a particular favorite in the Ross Island menu. Ponting wrote: "As for seal liver curry—like Kipling's cinnamon stew of the fat-tailed sheep, 'He who never hath tasted the food, by Allah! he knoweth not bad from good.'" [69] Although seal was not a standard component of the diet on the sledging trail, the men eventually ate the flesh of the ponies after the animals were put out of their misery on the polar journey. Both seal and pony meat could have lost some of its vitamin C value if overcooked, but fuel for cooking was typically in very short supply, especially on sledging trips. [70] The myth that Scott's team abhorred these foods or failed to understand their health value is a frequent but false entry in their legend, and there is evidence that Scott was insistent on fresh meat in the diet. Simpson noted that "Captain Scott made us eat seal meat to protect us from that dreaded enemy of polar expeditions, scurvy. . . . We also had a splendid cook. . . . Galantine of seal and penguin in aspic are not to be despised." [71]

On May 8, 1911, it was Captain Scott who lectured—on the topic of his plan for the south polar journey, to an audience consumed with "lively anticipation." [72] He expressed his opinion that "the problem of reaching the Pole can best be solved by relying on the ponies and man haulage." [73]

Scott's view of his transport options was heavily influenced by Shackleton. His rival had heard of the good work done by ponies in Arctic travel and had seen such animals in Shanghai. Shackleton enlisted the services of a representative from a leading firm of veterinary surgeons from that Chinese city to travel to Tientsin and select fifteen of the animals from among two thousand on sale. Shackleton also purchased nine dogs in New Zealand; these were descendants of Arctic animals that had been used by a previous Antarctic expedition. Finally, he also took one Arrol-Johnston four-cylinder motor car, capable of about twelve to fifteen horsepower—the same type of vehicle later brought by Scott. Because water cooling was impossible at the cold temperatures to be experienced, the polar cars' engines were air cooled. Scott's team improved on Shackleton's motor car by replacing the wheels with a broad revolving track, and in this respect Scott's vehicles were the ancestors of today's Snowcats and tanks. Shackleton's motor car suffered from numerous mechanical and traction problems, and he soon put his faith in his ponies. [74] Scott's experiences proved to be painfully similar.

Figure 25. From left, Wilson, Cherry-Garrard, and seaman Forde load a dead seal onto a sledge in midwinter. Photograph by H. Ponting. Scott Album, number 11347, Alexander Turnbull Library, Wellington, New Zealand.

Before beginning his southward trek, Shackleton weighed the advantages of dogs versus ponies, concluding that "a Manchurian pony can drag a sledge over a broken trail at the rate of twenty to thirty miles a day, pulling not less than twelve hundred pounds. It was a risk to take ponies from the far north through the tropics and then across two thousand miles of stormy sea on a very small ship, but I felt that if it could be done it would be well worth the trouble, for, compared with the dog, the pony is a far more efficient animal, one pony doing the work of at least ten dogs on the food allowance for ten dogs, and travelling a longer distance in a day." These estimates were overoptimistic. In practice, Shackleton's ponies pulled weights closer to six hundred pounds and achieved typical distances of at best about fifteen miles per day—less impressive than Shackleton had hoped but still comparable in principle to dogs.[75] Shackleton had gotten to within one hundred miles of the Pole using ponies and men, so Scott reasoned that success could be achieved with just a few more animals and men.

Figure 26. Iceberg grounded in McMurdo Sound. Note the seals on the ice at its base. The men found the animals to be unafraid and hence easy to hunt with rifles or even clubs. Photograph by H. Ponting. Scott Album, number 8685, Alexander Turnbull Library, Wellington, New Zealand.

The ponies hailed from the frigid plains of Manchuria and Siberia, regions where winter temperatures are often below −20°F.[76] Like Siberian sled dogs, they came from a land with harsh temperatures comparable to those that Scott expected to face on the polar trek. As Scott had already learned by painful experience on the depot journey, however, in spite of the potential for greater efficiency in terms of food required per mile for each pound of material transported, the ponies suffered from some drastic shortcomings compared with dogs. First, they went slower (implying that Amundsen, with his hundred dogs, would reach the Pole before Scott unless an accident befell the Norwegians). To make matters worse, the horses had weathered the blizzards of the depot journey poorly, so Scott would have to begin his polar journey later in the spring season to minimize risk to the animals. Finally, the ponies could not be safely taken up the heavily crevassed slopes of a steep glacier to reach the high plateau of the center of the continent. Thus their purpose was to transport large amounts of food and oil only as far as the base

Figure 27. Dog team passing a glacier. Photograph by H. Ponting. Scott Album, number 11380, Alexander Turnbull Library, Wellington, New Zealand.

of the glacier, so that the returning man-hauling parties could travel with relatively light loads. The remaining 740 miles to the Pole and back down the glacier would depend on grueling toil by men alone.

Four of Shackleton's eight ponies never even began their march, dying within a month of their arrival in Antarctica. Shackleton blamed the demise of these animals on the fact that "Manchurian ponies will eat anything at all that can be chewed."[77] Three of the four ate the salty sand and rock beneath their feet on the shore where Shackleton made his base. The fourth consumed shavings in which chemicals had been packed. Oddly, all the fatalities occurred in dark-colored animals, while the survivors were all white or light colored.[78] The random probability that in a group of eight animals the four dark-colored ones would die while the four light ones would live is one in seventy, so this loss suggests an important difference, perhaps in the tendency of the horses of differing color to engage in this dangerous behavior or in their susceptibility to the toxins.

Scott had studied Shackleton's book and therefore kept his animals off the beach at Cape Evans from the moment of arrival, ensuring that the surface beneath their feet was harmless snow and not fatal sand. His plan for the polar journey consisted of three stages—first, from Ross Island across the Barrier to the base of the Beardmore glacier; second, the ascent of the glacier from near sea level to the polar plateau near ten thousand feet; and finally, the trek across the high plateau from 86°S to the Pole. He assumed that the ponies could pull 550 pounds apiece at an average speed of about eleven miles per day as far as the base of the Beardmore glacier.[79]

Could the ponies, on whom so much depended, fulfill this role? There were reasons to doubt the quality of the animals, even before they began their journey to the bottom of the world. One of the geologists, Frank Debenham, noted that Oates "has been rather disgusted over the type of ponies provided for the expedition and rightly so, for only 3 or 4 are at all decent. The reason is a curious blunder. Capt. Scott, hearing that of Shackleton's ponies the dark ones died and the white ones lived, and in the popular belief that white animals resist cold better, ordered Meares to get only white ones if possible. Meares, who is no judge of horse flesh got a friend to pick the ponies for him at a fair in Mukden. There were only 200 to pick from so there was little choice, the white ponies forming about 15–20% of the lot." The seller of the nineteen ponies "went away with a plenty big smile on his face" according to the Russian groom Omelchenko, who was present at the sale.[80]

Hence Scott's ponies were poorly chosen, and he did not secure the services of an expert in horseflesh, as Shackleton had. Instead, Scott once again put his faith in his own man, but as in Bowers's near-fatal initiation into the instabilities of Antarctic sea ice, Meares had limited knowledge of the task before him. Cherry-Garrard believed that matters would have been different if Oates had chosen the animals.[81] The instructions to seek light-colored horses compounded the problem of Meares's inexperience. In its most extreme form, the myth of Scott the bumbler suggests that the choice of light-colored animals on the *Terra Nova* expedition was purely for the sake of presentation—that Scott enjoyed their attractive appearance as it complemented the snow. This footnote in Scott's legend is a false one; the decision to seek light-colored animals was logically rooted in the practical matter of Shackleton's bitter experiences with the deaths of all his dark-colored ponies. Unfortunately, the well-reasoned instruction to purchase light-colored ponies if possible made a bad situation worse.

Although Scott's light-colored animals arrived in Antarctica in poor health, they nevertheless ultimately fulfilled their role rather well. From November 15 to their deaths at varying stages of the journey across the Barrier, the ponies pulled between 450 and 700 pounds apiece and typically achieved distances of about fifteen miles per day.[82] As Cherry-Garrard wrote, "Some of these ponies were very poor material, and it must be conceded that Oates who was in charge of them started with a very great handicap. From first to last it was Oates' consummate management, seconded by the care and kindness of the ponies' leaders, which obtained results which often exceeded the most sanguine hopes." Elsewhere, Cherry-Garrard joked that "Oates trained and fed them as though they were to run in the Derby."[83] Lieutenant Evans also reflected on the devotion of the master of horse to his task, noting that "by the dim candle-light which illuminated our pony-shelter, one could see Oates grooming his charges, clearing up their stall, refitting their harness, and fixing up the little improvements that his quick, watchful eye continually suggested. At the far end of his stables he had a blubber stove, where he used to melt ice for the ponies' drinking water and cook bran mashes for his animals." With Oates's tender care, the animals' health improved markedly, and even the weakest of the animals hauled a considerable load for 280 miles across the Barrier on the journey to the Pole.[84] In response to Scott's expression of gratitude for his fine work in bringing the animals to the base of the Beardmore glacier, where the last met their end, Oates "grunted and was pleased."[85]

Scott's lecture at Cape Evans on the evening of May 8, 1911, included a detailed schedule for the polar trek. Originally he had hoped to reach the Pole as early as December 21, which would have resulted in a return date in February of the following year.[86] But although the ponies would prove able to do the work, the depot journey had convinced Scott of the need to start late enough to avoid exposing the animals to harsh weather. He revealed that his plan was to begin the southward march around November 3. Assuming that his team achieved average daily distances comparable to Shackleton's, the projected return date would be March 27, 1912.[87] By then the ship would have departed, so some of the men would have to remain in Antarctica for another year. All were asked to forgo their salaries in the next year because of the growing financial woes of the expedition; for the scientists this sum amounted to about four pounds per week.[88] Although they did not realize it at the time, much more important than the additional year's service or the loss of income was the fact that this schedule implied that the polar party would begin the next coreless winter deep in the heart of the Barrier.

For the Love of Science

The visitor is out for a walk on a clear, calm Antarctic day. Even though it's late morning according to the clock, the skies are as black as they were at midnight. It is early winter, and it will be many weeks before the sun rises and sets in the cycle of light and darkness that is normal except at the singular points of the Poles. But the starshine is surprisingly bright in the crystal clean air, and the visitor can make out the silvery shadows of the snow-covered hills that drape the horizon behind the old *Discovery* hut. He was comfortable yesterday at −22°F, even in a light breeze, and he congratulated himself then on getting used to the Antarctic weather. But it suddenly feels much colder. Today the −37°F air makes his balaclava stiffen with moisture as he breathes, and the woolen covering is becoming thick and heavy with ice near his mouth. His feet sweated a little in his thick woolen socks earlier today, and now there is a horrible clammy feeling centering on the big toe of his left foot. He will have to make this walk a short one or risk frostbite. As he strolls down the snow road, he passes a man moving rapidly in the opposite direction. The fellow waves as he bustles along, and the visitor notices that the other man's head is covered only in a woolen cap. His cheeks are bare and his parka hood is lying limply across his shoulders. As he pulls his own hood up tighter over his head, the visitor chuckles over this demonstration that some people acclimatize differently to the Antarctic than do others.

He reflects on what he has read and observed about the link between the wind and the temperatures in Antarctic winter. As soon as the warming rays from the sun dip below the horizon, the snow ceases to take up energy and instead radiates heat away, cooling to the vastness of space. The air near the ground can therefore become bitingly cold in the dark months of winter—much colder than it is a few hundred yards above. And so a steep temperature inversion layer can form, in which temperatures at the ground are far colder than those aloft. But windy conditions mix the warmer air from above into the inversion layer. The calm times and places are by far the coldest in the Antarctic winter, and the still air now is so cold that it hurts the visitor's exposed nose. He pulls his balaclava up higher to cover it.

The landscape is quiet, peaceful, and beautiful in its starkness, and he sighs with contentment. As he exhales, his breath forms a white fog around his face, blinding him for a moment. When the smoky swirls are gone, he sees a flash of green in the sky to his right. He turns and is treated to a spectacular curtain of flowing green auroral light. He breathes as shallowly as possible to keep his vision clear and is captivated by the dancing waves of bright green. After a few minutes they change shape from waves to narrower streaks, cutting the sky like celestial banners. He knows he is fortunate in being able to wear contact lenses to correct his poor vision. It is only these modern pieces of thin plastic that allow him to witness the beauty of this remarkable polar world, to drink in the glory of the aurora on a calm, cold day. The moisture from his skin and breath would make glasses a hazy misery under Antarctic conditions.

His foot is becoming numb, a dangerous sign that frostbite could follow. It is hard to force himself to walk toward his dormitory, leaving the spectacular light show behind. But he is a practical man, and he knows that he has been out longer than he ought to be in this weather—it has been almost an hour now. He trots up the hill toward the warm comfort of his room, but after five minutes of the steep uphill climb, he turns his ankle in a depression in the snow. The injury forces him to stop running, and as he slows to a walk he realizes that the small amount of sweat produced by his aborted effort at speed is rapidly freezing. There is soon a thin layer of cold ice on the balaclava where it presses on his forehead.

He limps into the warm building and moves quickly down the hall to his room. He strips off his cold parka, boots, socks, and clothing and dons a fresh set of warm, dry, long underwear and thick wool socks. It feels wonderful.

Then he glances at the Ross Island map he has hung on the back of his door. There is a spot on the chart marking the *Discovery* hut, just a few hundred yards from his room. Around the island to the north lies Cape Evans. To the east is Cape Crozier, across the Barrier. And between Hut Point Peninsula and Cape Crozier lies the area known as Windless Bight. He wonders idly whether that place is appropriately named. A region on the Barrier with little wind must be terribly cold in winter.

After careful thought, it was decided to celebrate midwinter day at Cape Evans on June 22, 1911, rather than the twenty-third. Solstice was to occur at 2:30 A.M. on the twenty-third, so the evening meal of the twenty-second would be the closest one to this important event.[1] The hut had been veiled in continuous winter darkness for weeks, and after the magical hour of winter solstice, the sun would begin its welcome progression back to them.

The holiday was chosen as the issue date for the *South Polar Times*, a sort of magazine replete with humorous poems, cartoons, and the like that served as an expedition archive as well as providing entertainment. The volume was lavishly illustrated by Wilson and carefully edited by Cherry-Garrard, who spent many hours at his typewriter to produce the document. Scott read it aloud "amidst much amusement" during lunch.[2]

Cherry-Garrard generously shared a cake that he had kept for the occasion, and the cook prepared a bountiful evening meal. Scott's men began their dinner with an excellent seal soup, but the highlight of the menu was Yorkshire pudding. As Ponting wrote: "Those who have never been deprived of it for many months have never relished the national dish of Old England as we did that day."[3] The liquor that was reserved for special occasions was given freely, and the rollicking evening that followed included a slide show of Antarctic pictures taken by their own photographer, raucous dancing, and a late night auroral display. The last of the revelers turned in at 2 A.M., and the next day was designated for rest and recuperation.[4]

On the other side of the Barrier, Amundsen and his men marked their

Figure 28. A midwinter work group at Cape Evans. From left, Atkinson, Cherry-Garrard, Bowers, Debenham, Taylor, and Gran. Photograph by H. Ponting. Scott Album, number 11352, Alexander Turnbull Library, Wellington, New Zealand.

holiday less boisterously, "by eating a little more than usual. . . . In the evening of a holiday we generally had a little gramophone, a glass of toddy, and a cigar." All were in their bunks by eleven at the Bay of Whales. Amundsen's men labored carefully over their boots, sledges, camp, and provisions during the winter, carrying out a series of refinements.[5] For the British team, winter was also a time for study of navigational methods, refitting of equipment, and consideration of the tasks ahead.

Like their British counterparts, the Norwegians were capable of the occasional blunder. In a midwinter diary entry Amundsen shamefacedly acknowledged that they had "forgotten to bring out that most commonplace of tools which is a necessity on a Polar expedition—namely a snow shovel." The Norwegians set to work to improvise some shovels using iron plate and wooden handles. When the spades were ready, they began to dig out the rather large drift that had built up near their hut door while this essential tool was lacking. The large mound gave someone the idea of hollowing out a snow hut, in which they constructed a very Scandinavian comfort: a steam bath.[6]

After the depot journey, Wilson secured Scott's permission to embark on a midwinter trip to Cape Crozier with two other men. Wilson asked Cherry-Garrard to serve as one of the hardy souls who would venture out on the Barrier in winter. Cherry-Garrard agreed, and the two discussed the critical question of the man to complete their trio. They concurred on the dauntless Bowers.[7]

Wilson's passion for birds was a driving factor leading him to attempt this dangerous trip, for he yearned to see whether examination of the unhatched embryos of the emperor penguins that nested there could give clues regarding avian evolution.[8] The origins and evolution of the world's fauna were a topic of great interest at the turn of the century, a time when many scientists were still intensely debating Darwin's theories.

Because emperor chicks had been seen in September during the *Discovery* expedition on trips to the rookery at Cape Crozier, Wilson believed that their eggs would be found there in July. Securing a group of eggs as specimens was Wilson's primary goal for their winter trek of about seventy miles each way.[9] Another important purpose of the journey was to test the rations on which the men would rely during the coming south polar march. They would all be allowed thirty-two ounces of food per day, but each of the three winter travelers would vary the amounts of butter, biscuit, and pemmican in order to find the optimum mix of fat, carbohydrates, and protein for arduous sledging journeys. Finally, they would gather "a wealth of other information . . . concerning the Barrier conditions, particularly the meteorological conditions," a goal that was to take on greater and greater importance as Simpson analyzed their findings.[10]

Three days after the midwinter feast, Scott and Wilson went for a walk and a private discussion. Scott impressed upon Wilson the importance of bringing Bowers and Cherry-Garrard back in good condition, for both were integral to his plan for the southern journey that would begin in October.[11]

Two nine-foot sledges were loaded with six weeks' food, a pickax, ice axes, an Alpine rope, camping and scientific equipment, sleeping bags, oil, and other gear. The team would be trudging across the Barrier pulling 253 pounds per man at a time of year when darkness would prevail nearly twenty-four hours per day.[12] Ponting captured the scene by flashlight just before they de-

Figure 29. From left, Bowers, Wilson, and Cherry-Garrard prepare to leave for Cape Crozier, June 27, 1911. Photograph by H. Ponting. Scott Album, number 11360, Alexander Turnbull Library, Wellington, New Zealand.

parted.[13] The trio timed the journey to get some light from the moon, but those hopes were largely dashed by the cruel interference of clouds, and the men marched in total blackness during much of the trip.[14]

In spite of heavy loads, the going was relatively easy when the three men set off over the smooth sea ice on June 27, 1911. The next day they marched past Hut Point and soon reached the edge of the Barrier. As they stood at the base of the snow-covered uphill slope to the Barrier, down came "a steady stream of very cold air which we noticed only a few yards from the bottom." Wilson documented the remarkable transition in temperature as they marched from Hut Point up the slope to the tip of the Barrier—from −26.5°F to −47°F in just a few miles.[15] Cherry-Garrard noticed the plunge into deep freeze in a more personal fashion. In an instant of poor judgment, he took off his fur mitts so that he could better pull the sledges up the hilly grade onto the Barrier. Although he had thin inner gloves on under the mitts, all ten of his fingers were quickly frostbitten. They were covered in inch-long blisters within a few hours. The pus inside the blisters subsequently froze, and his damaged fingers gave Cherry-Garrard a great deal of pain in coming days.[16]

As on earlier sledging trips, the critical reserves of oil were not meant to be used for anything other than cooking. But as conditions grew desperately cold, the men burned more in order to warm the air inside the frigid canvas tent. Eventually Cherry-Garrard managed to defrost his solidly frozen blisters over the cooking stove during supper one night. He pricked them and felt great relief when the liquid ran out.[17]

The three men struggled on in temperatures of −50°F. Wilson developed a frostbitten heel and sole on one foot, and Cherry-Garrard's big toes were bitten as well. Only the resistant Bowers was "never worried by frostbitten feet." They were beginning to enter the region between Hut Point Peninsula and Mount Terror (see map 3), which was known to be a place of little wind. Though sheltered from the flow of air off the Barrier, this bowl-like bight with its sandy snow was a place of torture for the trio. The very cold surface gave the sledges no glide, and the men were forced to begin the dreaded process of relaying their loads. The already difficult plod now became a misery of marching forward with half of their supplies, then going back to retrieve the rest. They steered their course by the light of Jupiter when the planet could be seen through the clouds. They spoke little, but one matter they did discuss was whether the conditions they were encountering were normal, or whether it was a particularly cold snap. They also discussed turning back, but each time the subject arose, they resolved to continue. Sweat and breath accumulated in their frigid sleeping bags each night as they tried to rest. Cherry-Garrard spent the last night of June in a dreadfully cold and damp reindeer bag, suffering a series of shivering fits and listening to Bowers snore.[18]

The evening of July 3 brought temperatures near −60°F and a magnificent aurora.[19] The three men lay on their backs with their faces to the wonderful light show in the sky, but only two of them could see the celestial display. The doctors had nearly refused to let Cherry-Garrard join the expedition because of his severe nearsightedness. In the extreme cold of the winter journey, the glasses on which he depended became useless, constantly fogged by moisture from his skin and breath. He was forced to give up wearing his lenses on most of the winter journey and was essentially blind except for close work.[20]

The Beaufort Scale

Beaufort Force Value	Wind Speed (miles/hr)	Wind Speed (km/hr)	Description
0	<0.6	<1	Calm
1	0.6–3	1–5	Light air
2	4–7	6–11	Light breeze
3	8–12	12–19	Gentle breeze
4	13–18	20–29	Moderate breeze
5	19–24	30–39	Fresh breeze
6	25–31	40–50	Strong breeze
7	32–38	51–61	Moderate gale
8	39–46	62–74	Fresh gale
9	47–54	75–87	Strong gale
10	55–63	88–102	Whole gale
11	64–73	103–18	Violent storm
12	74+	119+	Hurricane

Table 1. The Beaufort scale was developed by Cmdr. (later Adm. Sir) Francis Beaufort in 1805 as a means of estimating the strength of the wind from visual observations. At sea, factors such as the heights of waves were relied upon to gauge the wind.

The men's sleeping bags were becoming heavier with the ice of each passing day's perspiration and each night's fitful rest. Getting into the increasingly icy bags became a torturous process of slowly worming their bodies into the fur, gradually melting the ice with their own bodily warmth. This ritual of pain could take as much as an hour.[21] In spite of an eiderdown liner, Cherry-Garrard's sleeping bag was too big for him and hence even more uncomfortable than it would otherwise have been.[22]

The minimum temperature on the night of July 3 was −65°F, but a gusty wind began on the morning of July 4, and by 9:30 the temperature had risen to a relatively balmy −27.5°F. The trio stayed in their bags and waited for the wind to die down.[23] True to its modern name, Windless Bight that day had a relatively light breeze (only about 4 on the Beaufort scale, or about 13–18 miles per hour; see table 1). Meanwhile back at Cape Evans, the same wind

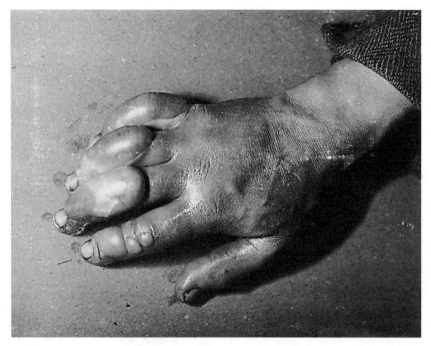

Figure 30. Dr. Atkinson's hand after his nearly disastrous mishap during the blizzard. Photograph by H. Ponting. Scott Polar Research Institute, Cambridge.

took the form of an intense blizzard; the peak wind there howled at fifty-two miles per hour.[24]

At about 4:30 in the afternoon that day, Dr. Atkinson took it upon himself to walk out to read the meteorology screens; because Bowers and Wilson were away, this duty required a new volunteer. With winds in excess of thirty miles per hour, the doctor decided to take readings not only from the screen nearest the hut but also from the one on the sea ice, about a mile to the northeast. When he had not returned by 6 P.M., a search began. As the hours passed the men grew more desperate. After first mistaking a dead seal for the body of the missing doctor, one searcher finally heard footsteps on the ice nearby, and the doctor was found at about midnight.[25] Doctor Atkinson had suffered serious frostbite on three fingers of his right hand as a result of his harrowing experience, and seaman Evans bandaged and cared for the wounds.[26] Twenty-four hours passed before sensation finally returned to all of the doctor's afflicted fingers.[27]

The air was calm again on the Barrier the next day, and Wilson, Cherry-Garrard, and Bowers pushed on. But the storm had left a fresh layer of cold and even less tractable snow on the surface.[28] Although the Cape Crozier trio did not use skis themselves (mainly to avoid breakage in the darkness), the runners of their sledges acted as skis carrying their provisions. The much greater friction of new snow compared with aged surfaces, a well-known characteristic to any skier, results from the sharp edges of new crystals. As temperatures fall below about $-20\,°F$, friction further increases because lubrication is impeded at cold temperatures. These were problems that Scott's expedition was to encounter with debilitating intensity in coming months. The Cape Crozier trio experienced them in vivid fashion on July 5, for they advanced a total of only 1.5 miles in eight exhausting hours of heavy pulling.[29]

On July 6 the air remained still and the noon temperature sank to an astonishing value of $-77\,°F$. To be sure of this remarkable figure, the men checked it with two thermometers. The intense cold now made every task a slow agony. The strings that tied their bags of pemmican, butter, and biscuits were like wire. It was impossible to handle any item with naked fingers, and every bit of camp work had to be done slowly while wearing fur mitts. By this time, the men's sweat and breath had begun to turn their clothing into armor plate. Cherry-Garrard made the mistake one morning of raising "my head to look round and found I could not move it back. My clothing had frozen hard as I stood—perhaps fifteen seconds. For four hours I had to pull with my head stuck up and from that time we all took care to bend down into a pulling position before being frozen in."[30]

Moisture also posed a threat to the all-important matches that were needed to light the cooking stove. The matches quickly collected condensation when taken from the dry cold outside into the wetter air of the tent. Sometimes four or five boxes were tried before one match successfully burst into precious flame.[31]

The Cape Crozier party's tent was double-lined, with an outer layer of windproof canvas and an inner light lining. Although the layer of air helped to insulate their shelter, the lining also collected rime from their breath, sweat, and cooking, becoming heavier with each passing day.[32] The young Australian Debenham thought about the lonesome trio absent on the Barrier, writing, "I should think that never before has such a tremendous discomfort been undergone for scientific research and the emperors should be highly honored."[33]

As the three men struggled along, the snow gradually became firmer and easier to negotiate, signaling that they were moving past the worst part of the windless area.[34] Wind is another key factor that influences the character of a skiing surface. Strong wind stiffens the surface of Antarctic snow, changing its dry character from soft and powdery to a porous but hardened texture that greatly eases ski or sledge travel.

July 9, 1911, was a relatively warm day at −36°F, but fog made the going difficult, and by afternoon the trio was surrounded by the crevasses that are spawned by the slow flow of the Barrier past the land near Cape Crozier. They "stood still and heard the ice creaking and groaning ever so deep down under us and all around."[35] They camped in a hollow that appeared to be more stable, although noises like "some giant . . . banging a big empty tank" came from under the tent. After supper a strong wind began to blow. It was to last three days and drive the temperatures up to a remarkable +9°F. For the first night in many, they all slept in welcome warmth.[36]

The men began marching again when the storm cleared on July 13. Temperatures were much warmer than they had been earlier in their trek—between −20°F and −30°F—and the trio managed seven and a half miles in seven and a half hours. But the next day was dark and foggy, and with the gloom came unseen and treacherous crevasses. Each of the three men fell in to the length of their sledging harnesses over the course of the ghastly day's marching, to be pulled out by his comrades. As Cherry-Garrard dryly wrote: "Crevasses in the dark *do* put your nerves on edge."[37]

A few more days of struggle amid crevasses in minimum temperatures near −35°F finally brought the party to its goal. Wilson had originally hoped to camp near the Adelie penguin rookery on the Cape Crozier beach, out of reach of the strongest of the winds that sweep down the slopes of Mount Terror. But that site was a long way from the emperor penguin rookery, and because a great deal of time had been taken up in the agony of reaching the cape, Wilson decided to put their base of operations on a closer ridge up a snow slope of a small volcanic cone. Here they would find stones with which to construct a primitive home. They planned to build a stone hut on the lee side of the ridge, a few yards from the top, in order to shield themselves from the force of the strong winds that were likely in this area.[38] The surface beneath their feet as they approached the site was a great "cup-like drift of wind-polished snow . . . so hard that we used our crampons just as though we had been on ice."[39]

The men had used a great deal of oil during the outbound journey, and a blubber stove like the one in the *Discovery* hut would be built to provide heat in the stone shelter. It was imperative that they obtain some penguin blubber quickly, in order to preserve their oil stores, for these were a critical part of the lifeline back to Cape Evans. The walls of the hut would be made of rocks banked with snow. One of the sledges would serve as the ridge beam, and a large sheet of canvas would provide a roof. Bowers "gathered rocks from over the hill, nothing was too big for him," while Wilson banked the walls in snow and Cherry-Garrard stacked the boulders.[40] The hard-blown snow wasn't easy to use for this purpose, but after a solid day as construction workers the men nearly finished their new home on July 17. Strong winds kept them in their bags in the tent on the next day, but the nineteenth dawned calm and relatively warm.

They decided to try to find the penguins. To reach the birds they had to traverse a series of dangerous crevasse-ridden pressure ridges where the Barrier met the island, then find a way down through them to the sea ice where the emperors roost. In the years since Wilson had last been in the area on the *Discovery* expedition, the ridges had moved and the going was "exciting work but it grew very much more exciting as the light got worse and worse." When darkness fell in the early afternoon, the men found themselves in a valley surrounded by towering, sixty-foot blocks of ice.[41] As they pondered the impossibility of going farther along this path, they heard the cooing calls of the emperor penguins echo off the rocks and ice around them. The birds were about a quarter of a mile below, on the frozen surface of the sea.[42] But it was too dark to go on, and the men had no choice but to turn around and return to their tent for the night.

The next morning before sunrise the three men carefully secured the roof onto the stone hut. They tied the canvas to rocks and covered it with slabs of hard snow. As soon as dim twilight appeared they went back to the pressure ridges, climbing over the steep slopes and repeatedly falling into crevasses. Finally, they happened upon a narrow opening between a cliff and a ridge of ice, just large enough for a man to wriggle through. This passage led to a cliff only twelve feet above the sea ice. The emperors could be seen nearby, huddled in a cluster for warmth. Cherry-Garrard stayed on top to help the others get back up the drop, while Wilson and Bowers jumped down to walk among the penguins.[43]

Wilson was disappointed to find only about one hundred birds, far fewer than the two thousand that had been gathered at this site in the *Discovery* days. The awkward gait of some of the penguins revealed that Wilson had been right about their reproductive cycle, however: some of the emperors had eggs, which they cradled carefully in the warmth between the tops of their feet and their stomachs. A few birds dropped their loads as Wilson and Bowers approached them, but examination quickly revealed that some of these were not eggs at all but just rounded lumps of ice of about the right size and shape. The two men were the first to witness this evidence of the phenomenal reproductive instincts of the emperor penguin, a bird that will try to incubate a piece of ice if it does not have a genuine egg. They did manage to collect five real eggs, and they slaughtered three large birds for their blubber before returning in the rapidly fading twilight to spend their first night in the stone hut.[44]

Two of the eggs were carried back by the nearsighted Cherry-Garrard, and these broke as he negotiated the difficult path back to camp. When the men arrived at their hut and filled their stove with the penguin blubber they had obtained, they were initially pleased that the fat burned brightly. But a blob of the hot burning blubber caught Wilson squarely in the eye, and he spent the night in considerable pain, "unable to stifle his groans."[45] During the night the wind rose to about forty miles per hour (force 8 on the Beaufort scale), and the men noticed that this had a disturbing lifting effect on the canvas roof.[46] At sunrise, in pain from his burned eye and disappointed by the loss of the eggs, Wilson said, "Things must improve. . . . I think we reached bed-rock last night."[47]

The men spent the next day putting more slabs of heavy ice on the roof and packing snow into as many cracks in the walls of their stone hut as possible. They pitched their tent at its door, so that they could cook and dry their clothing there instead of in the frigid stone hut.[48] They left their cooker in the tent that evening, along with a good deal of personal gear, including their fur boots and mitts. The temperature was in the minus twenties and there was little wind as they worked their way into their icy reindeer sleeping bags inside the stone hut.[49]

It was still pitch-black at 6:30 the next morning when the wind at Cape Crozier reached a screaming sixty miles per hour.[50] Bowers looked out the door of the stone hut into the maelstrom and saw that their tent—that most essential item of all the gear that stood between life and death on the Barrier during the return trip to Cape Evans—was gone.[51]

But instead of dwelling on their fate, the threesome immediately set to work recovering the equipment that had been left behind when the tent blew away. Fortunately, their fur boots and much of the remaining gear were still intact, and the men did battle with walls of "snow which flowed past us and tried to hurl us down the slope. . . . [Bowers was] knocked over once, but he clawed his way back just in time."[52] Two pieces of the cooker had been blown away, however, along with Wilson's fur mitts.[53]

The wind continued to assail their camp in ferocious gusts throughout the morning of July 22. The canvas of the stone hut's roof snapped and shuddered repeatedly. The men decided to cook a meal on their blubber stove while the storm raged outside, but the intense heat generated by the penguin blubber (which had proven to be a most efficient fuel), unsoldered a feed pipe that had not been adequately brazed. The blubber stove was rendered useless, for they had no equipment with which to fix it. There was only a bit more than one can of oil left for the cooker, and that now became their only source of heat. They had left Cape Evans with six cans of the life-giving oil but had been forced to use them more rapidly than planned in the deathly cold traverse of Windless Bight.[54] As the three men had prepared to leave Cape Evans weeks earlier, Scott had asked Wilson, "Bill, why are you taking all this oil?"[55] Wilson had made the decision to ensure a large margin of safety in their oil supplies, even though this meant carrying more weight. That oil had proven barely sufficient to allow them to come this far in the intense cold, and now the little that remained would be essential to their survival.

Snow crept in through every crevice in the stone walls of the hut. Soon everything was covered in six to eight inches of drift. The men had been forced to build their hut in one of the few places where rocks rather than only snow and ice could be found, and they had carefully placed their dwelling below the ridge, out of the full force of the wind. But Cherry-Garrard speculated that the wind flowing up the ridge and just over their heads created a suction that had spirited away their carefully secured tent and now accounted for the inflow of snow—more of which was building up on the lee than on the weather wall of the primitive stone structure.[56]

As long as the heavy snow blocks remained in place, the men reasoned that the roof of the stone hut would resist the pounding winds. They considered trying to go outside to further secure the canvas roof with the alpine rope. Bowers said that the job was impossible.[57] Bowers, who had led a pony to safety over drifting ice floes surrounded by killer whales and had furled the *Terra Nova's* sails in a furious gale, had finally encountered a task that even he deemed beyond reach.

For twenty-four hours the canvas roof crashed and banged, as the squalls built to Beaufort force 11, about seventy miles per hour.[58] The men tried to stop up the holes in the walls to stem the rising tide of snow, and they struggled to keep the rocks and snow supporting the roof from being dislodged. The brave canvas finally gave out at about noon on July 23. In a roaring gust the roof burst into tiny strips, "with a noise like a battery of guns going off."[59] The rocks that had helped to hold the roof in place showered down on the men as they dove into their sleeping bags, the only shelter that was left to them. When Cherry-Garrard was halfway into his bag, he turned to help Wilson, who told him to get into his own bag instead. The younger man acquiesced, realizing that Wilson "felt responsible, feared it was he who had brought us to this ghastly end." The wind roared all day while the men lay helpless in their bags, letting the snow drift over them. They sang songs and hymns. Occasionally they relieved their thirst by opening the flaps of their bags to bring a pinch of snow to their mouths.[60]

Cherry-Garrard lay contemplating death, wishing for a chance to relive at least a few of the years of his young life, and longing for peaches and syrup. They had survived a month of winter on the Barrier in a state of complete exhaustion and frigid cold, keeping themselves going and only slightly injured by frostbite through meticulous care and by burning large amounts of oil. Now they were down to their last can of oil, pinned down by a furious blizzard, and the tent was gone.[61]

The wind brought much warmer temperatures—about $-12\,°F$ at 6:00 P.M.

on July 24—and after a time the young Cherry felt warm for a change. Eventually he slept as the blizzard raged.[62] Wilson's view of their future was more optimistic, for he wrote, "We had time to think out a plan for getting home again now without our tent—in case we couldn't find it." They still had the floorcloth of the tent, which was under the sleeping bags in which they lay. Wilson reasoned that they could dig a hole in the Barrier each night and cover their heads with the floorcloth. If the canvas was placed flush with the Barrier surface rather than above it, then surely it would not be whisked away like their stone dwelling's ill-fated ceiling. Wilson "had no doubts about getting back so long as this blizzard didn't last until we were all stiffened with cold in our bags." The wind began to die down around midnight. Though frequently savage in their intensity, most Antarctic blizzards are mercifully short, lasting only a day or two. Thus did Edward A. Wilson celebrate the thirty-ninth anniversary of his birth, a day he described as "quite the funniest birthday I have ever spent."[63]

The next morning they managed to rig up their cooker for operation despite its missing pieces, and they prepared a meal of pemmican and tea—the first hot food they had eaten in forty-eight hours. They found the food delicious, even though it tasted strongly of the burned blubber still at the bottom. After eating, they settled back into their bags to wait for the light of dawn to aid their search for the tent. When the three men finally came out of their sleeping bags, Cherry-Garrard's eiderdown liner was thoroughly soaked. As he dragged it out of the bag, it rapidly froze into a solid heap of ice. The trio marched off downhill on the lee side of the slope to begin a desperate hunt for the tent. It was Bowers who found it, after only a quarter-mile search. The men reasoned that the tent must have snapped shut like an umbrella as it rose, for it was still in such a state when found. The tent was heavy because a massive amount of ice had accumulated on its walls, and in this closed position the weight had mercifully plummeted it back to earth nearly intact instead of sailing off to New Zealand. As Cherry-Garrard wrote, "Our lives had been taken away and given back to us." They pitched the tent as it had never been pitched before, in a spot farther down the slope, and they retrieved their gear from the stone hut.[64]

The men ate another meal in the safety of the priceless tent and discussed what to do next. Bowers was "all for another go at the emperor penguins."

Cherry-Garrard also voted for "one other tap at the Rookery," but Wilson was in charge and felt "defeated by the Cape Crozier weather and by the darkness." He decided that a return to Cape Evans the next day was their only choice. They cached a sledge, a pick, a variety of scientific supplies, some clothes, and Cherry-Garrard's now-useless sleeping bag liner.[65]

That night Cherry-Garrard's left big toe was frostbitten as he tried to sleep in his overlarge bag with no liner.[66] Wilson's bag was, in contrast, too small, and had begun to crack at both ends, displaying two large gashes across the middle.[67] None of the bags could be rolled up without risk of cracking the ice-covered leather into pieces, so as the three men left Cape Crozier on July 25, they laid their sleeping bags flat on the sledge. Lack of sleep was taking a heavy toll on Wilson and Cherry-Garrard, and Bowers was "much the strongest of us." Bowers was still sleeping well most of the night, and indeed his difficulty was to wriggle fully into his bag before drifting off. While the others shivered in restless agony, on some nights Bowers fell asleep before even finishing his dinner.[68]

As he had many times before, Bowers urged Cherry-Garrard to take his unused eiderdown liner. And although he "felt a brute to take it," the exhausted Cherry-Garrard finally accepted the inestimable gift and obtained a few nights of blissful rest before the new liner began to ice up like his first one. Bowers also tied a line from the tent around himself, determined that "if the tent went, he was going too."[69]

The trip back across the Barrier took seven days. Again the men fell deep into crevasses, and again the temperatures dipped down as low as −63°F in the still air of Windless Bight. This time there was no extra oil to burn, and they shivered and suffered even more than before. Wilson's hands particularly troubled him. With his fur mitts lost when the tent blew away, he had to rely on thinner woolen and dogskin gloves alone. Fortunately, the sun was gradually returning, and on July 28 "a wonderful glow stretched over the Barrier."[70] The twilight was a blessing in spite of the fact that the sun wouldn't fully emerge from below the horizon for about another month. Even with his fresh eiderdown liner, Cherry-Garrard spent many a miserable hour shaking from the cold in his sleeping bag. And although he lay awake much of the night, he still found it a pleasure to listen to Bowers snore.[71]

On the last day of July the threesome stopped for lunch in a temperature of −57 °F. As they continued marching toward the Barrier edge, the temperature rose to −43 °F. When they reached Hut Point it was −27 °F. A remarkable temperature difference of 30 °F had occurred in only a few miles, and Wilson again noted the numbers carefully in his diary, as he had when they began their journey.[72]

The three men slept not in a tent but in the relative comfort of the *Discovery* hut on July 31, 1911. They drank cocoa and warmed themselves with the plentiful supply of oil stored there. The next day, they marched on toward Cape Evans, stopping for lunch after eight miles. As they packed up their belongings for the last time, Wilson said, "I want to thank you two for what you have done. I couldn't have found two better companions—and what is more I never shall." Cherry-Garrard in turn wrote of Wilson and Bowers: "These two went through the winter journey and lived; later they went through the polar journey and died. They were gold, pure, shining, unalloyed. Words cannot express how good their companionship was."[73] While many remarkable friendships were forged among other members of the *Terra Nova* expedition, these three men's writings show that they developed a special set of bonds.

They reached the Cape Evans hut near ten that night. As Lieutenant Evans wrote, "It was pathetic to see them as they staggered into the hut. . . . I well remember undressing poor Wilson in the cubicle which he and I shared. His clothes almost had to be cut off him."[74] Cherry-Garrard fell asleep in warm blankets thinking that "Paradise must feel something like this." Although Bowers recovered the most rapidly, all three endured days of considerable pain in their hands and feet, presumably from the healing of many minor frostbites.[75] Debenham noted: "If a frostbite gets below the surface tissue of the hand or foot the result is a water blister, exactly as in the case of a bad burn. These are very inconvenient, to say the least of it, when sledging. If the frostbite is deep-seated then the blood-vessels do not recover and the last stage is gangrene and the only hope amputation."[76] One day after the return to Cape Evans, Bowers was, however, already talking of attempting the trip again to get more eggs the next year.[77] Scott described the state of the three travelers in his diary, noting Wilson's fatigue on the first night and Cherry-Garrard's haggard appearance. Scott noted that Bowers "has come through best, all things considered, and I believe he is the hardest traveller that ever undertook

Figure 31. From left, Wilson, Bowers, and Cherry-Garrard upon their return from Cape Crozier. Photograph by H. Ponting. Scott Album, number 11365, Alexander Turnbull Library, Wellington, New Zealand.

a Polar journey, as well as one of the most undaunted; [owing to] . . . his untiring energy and astonishing physique which enables him to continue to work under conditions which are absolutely paralysing to others. Never was such a sturdy, active, undefeatable little man."[78] Simpson related a conversation with Scott and Wilson in which Scott asked, "What should you have done if you had not recovered your tent, you could not possibly have got back." Wilson, with an expression on his face that Simpson described as unforgettable, replied: "I would have trusted Birdie to have got us out of anything."[79]

The three men had been away five weeks and had endured a journey of staggering tribulations. They brought back three emperor penguin eggs. Upon his return to England years later, Cherry-Garrard delivered the embryos to the Natural History Museum in London. He left the precious samples in the hands of the museum curators even though he was devastated by the lack of interest shown in the unique specimens that had been gathered at such an immense human cost.[80]

The ration testing was ruled a success. Wilson had lost the most weight, 3.5

pounds, while Bowers lost 2.5 pounds and Cherry-Garrard shed only 1 pound. It appeared that their planned food ration ought to suffice for even the hardest conditions to be faced on the coming journey to the Pole.

All of their sleeping bags had, on the other hand, amassed many pounds of ice. Cherry-Garrard began the journey with an eighteen-pound bag but returned with one weighing an astonishing forty-five pounds. Cocoa was suggested as an alternative to tea for the evening meal, in order to avoid the stimulation that would make sleep in an icy bag even more elusive.[81]

In the years to come, critics would decry this trip, arguing that the trek had no real scientific goal and that it was pure foolishness for the men who would face the demanding journey to the Pole to expend their vital energy on a midwinter junket to Cape Crozier.[82] But whatever the ultimate ornithological result may have been, there can be little doubt that Wilson was deeply motivated by the strongest of scientific passions, the same sometimes fateful passions that drive other scientists into dangerous places like the mouths of volcanoes, the jungles of New Guinea, or the bottom of the ocean. His fervor led the chief of scientific staff to frequent bouts with snow blindness and frostbite while sketching the frozen world around him, and to the safer but no less demanding pursuit of painstakingly dissecting thousands of Scottish grouse in an earlier year in England. And there was one more item in the scientific results that was pioneering, critical, and largely ignored by later analysts: the acquisition of winter meteorological data from the Barrier.

The connection between wind and temperature is difficult for visitors to the Antarctic to overlook, for except in summer each calm period brings the icy grip of frigid air, broken only when the wind blows. But this relation was driven home spectacularly on the Cape Crozier journey, and now the men had observations not only at Cape Evans but also on the Barrier. Scott remarked that "our party has shown the nature of the conditions which exist on the Great Barrier in winter. Hitherto we have only imagined their severity; now we have proof."[83]

Simpson meticulously analyzed the findings. Temperature and wind were measured hourly at Cape Evans, and Simpson set to work examining the differences between the temperatures observed at the base camp and those endured by the trio on the Barrier (figure 32). For the first five days of their struggle, the temperatures recorded by the Cape Crozier party averaged

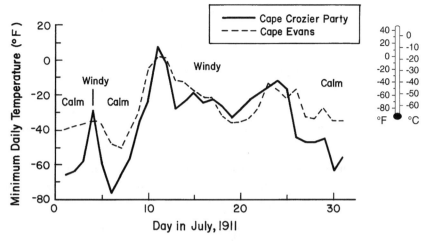

Figure 32. Minimum daily temperatures in July 1911 as documented by the Cape Crozier party, compared with those recorded on the same days at Cape Evans. Windy and calm periods are indicated. As noted by Simpson, the temperature difference between the coast and the Barrier is strongly dependent on the wind, ranging between no difference for very windy periods up to about 20°F to 30°F for very calm days on Windless Bight.

twenty-six degrees colder than those at Cape Evans—a gradient heralded by the perceptive Dr. Wilson's comments on the temperature change as they marched onto the frozen surface of the Barrier. On the day when a frigid minimum of −77°F had been recorded by Bowers, the air at Cape Evans also plummeted to the coldest value observed that winter—but it was about thirty degrees warmer than the trio suffered. The last five days of the month displayed temperatures near Windless Bight that were about twenty-three degrees colder than those at Cape Evans.[84] But on the blizzard days, the great equalizer of wind produced temperatures at Cape Crozier that were comparable to or even warmer than those at Cape Evans. Wind mixed warm air into the Barrier; it was the wind that provided warmth. The pieces of the puzzle of Antarctic winter meteorology were beginning to come together in the mind of Dr. Simpson, who now had excellent reasons to believe that in its coldest month the Barrier was about 25°F colder than Cape Evans. Armed with observations of the temperatures at Cape Evans throughout the year and information about the temperature differences between Cape Evans and the Barrier, the meteorologist could begin to piece together what the temperatures would probably be like on the upcoming journey to and from the Pole.

The frigid depths of winter at Windless Bight remained undocumented for the next seventy-three years after Wilson, Bowers, and Cherry-Garrard slogged across it in July 1911. An automated weather station then recorded winter temperatures there in 1984 and 1985. The machine subsequently proved to be no match for the harsh conditions, though a new machine is currently matching its ruggedness against Windless Bight's challenges. The remarkable chill of July 6, 1911, with a minimum of −77°F, has not yet been equaled by modern data in the Windless Bight area, but temperatures well below −60°F were measured in 1985. If Wilson and Simpson concluded that they had observed the worst face of a Ross Island winter on that still, dark day in 1911, they were correct.

The astute Dr. Simpson also studied the winds at Cape Evans and those recorded by the Cape Crozier party. He carefully deduced the prevailing wind direction and strength at many locations around Ross Island based upon the reports provided by sledging parties of the angles of the leaning pillars of sastrugi in the snow. The still air of the region that later became known as Windless Bight was evident both in the nature of the soft snow surface as described by the Cape Crozier party and in the remarkable observation of rather weak gusts there as recorded by Bowers on July 4, 1911 — a day when the wind roared at fifty-two miles per hour at nearby Cape Evans. Simpson concluded that "during blizzards the wind streams along the west of the Barrier parallel to the edge of the high land. When this southerly stream impinges on Ross Island it breaks up into two branches, one of which passes Cape Crozier as a S. W. or S. S. W. wind, and the other enters McMurdo Sound as a S. E. wind."[85] The wind pattern sketched by Simpson from this simple yet elegant analysis of mountain-parallel winds that flow south along the edge of the Transantarctic Mountains until they are split in two and deflected by the obstacles presented by Minna Bluff, Mount Erebus, and Mount Terror (see figure 33, map 3) is nearly an identical match to recent studies using such sophisticated methods as radar or networks of automated weather stations.[86] Simpson was thus the first to accurately outline the blocking topography that renders Windless Bight so remarkably still and hence so much colder than surrounding regions.

Simpson's Analysis (1919)   Recent Studies (1980s and 1990s)

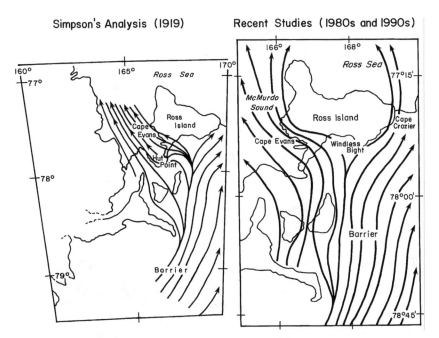

Figure 33. Simpson's 1919 estimate of wind patterns around Ross Island, left, based on such information as study of the sastrugi in the area, and a modern analysis from a detailed network of seventeen weather stations.

During August 1911, Simpson carried out some of the earliest balloon soundings of the Antarctic atmosphere, sending instruments up on hydrogen-filled balloons and recovering many of them by following a silken thread attached to the payload. A slow match fuse burned through a thread to detach the instrument on a small parachute from the balloon so that it fell safely to the ground bearing the data it had recorded. From these soundings, which sometimes reached as high as five miles, Simpson documented the remarkably steep surface temperature inversion that prevails under calm conditions in Antarctic winter. He correctly interpreted the very cold surface temperatures over the snow as a result of loss of heat that radiates away to space, writing that "near the ground the radiation is so great . . . that the air is abnormally cooled." In contrast, after strong winds, the temperature was found to be much warmer and nearly uniform in the lowest half-mile of the atmosphere, showing that mixing of warm air from above played a critical role in raising the surface temperature.[87] Again, modern studies have confirmed

Figure 34. Dr. Simpson inflates one of his balloons, April 7, 1911. Photograph by H. Ponting. Scott Album, number 30599, Alexander Turnbull Library, Wellington, New Zealand.

Simpson's insightful reasoning.[88] Simpson laid the groundwork for understanding the factors that control surface temperature in Antarctic winter, the conditions that would determine the survival of any party trying to attain the Pole.

The Norwegian ski-runner Gran listened to the British explorers talk about the temperatures and speculate about Amundsen's chances. He wrote: "The hut rings with discussion about the low temperature and the weather. 'Poor Amundsen,' I hear them say, but he will make it."[89] Although the men at Cape Evans did not know it, Amundsen had already endured temperatures below −40°F on his depot journeys in March. Although the severe cold of autumn surprised him, its nighttime cold did not torment him as it did the British explorers, in part because of his excellent sleeping bags.

Amundsen's sleeping bags were a three-part affair. Outside the bag went a cover of very thin canvas, which "protected the bag from the moisture of the breath. Instead of condensing on the skin and making it wet, this settled on the cover, forming in the course of the night a film of ice, which disappeared again during the day, breaking off while the bag lay stretched on the sledge." Next came an outer bag of heavy buck reindeer skin, weighing about thirteen pounds. Inside this was placed an inner bag of calfskin or thin reindeer doeskin, and thanks to this arrangement Amundsen and his men slept with a warm dry layer of fur next to their bodies, rather than one of ice.[90]

Amundsen's reindeer skins came from the Lapps and were selected with extreme care by a buyer who had served Amundsen on previous expeditions to the Arctic. The man searched the stocks of the far northern Norwegian towns of Tromsø, Karasjok, and Kaatokeino to find 250 of the finest skins, which would be sewn into clothing, boots, and sleeping bags. Amundsen wrote:

> We attached great importance to having the bags made of the very best sort of skin, and took care that the thin skin of the belly was removed. I have seen sleeping bags of the finest reindeer skin spoilt in a comparatively short time if they contained a few patches of this thin skin, as of course the cold penetrates more easily through the thin skin, and gives rise to dampness in the form of rime on meeting the warmth of the body. These thin patches remain damp whenever one is in the bag, and in a short time they lose their hair. . . . One cannot be too careful in the choice of skins.[91]

Captain Scott had selected the fur gloves, sleeping bags, and fur boots of the *Terra Nova* expedition on a trip to Norway, assisted by Gran and another of his lieutenants.[92] Cherry-Garrard gamely wrote in his report of the winter journey to Cape Crozier that the sleeping bags "were as good as could be wished as regards the skins."[93] All reindeer skins shed hair to some degree, but Amundsen's remarks show that there are great differences between the best and worst furs. Debenham showed some dismay at the quality of the British expedition's sleeping bags, writing that "our bags like the . . . fur boots, have been badly selected and moult continually."[94] And on that awful day after the blizzard stripped the Cape Crozier party first of their tent and then of the canvas roof of their cold stone hut, the tea that Cherry-Garrard so enjoyed for its warmth not only tasted of burnt penguin blubber but also "was full of hairs from our bags."[95]

In October 1911, Captain Scott sent a detailed set of instructions to Pennell, the commander of the *Terra Nova*, specifying supplies required for the next year. He asked Pennell to secure reindeer pelts to be used for repairs to the sleeping bags and fur boots. He wrote: "I very much fear you will not have brought any: anything you can provide to make good the want would be acceptable."[96] More dramatic incidents, like the sinking of the third motor sledge, form the cornerstone of the legend of Scott's mistakes. But the experiences of the Cape Crozier party bear witness to the miserable limitations of the sleeping bags. This was a problem that even the valiant Bowers could solve only for a few nights—by giving Cherry-Garrard his fresh eiderdown liner, which would stay dry for a short while. Better skins were out of reach, on the other side of the world, in Scandinavia, Canada, Alaska, and Greenland, and worse, they were not on the mind of the scientific but still inexperienced leader.

SEVEN

In the Footsteps of Shackleton

The blizzard has raged outside the visitor's dormitory for three full days. The wind howls like an animal as it races past the building. A stream of fine snow comes into his room through a tiny crack between the window and its frame, and it coats the sill with a layer of cold crystals. It is early spring now, and warmer and more changeable weather has arrived along with the return of sunlight. He stands at the window and runs his finger through the white powder, and he tries to make out the shape of the administrative building next door. He knows that it is no more than forty feet away, but although he squints and strains, he can see nothing but a formless white wall of snow. He puts on his boots and parka and goes down the hall to the vestibule. Then he opens the door and the full force of the storm hits his face.

The ferocious wind has made the air quite warm; it must be near +20°F. The air feels strangely damp, in sharp contrast to its normally parched touch. The texture of the snow is different, too—not fine and powdery, as it generally is, but wet. A sudden gust nearly knocks him off his feet. He staggers but steps outside anyway, knowing that he is doing something very foolish. He tells himself he won't go far, he just wants to see what it really feels like to stand alone in an Antarctic blizzard, to experience it at least for a moment as Scott and his companions did. He takes five steps forward and glances back over his shoulder. The building is still visible behind him through a shifting haze of snow. He takes five more, and now the building has completely disappeared. Indeed, the whole world has disappeared, and there is nothing but a formless white in all directions. He cannot even see the ground when he looks down, so dense is the rush of snow.

He spreads out his arms and the wind seems to claw at his torso as it flows around him. The snow fills his throat, and breathing becomes difficult. A thin trickle of cold water runs down his neck. The snow has somehow sneaked past his tightly closed parka hood into his hair, and now it is melting there. He swallows to fight the fear that is rising in his throat. He tells himself that he is ten steps away from a safe, warm building, so logic dictates that there is nothing to worry about. Compare this to the plight of the men of the *Terra Nova* expedition, who felt their way through blizzards across the remotest part of the Barrier. It is almost unthinkable. Perhaps the species of man has changed since those remarkable men walked on this hostile land; perhaps we are lesser beings now than we were nearly a century ago. Or perhaps the will to survive can still bring out such strength and courage, but in our well-insulated world of technological prowess we seldom probe these raw edges of ourselves.

He turns, careful to rotate one hundred and eighty degrees, and begins to walk slowly back in the direction he thinks must be correct. As he walks, he loses his awareness not only of right and left but even of up and down. All sense of direction has been shrouded by the snow. It is a terrifying sensation. Tears of relief come to his eyes when he sees the building again. The wind pushes hard against his body, and he lurches to fight its pressure for the last few steps to shelter. He opens the door to the vestibule, gripping the handle tightly to keep it under control in the wind. As he closes the wooden door behind him, the din of the storm changes pitch, like a freight train roaring past and then receding into the distance. All that stands between him and the maelstrom outside are the walls of this man-made structure, which suddenly seem very flimsy. A powerful gust pounds against the wall, which shakes and groans under the force.

The next morning he opens the same door to a remarkably different Antarctic world: still, beautiful, and peaceful. The sky is red with the light of dawn, and the weather is glorious, a warm −5 °F with little wind. The twilight glows pale magenta on the hills behind him and blazes a deep salmon on the tall peaks of the distant mountains to the west. The unusual storm has deposited ten inches of heavy snow over the station. He has never seen such a wet, thick snowfall here before, and later today the station meteorologist will tell him that the last one was more than ten years ago. As he steps out for a morning walk, he sinks deeply into the soft surface. He tramps down the hill toward the frozen Sound. The snow makes for rough going. He has to lift his feet high with every step, and soon there is clammy sweat on the back of his neck. He opens his parka and slows his pace so as not to get overheated.

It's only September, and the ice still holds the ocean solidly in its cold grip. Out on the Sound is a cluster of heavy equipment—huge snowblowers and bulldozers are sweeping back and forth, preparing the ice runway for the planes that will soon begin arriving. The population of the station will double in just a few days. The visitor grimaces. It has been pleasant not to worry about catching colds or other illnesses. Even when he was run down from overwork last month, he ran no risk of sickness because the station population had long since shared and become resistant to one another's germs. All that will change when the new folk arrive, carrying with them a fresh group of cold and flu viruses to which those here will be particularly vulnerable. But the planes will also bring delicious fresh fruit and vegetables, and the all-important mail from home.

Movement of something dark on the ice about a mile away catches the visitor's eye amid the white. At first it looks like a group of men bunched together, perhaps the supervisors discussing runway preparations. But then the figures spread out a little, and he realizes that it is a cluster of emperor penguins. He shades his eyes with his hand, and now he can make out about fourteen of the large birds. One penguin separates from the others and begins to walk due south in a slow, waddling gait, trudging slowly across the ice. The birds are about fifteen miles from open water to the north, but they are inexplicably headed south. There is no warm ocean that way, no food, no comfort, nothing but the endless snows of Antarctica. But the leader continues and the others rush to follow. The visitor keeps watching, hoping the birds will turn around, but they march steadily southward, and soon he loses sight of them behind an immense grounded iceberg. He sighs and walks back up the hill to the cafeteria, where all the warm breakfast he can eat will already be there for the taking.

Figure 35. From left, Bowers, Atkinson, and Cherry-Garrard bag the provisions to be used for the southern journey. Photograph by H. Ponting. Scott Album, number 11358, Alexander Turnbull Library, Wellington, New Zealand.

The sun returned to Cape Evans after its long winter absence in late August. A blizzard kept the men of the *Terra Nova* expedition from seeing the thin red arc peep above the horizon until August 26, when Lieutenant Evans and Simpson both spotted it. The return of the sun changed not only the colors around them but also their outlook, lifting the monotony of dark and cold that had shrouded the Cape Evans base throughout the winter. As Evans wrote: "Erebus's slopes were now bathed in every shade of orange, pink, and purple. To begin with, we had very little of this lovely coloring, but soon the gladdening tints stretched out over morning and afternoon. We were never idle in the hut, but the sun's return seemed to make fingers lighter as well as hearts."[1]

Preparations for the southern journey were already under way, but urgency increased with the return of the sun. Bowers turned the central table inside the hut into "a grocer's shop . . . bagging provisions for the sledge journeys."[2] The brown lumps of precooked pemmican, for example, were removed from cans and placed into cloth bags designed to feed four men at lunch and dinner over seven days. One of the challenges on the sledging trail was the job of guessing how much of the fat-and-meat mixture formed the portion designated for one meal.[3]

On September 9, 1911, Lieutenant Evans, the Norwegian ski-runner Gran, and seaman Forde left the main hut to dig out Corner Camp, about fifty miles away on the northern edge of the Barrier. Just as Wilson had on the Cape Crozier journey, the lieutenant noticed "an extraordinary change in the temperature" that occurred in a few short miles as his party sledged southward onto the Barrier: "Although only twenty miles from our winter quarters at Cape Evans, the temperature was 21° lower."[4] The seaman's nose was frost-bitten the first day out in temperatures near −40°F. By the time the men were in their sleeping bags that night, the temperature had plummeted to −60°F, and "all night we shivered and fidgeted, feeling the want of extra heat in the small of our backs. . . . We got little or no sleep . . ."[5] Those minimum temperatures were colder than average for the region near Corner Camp (fig. 36), but within the range of typical variability for the coreless winter's September.

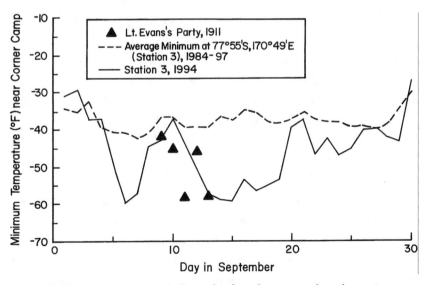

Figure 36. Minimum temperatures in September from the automated weather station at 77°55′S, 170°49′E, near Corner Camp (station 3; see map 2), compared with Lieutenant Evans's 1911 data.

Four hundred miles to their east, Amundsen led his men away from their camp just one day before Lieutenant Evans ventured onto the sledging trail. Thus both March and September of 1911 found two parties enduring the hardships of the Barrier—in each case, one led by the lieutenant and the other by Amundsen. But rather than digging out a depot, the Norwegian team was now testing whether it was already time to strike out due south for the Pole.

On the morning of September 11, 1911, Amundsen and Lieutenant Evans both recorded temperatures below −60 °F.[6] Evans and his men reached Corner Camp two days later and dutifully dug out the cached supplies from under the immense snowdrift that had amassed over the winter, a labor Evans described as "about the coldest day's work I ever remember doing."[7] After conducting an inventory of the supplies stored at the depot, Evans led his men back to the relative warmth of Hut Point as rapidly as possible. They ate well and slept much better in the *Discovery* hut, and the next day they skied the fifteen miles across the frozen sea ice to Cape Evans.

After a brief pause for a few days' rest at Cape Evans, the lieutenant struck out again on a surveying journey of the area near McMurdo Sound.[8] He was to spend far more time in September and October 1911 away from the base camp (and therefore eating sledging rations containing almost no vitamin C) than any other man going south toward the Pole.

When September 12 dawned with a temperature of −61.6°F, Amundsen decided that it would not be possible to continue his drive southward so early in the season. His normally eager dogs had to be lifted into their harnesses, and the fluid in his compasses had frozen solid. He decided to go only as far as his first major depot at 80 °S, where he would drop his loads and follow his tracks back home.[9]

As Amundsen and his team cooked their dinner just after turning northward, one of his men reported a loss of sensation in his heel. Inspection revealed that the flesh was the color of tallow, badly damaged by frostbite. Another man was plagued with the same problem. Three men had frozen heels by the end of this ghastly trip, and although the flesh did eventually recover, the pain was severe, and serious damage was averted only by their prompt return to base. They also lost several dogs to the cold. As a result of this trip, Amundsen decided to take five men to the Pole rather than eight, citing matters of efficiency, such as the need to reduce complexity and thereby the time needed for camp work.[10] There are indications, however, that serious personality conflicts also emerged on this trip, and that these strongly affected the great explorer's choice of men for the final polar party.[11]

Perfecting his boots was as great a concern to Amundsen as perfecting his team of companions. A boot that constricted circulation in any way could cause the agony of frostbite in extremely cold weather. Amundsen spent two years designing, testing, and modifying his ski boots.[12] Any shortcoming in the design of the boots could prove fatal, as shown by the frozen heels of September 1911. The experienced Amundsen therefore devoted meticulous attention to improving his footgear before venturing out across the Barrier again.

In midwinter 1911 Scott also expressed concern with the ski boots and bindings he had brought to Antarctica: "With this arrangement one does not have good control of his ski and stands the chance of a chafe on the 'tendon Achilles.'" In the British team, it was seaman Evans whose considerable skill with tools led to a remarkably rapid solution to the problem that had plagued Amundsen for years. Evans rose "to the occasion as a boot maker," fashioning a ski boot using a sole of sealskin stiffened with wood. Soft fur boots were then accommodated inside these outer shoes. The arrangement allowed the feet to move relatively freely in a loose and warm inner boot, while furnishing the rigidity underfoot that was required for skiing.[13] Just as Oates had labored long and skillfully to better the condition of the poorly chosen ponies, so did seaman Evans play a key role in improving boots and other critical sledging gear. As his Australian friend Debenham wrote, "His position is that of sledgemaster. . . . He is in charge of all sledging gear of every sort, makes and repairs sledges, tents, etc., and is Scott's general court of appeal when anything requires to be rigged."[14] Scott appreciated the seaman's work, writing that "our ski shoes and crampons have been absolutely indispensable, and if the original ideas were not his, the details of manufacture and design and the good workmanship are his alone."[15]

Seaman Evans hailed from Swansea in Wales and was among the largest of the men, weighing in for his second trip to the Antarctic at nearly two hundred pounds. He was described by the young Australian geologist as "a great companion, always ready with a yarn or a song, always ready for hard or dirty jobs and yet not at all self-asserting. . . . He is a product of Old South Wales and had many a wordy battle with me as representative of New South Wales." [16] But seaman Evans had more to offer to the expedition than banter, more even than excellent ski boots. When Debenham's toes became frostbitten during the journey to the western mountains in early 1911, seaman Evans "sat down on a pinnacle of ice, made me lie on my back and put my bare feet against his tummy underneath his windproof blouse and his jersey. Gradually feeling came back." [17] This man deemed by Scott "a giant worker with a really remarkable headpiece [brain]" was among those chosen for the honor of going all the way to the South Pole.[18]

One of the most important results of Lieutenant Evans's September trip to Corner Camp was the collection of meteorological data. With this last piece of information, Scott's men had now seen the Barrier in all its seasons. They had been on its frozen surface to lay their depot in January and February, and Lieutenant Evans had braved it again in March 1911. Wilson, Bowers, and Cherry-Garrard had barely escaped its appalling cold in July. And now the lieutenant and his men had shivered and suffered in their tent through September lows in the minus sixties.

The Barrier's meteorology was becoming clearer to the men of the *Terra Nova* expedition, thanks to these forays onto its surface and the accompanying continuous record of hourly data at Cape Evans. Temperatures had been relatively cold at Cape Evans while Lieutenant Evans swung the sling thermometer at Corner Camp. Simpson found a mean difference between conditions at Cape Evans and those on the Barrier in September 1911 of about seventeen degrees, close to the twenty-one-degree temperature difference measured during the lieutenant's Barrier trek in March 1911. In the winter depths of July, the average temperature difference had also typically been between twenty and twenty-five degrees. Only a few days displayed larger gradients. Those occurred in July, when the Cape Crozier trio had slogged their way across the most windless, and therefore presumably coldest, regions.[19] Putting this information together, Simpson estimated the average annual cycle of temperatures to be expected on the Barrier. About seventy years passed before the conditions on the Barrier began to be systematically measured, allowing a test of Simpson's predictions based on this simple analysis. Recent data reveal that Simpson's 1919 estimate was stunning in its accuracy,

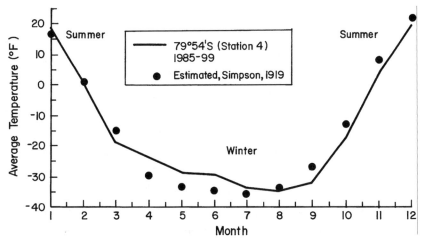

Figure 37. Contemporary measurements of the typical cycle of temperatures at 79°54′S (near One Ton Camp, station 4; see map 2), compared with Simpson's 1919 estimate based on meteorological reasoning.

as shown in figure 37. Scott and his men had gathered enough data for Simpson to surmise precisely what average conditions would be like deep in the heart of the Barrier throughout the year.

Scott's design for the polar journey was intimately tied to the weather. October was warm at Cape Evans in 1911, with an average temperature near −3°F, but blizzards confirmed Scott's concerns that an early departure would not be safe for the ponies.[20] He would wait until the end of the month to begin the polar trek.

Starting late for the ponies' sake dictated a return in mid- to late March for the team of men who would make the full circuit to the Pole. Scott and Simpson had every reason to believe, based upon their hard-won experience and careful measurements during journeys in every season, that the Barrier temperatures in March would be about twenty degrees colder than at Cape Evans. This meant that the last stage of the polar journey on the Barrier should be expected to take place in challenging but endurable temperatures averaging near −20°F.

Preparations continued apace throughout October. The ponies were exercised whenever possible. The motor sledges were brought out, only to have one suffer a broken axle. Scott brooded over the problems with the potentially wonderful motor vehicles, writing: "I am secretly convinced that we shall not get much help from the motors, yet nothing has ever happened to them that was unavoidable. A little more care and foresight would make them splendid allies. The trouble is that if they fail, no one will ever believe this." [21] His concerns were growing to encompass not only the likely outcome of his expedition, but also how it would ultimately be viewed by the world.

Scott held his photographer Ponting in high esteem, writing of his "wonderfully fine cinematograph work," and adding, "What a very good fellow he is." [22] Ponting in turn glowingly described Scott in his account of the expedition published in 1921, noting, "I was drawn strongly to the famous explorer at my first meeting with him." [23] The two men interacted frequently in September and October 1911, when Scott realized that "it would largely devolve upon himself" to photograph the polar journey. Bowers, Gran, the Canadian physicist Wright, Debenham, and Scott all began to learn photography under Ponting's tutelage, and by early October, Scott wrote that "the photography craze is in full swing." [24]

Years after the expedition, Ponting wrote a description of these lessons in which he sought to highlight Scott's charming and human side. But those paragraphs also provide a vivid illustration of some important limitations of the man who was about to lead his companions south into the most desolate place in the world:

> In that nice way in which he always asked a favour of anyone, he said that I should render a very great service to the expedition if I would take him, and a few others in hand, and coach them in photography. I replied that nothing would give me greater pleasure than to do anything in my power to help him and any of my comrades. . . .
>
> Captain Scott and Bowers applied themselves to the work with extraordinary enthusiasm. Indeed, Scott's zeal outran his capability; he craved to be initiated into the uses of color-filters and telephoto lenses before he had mastered an exposure meter. I had to express my disapproval of such haste, and firmly decline to discuss these things until he could repeatedly show me half-a-dozen correctly exposed

Figure 38. The photographer Ponting with his telephoto apparatus, January 1912. Photographer unknown. Scott Album, number 30597, Alexander Turnbull Library, Wellington, New Zealand.

negatives from as many plates. When he had achieved this result under my guidance, he would sally forth alone with his camera.

He would come back as pleased as a boy, telling me quite excitedly he had got some splendid things, and together we would begin to develop his plates—six in a dish. When five minutes or more had elapsed and no sign of a latent image appeared on any of them, I knew something was wrong, and a conversation would follow, something in this wise:

"Are you quite sure you did everything correctly?"

"My dear fellow (a great expression this of Scott's), I'm absolutely certain I did. I'm sure I made no mistake."

"Did you put in the plateholder?"   "Yes."

"Did you draw the slide?"   "Yes."

"Did you set the shutter?"   "Yes."

"Did you release the shutter?"   "Yes."

"Did you take the cap off the lens?"   "Yes."

Then he would rub his head, in that way he had, and admit:

"No! Good heavens! I forgot. I could have sworn I had forgotten nothing."

He would fill up his holders again and be off once more. He fell repeatedly into every pitfall in his haste—with unfamiliar apparatus. One time he would forget to set the shutter, another time he would forget to release it, and each time he would vow not to make the same error again—and then go out and make some other. But I liked him all the more for his human impatience and his mistakes. How often have I not made them all myself, in my own early days with the camera![25]

As October drew to a close, Scott turned his attention away from photography and onto the final preparations for the polar journey. In a series of letters he again revealed the extraordinary depth of his personal touch. He wrote to the families of his men, among them Bowers's mother, to whom he said: "I must send you a line on the eve of our departure for the South to tell you how fortunate I consider myself in having secured the services of your son for this expedition. He is just splendid, no praise from me could do him justice."[26] Scott left Simpson in command of the base at Cape Evans, underscoring the need to be cautious on the unstable sea ice in summer. He also provided detailed instructions for the ship, describing the conditions he had observed during the previous fall and winter—information that could be useful in ensuring that the Terra Nova would not become trapped in the ice of the Sound in the coming season. And he asked the captain of his vessel to lend assistance to Amundsen if the Norwegians were in need of aid.[27] Even as Scott wrote these generous instructions, Amundsen was on his way to the Pole, having left his camp with four other men and fifty-two dogs on October 19, 1911.[28]

Scott's transport relied on multiple methods, each with a greatly different speed. Scott would lead the pony party on which so much depended. The ponies could not be taken up the crevassed surface of the Beardmore glacier to the plateau, but they would pull the bulk of the load as far as its base. The motors traveled slowly and would therefore depart about a week before the ponies. The motor party was placed under the command of Lieutenant Evans, assisted by Lashly, the mechanic Day, and a young seaman named Hooper. Evans was given a letter instructing him to proceed to One Ton Camp and from there to about 80°30′S, where he and his men would await the arrival of the other parties. Their early departure would allow time to stop for repairs if needed. If the vehicles broke down completely, then Lieutenant Evans and his men were ordered to abandon them and advance on foot, man-hauling as much food as possible to the rendezvous point.[29]

The dogs were the fastest means of transport, but Scott still did not believe that the canines would be reliable over long distances. His plan called for them to make a series of limited trips south, never going beyond the Barrier. He instructed his master of dogs, Meares, to leave after the ponies and haul their first load to One Ton Camp, where the dog and pony parties would meet. The dogs were to return from this journey no later than December 19. They would then make a second journey south to One Ton Camp in January, to bring out the supplies that would be critical for the returning parties: five weeks' worth of food and oil for five men, and as much dog food as possible. The dogs would begin their third and final journey south around the beginning of February 1912, with a goal of "meeting the returning party about March 1 in latitude 82 or 82.5°S," so that Scott and the polar party might perhaps manage with the dogs' assistance to return in time to catch the ship before the encroaching winter ice forced its departure. In closing this letter, Scott emphasized that the second of these journeys was vital, while the third was less so. Regardless of what else occurred, it was imperative that provisions be brought to One Ton Camp in January; otherwise the returning parties would starve. Scott's letter to the captain of the *Terra Nova* noted that Meares might leave Antarctica with the vessel, depending upon letters from home.[30] In this case the responsibility for the third dog journey must fall to someone else, an individual not specified.

Scott also wrote to Kinsey, his agent in New Zealand, frankly expressing his views regarding his own and his rival's prospects:

I am fully alive to the complication of the situation by Amundsen, but as any attempt at a race might have been fatal to our chance of getting to the Pole at all, I decided long ago to do exactly as I should have done had Amundsen not been down here. If he gets to the Pole, he is bound to do it rapidly with dogs, but one guesses that success will justify him and that our venture will be "out of it." If he fails, he ought to hide! Anyway, he is taking a big risk, and perhaps deserves his luck if he gets through—But he is not there yet! Meanwhile you may be sure we shall be doing the best we can to carry out my plan.[31]

Lieutenant Evans and his three companions began the trek poleward on October 24, 1911, hauling three tons of provisions with the two fourteen-horsepower motor sledges at speeds of a few miles per hour. If the motors could be coaxed past the sea ice, the first part of the trek would be easier on the ponies, which could then travel lightly loaded over this first section of difficult terrain. Two men controlled each sledge, with one handling the engine and the other pulling on a steering rope in front. The vehicles advanced well on snow, but when they reached smooth ice their progress stalled. The tracks slipped and the hard surface began to spoil the wooden rollers. Scott and seven others came out to assist and returned after one day, when the surface improved, and the motor vehicles began again to advance steadily southward.[32]

While traction posed a relatively minor problem, regulation of the engine temperatures was the major challenge faced by the motor party. The air-cooled engines had been tested in Norway, but in the far more severe weather of Antarctica the cylinders tended to overheat while the carburetors became too cold. The men frequently were forced to stop, cover the engines, and wait for the temperatures to equalize between the two extremes.[33] A gasoline lamp was also employed to warm the reluctant carburetors. The motor party lurched south in fits and starts, constantly struggling with breakdowns. To ease the strain on the vehicles, all four of the men "would heave with all our might on the spans of the towing sledges."[34] But worst of all were the repairs, which involved handling frigid metal in temperatures that were frequently below −10°F.[35] On October 27 Lashly wrote that on "opening the crank chamber we found the crank brasses broke into little pieces so there is nothing left to do but replace them with the spare ones; of course this meant a cold job for Mr. Day and myself, as handling metal on the Barrier is not a thing one looks forward to with pleasure."[36] The strict conventions of class

Figure 39. The motor party prepares to depart from Cape Evans: from left, Lashly, Day, Lieutenant Evans, and Hooper. Photograph by H. Ponting. Scott Album, number 11406, Alexander Turnbull Library, Wellington, New Zealand.

followed the expedition onto the Barrier, and Lashly's diary carefully distinguishes officers and scientists, who are always politely designated "Mister," and the seamen, who are called simply by their last names.

Soon a connecting rod broke through a piston on one sledge, forcing the men to depot some of the supplies and continue with the remaining vehicle. Just past Corner Camp on November 1, the second motor was also abandoned after hours of frigid but fruitless labor trying to fix it. Thus ended the brief career of the motor sledges, fifty-one miles from Cape Evans. At least they had gotten a heavy load past the sea ice as hoped.[37]

Before the winter, a wind vane had been positioned at Corner Camp. The instrument featured an aluminum base plate that was scratched by the motion of the vane to provide a simple yet effective measure of the prevailing wind direction. It strikingly confirmed the strong southwesterly winds of the Barrier, the flow from behind that should help speed the return journeys.[38]

Lieutenant Evans left a note for Captain Scott at Corner Camp, and he and his men began man-hauling 185 pounds apiece toward the south. The lieutenant was determined that his group would not be overtaken by the

Figure 40. The dog party departs from Hut Point. Vince's cross is visible on the hill in the background. Photograph by H. Ponting. Scott Album, number 8296, Alexander Turnbull Library, Wellington, New Zealand.

pony party now following them. At first the man-haulers made fifteen and a half to seventeen miles per day on good surfaces. The weather was relatively warm (−12.4°F on November 4), and the four men rose early to make long marches, a habit that Evans later credited with saving his life. The snow became deeper and the going harder after they passed One Ton Camp at 79°29′S. They picked up still more supplies there, and in the days that followed they managed marches of about twelve miles. The team reached the appointed spot at 80°32′S on November 15. There they waited a week for the others to join them, enjoying calm Antarctic summer weather with temperatures sometimes above zero and seldom below −10°F.[39] The party passed the time by building an enormous snow cairn, jokingly dubbed Mount Hooper after their youngest member, and reading *The Pickwick Papers* aloud.[40]

Scott delayed the planned departure of the pony party by one day after helping the motor party. Before leaving on the southern journey, Wilson found time to examine the emperor penguin eggs collected from the winter journey to Cape Crozier. He was pleased to find "well formed chicks of three different sizes, fairly young, but a good deal older than I had ever expected which is all the better for my work. I got these well pickled. . . . They are quite unique and probably the most primitive embryos of this most primitive bird." The careful Wilson hedged his bets with *probably* in case Amundsen, too, had collected penguin eggs.[41] He need not have worried, for Amundsen was focused completely on the Pole, with limited interest in the scientific pursuits that fascinated Wilson and Scott.

Ten ponies and their leaders left Cape Evans on November 1, 1911. They regrouped at Hut Point, where it was discovered that one important item had been forgotten: the Union Jack that was to be planted at the South Pole. Scott used the telephone to request that it be brought to him at the *Discovery* hut, and the Norwegian ski-runner swiftly delivered the flag to the British leader.[42]

The main party began the long trek south late on November 2. They marched at night, as they had done on the depot journey, in order to have the best surface for the ponies. Dr. Atkinson was the leader in a first group of three, which included Wright and an Irish seaman named Keohane, leading the three weakest ponies. These animals were dubbed "the Baltic Fleet," after the Russian ships that had taken seven months to sail to the relief of Port Arthur during the Russo-Japanese war of 1904–5.[43] Two hours later came Scott, Wilson, and Cherry-Garrard with their animals. Last were Oates, Bowers, and seamen Evans and Crean with the swiftest ponies.[44]

Only Oates could control Christopher, the demon horse. This pony's front leg was tied up to his shoulder each day so that he could be thrown to the ground. Then he was harnessed to his load, with his head carefully held down on the ice so that he could not bite. He was brought up on three legs and allowed to kick the fourth free of its rope. It took all of Oates's considerable skills and patience to keep the unruly horse under control on the march.[45]

The weather was relatively warm on the Barrier in the beginning of November, and Cherry-Garrard's impression was that of "constant wonder at its comfort. One had forgotten that a tent could be warm and a sleeping bag dry: so deep were the contrary impressions that only actual experience was convincing."[46] Temperatures soared above zero on most days as the troupe of ten ponies and their leaders marched along on the snow-covered Barrier toward their rendezvous with the motor party ahead of them.[47] The sun had ceased setting weeks earlier, so that even as they halted for "lunch" at midnight, camp work was carried out in full daylight.

But as the men stopped to camp on November 6, the wind picked up and a blizzard began that kept them in their tents for two days. They built snow walls around the ponies and covered them with blankets, but the animals suffered as they had on the depot journey, even though temperatures remained above zero.[48] Scott wrote, "It is not easy to understand at first why the blizzard should have such a withering effect on the poor beasts. I think it is mainly due to the exceeding fineness of the snow particles, which, like finely divided powder, penetrate the hair of the coat and lodge in the inner warmths. Here it melts, and as water carrie[s] off the animal heat."[49]

The dog party started later and caught up with the horses on November 7. After the storm cleared, the combined horse and dog column continued its march in warm weather with good surfaces. On November 9 Scott wrote, "Things look hopeful. The weather is beautiful: +12°F with a bright sun," but only one day later he lamented "a very horrid march . . . strong head wind . . . then a snowstorm." Steering became difficult in the bad weather, but fortunately they picked up the tracks left by Lieutenant Evans and his companions. The heavy pulling continued to wear on the ponies, and on November 13 Scott wrote that he was "anxious about these beasts—very anxious, they are not the ponies they ought to have been and if they pull through well, all the thanks will be due to Oates."[50] The party plodded on to the south, sinking in at times up to their knees.[51] Pony snowshoes had been brought, but they proved ineffective in the deep, soft snow, and the very difficult surface sapped the energies of both men and animals. While Scott worried about the weather, Wilson enjoyed its effects of light and color, noting "parts of fine parhelion. . . . The clouds and light and shade effects have been very beautiful."[52]

The pony and dog parties reached One Ton Camp on November 15. They dug out the depot and looked for the oats that had been sprinkled on the surface in February to measure the accretion of winter snow. These were nowhere to be found, but they did find the minimum thermometer, which had also been carefully placed there on the depot journey. It showed a minimum winter temperature at One Ton Camp for 1911 of −72°F, a value that can now be shown to be typical of this part of the Barrier as measured over multiple years by the nearby automated weather station at 79°54′S (fig. 41).[53]

Although he did not remark upon it in his diary, Wilson must have noted with satisfaction that a winter minimum of −72°F was comparable to the harshest value of −77°F that he, Bowers, and Cherry-Garrard had experi-

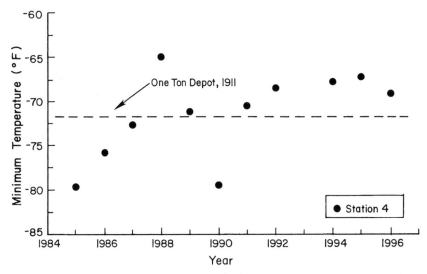

Figure 41. Modern measurements of the minimum winter temperature in the heart of the Barrier (station 4; see map 2), compared with Scott's 1911 observations based on the minimum thermometer left at One Ton Camp the previous summer.

enced during their winter journey to Cape Crozier. It was twenty-two degrees colder than the coldest value measured at Cape Evans in July 1911, again pointing to a temperature difference of roughly twenty degrees between the Sound and the middle of the Barrier, even in the coldest depths of a bitter Antarctic winter.[54]

The men depoted a supply of seal liver and rested the ponies for a day at One Ton Camp.[55] The stronger ponies were now pulling loads of about 580 pounds each, while the weaker animals pulled 400 pounds, and the two dog teams dragged 1,570 pounds between them.[56]

On November 21 the pony and dog parties arrived at 80°30′S, where they met Lieutenant Evans and the motor party. The lieutenant's group had been man-hauling for weeks and were hungry and thin, while those driving dogs and ponies had felt satisfied by the same rations of food, as they had been on the depot journey.[57]

The weakest pony was shot on November 24 to provide food for the dogs, and the next morning the motor mechanic Day and seaman Hooper turned for home. The other men and animals continued their march to the south across the white monotony of the Barrier. At least the surface was relatively even and the area showed little sign of serious crevasses. But the sky was often cloudy, and there was frequently driving snow from the south, so that they plodded on through a formless blank landscape of unending white in all directions. Sky and horizon merged, and steering was a constant challenge. At times the only indicator for navigation was the sastrugi, whose leaning forms revealed the dominant wind direction.[58]

Another pony was slaughtered on November 28. Scott had decided that the dogs should continue to push on to the south, and they therefore had to be fed. The dogs were going well, and their labor would delay the need for heavy man-hauling as long as possible. The men also partook of the pony meat, finding it "sweet and good, though tough." Cherry-Garrard wrote that because cooking oil was rationed, "we could not do more than heat the meat by throwing it into the pemmican."[59] Eaten in such a semiraw state, the animal meat would have provided significant amounts of vitamin C.[60]

As the stories of Scott's errors evolved and grew over the decades that followed, legend suggested that the sentimental men of the *Terra Nova* expedition contracted scurvy and perished because they refused to eat their ponies. Scurvy did occur in at least one man in spite of the consumption of pony meat, and it is certainly true that the men became fond of their animals. But the delights of dining on horseflesh are emphasized in many of the diaries. Bowers, for example, did indeed become fond of his horse, whom he described as "a steady goer, and as gentle as a dear old sheep." But he was also practical about the necessity of eating the animal, writing: "I must say that pony flesh is A-1."[61]

The endless white of the Barrier gave way to better weather and the welcome sight of the Transantarctic Mountains on November 29. The change in the vista lifted the men's spirits. But the food brought for the ponies began to run out. The next horse to go was the fiend, Christopher. The dogs had been taken much farther than planned but were "doing splendidly." On December 2 the team of twelve men dined on horse meat and were "so well fed that hunger isn't thought of." An optimistic Scott wrote, "We have reached the 83rd parallel and are practically safe to get through. . . . Everything looks well if the weather will only give us a chance to see our way to the Glacier."[62]

The men were now marching where only Shackleton had been before—along nearly the same route three years earlier. Although the weather continued to threaten, Scott noted with satisfaction that "the ponies marched splendidly. . . . They must be in very much better condition than Shackleton's animals." But after each march the wolflike dogs were ravenous, and in the next two days both Bowers's and Cherry-Garrard's equine companions were sacrificed as dog food. December 4 began with a strong wind and a thick blizzard, but a lull set in later in the day, allowing the column to advance thirteen miles. Scott noticed "a phenomenal rise" in the barometric pressure and speculated that "there is a very great disturbance of atmospheric conditions." He lamented the difficult winds and surfaces he was finding compared to the easy journey that he felt had been reported by Shackleton, writing that "it makes me feel a little bitter to contrast such weather with that experienced by our predecessors."[63]

The men awoke the next day to a wind that howled at speeds of about fifty miles per hour.[64] This blizzard was quite unlike those they had earlier endured. The snow was "not fine as usual, but in big flakes driving in a hard wind."[65] Bowers swung the thermometer that day and then swung it again, unable to believe that the temperature was really +33°F. The remarkable warmth of the maritime air pelting them with wet, heavy snow was confirmed by the water that "trickle[d] down the tent poles and only form[ed] icicles in contact with the snow floor."[66] Lieutenant Evans described "the poor ponies cowering behind their snow walls the picture of misery."[67] The blizzard raged for four full days, December 5–8, 1911. Most of the men rested in their sleeping bags; Wilson, for example, read Tennyson.[68] But even though the thick walls of rushing snow made it impossible to see the next tent most of the time, one dedicated man "set himself to better the ponies' state during the bad weather. . . . Whenever one peeped out of the tent door there was Oates, wet to the skin, trying to keep life in his charges."[69]

Men, dogs, and horses had to eat while they waited, though they did so as sparingly as possible. But by December 7 they had begun consuming the rations that had been reserved for the ascent of the glacier. Scott wrote that "resignation to misfortune is the only attitude, but not an easy one to adopt. It seems undeserved where plans were well laid and so nearly crowned with a first success."[70]

At noon on December 8 the weather improved enough for the men to dig out and reposition their tents. The sledges were pulled out from under four-foot drifts. Everything that had been left on them was now dripping wet. The ponies sank in to their bellies and the men to their knees. But they found that four men on skis could pull a heavily loaded sledge. Cherry-Garrard and the Canadian Wright traded the books each had finished reading, and Cherry-Garrard now had Dante's *Inferno* for his bedtime reading while "the steady patter of the falling snow upon the tent" continued that night.[71]

Although Scott had complained earlier in the journey about his luck compared to that of Shackleton, it was only with this storm that he and his party experienced truly unusual conditions. A wet, warm blizzard of such extended duration with winds in excess of fifty miles per hour has not yet been observed in eight years of December data at the nearby automated weather station at 83°8'S, 174°10'E, or in fourteen years of December data at the station at 79°54'S, 169°58'E (see map 2). The longest and windiest storm recorded by modern instruments in this region of the Barrier occurred in December 1995. It lasted about two days and displayed peak winds of about forty miles per hour—comparable to storms experienced earlier by Shackleton and Scott. But Scott and his men were tentbound while the blizzard dumped heavy snow for four full days, December 5–8, 1911, and they estimated the wind speed at up to eighty miles per hour.[72] Scott and his men were the victims of bad luck in this exceptionally severe and prolonged storm, which must have been due to a tongue of warm, wet air from the ocean that pushed unusually far across the Barrier.[73]

The continent of Antarctica is one of the largest and driest deserts in the world. Wet air seldom pushes into its interior as it did in December 1911, and over most of the Barrier the typical annual precipitation is believed to be between four and six inches per year, close to the amount falling upon the Nevada desert.[74] The high continental interior is drier yet, for moisture is thoroughly wrung from any air that does manage to ascend from sea level to the plateau at more than ten thousand feet elevation. As a result the annual precipitation near the South Pole averages only a bit more than one inch per year, comparable to some stations in the Sahara.[75] The city of Plymouth, England, by contrast, receives about forty inches of moisture in an average year.[76]

Figure 42. Looking up the Gateway from Pony Camp. Note the footprints in the snow. Photographer unknown. Scott Album, number 11452, Alexander Turnbull Library, Wellington, New Zealand.

While Scott and his men wallowed in deep snow, conditions in the middle of the high dry desert on the plateau during December 5–6, 1911, were documented by Amundsen and his party. The Norwegian party reported light drifting snow at their location near 88°S, but not severe enough to stop the men and their dogs from continuing southward. They were already well up on the polar plateau at high elevation and, simply put, safely above the reach of the wet storm (see map 1). By the end of December 7 Amundsen and his men were enjoying mild weather again, and on December 8 Amundsen's team paused in good weather for a photograph to mark the point where they passed Shackleton's southernmost point at 88°23′.[77] Meanwhile, Scott and his men lay in their tents, waiting for the driving snow on the Barrier to subside. The legend of the bumbler may suggest to some that Scott failed to march at times that Amundsen thought easy.[78] But the case of the storm of December 1911 reflects not the skills of the two leaders in dealing with the weather but rather their fortunes in geographic placement. If the same storm had occurred three weeks earlier, both teams would have been pinned down by it on the Barrier. Amundsen's faster pace did, however, reduce his time spent at sea level on the Barrier and therefore his vulnerability to the possibility of such an event.

On December 9 Scott and his men finally were able to continue southward. The pony food had been completely exhausted during the blizzard, and the soft-hearted Wilson gave his animal all of his own biscuits that morning as well as the night before. Bowers's and Cherry-Garrard's ponies had already been shot, and the two men formed a man-hauling party to blaze the trail on skis through the heavy snow. Wilson led his pony on its last march along with the other four drivers and their animals. He wrote, "It was horrible work flogging them on, floundering belly deep as they were. . . . We were ploughing along knee deep alternately hammering and dragging and encouraging our poor beasts. . . . The horses constantly collapsed and lay down and sank down. Then we camped. Shot them all." [79] Pony meat was cached at the site, which they called Shambles Camp or Pony Camp. [80]

The ponies' death march had lasted for eleven long hours, covering about seven miles and completing the animals' appointed task of dragging the bulk of the supplies over the Barrier. When it was over Scott and his men were within two miles of the "Gateway" to the Beardmore glacier discovered by Shackleton. The base of that huge glacier is heavily crevassed, and this snow-filled notch is one of the few places where it can be approached in relative safety. [81]

Here Shackleton and his men had found hard blue ice that could be scaled in crampons, though they also encountered numerous crevasses that made progress difficult at times. [82] Scott and his party were now several days behind Shackleton's mark, and the glacier before them was buried in deep snow. Scott defensively explained his position, writing that "no foresight — no procedure — could have prepared us for this state of affairs. Had we been ten times as experienced or certain of our aim we should not have expected such rebuffs." [83]

It was only the beginning of December, but the sledging season had started with what has been shown here, based upon many years of modern data, to be a highly unusual storm. Scott bemoaned his luck, writing that "one has a horrid feeling that this is a real bad season." [84]

EIGHT

Beyond the H of Hell

The snow is deep at the makeshift airport, and the visitor sinks in up to his calves as he trudges over to the runway. It is late January, and McMurdo Sound is basking in a +20°F day. He feels much too warm in his heavy Antarctic parka, but he doesn't have far to go. After a few hundred yards he climbs a few steps into the waiting plane. There are a dozen other passengers on this flight to the South Pole, but by now the visitor knows the ropes, and he snares the best seat, next to one of the cargo plane's few side windows. A huge black crate dominates the belly of the plane, behind the passenger area. The visitor has heard that it is a sensitive piece of equipment, destined to be part of a new astronomy experiment. The lack of water in the heart of this crystalline desert makes the Pole the next best thing to outer space for astronomical work. As he ponders the size of the enormous box, the visitor can't help thinking that the weight of this container and the space it occupies have displaced the letters that would have been so welcome to the people who have spent the past nine months in isolation at the bottom of the world. They will have to wait for another flight in order to hear from their loved ones. The demands of science and humanity are still in competition, just as they were during Scott's expedition.

The plane roars as it leaves the runway, winging its way south on four powerful propeller engines. It can fly on just one if necessary, ensuring safe passage across the forbidding landscape below.

Soon they have left the majestic mountains of the coast behind and are traversing the endless plain of the Barrier. The sky is nearly cloudless, and there is nothing to interfere with the awe-inspiring views of pristine white in all directions. Occasionally the visitor spots jagged furrows on the surface far below, the sure sign of crevasses. The automated weather stations are far too small to make out at this distance, but he knows that they are down there somewhere, dutifully measuring the temperatures on the immense snow plain, as they have for years. He learned just two days ago that purely by chance one of them lies within a few miles of the location where Scott and his men perished. Another happens to sit very close to the place where Scott brooded as he waited for the end of the awful snowstorm of December 1911. The scientists who positioned these devices looked simply for safe spots to land on the Barrier where there were not too many crevasses. And so through remarkable fortune these modern scientific instruments now touch upon history.

The jutting slopes of high mountains suddenly pierce the snowfield to the south, and after a few moments the sound of the engines changes pitch as the airplane begins to climb up to the continental interior. Below is a glacier of enormous proportions, a beautiful wide white Mississippi up to thirty miles across. Amid the rolling snow are steep icefalls and the deep black cracks of crevasses. It is truly a marvel that nobody was lost when Scott, Shackleton, and their men struggled up and down this dangerous maze that is the Beardmore.

The plane drones on ever southward, and the glacier gives way to the high plateau. The surface is scoured by the wind, and the visitor can see swirling rivers of snow whipping along the forbidding expanse below. Then the geodesic dome of South Pole Station can be seen up ahead. The man-made structure seems incongruous and terribly fragile in the vast empty landscape. The plane descends quickly and lands with a soft bump on the snow, then glides to a stop on skis. It has taken just three hours to get here. The visitor's back feels stiff and painful as he stands up. He stretches to get out the kinks, and he scowls in annoyance at the discomfort. Then he laughs at his modern softness. Scott and his men toiled in anguish for two months to make the same journey, and then they had to begin the grim task of the return.

He steps out of the plane into bright sunshine. But in spite of the sun, the air is frigid at the 10,000-foot elevation of the Pole. He will later learn from the station meteorologist that the temperature today is −23°F. The difference in conditions between this lofty plateau and the relative warmth of sea level at McMurdo just a few hours earlier is a striking reminder that the Pole is always a challenge, even in summer. A cold breeze brushes his face, and he pulls his parka hood up over his cheek. As he walks toward the dome, he squints against the intensely white light. Then the visitor stops for a moment, letting the other passengers go by. Even though the sun is always low, never getting more than twenty-three degrees above the horizon in summer at the Pole, the light is blinding because of reflection off the snow. He fishes his protective sunglasses out of his pocket with a gloved hand and quickly dons them.

The visitor knows that Scott and his men suffered greatly from snow blindness. Like others conversant in the legend of Scott's purported gaffes, he knows that the polar parties marched north during the day on their desperate return from this place, even though nighttime travel would have put the relentlessly bright sun at their backs instead of in their faces. Could they all have been so exhausted or stupid that they did not recognize this simple alternative? Even if one chose to believe this of Scott, what of the observant Wilson, the remarkable Bowers, the practical seaman Evans, and the meticulous Lieutenant Evans? The visitor is finding this question hard to understand now that he has begun reading about these intelligent and observant men.

He glances toward the bright disk of the sun, then rotates and puts it behind him. As he does so, he casts a long shadow onto the snow before him. The low angle of the sun gives his specter remarkable length. The black stripe is distorted by slight undulations in the surface, and in some places it looks like the black furrow of an open crevasse. As Scott and his men struggled to find their way home from this terrible place to the safety of the coast, they would have desperately scanned every nuance of shape and texture of the surface in order to avoid the crevasses hidden below. Their own shadows therefore had to be placed behind rather than in front of them, despite the risk of snow blindness. It is a problem the visitor had never considered before, but one that has become obvious within minutes of arrival at the unique environment of the Pole.

The visitor turns again, watching his long black shadow dance across the snow and pondering the terrifying choice of snow blindness versus death in an icy crevasse. Then he notices that his rotating boot is squeaking on the dry snow surface. It is so cold and dry here that the snow is completely unyielding, just as he has noticed a few times at McMurdo when the temperature dipped below about −20°F. And temperatures of course tend to be coldest at night, especially on the Barrier. As Scott and his men struggled to return from the Pole to the coast while dragging their heavy loads behind them, every scant degree of warmth would have meant a slightly easier glide. Perhaps this was an even more essential element in choosing whether to march during the relative warmth of the day or at night. Perhaps the risk of snow blindness was among the smallest of their towering burdens, and perhaps it is the modern believers in the legend of Scott the bumbler who are themselves blind to the much larger threats to the survival of the men who walked alone in this otherworldly place more than eighty years ago.

The men of the *Terra Nova* expedition began to ascend the Beardmore on December 10, 1911. Three groups of four heaved 170 pounds per man up its slopes. Scott chose Wilson, Oates, and seaman Evans for his team, while Lieutenant Evans pulled with Lashly, the Canadian Wright, and Dr. Atkinson. The last foursome was led by Bowers, accompanied by Cherry-Garrard and two seamen, Crean and Keohane. Scott decided to take the dogs on farther than had originally been planned, for the canines had been feeding well on fresh horseflesh and were pulling strongly. Meares and the young Russian Dimitri drove the two dog sleds, each of which pulled about 800 pounds of supplies.[1]

As the men and dogs dragged their food and gear up the glacier, the summer weather was generally warm, with daytime highs often near +20°F and nighttime lows seldom below −10°F. At times, the weather was so easy that the men "marched in singlets." But the surface over which they pulled their loads for the next several days was deeply covered in the wet snow deposited by the remarkable storm they had just experienced a few miles away. The pulling became "extraordinarily fatiguing. We sank above our finnesko everywhere and in places nearly to our knees. The runners of the sledges got coated with a thin film of ice from which we could not free them, and the sledges themselves sank to the crossbars in soft spots." Scott lamented the circumstances and again compared his unhappy lot to the apparently easier one of his predecessor, writing that "hereabouts Shackleton found hard blue ice. It seems an extraordinary difference in fortune, and at every step S's luck becomes more evident."[2]

The dogs were in excellent shape, and Cherry-Garrard later wrote that "it began to look as if Amundsen had chosen the right form of transport."[3] But food supplies were not sufficient to support the further advance of the dogs and their drivers—there was nothing for either to eat on the southward trail. On December 11, 1911, the men built a large depot of supplies for the parties of men who would return this way (Lower Glacier Depot, see map 5), and the dog teams turned for home. They had already gone so much farther than planned that Meares and Dimitri, to avoid depleting the depots, would have only two meals a day. As Lieutenant Evans wrote, "It is a dreadful thing on an Antarctic sledge journey to forfeit a whole meal daily, and Meares' generosity should not be forgotten."[4]

As they bade farewell to their companions, Scott wrote that he expected the dog party to "get back quite easily."[5] But the dog party's journey of more than 450 miles back to Cape Evans proved to be a battle with both the heavy snow that now blanketed the entire Barrier and with the challenges of navigation. Meares dutifully recorded a warm lunchtime temperature of +25°F on January 1, 1912. But in the column normally used for such meteorological remarks as "band of clouds to S," he wrote the poignant note, "no idea where we are."[6] In spite of limiting their meals, the delays that Meares and Dimitri suffered because of heavy snow and losing their way forced them to take some food from the depots that had been meant for the other returning parties. The two dog drivers completed their harrowing trip back to the coast on January 4, 1912.[7]

When the dogs departed, the remaining twelve men took on more weight —now pulling more than two hundred pounds apiece.[8] They worked long hours in the deep snow to make meager distances of four to ten miles per day for the next week—a sharp contrast to the weeks before the storm, when they had routinely covered fifteen miles per day, about what Shackleton had

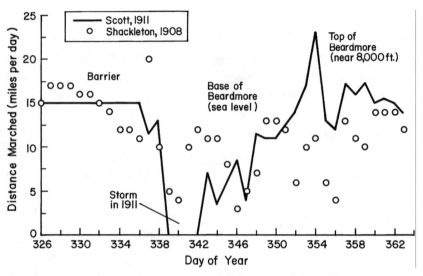

Figure 43. Rates of progress on the Barrier and on the Beardmore glacier by Scott's and Shackleton's expeditions in late November and December of 1911 and 1908, respectively. The storm of early December 1911 drove Scott's progress to zero on those days. Data taken from tables presented in Shackleton's *Heart of the Antarctic* and Scott's *Last Expedition*, vol. 1.

averaged (fig. 43). Lieutenant Evans wrote that when it was possible, the men "worked on ski, and . . . tremble to think what we should have done here without them."[9] On December 16 an unhappy Scott lamented the fact that his party was now "6 days behind Shackleton, all due to that wretched storm." The unusually wet blizzard had left Scott completely tentbound for four days, after which the party had struggled in deep snow to make a few miles per day. Its occurrence just before the men began the ascent of the steep glacier added to the challenge they faced in attaining more than eight thousand feet of elevation between December 10 and December 21.[10] Even the hardy Bowers found the going excruciatingly difficult, writing: "It was all we could do to keep the sledge moving for short spells of a few hundred yards, the whole concern sinking so deeply into the soft snow as to form a snow plough. The starting was worse than pulling as it required from ten to fifteen desperate jerks on the harness to move the sledge at all."[11]

The two trained physicians discussed the men's health following this period of enormous toil, and Atkinson expressed some concern regarding fatigue in Lashly and Wright. But as they inched their way out of the deepest snows, Wilson pronounced the party to be generally "very fit and enjoying it." Wilson took delight in the geologic features of the landscape around them, writing that he "visited a large boulder isolated in the pressure ridges and found it to be very coarse granite full of large quartz crystals an inch and a half square and white quartz veins, very full of mica and hornblende and quartz, and some isolated sort of inclusions of fine grey gneiss." [12] Wilson reserved his greatest scientific passion for Antarctic birds and most especially the emperor penguins, but the chief of the scientific staff expressed a broad interest in all aspects of the unique natural world around him.

As they climbed up the face of the Beardmore, the surface became firmer, but with the welcome sight of smooth blue ice also came the fearsome crevasses and pressure ridges. The men's goggles clouded up frequently because of the exertion of hauling their loads in the warm temperatures, and "our eyes had to be used for long periods without glasses for clearing crevasses. . . . The clouding of our goggles made the crevasses more difficult to spot, and one or other of the party got legs or feet down pretty often." [13] As they pitched their tent one evening, Cherry-Garrard described how they "broke into a crevasse which ran about a foot in front of the door and there was another at Scott's door. We threw an empty oil can down and it echoed for a terribly long time." [14] Thus the snow was a mixed blessing: it made for rough going, but it also helped to stand between the men and a similar plunge. Wind and warm weather removed the protective blanket of snow in the coming weeks and exposed the maze of crevasses beneath, and the route posed a different set of challenges on their return.

Lieutenant Evans and Lashly had been man-hauling since leaving Corner Camp, and the sustained exertion had often made them ravenously hungry. But as the party ascended the Beardmore, the lieutenant "felt that our ration was sufficient; we had now commenced the 'Summit Ration' which contained considerable extra fats" — the food allowance that had been tested on the Cape Crozier journey during the winter. Although they were six days behind Shackleton's mark in distance, Scott's men felt that they had an advantage in supplies: "We often discussed Shackleton's journey, and were amazed at his fine performance. We always had full rations, which Shackleton's party never enjoyed at this stage." [15]

Figure 44. Camp on the Beardmore glacier. Photographer unknown. Scott Album, number 11444, Alexander Turnbull Library, Wellington, New Zealand.

But while food was sufficient, water was scarce. On December 17 Scott wrote, "We get fearfully thirsty and chip up ice on the march, as well as drinking a great deal of water on halting. Our fuel only just does it, but that is all we want."[16] Certainly there was plenty of frozen water all around them, but the metabolic cost of obtaining moisture by eating snow and ice is far too high to allow this approach to meet daily needs for quantity. This problem had long been recognized by polar explorers, including Peary's men, one of whom, Henson, wrote: "To eat snow to quench our thirsts would have been the height of folly. . . . For the result of eating snow is death."[17] Scott's men were completely dependent on their stoves to provide the water they craved, and their allotment of oil was barely sufficient for the task. On some days their thirst was "overpowering."[18] As they ascended still higher to the plateau, the physiological demand for water even while resting increased dramatically. The much thinner air of high elevation sharply increases metabolic and respiration rates and hence the body's need for water. These aspects of working at high altitude were not understood in 1911 and are still a subject of study.[19]

Scott's men were advancing into the great unknown of the world's coldest, highest, driest desert, a region where thirst struck early and dehydration could follow.

Scott's plan called for eight men to advance past the top of the great glacier at 85°S. In order to take into account the men's health and ruggedness at the critical time, he had kept his options open as to the makeup of the party. Now he began evaluating the performance of each sledging team. On December 10 he noted his concern about Lieutenant Evans's men, who "fell a long way behind, had to take off ski, and took nearly half an hour to come up a few hundred yards. True the surface was awful and growing worse every moment." He deemed his own party in the best shape, writing: "As for myself, I never felt fitter and my party can easily hold its own. . . . [Seaman] Evans, of course, is a tower of strength, but Oates and Wilson are doing splendidly also." Some of the men's boots were part of the problem, and seaman Evans once more proved his worth, for it was he who "put them into shape again." By December 13 Scott was reaching the conclusion that his group was much the strongest of the three, writing, "We got our load along, soon passing Bowers, but the toil was simply awful. . . . Again and again the sledge got one runner on harder snow than the other, canted on its side and refused to move. At the top of the rise, I found [Lieutenant] Evans reduced to relay work, and Bowers followed his example soon after. We got our whole load through [without relaying]."[20]

Lieutenant Evans realized that his team's extra weeks of man-hauling following the early failure of the motor sledges had taken a toll on their strength. But when Scott's team "offered to take on more weight . . . Evans's pride wouldn't allow such help." Scott continued testing, writing that "later in the morning we exchanged sledges with Bowers and pulled theirs easily, whilst they made quite heavy work with ours. I am afraid Cherry-Garrard and Keohane are the weakness of that team, though both put their utmost into the traces."[21] Cherry-Garrard acknowledged the greater speed and strength of Scott's team, writing that "Scott's was the faster, as it should have been," for that foursome included the largest and heaviest men of the party—seaman Evans and Captain Oates.[22]

Bowers took the time to write a letter to his sister Edie as the party slogged its way up the glacier. In it he expressed his belief that he would soon be asked to turn back, and his willingness to do so in the interests of the expedition's success: "Naturally none of us like to turn back and in another 16 days or so another four will have to turn back. I am expecting to be in charge of that detachment but one never knows. However I am here to do what I am told and I am all for Capt. Scott anyhow—honestly think he will win through. May the Lord be on our side."[23]

On December 17 the men wore crampons all day, and Scott was "delighted with them. . . . [Seaman] Evans, the inventor of both crampons and ski shoes, is greatly pleased and certainly we owe him much." The next day brought snowfall, but the weather was not severe enough to stop the column from marching. After a period spent in "annoying criss-cross cracks" of crevasses in which many a leg was dropped on December 19, the men were finally drawing close to the summit. Bowers's sledgemeter broke and fell off on the following day; after a fruitless search, it was given up for lost.[24] This compounded the navigational challenges to be faced by one of the returning parties, for they would have to estimate rather than measure the distance traveled each day.

As they marched, the men were relieved to see no signs of Amundsen, for they thought that the Norwegians might use the Beardmore glacier for their approach to the Pole.[25] They began to hope that they might therefore be first at their goal, not knowing that Amundsen had climbed to the plateau along an entirely different route and indeed was already at the Pole.

Scott had now reached 85°S, the point of deciding who would return and who would share in the glory of the next stage of the journey. He "dreaded this necessity of choosing—nothing could be more heartrending." But he gave the order for Cherry-Garrard, Keohane, Atkinson, and Wright to return.[26] Scott instructed Atkinson that he must ensure that the dog teams come out to meet the polar party even if Meares were to return home.[27]

Scott wrote that "all are disappointed—poor Wright rather bitterly, I fear."[28] Indeed, the Canadian deeply resented not being chosen to continue. He had written in his diary of numerous personality conflicts with Lieutenant Evans, whom he deemed a posturer and far less fit to continue than himself. When given the order to leave, Wright wrote: "Scott a fool." Scott pointed out that each of the returning groups would require a talented navigator, and when Wright learned that he was to play this critical role, he was somewhat mollified.[29] Lieutenant Evans worked until midnight that night, "getting out copy of route and bearings for Wright to navigate back on."[30]

In spite of Wright's considerable skills in navigation, he later wrote of leading this party in a semicircle in blowing snow on the Barrier during the return trek: "I turned a complete (half) circle and came back to meet our own tracks on a dreadful day with no horizon, no wind, no sastrugi or drift to help the navigator."[31] As the party of men realized that the tracks in the snow were their own, terror probably mingled with an improved understanding of Scott's decision to send Wright back with the first return party.

Cherry-Garrard seemed less angry about Scott's decision, although no less surprised. He wrote that "Scott . . . said he had been thinking a lot about it but had come to the conclusion that the seamen with their special knowledge, would be needed: to rebuild the sledge, I suppose. Wilson told me it was a toss-up whether Titus [Oates] or I should go on: that being so I think Titus will help him more than I can. . . . I said I hoped I had not disappointed him, and he caught hold of me and said 'No-no-no,' so if that is the case all is well."[32] It therefore appears that neither Cherry-Garrard nor Wilson deemed Oates less fit than others to continue at this point in the journey, but rather more so.

December 20 was the last day the twelve men marched together. They spotted sandstone and red granite on the rocks around them, as well as stratification that may have been coal.[33] Wilson found the rocks "magnificent everywhere" but lamented that there was "little chance of doing anything at it" — that is, of collecting samples.[34]

When they camped that evening, Cherry-Garrard felt a special pain in parting from Wilson and Bowers, the two friends with whom he had shared so much on the winter journey. He did not know that it was the last time he would see them alive as he wrote: "There is a very mournful air tonight — those going on and those turning back."[35] Wilson expressed similar feelings: "It was wretched parting with the others."[36] And Bowers wrote: "It was quite touching saying farewell to our good pals. . . . I am sending this [journal] by my friend Cherry, whose going I feel muchly, though we cannot all go on, worse luck."[37] To his sister Edie, Bowers wrote: "The first four go back tomorrow. They are Surgeon Atkinson, R. N., C. S. Wright, A. Cherry Garrard (my great friend) and P. O. Keohane, R. N. I am delighted to be here."[38]

On December 22 two teams of four continued southward, pulling 190 pounds per man, while the others turned for home. Scott's team was unchanged (Wilson, Oates, and seaman Evans), while Lieutenant Evans now led Bowers, Lashly, and Crean.[39] The group made twelve miles in good time, and Scott concluded that "we have weeded the weak spots and made the proper choice for the returning party." The next day the group found themselves among "crevasses as big as Regent Street." They managed to cross these on the snow bridges that frequently span such structures, but they steered farther to the west than to the south. The afternoon brought still more "vicissitudes of fortune" in the form of a difficult surface covered with crevasses in all directions into which many legs were dropped.[40]

One member of Scott's expedition dryly remarked, "It is shock to a party, returning in their steps after traversing a level plain like the Ross Barrier with a heavy motor sledge to see . . . the tracks of their motor leading to and from an apparently bottomless chasm several yards wide."[41] A crevasse may be safely bridged by snow at one time but collapse later. The dangers faced by Scott and his men in traversing the bottomless voids around them were compounded by their race against time, for there was not enough food to allow delays caused by careful testing of the surfaces, or for choosing alternative longer and safer routes.

In spite of the challenging surface, Scott felt "very cheerful about everything. . . . To me for the first time our goal seems really in sight. . . . We can pull our loads and pull them much faster and farther than I expected in my most hopeful moments. I only pray for a fair share of good weather."[42] The going was relatively easy for the nine hours spent in marching fourteen miles on the next day, Christmas Eve, and Wilson "thoroughly enjoyed the afternoon march."[43]

Christmas Day, 1911, brought bright sunny weather, a temperature of −7.5 °F at its end, and light winds of about fifteen to twenty miles per hour.[44] It was Lashly's forty-fourth birthday, and he celebrated part of it by falling into a deep crevasse up to the full length of his sledging harness.[45] The abyss below him was fifty feet deep as he spun in midair. He wrote: "It was not of course a very nice sensation especially on Christmas Day. . . . When I collected myself I heard someone calling from above 'Are you all right, Lashly?' I was all right it is true, but I did not care to be dangling in the air on a piece of rope. . . .

Mr. Evans, Bowers and Crean hauled me out and Crean wished me many happy returns of the day, and of course I thanked him politely and the others laughed, but all were pleased I was not hurt bar a bit of a shake."[46] Lieutenant Evans described Lashly's response not as polite but as unprintable.[47] The enigmatic Lashly may have owed his survival to the capable management of the supplies by Bowers, who "was glad that having noticed [Lashly's] rope rather worn . . . had given him a new one a few days before."[48]

That night all enjoyed a Christmas feast that included pemmican with slices of pony meat, biscuits, cocoa, raisins, caramels, ginger, and plum pudding.[49] Before Bowers went to sleep replete with food, he turned to Lieutenant Evans and said, "Next Christmas we will get hold of all the poor children we can and just stuff them full of nice things, won't we?"[50] The temperatures were warm that night, about −10°F, and the men "all slept splendidly and feel thoroughly warm" on full stomachs.[51]

By December 27 Scott had begun to worry about the other sledging group, which "had great difficulty in keeping up" as they struggled up and down grades covered in sastrugi. Lieutenant Evans's team found the going rough on the next day as well. First Scott traded places with the lieutenant. He noted with characteristic frankness that he himself found the other sledge difficult to pull. Then he exchanged seaman Evans for Lashly, and with this change, the sledge pulled more easily.[52] That was probably the moment when the fates of these two members of the "lower deck" were decided: the strong man Evans would soon be chosen to continue on to the Pole and perish on the return, while Lashly would turn back with the second return party and live.

After lunch the two teams exchanged sledges. This test revealed that the second team's sledge had been poorly loaded.[53] The sledge was repacked, and the next day both pulled evenly, but the surface was like sand and the going extremely difficult. On December 30, however, a disparity was again evident between the two sledging teams. Wilson wrote: "The other sledge fell back a long way and came in in the evening three quarters of an hour later than we did."[54] They were now pulling over rough surfaces at an elevation of 9,200 feet, and minimum daily temperatures had dropped to about −15°F. The men made thirteen miles nonetheless. The next day Lieutenant Evans's team depoted their skis, ski shoes, and alpine rope, saving about one hundred pounds. Scott then sent them ahead to break trail.[55]

Why were the skis of Lieutenant Evans's team left behind? Certainly the wooden skis were heavy, and Scott had earlier written, "It is difficult to know what to do about the ski; their weight is considerable and yet under certain circumstances they are extraordinarily useful." A few days later, on January 6, 1912, Scott expressed concern that the need to carry skis rather than wear them in rough sastrugi created a grave risk of breakage. On January 7 Scott depoted his own skis, but he later went back to retrieve them.[56] Perhaps Scott deliberately and cruelly wished to wear out the other team by depoting their skis at this stage. Or perhaps he was simply unsure what the best course of action would be and opted for real-time testing, as he had many times before. Whatever the leader's reasons may have been, Bowers paid dearly for this decision in the weeks to come.

At lunch the men made a depot (Three-Degree Depot) and then seamen Evans, Lashly, and Crean set to work to cut down the twelve-foot sledges to ten-foot lengths to save still more weight. The three labored in the cold until after midnight.[57]

Travel on skis was better than expected the next day, with relatively good gliding surfaces. The men celebrated New Year's Day, 1912, with a stick of chocolate. On January 2 both teams did fifteen miles, but Scott acknowledged that "it's been a plod for the foot people and pretty easy going for us." Remarkably, the party was visited by a skua that day in a latitude beyond 87°S and an elevation near ten thousand feet.[58]

On January 3 Scott came into Lieutenant Evans's tent to inform him that Scott would be taking his own team south to the Pole. He asked whether Bowers could be spared to accompany him. This would leave Lieutenant Evans shorthanded, pulling the weights of sledge, cooker, tent, and other supplies normally dragged by four men.[59] But Evans consented, probably knowing that it was Bowers's fondest hope to go forward. Indeed, Bowers later reflected upon "how glad I was to change over" to the team that would continue.[60] Wilson wrote that he was sorry for Lieutenant Evans, who had spent two and a half years working for a place on the polar journey.[61] But the lieutenant acknowledged that he and Lashly "could never hope to be in the polar party after our long drag out from Cape Evans itself. . . . It was a disappointment, but not too great to bear."[62] Lieutenant Evans had been repeatedly used to advance the cause of the expedition at high cost to himself—when he sledged to Corner Camp in March and September 1911, when he led the motor party on its brief journey and subsequently began man-hauling a month before the pony leaders, and when he blazed trail on foot in the last days of his southern march.

Lashly wrote that Scott "seemed pretty confident of success. He seemed a bit afraid of us getting hung up, but as he said we had a splendid navigator. . . . He also thanked us all heartily for the way we had assisted in the Journey."[63] The Pole was now just over 160 miles away, and they had caught up with Shackleton's dates in spite of the setback of the Barrier storm in December.

Scott does not explain why he decided to take five men to the Pole rather than four. Cherry-Garrard guessed that he wished to share the glory of the achievement with as many men as possible.[64] Lieutenant Evans surmised that because Scott had hoped to be ahead of Shackleton's mark rather than even with it at this point, he decided that he needed Bowers's strength to make the march.[65] Certainly Bowers had repeatedly proven his remarkable physical qualities and his value to the expedition. His endurance as a navigator who could take sightings when others found their fingers no match for the weather would also be extremely valuable to Scott. Without Bowers, the demanding task of taking sights for position would have fallen largely to Scott himself. Bowers could have been exchanged for Oates rather than added to the party, but Cherry-Garrard and others have speculated that Scott may have wished to have the army represented at the Pole along with the navy, or to reward Oates for his excellent work with the ponies.[66] Oates also had some ability in navigation and was known as a man of considerable physical strength. In a letter to his mother, to be carried back by Lieutenant Evans's party on January 3, 1912, Oates himself said: "I am very fit indeed and have lost condition less than any one else almost."[67] Whatever Scott's reasons may have been, there can be little doubt that his decision to take five men on to the Pole was a change of mind at the last moment, for Bowers's skis were many miles away, having been depoted along with the rest of those of the lieutenant's group. When Lieutenant Evans, Lashly, and Crean watched the group of five men pull away, Bowers marched on foot behind Wilson and Scott.[68]

Lieutenant Evans later wrote of being "the last living man to speak to Scott."[69] Optimism ran high as the two teams prepared to part: "Since no traces of the . . . Norwegian had been found so far, we fondly imagined that our flag would be the first to fly at the South Pole. . . . The excitement was intense, for it was obvious that with five fit men, the pole being only [163 miles] away—the achievement was merely a matter of 10 or 11 days' good sledging."[70] Lieutenant Evans and his men "made a short march with Scott's team to see that, with their load increased by what we had brought along, they could manage without unduly straining. They got along finely for three or four miles, then they halted and said good-bye. We shook hands all round, and we felt very moved as we looked into their eyes and at their smoke-begrimed, bearded faces."[71] Scott expected Evans's party to "make a quick journey back."[72] But the return journey experienced by the lieutenant, Lashly, and Crean was anything but routine.

Shackleton and his men had turned back from 88°23′ on January 9, 1909, while Lieutenant Evans and his companions turned their faces northward from 87°35′ on January 4, 1912. Shackleton and his party marched largely on short rations from December 20, 1908, until near the end of their harrowing journey on February 22, 1909, enduring many "dark days of hunger."[73] Scott's expedition carried and depoted considerably more food per man on the trail—and the greater food supply boosted their confidence that this British Antarctic expedition would succeed in the quest for the Pole. Loads would be light for all parties on the northbound track, because the required food had largely been cached ahead of them. But they would have to travel about sixteen miles per day on average to reach each depot on full rations. Lieutenant Evans quickly came to the disturbing realization that his short-handed team could not achieve such distances by marching only nine hours per day. He therefore began a practice of setting his watch forward an hour to wake the seamen earlier than normal, then setting it back later. Thus they marched from ten to twelve hours daily.[74] With only one chronometer and no sledgemeter, Evans's party was critically dependent on his skills as a navigator to avoid becoming hopelessly lost.

On January 6 the team retrieved its skis from the Three-Degree Depot and picked up food for the next 120 miles—about seven days' worth.[75] On January 7 they covered nineteen miles in a temperature of −16°F and blinding snow. They tried to follow their outbound footsteps back to the safety of their precious food stores, but on January 8 "the weather was so bad that we entirely lost the track." By the thirteenth, they were at the top of the glacier, where they looked down on hundreds of feet of icefalls. During the ascent, Scott had chosen to go around these falls, but Lieutenant Evans thought that the risks of traversing them directly were outweighed by the gain of three days' time. Evans strove to include his men in the difficult decision they were now facing, so he first asked Lashly, the senior of the two, what he thought the best course of action would be. Lashly responded, "You're the officer, you must decide, Sir." He then turned to Crean, who answered that "Captain Scott would never do a damned fool thing like that." Crean's answer shows that his men considered Scott to be a cautious and deliberate leader. Evans was a different sort of man, one who would take many risks in a brilliant military career—among them a broadside ramming of a German ship in an important World War I battle just a few years later. The lieutenant said simply, "Captain Scott's not here, jump on," and off they went.[76]

The three men glissaded down the icefalls, hanging onto their sledge as it roared downward at speeds up to sixty miles per hour. Evans described the descent as "exciting," because "to brake was impossible, for the sledge had taken charge. . . . To stop it in any way would have meant a broken leg. . . . We held on for our lives, lying face downwards on the sledge." Near the bottom, they "shot over one yawning crevasse before we had known of its existence almost," after which the sledge-turned-toboggan crashed into a ridge, rolled over and over, and finally stopped.[77]

"How we escaped entirely uninjured is beyond me to explain. . . . That night in our sleeping bags we felt like three bruised pears," wrote Evans. The next day, the three men reached Upper Glacier Depot, where they again took on supplies.[78]

For the next two days the trio covered ground quickly in above-zero temperatures, but they camped in "very rough ice and pressure ridges" on January 16. Lashly worried that they were "slightly out of our proper course."[79] That evening they discussed "what luxuries Lashly, who was a famous cook, should prepare on our return." Lieutenant Evans set his heart on steak and kidney pudding, and Lashly promised to make it for him. The three men found their sleeping bags to be luxuriantly comfortable that night, as "the recent fine weather had given us a chance to dry thoroughly the fur and get the bags clear of that uncomfortable clamminess."[80] Even the past week's nighttime minimum temperatures had been warm, typically between −10°F and

0°F, and the men no longer had to battle the ice in order to sleep in their reindeer bags.[81]

The next day's march proved Lashly's concerns about their position to be correct. The glacier was draped in an ice fog that rendered steering difficult, and as they struggled along through "tiny floating ice crystals . . . great hummocks of ice stood weirdly shapen as they loomed through the frozen mist. . . . The uncertain light of the mist worried us all three, and we were forced to take off our goggles to see to advance at all." The sun came out, but rather than cheering the three hapless men, it revealed that they were now in the midst of "the most disheartening wilderness of pressure ridges and disturbances." The summer's sun and heat had cleared off the snow from this region since they last visited it, "laying bare the great blue, black cracks."[82] They were in the heart of the huge icefalls that lie in the middle of the Beardmore glacier, and they were flanked by "fathomless pits each side of us . . . where it was possible to drop the biggest ship afloat and lose her."[83]

After hours of marching along the lengths of the abyss, it became clear that to progress past the chasm before them would require crossing a snow bridge that stretched across two enormous crevasses. As Crean described it later, the three men "went along the crossbar to the H of Hell." They put the four hundred–pound sledge carefully on the inverted V-shaped snow bridge. The apex of the V was narrower than the sledge, and so the runners draped its two sides. First Lashly went ahead alone. He shuffled his way across, letting out the alpine rope as he went. Lieutenant Evans did not specify the width of this particular "stupendous open gulf," but as Lashly worked his way along, Evans hoped that the ninety-foot rope would do the job. Fortunately, the cord "was sufficient in length," the snow bridge held, and Lashly crossed over to firmer ground. The bridge had held the weight of one man, but now they were faced with the grim task of trying to work their heavy sledge across it. Lashly may have longed for a rock or a tree with which to secure the alpine rope, but there was nothing but ice, snow, and his own strength to aid the effort. Lashly "sat gingerly on the opposite ridge, hauling carefully but not too strongly on the rope" attached to the sledge. Crean held onto one side of the sledge and perched on one side of the V. Evans balanced him on the other side, while Lashly slowly pulled on the rope. Thus with repeated calls of "one, two, three—heave," the men inched across the expanse above the great blue void below, carefully balancing the sledge each time they moved.[84]

Lieutenant Evans later praised "the hearts of lions" of both his stalwart companions. After the three men had cleared the "H of Hell," he wrote: "I remembered the poor ponies after their fourteen hours' march, their flanks heaving, their black eyes dull, shrivelled and wasted. The poor beasts had stood . . . mere wrecks of the beautiful little animals that we took away from New Zealand, and I could not help likening our condition to theirs on that painful day. The three of us sat on the sledge—hollow-eyed and gaunt looking."[85] Lashly's diary expressed the same feelings; but in words that reflected the chasms of class and education between himself and his lieutenant, he wrote only: "What a day this have been for us all."[86]

Evans suffered from severe snow blindness the next day, for he had kept his goggles off during the journey through hell, writing explicitly that "it was a matter of life or death with us, and snow blindness must be risked."[87] Although the wisdom of choosing to march in daytime may be arguable, the fact that the explorers made the choice consciously is clear.[88] The trio reached the next depot (Mid-Glacier Depot) and rested. There they left a note for Scott but did not tell him of their narrow escape from the crevasses. For the next several days Lieutenant Evans's eyes gave him great pain, but the three men continued to trudge on, making good daily distances. On January 21, 1912, seaman Lashly wrote: "Tomorrow we hope to see and reach the Barrier, and be clear of the Beardmore for ever. We none of us mind the struggle we have been through to attain the amount of success so far reached. It is all for the good of science, as Crean says."[89]

But the next day Evans complained of stiffness at the back of his knees, one of the first signs of scurvy.[90] The men took some pony meat when they reached Shambles Camp at the foot of the glacier, the site of the final pony slaughter. The next day Evans was somewhat better.[91] While the onset of scurvy is slow—typically occurring after many weeks without adequate nutrition—it has been known since the first studies of the dread disease that recovery begins within days after consumption of vitamin C.[92] But Evans's party deliberately took only a small amount of the life-giving meat.[93] They left the rest for the others following behind them, even though Oates's parting words to them had been: "Old Christopher is waiting to be eaten on the Barrier when you get there."[94]

The wind began to blow from the south, so the three practical navy men fitted up a sail for their sledge. The weather remained mild. For the next week they enjoyed warm days and nights, with temperatures ranging between about +4°F and +35°F.[95] The beneficent southerly wind frequently made for very easy marching, as on January 27, a day when "we had a good run . . . with the sail up. It only required one of us to keep it straight, no need whatever to pull."[96] The winds on the Ross Ice Shelf are persistently from the south, mainly reflecting the gravity-driven flow of dense air down from the high continental interior to the coast, and the welcome breeze that filled the second return party's sails was typical of this region at that time of year.[97] Scott and his men were well aware of this key aspect of Barrier meteorology, and they looked forward to using sails to speed their return, as they had on the *Discovery* journey in 1903. Bowers, for example, wrote to his mother that after reaching the Pole, "we shall be able to get this wind behind our backs and streak for home."[98]

But on January 29 Evans's legs were getting worse again, turning black and blue. On January 30 the party reached Mid-Barrier Depot to find a shortage of oil. Lashly wrote, "There seems to have been some leakage in the one can, but how[,] we could not account for that." By February 2 Lashly realized that "Mr. Evans is no better but seems to be in great pain." The next day, the lieutenant was unable to lift his legs, so the two seamen put him on his skis and strapped them on.[99]

On February 4 the three men reached Mount Hooper Depot at 80°32'S, the spot where Lashly and Lieutenant Evans had waited for Scott two months earlier. The lieutenant was growing weaker daily but continued to trudge alongside the sledge while he "suffered absolute agonies."[100] Lashly wrote, "He is a brick, there is plenty of pluck: one cannot but admire such pluck. . . . He is suffering a good deal and in silence." Evans's gums were now ulcerated and his teeth were becoming loose. He could no longer eat pemmican at all. The weather continued to be mercifully warm, with temperatures between about −4°F and +12°F, which not only provided great comfort but also reduced the men's hunger. Even Lashly and Crean found that "the pemmi-

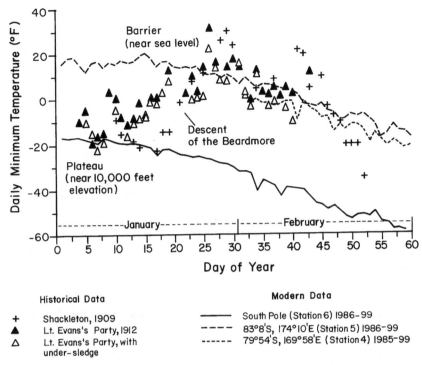

Historical Data

+   Shackleton, 1909
▲   Lt. Evans's Party, 1912
△   Lt. Evans's Party, with
       under-sledge

Modern Data

———   South Pole (Station 6) 1986-99
– – – –   83°8'S, 174°10'E (Station 5) 1986-99
------   79°54'S, 169°58'E (Station 4) 1985-99

Figure 45. Daily minimum temperatures experienced on the return trek by Lieutenant Evans's party, compared with the modern record and with data from Shackleton's farthest-south trip in 1909. The measurements taken by each of these two groups of early explorers compare well to the averages of the modern record, suggesting that the meteorological conditions they encountered on their return journeys were typical.

can is too much, especially when the weather is warm," so the trio left their share of the rich meat and fat mixture at Mount Hooper Depot for the others following behind them.[101]

The generally warm weather that Lieutenant Evans's party enjoyed since leaving 87°S was a great blessing to their journey but quite typical for the location and time of year (fig. 45). Indeed, the temperatures they experienced were similar to those encountered by Shackleton three years earlier and by Scott in January of 1903 on the *Discovery* expedition's farthest point south. Nature had dealt Evans and his companions a typical summer hand in terms of warmth, helpful southerly winds, and ease of travel over a period of weeks. At these temperatures, the sledge ran relatively easily over the snow even when the wind was not strong. As Evans grew weaker and only two men pulled the sledge, progress was still fairly good, thanks to the beneficent weather.[102]

On February 6 Lashly wrote that the "sun was very hot and caused us to sweat a good deal," and on February 7 the seaman recorded that "the day have been simply lovely." But that night the two sailors had to help their lieutenant into and out of the tent, and Lashly sadly noted that "it is difficult for him to stand." The next day Lashly recorded that "Mr. Evans have passed a good deal of blood . . . which makes things look a lot worse."[103] February 9 marked the last day on which Evans carried out his meteorological observations. He apologized to all who might one day be curious about Antarctic weather: "Observer too bad with scurvy to continue observations—sorry!"[104]

Surely the excellent weather had been a key factor that allowed Evans to continue marching during this period in spite of his increasingly debilitated condition. But the weather's kindness finally faded on February 10–12, when the men marched in a mild blizzard. Perhaps as a result, Evans could no longer continue to drag himself along on the morning of February 13. He asked Lashly and Crean to leave him, but even though they were still about one hundred miles from Hut Point, Lashly wrote that "this we could not think of. We shall stand by him to the end one way or other." The two seamen depoted nearly every item that was not critical in order to devote their strength to the awesome task of pulling the sick man; among some non-essentials that they kept was the meteorological log book. As they prepared to depart, Lashly changed his socks. In the process his foot became badly frostbitten, and the only available remedy was physical contact with warmer flesh. Lashly wrote that "although Mr. Evans was so bad he proposed to stuff it on his stomach to try and get it right again. I did not like to risk such a thing as he is certainly very weak, but we tried it and it succeeded in bringing me round. . . . I shall never forget the kindness bestowed on me at a critical time in our travels but I think we could go to any length of trouble to assist one another."[105]

Lashly and Crean then wrapped Lieutenant Evans in his sleeping bag and strapped him on the sledge. Lashly wrote: "It is a painful piece of work . . . but he don't complain. The only thing we hear him grind his teeth."[106] For the next five days, the two sailors dragged their lieutenant on the sledge. By

Figure 46. Drawing of a Barrier camp by E. A. Wilson, with depiction of a "fogbow" effect caused by ice crystals. Scott Polar Research Institute, Cambridge.

raising his head, the sick man could see "how slowly their legs seemed to move—wearily but nobly they fought on."[107] The weather was getting colder now, with Lashly concerned that "if the temperature goes much lower it will be a job to keep him warm. . . . I don't think we have the go in us we had, but we must try and push on."[108]

For five excruciatingly long days, the two seamen trudged through the snow, carrying Lieutenant Evans on the sledge. But when they tried to lift the sick man to put him onto the sledge on the morning of February 18, he collapsed and fainted. They were still more than thirty miles from Hut Point.[109]

Evans wrote that "seriously and sadly they re-erected our tent and put me once again inside. I thought I was being put into my grave. Outside I heard them talking. . . . They were discussing which should go and which should stay."[110] Finally Crean came in to say goodbye. Then he struck out alone in "splendid weather" for Hut Point. Provisions were running low, and Crean took only a small amount of chocolate and biscuits to carry him through on a solo march to seek rescue.[111] With no tent or sleeping bag, Crean would certainly perish if a blizzard swept in before he could reach the safety of the *Discovery* hut.

The seamen's decision not to leave the lieutenant is a testimony to their remarkable loyalty. One man alone could fall into a crevasse and then all three would be lost. But the notion of both of them abandoning Evans, even for the purpose of seeking rescue, was unthinkable. Lashly left Evans's side only long enough to walk a mile to Corner Camp, where he found a few scraps of food. He also found a note warning that there were many bad crevasses between this spot and the sea ice—just the route where Crean would be traveling. Lashly prudently took some oil from the defunct motor sledge he had abandoned months earlier on the outward trek. Then he returned to the tent, informing Evans only that he had found a note indicating that all was well.[112]

Crean walked eighteen hours nonstop to reach help in the welcome form of Dr. Atkinson, Dimitri, and the dogs at the *Discovery* hut.[113] It was a stroke of luck that the dog teams and drivers were there at all. Meares was preparing to board the ship for home, and the doctor had taken on the task of meeting the returning polar party as ordered. The doctor was concerned that the ice between Cape Evans and Hut Point might go out (as it had in 1911, just after the start of the depot journey), so he and Dimitri had gone early to the *Discovery* hut to ensure safe passage. In another week, he and Dimitri would have set out to the south, and Crean would have been forced to continue his desperate walk to try to reach Cape Evans—another fifteen miles—unless he had by good fortune been seen by them along their trek. And it was only through good fortune in the weather that Crean himself survived his solo journey, for as he got within sight of Hut Point the wind began "blowing very hard with drift," and a blizzard swept in just a half-hour after his arrival.[114]

The next day Lashly wrote that "the temperature is dropping rapidly. Our tent was all covered in frost rime today, a sure sign of colder weather. . . . I wonder if poor old Tom [Crean] reached alright. . . . We have got ½ gallon [of oil] and if relief don't come for some time we shall be able to have hot water when all other things are gone." The storm held up the departure of the rescue team for two days, but on February 20 Lieutenant Evans and Lashly finally heard the wonderful sound of barking dogs. The doctor brought food,

Figure 47. Lieutenant Evans and one of the sledging theodolites, October 1911. To complete his surveying of McMurdo Sound, Evans spent much of September and October sledging, which probably contributed to his bout with scurvy. Photograph by H. Ponting. Scott Album, number 11401, Alexander Turnbull Library, Wellington, New Zealand.

including cake and a scurvy remedy favored by sailors of the day, onions.[115] These would have provided Evans with a small amount of much-needed vitamin C.[116]

Yet another blizzard howled on February 21 while the men ate and rested in the tent. The weather had turned colder with the advancing season, and although the strong wind of the blizzard would have warmed the air somewhat, the men noticed the seasonal drop in temperature. But the next day they were able to set off with Evans strapped on Dimitri's dog sled. Remarkably, Lashly was still well enough to take turns with Dr. Atkinson in running alongside the second dog team. Only the lieutenant succumbed to scurvy, and he had been sledging far longer than the others. With the exception of the pony meat eaten on the southern journey, he had been on sledging rations almost continuously since September, many weeks longer than any of the other members of the southern party.

When they reached the safety of Hut Point on February 22, 1912, Lashly began to prepare some seal meat while Lieutenant Evans peacefully slept.[117] The ordeal of one of the last two returning parties was over. In typical Antarctic summer weather, they had just barely returned from the gate of Hell.

NINE

This Awful Place

The visitor sits in the bar at South Pole station, nursing a beer and contemplating the plaque on the wall. The air inside is warm, and his chair is soft. Outside the wind is blowing a brisk thirty miles per hour, and the temperature is −25°F without adjusting for wind chill. The engraved plaque above the bar bears a quotation from Robert Falcon Scott: "Great God, this is an awful place." It has been placed here as a joke, perhaps to remind the station's inhabitants that drinking is bad for their health.

The visitor leaves the comfortable bar just before midnight. He dons his parka, gloves, and boots, and makes his way outside to walk a half-mile to the rubberized canvas Jamesway tent where he will sleep in a barracks arrangement, surrounded by a dozen others. The tent walls are cold to the touch, but diesel-powered heaters keep the interior of the structure surprisingly warm. The January sun is above the horizon and will remain so all night and day for months on end, but the air feels cold tonight, and the stiff wind tugs at the visitor's parka. He stops to use the toilet. As he leaves the bathroom he looks longingly at the nearby Jamesways, just a few feet from this relief. Plumbing is a complicated problem in Antarctica, and places with the blessed luxuries of running water and flush toilets are few and far between. His own bed is far down the line of tents, several hundred feet away from such comfort.

He strips off his boots and clothing when he reaches his bunk. He climbs into bed dressed in his long underwear, and he pulls the heavy woolen blankets over himself. But although it is warm enough in the tent, he finds sleep elusive. His heart is racing much faster than normal, and his breathing is rapid and labored. Finally he falls asleep, only to wake with a start, gasping for air after what seems only moments. Someone warned him that this might happen in the thin air of the Pole. He has heard that the elevation here is 2,835 meters, or about 9,200 feet. And the circulation of the wind around the continent forms a swirling vortex that further lowers the pressure at the Pole, rendering its effective elevation even higher—typically above 10,000 feet in summer.

He wakes to a splitting headache at about three in the morning. After struggling to get back to sleep, he finally gives up, puts on his boots and parka over his long underwear, and trudges outside. It feels colder now, but the air is still. In his drowsy state he has forgotten to put on his gloves, and as he turns the handle on the door to the bathroom, he feels the skin of his hand stick tightly to the frigid metal. He pulls it away quickly, but already a burning feeling bites at three of his fingers. It is still an awful place, he thinks to himself as he gets back to his bunk a few minutes later. He cradles his smarting hand, cursing his carelessness.

He sits sullen and alone in the cafeteria eating breakfast the next morning. The headache has gotten worse, and he is in no mood for company. But the South Pole station doctor seats herself bravely across from him despite his best efforts to look unfriendly. He shrugs and continues eating. She asks him to pass the sugar. As she pours the white grains into her coffee, she says in a gentle voice that he doesn't look well. Is he suffering from a headache, she inquires, and is he having difficulty sleeping? Perhaps he feels his heart beating loudly, the blood rushing in his ears? He ignores her and goes on eating the toasted bread, which tastes like cardboard. She puts two large glasses of water in front of him. Your body is trying to help you, she advises. You are breathing faster to get more oxygen, but this means more carbon dioxide is also flowing through you, and your blood is becoming alkaline. Your kidneys are working hard to get rid of the alkalinity, but they can succeed only if you drink—even though the bathroom is a long walk. Between the dry air and the increased respiration, your body is also losing moisture at a furious rate. Dehydration is the biggest problem we have here. I know you don't feel thirsty, she says. But that's part of the problem. She eyes him critically. Your bad mood is a sure tipoff. I see it all the time.

She has described his condition exactly, and he reluctantly nods his admission. She pushes the water closer to him. A normal man doing moderate exercise at the South Pole needs at least a half-gallon of water a day to stay healthy, she says. If you're exercising much, a gallon and a half is better.

She has gotten his attention now. Scott drank only a few glasses of tea a day, he says slowly. The doctor casts her practiced gaze over the others in the cafeteria. Which one is Scott? she asks in a worried tone.

The visitor shakes his head. He's gone now, he says, gone a long time. The doctor turns her focus back to him. She tells him to drink the water immediately, and to come to the clinic so she can look him over in an hour. He agrees and begins to drink as she walks out. Scott had barely enough fuel to warm the pemmican and make a mug of tea for each man at each meal, he thinks, as he drains the big glass.

By December 11, 1911, Amundsen and his four companions had passed the 89th parallel and were continuing south in temperatures near −15 °F, under skies that were "calm with sunshine." He and his men carefully measured the elevation of the sun versus time of day to deduce a latitude of 89°30′S on December 12. They also calculated their location based on "dead reckoning"—that is, by adding up the daily distances traveled as recorded by their sledgemeters. The two methods agreed to within 1,000 yards. As they approached the Pole, Amundsen and his men searched for signs of Scott's team but "could not descry anything but the endless flat plain ahead of us." [1]

At three in the afternoon of December 14, dead reckoning suggested that the Norwegians were at the Pole. But their leader, a man who had long cherished the dream of being first at the other end of the world, had mixed feelings. Amundsen wrote: "I have never known any man to be placed in such a diametrically opposite position to the goal of his desires as I was at that moment. . . . The North Pole . . . had attracted me from childhood, and here I was at the South Pole." All five "frost-bitten fists" grasped their national emblem as the Norwegian team planted a flag to celebrate their attainment of the Pole. After this brief moment of ceremony, the Norwegians set about the serious work of fixing the Pole position more accurately, well aware that the sledgemeter reading confirmed only that they were close. They took a brief rest and arose at midnight to train their sextants on the sun. This datum suggested that their latitude was about 89°56'S, within striking range of their goal.[2]

The Norwegians knew that a series of careful measurements of the solar elevation above the horizon was essential to accurately determine the Pole position. To ensure that at least one of their team would pass very close to the Pole no matter what else occurred, Amundsen sent three men out skiing to bracket a circle with a 12.5-mile radius around their position. The men skied in three directions—two perpendicular to the line along which they had come, and the third farther south along the meridian. Although the weather was fine when they left, the three skiers ran a significant risk of being lost if a storm had swept in during their twenty-five-mile journeys along the highest and loneliest cross-country ski runs in the world. Meanwhile Amundsen and his remaining teammate meticulously measured the elevation of the sun every hour from 6 A.M. to 7 P.M.[3]

At Cape Evans in mid-January, the sun dips to ten degrees above the horizon at midnight and rises to its zenith of thirty-five degrees at local noon, circling the sky over twenty-four hours and never setting. As the Norwegian and British explorers approached the Pole, the sun's daily arc around the sky became flatter and flatter. At the singular points of the true Poles of the Earth, the sun remains at a constant angle over twenty-four hours; in mid-January, for example, the sun is twenty degrees above the horizon at the South Pole throughout the day. Explorers can therefore document their attainment of the Pole through repeated and careful measurements of solar position. Measurements of the positions of stars or planets are invaluable aides to navigation at lower latitudes, where dark nights reveal other celestial objects, but for the two teams of explorers who raced to the South Pole near the end of 1911 only the solar disk could be seen in the continuous bright sunshine of the polar summer.

On December 16, 1911, Amundsen's five men skied together a few miles to what they calculated to be the true Pole. Here they put up a tent, which they christened Polheim, and they labored in shifts to take detailed observations of the angle of the sun above the horizon each hour for the next twenty-four. The data indicated that they were as close as they could come to the Pole within the limitations of accuracy of their instruments—there was a finite uncertainty in their ability to read the scales on their sextants, just as there is uncertainty in reading a common ruler. Two skiers again went out along the directions of those uncertainties to a distance of 4.5 miles, in order to be certain to pass as close as possible to the true Pole. One analysis of Amundsen's surveying data gave the latitude of Amundsen's Polheim as 89°58.5′S, longitude 60°E, and suggested that the two skiers may have passed within about six hundred yards of the Pole, perhaps even within one hundred yards.[4] Another study of the same data emphasized the difficulty of accounting for such factors as the refraction of light through an atmosphere at extreme cold temperatures, but concluded that Amundsen's Polheim was indeed no more than a mile from the true geographic Pole.[5]

Amundsen and his men ate dinner and celebrated simply afterward with cigars. They left the extra tent they had brought along to mark the Pole, placing inside it a letter addressed to their king and another for Captain Scott, along with a sextant and some other unwanted equipment. They turned north on December 17, 1911, in a temperature of −2.2°F and a "mild summer-like wind." They began their journey home "in good spirits, so we went along at a great pace."[6] They descended from the plateau to the eastern edge of the ice shelf on the glacier they had christened the Heiberg. They encountered crevasses and blizzards but enjoyed typically mild summer Antarctic weather. They traversed the Barrier in daily minimum temperatures generally between zero and +10°F.[7] The amiable weather the Norwegians experienced was similar to that encountered at the same time by Lieutenant Evans's team a few hundred miles to their west. Their dogs carried them along briskly at an average speed of about twenty-three miles per day, and Amundsen and his men reached their home base at the Bay of Whales on January 25, 1912.[8]

When Wilson learned on January 3, 1912, that he was among the five men chosen to go on to the Pole, he wrote a quick note to his wife to be taken back by Lieutenant Evans's party: "I am glad for your sake that I am one of the five . . . all fit and strong and well. . . . Our five are all very nice together

Figure 48. From left: Scott, Wilson, Oates, and seaman Evans, sledging on the high plateau. Photograph by H. Bowers. Scott Album, number 2931, Alexander Turnbull Library, Wellington, New Zealand.

and we shall be a very happy party."[9] Captain Oates mirrored Wilson's views, writing to his mother, "I have been selected to go on to the Pole with Scott. . . . I am of course delighted." Oates's letter also remarked upon temperatures near $-20\,°F$ that they had endured the previous night in the rarefied air of the plateau, but he closed by reassuring her, "We get plenty of food & as soon as we start back we have plenty in the depots." Along with his final words home to his mother, the dragoon's thoughts were of horses in England, and he took the time to enclose a note to his brother regarding a filly.[10] Bowers was also confident about the food stores, telling his mother in a letter written on January 3, 1912, that "it will be possible to accomplish the whole journey without short rations of any sort. . . . We shall be a happy party though rather squeezed up in a 4 man tent."[11]

The day after Lieutenant Evans's team departed, Wilson wrote of "sastrugi getting decidedly heavier." It became increasingly difficult to pull the sledge over the rough surface. As the men slogged on over the plateau at an elevation near ten thousand feet, Wilson wrote that "we sweat freely on these occasions."[12] At this point Scott and his men felt "the cold very little, the great comfort of our situation is the excellent drying effect of the sun." But Scott also noted that "cooking for five takes a seriously longer time than cooking for four; perhaps half an hour on the whole day. It is an item I had not considered when re-organising."[13] Cherry-Garrard summarized the impact of this belated realization succinctly: "Half an hour off your sleep, or half an hour off your march?"—either was a burden that would compound dramatically in the coming days. Furthermore, their tent was intended for four men rather than five. The additional man would push those on the edges past the floorcloth to the snow outside, further increasing the discomforts of their already-miserable nights in icy sleeping bags. Extra rime from the added man's breath would deposit nightly on the walls of the tent, to be brushed off on their heads and clothing as all maneuvered in the cramped space.[14] Scott's admission that he had not considered the increased cooking time is reminiscent of his failure to remove the lens cap when learning photography, but this time the oversight was one of a number of growing threats to their survival. As he had many times before, Scott noted the obviously damning point quite honestly in his diary.

On January 6 at an elevation estimated at 10,500 feet, Scott and his men encountered "a sea of fish hook waves" of sastrugi that rendered passage on ski impossible. They all pulled hard on foot, with their skis carried on the sledge, but they achieved only 6.5 miles for the day, far less than their planned distances.[15]

When the surfaces of January 7 again presented difficult sastrugi, Scott decided to depot the skis of the polar party. There would be little point in dragging an extra weight of about one hundred pounds when the furrows of sastrugi were too deep and rough to allow their use. But after a mile, the sastrugi disappeared, and the men went back and retrieved the skis. That night Scott wrote, "I am awfully glad we have hung on to the ski; hard as the marching is, it is far less tiring on ski. Bowers has a heavy time on foot." Scott also noted that seaman Evans had a deep cut on his hand due to the sledge-making work of a few days before, and with concern he wrote: "I hope it won't give trouble."[16] Wilson examined the big seaman's wound that evening and noted "a lot of pus in it."[17]

The next day brought a mild blizzard, and Scott chose to take a day of rest. He wrote glowingly of all of his companions, noting Wilson's work "first as doctor, ever on the lookout to alleviate the small pains and troubles incidental to the work." He praised seaman Evans: "It is only now that I realize how much has been due to him." Of Bowers he said: "Nothing comes amiss to him, and no work is too hard. It is a difficulty to get him into the tent; he seems quite oblivious of the cold and he lies coiled in his bag writing and working out sights long after the others are asleep." And finally, he noted that Oates "goes hard the whole time, does his share of camp work and stands the hardship as well as any of us." In summary, he concluded that "our five people are perhaps as happily selected as it is possible to imagine."[18]

On January 9 Scott's party passed Shackleton's farthest point south, exactly three years to the day after that British expedition braved the plateau. When they pitched their tent at a point beyond Shackleton's most southerly encampment, Scott wrote that they had on that day made a record for the southernmost camp, not knowing that Amundsen had already established one at the Pole itself.[19] As Scott and his men struggled southward taking theodolite readings, a twenty-six-minute discrepancy occurred between Scott's and Bowers's watches used for determining position. These were the only two watches carried by the party, and knowledge of the time was essential for navigation. Wilson wrote, "Question is which has gone wrong," but an irritated Scott lamented that "Bowers' watch has suddenly dropped 26 minutes."[20] A later report on the surveying work of the expedition suggests that Scott's watch was indeed the correct one.[21]

The men built a depot the next day, going forward with eighteen days' food. Scott wrote that he would have been confident with this allotment earlier, but "now the surface is beyond words, and if it continues we shall have the greatest difficulty to keep our march long enough. The surface is quite covered with sandy snow." The next day he remarked that "the forenoon was agonising. . . . We have covered 6 miles, but at fearful cost to ourselves." Both Wilson and Scott noted the softness of the snow in the next several days, and the going on foot for Bowers can only have been excruciatingly difficult. But on the night of January 12, Scott wrote of the smallest man in his party: "Little Bowers is wonderful; in spite of my protest he would take sights after we had camped tonight, after marching in the soft snow all day where we have been comparatively restful on ski."[22]

On Sunday, January 14, the party passed latitude 89°20' at lunch, and Scott noted that they were all feeling the cold. The lunchtime temperature that day was −19°F, considerably colder than the conditions Amundsen had

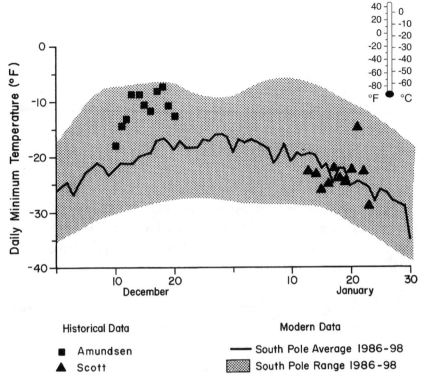

Figure 49. Daily minimum temperatures recorded by Amundsen's and Scott's parties within one degree of latitude of the South Pole, compared to the averages and the ranges recorded by automated weather station data. Amundsen's data happen to lie on the warm edge of the range, while Scott's are generally near the mean, with the exception of one warm day. This difference in the luck of their circumstances, combined with Amundsen's earlier arrival, led to an overall difference of more than ten degrees in the average minimum temperatures experienced by the two groups at the Pole.

experienced a month earlier (see fig. 49). Now it was past the summer solstice, and the relative warmth provided by the sun was quickly retreating from the Pole. The men's discomfort was exacerbated by the "bald state of our finnesko." Scott remarked that "Oates seems to be feeling the cold and fatigue more than the rest of us, but we are all very fit. It is a critical time, but we ought to pull through . . . so close it seems and only the weather to baulk us." Between the cold temperatures, accompanying sandy surfaces, and high elevation, advancing ten to fourteen miles per day was now a struggle.[23] On January 15 they determined their elevation as 9,920 feet, and they depoted more weight. They had found, as had Amundsen before them, that the Pole actually sits in a slight depression, and they were past the highest point they would cross.[24] After lunch "the sledge came surprisingly lightly . . . something from loss of weight . . . most of all perhaps as a result of tea. . . . Anyhow we made a capital afternoon march of 6.2 miles."[25]

Tea may very well have had a significant role in the men's renewed energy on this day. The fuel they carried was scarcely sufficient with good management on the part of the cook to provide each man with his daily portion of food and liquids, which consisted of one mug of warm food (pemmican stew) and one of tea at breakfast and dinner, and one mug of tea to accompany the lunchtime biscuit.[26] Each man had two aluminum mugs used for pemmican and tea; the smaller one could be stacked compactly inside the other. The volume of the larger tea mug was about two cups.[27] Between the tea and the liquid in their pemmican stew, the men were consuming only about two and a half quarts of water per day. But they were losing moisture at a furious rate. Not only were they marching many miles per day dragging a heavy sledge behind them across an intractable surface, they were doing so at high elevation in the middle of the high, cold desert of Antarctica. In spite of increased need for water, visitors to cold and high altitude environments often experience decreased thirst. Like many of today's residents of the South Pole, Scott and his companions likely did not recognize early signs of dehydration. Relatively sedentary individuals require about two to four quarts of water per day at high altitudes, whereas strenuous exercise can boost water needs to as much as two quarts per hour.[28] As Lieutenant Evans wrote, "Water is always short on a sledging trip."[29]

When they camped that night, an optimistic Scott wrote: "It is wonderful to think that two long marches would land us at the Pole. We left our depot today with nine days' provisions, so that it ought to be a certain thing now, and the only appalling possibility the sight of the Norwegian flag forestalling ours. . . . We ought to do it now."[30]

On January 16, 1912, that appalling possibility was realized. It was Bowers whose "sharp eyes detected what he thought was a cairn. . . . Half an hour later he detected a black speck ahead. Soon we knew that this could not be a natural snow feature. We marched on, found that it was a black flag. . . . Nearby the remains of a camp; sledge tracks and ski tracks going and coming and the clear trace of dogs' paws—many dogs."[31] The analytical Dr. Wilson accurately estimated the age of the tracks at a few weeks—probably three or more, and noted that "the flag was fairly well frayed," indicating stiff winds.[32]

Scott and his four companions reached the Pole the next day, according to their own dead reckoning. That night Scott wrote, "Little Bowers is laying himself out to get sights in terrible difficult circumstances; the wind is blowing hard, T. −21°, and there is that curious damp, cold feeling in the air which chills one to the bone in no time. . . . Great God! this is an awful place and terrible enough for us to have laboured to it without the reward of priority." Where Amundsen had celebrated his triumph with a cigar, Scott, Oates, and seaman Evans enjoyed cigarettes that Wilson had brought. The three smokers probably had increased difficulty breathing the thin air, but like today's visitors to the Pole, they nevertheless enjoyed the tobacco.[33]

Next the British explorers carried out their own careful determination of the Pole position. An initial set of observations suggested that the true Pole was behind them and to the right of their track. The men marched back that way on the next day, and there they found Amundsen's Polheim tent. Scott left a note in the Polheim tent and took the one Amundsen had left for him. Amundsen's letter is quoted as follows:

> Dear Captain Scott—As you probably are the first to reach this
> area after us, I will ask you to kindly forward this letter to King
> Haakon VII. If you can use any of the articles left in the tent please
> do not hesitate to do so. The sledge left outside may be of use to
> you. With kind regards I wish you a safe return. Yours truly, Roald
> Amundsen.[34]

There was no sign of the sledge to which Amundsen referred; it must already have been buried by drifting snow. Amundsen also left behind three reindeer bags containing fur mitts and other clothing, as well as a sextant and other supplies. Scott noted with some surprise that an English-made hypsometer, a meteorological instrument for measuring pressure, had also been discarded by the Norwegians.[35] He had no way of knowing that this last item was very likely the parting gift given to Amundsen by his own former sledgemate and rival, Ernest Shackleton.[36]

Figure 50. The British team at Polheim. From left, Scott, Oates, Wilson, and seaman Evans. Photograph by H. Bowers. Scott Album, number 2930, Alexander Turnbull Library, Wellington, New Zealand.

The British team then continued the labor of precisely locating the Pole. Bowers stood out in a stiff wind recording temperatures as low as −24°F on January 18, 1912, and taking repeated sights.[37] His navigational data and calculations were checked by Scott, who made several corrections in the complex computations. One study suggests that their final determination was within 1,500 yards of the true Pole.[38]

Unlike the acrimonious debate a few years earlier between Cook and Peary regarding which, if either, had truly attained the North Pole, Scott and his colleagues frankly described the Norwegians' achievement in polite and respectful terms. Scott wrote: "There is no doubt that our predecessors have made thoroughly sure of their mark and fully carried out their program."[39] According to Lieutenant Evans, the British fixed their own Pole position half a mile from Amundsen's mark, which implied that the two teams' evaluation of the Pole position differed by about one scale division of the theodolite — which he deemed a stunning demonstration of navigational skills by both.[40]

Scott and his men toiled within one degree of latitude of the South Pole

from January 13 to January 23. The daily minimum temperatures they recorded during this time averaged −23 °F.[41] The average of the daily minima
for January 13–23 recorded annually by the automated weather station at
the Pole since 1986 is −22.6 °F and shows only a few degrees of mean variability when averaged over these eleven days. The good quantitative agreement between Scott's 1912 data and modern observations provides further
support for the accuracy of the calibration of their thermometers as carried
out by Simpson. The average minimum temperatures reported by Amundsen while within one degree of the South Pole a month earlier were considerably warmer, about −10 °F. These temperatures were in the high range
of normal for that time of year. The contemporary meteorological data presented in figure 49 show that the colder weather encountered by Scott was
caused both by the advancing season and by where luck placed him within
the range of variable conditions that prevail in summer at the Pole.

Bowers took a few moments to write a letter to his sister before leaving the
Pole, noting that he was "awfully sorry for Captain Scott who has taken the
blow very well indeed."[42] Even Bowers felt the cold as Scott's team established its Pole position—so much so that during breakfast that day he "sewed
a flap attachment to the hood of my green hat so as to prevent the wind from
blowing down my neck on the march."[43] The amazing Bowers apparently
had not felt the need to keep the wind off of his neck earlier in the trek.

The faces that looked into the camera at the South Pole were weathered,
and some were frostbitten, but all except one were taking the trouble to continue to trim or shave their moustaches and beards up to this point in the journey, suggesting that their straits were not yet desperate. Only Oates peered
into the lens past facial hair heavily encrusted with ice. Oates had also confided to his diary a month earlier that his feet were often cold and wet.[44]

A strong wind and a sail eased the task of hauling the sledge, just as
planned, when Scott and his men turned northward. They followed their
own tracks, and Bowers was pleased shortly after leaving the Pole when "we
then with much relief left all traces of the Norwegians behind us, and headed
on our own track." On January 20 Bowers's tone seemed as optimistic as ever
as he wrote of "a good sailing breeze again this morning." On this day he also
noted, "We are absolutely dependent upon our depots to get off the plateau
alive, and so welcome the lonely little cairns gladly." On January 21 Bowers

Figure 51. The British team at their own Pole position. Photograph taken remotely, by pulling a string. From left, Oates, Bowers, Scott, Wilson, and seaman Evans. Scott Album, number 2932, Alexander Turnbull Library, Wellington, New Zealand.

struggled with "soft plodding for me on foot. I shall be jolly glad to pick up my dear old ski[s]. They are nearly 200 miles away yet, however." [45]

Favorable breezes from behind filled their sail on January 23, and Bowers wrote that "we sped along merrily. . . . In the afternoon it was even stronger, and I had to go back to the sledge and act as guide and brakesman. We had to lower the sail a bit, but even then she ran like a bird. . . . Evans got his nose frost-bitten, not an unusual thing with him." [46]

Seaman Evans had suffered from frostbite frequently in his polar travels. Scott had first remarked upon the big seaman's bouts with it on the sledging journey into Victoria Land in 1903 during the *Discovery* expedition. Scott had also commented upon Oates's susceptibility to frostbite. But in spite of this tendency, both men were among those chosen for the Pole, and now Scott wrote: "Evans is a good deal run down—his fingers are badly blistered and his nose is rather seriously congested with frequent frost bites. He is very much annoyed with himself, which is not a good sign. I think Wilson, Bowers, and I are as fit as possible under the circumstances. Oates gets cold feet." [47] That night, Wilson was also suffering from a recurrent problem of his own, snowblindness. [48] The next day, Bowers wrote: "Evans has got his fingers all blistered with frostbites, otherwise we are all well, but thinning, and in spite of our good rations get hungrier daily." [49]

Cold temperatures such as those the men were now experiencing increase the body's need for nourishment in many ways. First, basic body functions require more energy to maintain thermal regulation in extreme cold. Locomotion over snow-covered terrain is more difficult and strenuous than in other environments, as anyone who has walked through deep snow has surely experienced. Shivering also increases the body's metabolic rate, helping to prevent the danger of a decreased body core temperature that could be fatal, but increasing the need for food. Extra energy is also required simply to bring very cold air up to body temperature in every breath. And all of the added food requirements in cold temperatures depend upon both the weight of the individual and on the level of physical activity. [50] Seaman Evans was the biggest man in the party, and Scott relied upon his great strength. Cherry-Garrard later wrote, "I do not believe that this is a life for such men, who are expected to pull their weight and to support and drive a larger machine than their companions, and at the same time to eat no extra food. . . . It is clear that the heaviest man will feel the deficiency sooner and more severely than others who are smaller than he. Evans must have had a most terrible time: I think it is clear from the diaries that he had suffered very greatly without complaint." [51] At close to 200 pounds, seaman Evans would have required at least three hundred to five hundred food calories more per day for his basic needs in cold conditions than a 150-pound companion, and he would therefore have tended to lose more weight. [52]

But Evans was not the only man who now was hungry. Why were the smaller men also terribly ravenous and losing weight, when their rations had been carefully tested under even colder conditions during the torturous winter journey to Cape Crozier? Three men had dragged two hundred pounds per man across Windless Bight in midwinter temperatures as low as −77°F but had lost only a few pounds in a journey of six weeks. The polar trek was now into its eleventh week, but the main problem was probably not the longer period but rather the dramatically higher elevation. Scott's party was now engaged in man-hauling not at sea level but on the high plateau near ten thousand feet. The problems of weight loss at high altitude are incompletely understood even today, and Scott and his men could not have foreseen them. We do know that keeping up with the body's demand for oxygen at high altitude increases both respiration and heart rates. The calories required to maintain basic bodily functions increase by three hundred to five hundred calories per day at high altitude even in sedentary individuals. Greater increases would be expected for persons engaged in strenuous exercise, such as the daily struggles faced by the men of the polar party, particularly the strong-man Evans.[53] There is also some evidence that food is absorbed less efficiently by the body at high altitudes, though this has not been proven. And there are suggestions that fat is more difficult than other foods to metabolize at high altitudes.[54] The rich pemmican that staved off the men's hunger was heavily loaded with fat and thus perhaps a poor high-altitude nutrient. A doctor who walked to the Pole with two companions in 1985 documented weight losses of up to twenty-three pounds in his party, and this team of modern explorers did not attempt the return journey on foot.[55] In short, the ration testing that Scott's men had so scientifically performed the previous winter at sea level could not provide a basis for gauging their increased needs on the high polar plateau, and they were all getting "pretty thin, especially Evans."[56]

Scott's approach to evaluating ration needs based upon the Cape Crozier journey again illustrates that he was a man of strong scientific leanings who experimented and then used the findings to formulate his plans logically, but often at the very margins of safety. Amundsen took a different tack, making certain to achieve his goals by preparing for conditions far more extreme than those he expected to encounter. The Norwegian team ate more calories per day than Scott's men while doing less strenuous work; one team member noted that the Norwegians actually gained weight on their polar journey.[57] They also left extra fur clothing in the tent at Polheim. Bowers gratefully took a discarded pair of reindeer mitts from the Polheim tent, for he had lost his own on the trail a few days earlier.[58]

Scott and his hungry men trudged northward for home in daily minimum temperatures now near $-20\,°F.$[59] They prayed for the wind to blow behind them and lighten their load. Even with their now-light sledge, the men frequently found the task of pulling far more difficult than before. The cold temperatures began to exact a terrible price not only in their comfort but also in the rate of progress possible on the cold, sandpapery snow—a problem that had also been encountered on the Cape Crozier journey as temperatures plummeted. Even the optimistic Bowers wrote that "the light sledge pulled by five men came along like a drag without a particle of slide or give," and Scott wrote that the cold dry snow led to "the most tiring march we have had. . . . By Jove! it has been a grind." [60] Recreational downhill and cross-country skiers who generally enjoy their sport at temperatures above freezing have little experience of the remarkable change that occurs in snow at very cold temperatures. As temperatures dip below about −20°F, the glide is gone— destroyed by the basic thermal properties of ice. Even modern waxes and Inuit methods of icing the runners have limited value under very cold conditions when the snow surface not only becomes rough but also can lose its underlying stiffness. Peary and his men in Greenland were assisted by Inuit companions who employed a wealth of traditional knowledge regarding ski techniques, but they still found that the snow at very cold temperatures sometimes took on the character of granulated sugar, rendering skiing a grueling task. [61]

New snowfall of sharply faceted crystals further compounds the problem, as the Cape Crozier party had already experienced in July. As he trudged northward, Scott noticed that the snow that fell on the plateau before him at temperatures around −25°F dropped "very minute crystals. . . . The fine crystals absolutely spoil the surface; we had heavy dragging during the last hour in spite of the light load and a full sail." [62] Scott had originally hoped to reach the Pole around the solstice, on December 21, correctly reasoning that warmer temperatures would prevail then and make for easier going as well as greater physical comfort. Now he and his men were engaged in a race with the rapid advance of the coreless winter, and temperatures at the South Pole were beginning to drop. The act of skiing suddenly became a monstrous challenge for Scott's party, and they knew that their survival depended upon descending the glacier and reaching the warmer conditions expected at sea level. Amundsen's team did not experience these rough surfaces because they were long gone before the temperatures turned cold, already back at their base by late January. They certainly were far more experienced skiers, and their task was surely easier because they skied unencumbered, without pulling a heavy sledge. But even Amundsen once described the problem of skiing in frigid conditions, writing that "the cold affected the going at once; it was slow and unyielding." [63]

On January 24 Scott's progress northward was brought to a halt at lunch, when a blizzard developed and the men could no longer navigate with confidence. The storm abated the next morning, and the weary team again plodded northward. But Scott wrote that "Oates suffers from a very cold foot. . . . Evans' fingers and nose are in a bad state and tonight Wilson is suffering tortures in his eyes." For the next several days, the men marched on in misery. They were able to pick up their cairns and depots but frequently found no trace of their outbound tracks between these markers. The wind had already begun to eradicate their footsteps from the plateau. But the wind was also a boon to their progress across the cold snow, as on January 29, when Scott wrote that "the sledge with our good wind behind runs splendidly." [64] Progress across the frigid surface to this point was monotonous and painful, but steady.

Wilson strained a tendon in his leg on January 29 and for the next several days was forced to walk in pain by the sledge instead of helping to pull. He gave his skis to Bowers while he marched. In the afternoon of January 31 Bowers's own "dear old ski[s]" were at long last retrieved from the depot where they had been left. The remarkable little man had trudged through deep snow for exactly a month, covering about four hundred miles on foot while the others had skied. The disappointment of being beaten to the Pole does not appear to have stifled Bowers's spirit; the tone of his diary remained cheerful even after the party discovered the Norwegians' camp. His entry for January 25 dwelled with a humorous slant on his feelings of "tribulation as regards meals now as we have run out of salt, one of my favorite commodities." But perhaps the return journey on foot took a great deal out of him, for January 29 marks Bowers's last detailed entry in his diary. He wrote optimistically enough that night of a good breeze and improving surface, but after this date he recorded only a few brief remarks until he ceased his daily entries entirely on February 11.[65] On some occasions around this period and in the weeks to come, he failed to record the times of his meteorological measurements. This may indicate not fatigue but rather the fact that his watch was the one that had gone awry. However, there is also a marked change in the level of detail in the remarks he recorded in his meteorological log book after January. On January 30 Bowers commented in detail, as he had in earlier entries: "Slight mist on the horizon. Stiff breeze with surface drift all day. 20h 30m: ice crystals falling. Hazy on horizon." But from February 1 on, many days passed with very terse or no meteorological remarks by the diligent Bowers.[66]

As January drew to a close, the biggest man of the party was the one in the greatest trouble. Wilson's and Scott's writings described seaman Evans's decline. On the thirtieth Scott noted that "Evans dislodged two fingernails tonight; his hands are really bad, and to my surprise he shows signs of losing heart over it. He hasn't been cheerful since the accident."[67] The big seaman had always been known for his cheerful good nature, but something had changed. A day later, Wilson wrote of "Evans' fingernails all coming off, very raw and sore."[68]

The polar party picked up more food at Three-Degree Depot on January 31, making possible a welcome increase in rations as the men began the descent down the glacier, following in the tracks of the second return party. They managed good marches of eighteen, twenty-one, and twenty-one miles, respectively, on February 2, 3, and 4, similar to those of Lieutenant Evans's party almost a month before. This excellent progress was achieved partly through the grace of a helpful southerly wind; the daily minimum temperatures were near −20°F, which would have made such distances difficult in its absence.[69]

On February 2 Scott fell and hurt his shoulder, but a more serious accident occurred two days later, when both Scott and Evans fell into a crevasse together. The two men had also plunged into a crevasse in December of 1902 on the *Discovery* expedition, to be pulled out on that occasion by Lashly. Nine years earlier the big seaman had laughed about the experience, exclaiming, "well, I'm blowed," but this time his reaction was different.[70] On February 4, 1912, Scott wrote that Evans was becoming unfit.[71] The worried Dr. Wilson continued to dress Evans's suppurating fingers and noted that the seaman was "feeling the cold a lot[,] always getting frostbitten," while Oates's toes were blackening.[72]

On the evening of February 4 Scott wrote with concern, "I hope we are not going to have trouble with ice falls," but two days later the polar party, like Lieutenant Evans's team before them, found themselves in "a beastly position amidst crevasses" and "huge open chasms." They threaded their way past these hazards and dragged the sledge through high sastrugi. Evans's nose was further frostbitten in the process, perhaps through Scott's insistence on a hurried pace, for Wilson noted with irritation that "we again had a forenoon of trying to cut corners."[73] Scott wrote, "Evans is the chief anxiety now; his cuts and wounds suppurate, his nose looks very bad, and altogether he shows considerable signs of being played out. Things may mend for him on the glacier, and his wounds get some respite under warmer conditions."[74]

In the next few days, the men steered toward the mountains and spent time "geologizing." Wilson's diary for this day is unusually animated with the thrill of scientific excitement as he writes of "magnificent Beacon Sandstone cliffs . . . masses of limestone in the moraine, and dolerite crags in various places. Coal seams at all heights in the sandstone cliffs and lumps of weathered coal with fossils, vegetable. Had a regular field day and got some splendid things in the short time."[75] Wilson collected several samples of the coal, including "beautifully traced leaves in layers."[76] These were among the early pieces of evidence that the continent of Antarctica once lay in much warmer climes where plants had flourished. And although temperatures in the Antarctic of 1912 were much too cold to support plants, all the men enjoyed the warmer air and easier conditions of the lowered elevation.

They were now free of the intense cold of the dreaded plateau, and their diaries expressed greater optimism. Wilson wrote, "We are all thoroughly enjoying temps. of +10 or thereabouts now."[77] On February 9 Scott wrote that "tonight it is wonderfully calm and warm." For the first time in weeks, he found that "our food satisfies now."[78] Lieutenant Evans suggests that Scott's purpose in the less frenzied pace of February 8 and 9 was not only to collect the treasured geologic specimens but also to allow seaman Evans a much-needed rest in warmer weather that might bring him back from the brink.[79]

Although the weather was now much kinder than it had been on the plateau, more crevasses lay ahead. For the next three days, the party maneuvered through the ice falls, "falling into crevasses every minute" among "huge chasms, closely packed and most difficult to cross." As they struggled to find their way through, food began to run perilously short. On February 13 the party managed to find Mid-Glacier Depot just as they were nearly out of food, and "the relief to all is inexpressible."[80] Temperatures were rather typical when they finally returned to sea level on the Barrier, just a few degrees warmer than the modern average for this time of year, and close to those enjoyed by Amundsen's and Lieutenant Evans's teams a few weeks earlier.

But on February 14 Evans "disclosed a huge blister on his foot. It delays us on the march, when he had to have his crampon readjusted. . . . He is hungry and so is Wilson. We can't risk opening out our food again." Two days later Scott wrote, "A rather trying position. Evans has nearly broken down in brain, we think. He is absolutely changed from his normal self-reliant self. . . . It is anxious work with the sick man."[81] Wilson provided more medical details, writing that "Evans collapsed, sick and giddy, and unable to walk even by the sledge on ski, so we camped."[82]

Scott described in detail the "very terrible day" of February 17, 1912, the day on which the big seaman

started in his place on the traces, but half an hour later worked his ski shoes adrift, and had to leave the sledge. The surface was awful, the soft recently fallen snow clogging the ski and runners at every step, the sledge groaning, the sky overcast, and the land hazy. We stopped after about one hour, and Evans came up again, but very slowly. Half an hour later he dropped out again on the same plea. . . . I cautioned him to come on as quickly as he could, and he answered cheerfully as I thought. We had to push on, and the remainder of us were forced to pull very hard, sweating heavily. . . . We stopped, and seeing Evans a long way astern, I camped for lunch. There was no alarm at first, and we prepared tea and our own meal, consuming the latter. After lunch, and Evans still not appearing, we looked out, to see him still afar off. By this time we were alarmed, and all four started back on ski. I was first to reach the poor man and shocked at his appearance; he was on his knees with clothing disarranged, hands uncovered and frostbitten, and a wild look in his eyes. Asked what was the matter, he replied with a slow speech that he didn't know, but thought he must have fainted. We got him on his feet, but after two or three steps he sank down again. He showed every sign of complete collapse. Wilson, Bowers, and I went back for the sledge, while Oates remained with him. When we returned, he was practically unconscious, and when we got him into the tent quite comatose. He died quietly at 12:30 a.m.[83]

Cherry-Garrard later speculated that seaman Evans's hunger and starvation could have been the deciding element in his death, but the extreme rapidity of his final decline suggests that other factors must have been at work.[84] The suppurating cut on his hand and his frostbitten nose inflicted terrible pain, but modern medical experts have argued that his collapse, inability to walk, and giddiness suggest that the proximate cause of his death was a brain injury.[85] The question is then what was the ultimate cause of such debilitating damage to the brain.

Wilson conjectured that seaman Evans could have injured his brain in the fall he suffered in a crevasse on February 4, but a more recent medical study stressed that the symptoms of a concussion would have been apparent soon after such a fall rather than weeks later.[86] Others have emphasized that scurvy could have been involved as the underlying ultimate cause, for that condition could have exacerbated the damage to the brain following the fall, perhaps leading to a slow hemorrhage that would not have occurred in a well man.[87] But if Evans had been suffering from the advanced stages of scurvy, then it seems surprising that the observant Wilson did not remark upon the appearance of its many warning signs. Dr. Wilson's description of Evans's symptoms dealt openly with his suppurating fingers and his numerous painful frostbites, but the doctor made no mention of reddening of the gums nor of painful joints—symptoms that he had meticulously reported in Shackleton, Scott, and himself on the *Discovery* expedition in December 1902. There was no stigma attached to scurvy, as is evident in Lieutenant Evans's frank account of the progression of the disease in himself, and in Scott's writings on the struggles with the illness during the *Discovery* expedition. If seaman Evans had scurvy, it probably was in its earliest stages, with no apparent signs.

Unlike the lieutenant, seaman Evans had been sledging only briefly before the start of the polar trek, so a much longer period on sledging rations cannot explain an early onset of the disease in the big man. But seaman Evans did probably start the fatal journey with far fewer reserves of vitamin C than his companions, because he is the only member of the polar party who had a

Figure 52. Seaman Edgar "Taff" Evans. Photograph by H. Ponting. Scott Polar Research Institute, Cambridge.

documented distaste for eating seal. When he sledged to the western mountains along with the geologists in March 1911, the geologist Debenham, who befriended Evans, wrote: "For supper we had seal liver fried in blubber, excellent. Evans was much averse to tasting it as the slightest taste of blubber offends him."[88] While the others relished the vitamin C–rich seal liver, it appears that seaman Evans probably avoided it. The onset of scurvy in its earliest stages, undetected by Dr. Wilson, could therefore have been a factor in his death when combined with a brain injury. In contrast, Bowers enthusiastically wrote to his sister in October of 1911 from Cape Evans that in his view, "penguin and seal meat is topping stuff."[89]

But scurvy and crevasses were not the only threats to the men's survival. Perhaps because the South Pole is notorious for its extreme cold, its extreme dryness is seldom remarked upon. Scott's party had just completed a strenuous journey across one of the world's great deserts, and with limited water. If seaman Evans was dehydrated, then this debilitating condition could have contributed to his death. The biggest man and the one expected by Scott to pull to the limit of his tremendous strength may well have suffered more from the party's minimal allotment of fluids than did his companions.

And there is another way in which the South Pole is a land of extremes. It is not only cold and dry, but it is also at high elevation, even though it sits on a broad plateau rather than on the sharp outline of a mountain peak. Three years earlier, as Shackleton led his men over the same terrain, he wrote of unusual and painful headaches and nosebleeds. On December 31, 1908, Shackleton recorded that his head was "very bad all day"; two days before he had written, "I have been suffering from a bad headache. . . . I think that these headaches are a form of mountain sickness, due to our high altitude. The others have bled from the nose."[90] Scott did not comment about headaches, but it is unlikely that his party avoided them. Headaches are one of the first signs of mountain sickness, as Shackleton correctly surmised. In most people the headaches subside as acclimatization takes place or when they descend to lower elevation. But the reduced pressures of high altitude can also cause far more serious problems of swelling of the capillaries in the lungs and brain in some individuals, even at relatively modest elevations of ten thousand feet—comparable to the Pole. Dehydration increases the danger that mountain sickness will progress to the stage of edema in the brain and the related problems of blood clots and strokes.[91]

One of these high-altitude problems could have been fundamentally responsible for the injury to seaman Evans's brain, and again incipient scurvy could have aggravated the condition. Today's traveler to the South Pole is advised to drink plenty of fluids and to avoid strenuous exercise, but the Englishmen who were among its first visitors could enjoy neither of these luxuries. In spite of the relative ease with which contemporary visitors travel to and work at the South Pole, and the ready availability of abundant food and water, some suffer from serious altitude sickness. On average one individual per year must be evacuated from the Pole station to lower elevations.[92] It is possible that a dehydrated seaman Evans succumbed to high altitude cerebral edema, the most dangerous form of mountain sickness, which directly affects the brain through swelling. The symptoms of this condition include the malaise that began to change Evans's previously cheerful personality shortly after arrival at the Pole; his unsteadiness of gait, as noted by Wilson on February 16; and confusion and disorientation, as was evident in the seaman's final breakdown on February 17. Loss of consciousness and death can follow if the condition is not treated. Descent to lower elevation does not always reverse the damage done to the brain in cases of high altitude cerebral edema, and death can occur even after descent to sea level, consistent with Evans's death at the base of the glacier.[93]

The sketchy medical evidence thus suggests that seaman Evans died of brain damage, brought on, perhaps, by scurvy, dehydration, high altitude, or a combination of these factors. Although the clinical question of the ultimate cause of his death remains uncertain, there can be no doubt of the suffering that both he and the remaining members of the polar party endured as he perished. These were recorded by Cherry-Garrard: "At home he would have been nursed in bed: here he must march . . . until he was crawling on his frost-bitten hands and knees in the snow — horrible: most horrible perhaps for those who found him so, and sat in the tent and watched him die." [94]

Sunset on the Barrier

The visitor's headaches and foul mood have subsided now that he is drinking more water, but he still finds sleep elusive in the rarefied air of the Pole. After a few hours of tossing and turning, he decides to take one of his now-frequent trips to the toilet. He opens the door to the Jamesway and blinks in the midnight sun. It is late January and the air is unusually cold, about −35°F. He has become accustomed to −20°F, but there is something about temperatures below −30°F that gives the air a special bite. It's only a few more degrees, but for him these are the critical ones that cross the line between ease and pain. For some people it occurs at a colder point, but his personal threshold of comfort seems stuck at −30°F, even though he has now spent months in the Antarctic.

He is careful this time to put on his gloves as he walks to the bathroom door. Once outside again, he decides to go to the true Pole in spite of the late hour and the cold weather. He walks toward the Pole marker to his left. He has stopped thinking of directions as north, south, east, or west; only left and right seem to have any meaning here at the bottom of the world.

Amundsen's and Scott's markings were covered up by drifting snow soon after their visits, and this place was untouched for many years after them. Now the Pole is identified by a metal sign planted deep in the snow. The marker carries words that honor the achievements of those who were here first, but it bears neither the Norwegian nor the British flag that flew briefly at this spot in 1911 and 1912. Instead, it carries the ensign of the Americans who now maintain the outpost. The visitor marches to the Pole with awkward steps, sinking several inches into the snow on each stride. The station is quiet, and the only sound he hears is the rush of the wind past his parka hood. Behind him sit the domed structure of the station and the canvas tent where he sleeps. Ahead there is nothing but the same desolate snow plain that Scott and his men struggled across, marked only by a series of metal sticks that show the slow movement of the Pole marker. Each year the massive ice sheet slides by a little more than 3 yards relative to the true geographic pole of the solid Earth far below. A marker is left behind and the sign proclaiming the position of the true Pole is moved accordingly each New Year. The sticks of past years recede far into the distance, and he tries to count back along their snakelike path, but it is too hard to be sure of the sequence after the first ten or so. The visitor reflects that while it is hard to see just now where the Pole marker has slid, it is much harder to know what really happened to seaman Evans after he left this desolate place nearly ninety years ago.

A loud voice behind him intrudes on the visitor's reverie. A group of five men has emerged from the station, and they are heading toward the Pole. As they come closer he can smell liquor on their breath. In a gloved palm, one man holds a small electronic device. At first it looks like a calculator, but then the visitor realizes it is that most modern of navigational tools, a hand-held global positioning system (GPS) unit. The owner punches some buttons while his friends look over his shoulder. One complains that the unit isn't working, but another cautions that they must wait a few seconds while the device finds multiple satellites. After about a minute the owner holds up the GPS, smiling. Not bad, he says, 89.998. They discuss the uncertainties in the measurement. Then they push the buttons again and this time the readout says 90.000. The men cheer triumphantly and then walk back over the snow to the station, probably to return to the bar. In the space of a minute they have found the Pole, without the need for repeated and meticulous measurements of the solar position or for the dispatching of skiers.

The visitor enjoys the silence for a time after the voices have died away. Then the cold air begins to chill his face, and he starts back toward his warm bed. But the snow is uneven, and he again turns the ankle that he weakened in his fall weeks ago at McMurdo. The pain is intense this time, and he collapses on the snow. He tries to get up but it hurts too much, and he sits down again to rub it. He is too far from the station and from the tents for anyone to hear him shout. Suddenly it occurs to him that it would not be impossible to die of exposure here if he cannot get up by himself and if nobody happens to come along within the next few hours. There are, of course, many legends of drunken men who have perished in this fashion, but like the legends of Scott, it is hard to be sure which, if any of them, are true.

His legs are covered only in blue jeans and long underwear. As he sits on the snow and rubs his ankle, his thighs begin to feel terribly cold. But after a few minutes the pain in his ankle subsides considerably, and he is able to get up and hobble to the station. He finds an acquaintance inside, and the other man gets a snowmobile to drive him to his warm bed. If the ankle still hurts in the morning, he will go see the doctor to have it wrapped. And if it gets very bad, he might have to take the next flight home.

Scott and his three remaining companions reached their depot at the base of the Beardmore glacier the day after seaman Evans died. They passed through the Gateway between the glacier and the mountains easily and continued to the site where the last horses had been slaughtered on the outbound journey. There "with plenty of horsemeat" the men enjoyed "a fine supper." Scott expressed optimism about the increased food now available from the depoted pony meat, noting that "new life seems to come with greater food almost immediately," but he also remarked, "I am anxious about the Barrier surfaces." The next day his fears were realized, as the "surface was every bit as bad as I expected. . . . It has been like pulling over desert sand, not the least glide in the world." Wilson wrote of "a very heavy surface indeed." The stew of pemmican and horseflesh consumed that night was voted "the best hoosh we had ever had." Scott noted honestly and somewhat shockingly that "the absence of poor Evans is a help to the commissariat, but if he had been here in a fit state we might have got along faster."[1]

On February 20 the four men struggled across the "same terrible surface" and the minimum temperature that day was −15 °F.[2] Although they were pulling as hard as they could and eating relatively well, they were managing only about nine miles per day at great effort, for the cold surface was again becoming intractable, and the calm air lent no southerly wind to assist them.[3]

The wind picked up on February 22, and although a full sail improved their progress, the breeze also caused the men to lose their track in the drifting snow. That evening they again partook of a "great pony hoosh," but the failure to find their trail meant that they were in grave danger of missing their next depot.[4] Scott was convinced that they were too far to the east, but the next day Bowers managed to take a set of sights with the theodolite that suggested they were instead too far to the west. They marched along in uncertainty and fear until "Bowers' wonderful sharp eyes detected an old double lunch cairn, and the theodolite telescope confirmed it." Once again the little man had proven indispensable in trying circumstances. Scott wrote that "things are looking up again, as we are on the regular line of cairns with no gaps right home."[5] The last Barrier stage was expected to be the easiest part of the journey. They had dragged heavy sledges on the way out, but now they had a much lighter burden, carrying only enough food to get to the next depot. There was plenty of food in those depots, carefully cached on the way out. The temperatures were expected to be warmer here at sea level than those they had endured on the high plateau, and the prevailing southerly wind would be there to fill their sails and whisk them to the blessed relief of home base.

Although they picked up the South Barrier Depot as planned on the next day, there they found a shortage of oil. The daytime temperatures were "quite warm" in the tent on February 24, but Scott noticed that there was a larger difference between day and night temperatures as the season advanced. Wilson suffered a bad attack of snow blindness, and the men covered only four miles in the afternoon on a "really terrible surface" with no helpful wind.[6]

On February 26 Wilson wrote of a "good day's going on ski with little breeze from S. S. E. Fat pony hoosh. Temp down to −37 in the night." His last diary entry, dated February 27, simply ends with the words: "Turned in at −37." Wilson, who had kept a diary since he was a young schoolboy, stopped recording his daily thoughts on this date, perhaps because of his added burden as doctor, as emphasized by Cherry-Garrard: "As things got worse Bill's work as a doctor became heavier. . . . Wilson had to look after himself and at the same time devote time to others." [7]

Scott wrote on February 26 of "very cold nights now and cold feet starting march, as day footgear doesn't dry at all." Wet gear in cold conditions remains among the Antarctic traveler's greatest enemies, and with this diary entry Scott described a new threat of enormous proportions. Although frostbitten noses could be endured, frostbitten feet could bring an end to the march on which the men's lives depended.

The next several days brought weather that marked the beginning of the end for at least one man. The minimum temperatures dipped below −30°F every day from February 26 through March 2, the day when "Oates disclosed his feet, the toes showing very bad indeed, evidently bitten by the late [recent] temperatures." [8] That morning in temperatures of −35.5°F, as documented by Bowers's meteorological log, the simple task of putting on fur boots became an agony that required an hour and a half. [9] Although Oates had experienced frostbite earlier in the journey, the severity of the conditions now allowed little or no opportunity to thaw out new damage, and flesh that has been frostbitten before is more susceptible than it would otherwise be. The next morning arrived with even more frigid temperatures of −41°F, and Scott described in detail the deadly change that these conditions produced in the snow that now ground like sandpaper against the runners of their sledge and their skis: "The surface, lately a very good hard one, is coated with a thin layer of wooly crystals. . . . These are too firmly fixed to be removed by the wind and cause impossible friction on the runners. God help us, we can't keep up this pulling, that is certain. Amongst ourselves we are unendingly cheerful but what each man feels in his heart I can only guess. Putting on foot gear in the morning is getting slower and slower, therefore every day more dangerous." [10] Each day the sun also dipped lower and lower. By about March 4 it would have been below the horizon for a few hours at midnight. The bright light of twenty-four-hour polar summer was fading quickly, along with their hopes for survival.

Over the next few days, a helpful wind brought somewhat higher daytime temperatures, but nights remained extremely cold. Progress was a torture across the sharp hoarfrost that now covered the Barrier, and the men toiled with all their might to achieve only three and a half miles in four and a half hours. Scott lamented that "under the immediate surface crystals is a hard sastrugi surface, which must have been excellent for pulling a week or two ago." [11] Short of oil, the party went to bed on March 4 with a cup of cocoa and solid pemmican, for there was not enough fuel to make a normal hot stew. Thus their already-limited daily intake of water decreased, and the possibility of dehydration mounted.

March 5 dawned with the temperature a grim −37.5°F.[12] Oates awoke that morning with feet

> in a wretched condition. One swelled up tremendously last night and he is very lame this morning. . . . We none of us expected these terribly low temperatures, and of the rest of us Wilson is feeling them most; mainly I fear, from his self-sacrificing devotion in doctoring Oates' feet. We cannot help each other, each has enough to do to take care of himself. We get cold on the march when the trudging is heavy, and the wind pierces our worn garments. . . . It's tough work to be pulling harder than we ever pulled in our lives for long hours, and to feel that the progress is so slow. One can only say "God help us!" and plod on our weary way, cold and very miserable.[13]

In spite of a good breeze on March 6, the men progressed at a rate of only about a mile per hour, and "the sledge came as heavy as lead." Scott wrote that Oates "is wonderfully plucky, as his feet must be giving him great pain. He makes no complaint, but his spirits only come up in spurts now, and he grows more silent in the tent. . . . If we were all fit I should have hopes of getting through, but the poor Soldier has become a terrible hindrance, though he does his utmost and suffers much I fear." [14] Daily minimum temperatures continued to drop down to the low minus thirties, and the party managed only six to eight miles per day with light loads in a region where they had achieved fifteen miles per day on the outbound march.[15]

As Scott and his men approached the Mount Hooper Depot at 80°32′S on March 7 and 8, they hoped for relief in the form of men and dogs, or at least the supplies brought by them. Upon reaching the depot, Scott wrote that "the dogs which would have been our salvation have evidently failed."

The amount of oil in the can retrieved from this depot was shockingly low, and spirits plummeted even further.[16]

On March 10 Oates asked Wilson whether he had any chance of pulling through. The doctor responded that he didn't know, but Scott wrote in his diary: "In point of fact he has none. Apart from him, if he went under now, I doubt whether we could get through. . . . The weather conditions are awful, and our gear gets steadily more icy and difficult to manage."[17]

With the exception of March 4, the party had endured minimum temperatures below −30°F every day since February 27.[18] The coreless winter had begun, and at the moment when Scott and his companions were most vulnerable to its ravaging effects on their bodies and on the surfaces over which they had to travel. Comparison of the polar party's progress to that of the other two returning parties as each marched northward from 86°S illustrates these desperate straits. Lieutenant Evans and his two seamen companions reached 86°S on January 10; the short-handed, three-man party then had to descend the great glacier and traverse the plain of the Barrier to reach home. Scott and his four companions arrived at the same point after completing the journey to the Pole a little less than a month later, on February 4. For about the next two weeks after passing 86°S, both groups enjoyed several days with minimum temperatures as warm as +10°F, and the two teams made comparable daily progress. Their speeds of daily travel were roughly matched by the first return party, led by Dr. Atkinson. The legend of Scott as a bumbler suggests that he may have decided to die, perhaps even at the moment when he learned that Amundsen had beaten him to the Pole, but the rate of progress shown in figure 53 belies such an interpretation. Although

Figure 53 (facing page). The top panel shows the relative rates of progress of the first return party, led by Atkinson, the second return party, led by Lieutenant Evans, and Scott's party at various positions on the Beardmore glacier and on the Barrier as a function of days since passing 86°S, just above the top of the glacier. Each group returned progressively later, but the conditions they experienced are plotted as a function of days since passing 86°S. The first return party turned north from about 85°S, and their position data are offset to correspond to the other two at that point. The panel also notes the corresponding points when some of the major events befell each party. Positions of various depots are shown on the right. The bottom panel shows the corresponding daily minimum temperatures experienced by each party. Data taken from the tables in Simpson, *Meteorology*, vol, 3.

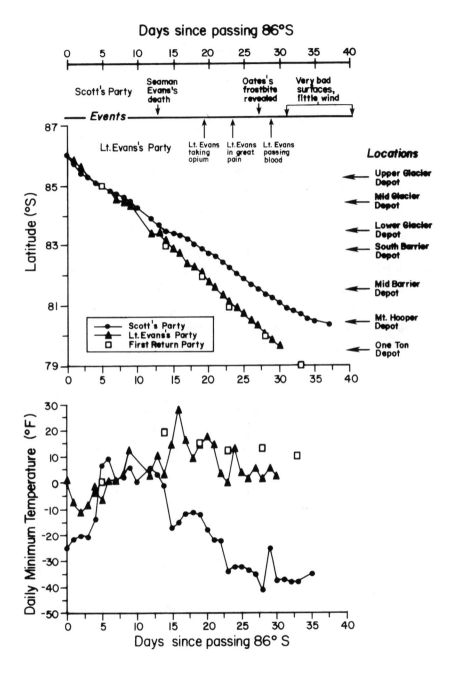

Days since passing 86°S

0   5   10   15   20   25   30   35   40

Scott's Party

Seaman
Evans's
death

Oates's
frostbite
revealed

Very bad
surfaces,
little wind

— Events —

Lt. Evans's Party

Lt. Evans
taking
opium

Lt. Evans
in great
pain

Lt. Evans
passing
blood

Locations

Latitude (°S)

87

85

83

81

79

● Scott's Party
▲ Lt. Evans's Party
□ First Return Party

Upper Glacier
Depot

Mid Glacier
Depot

Lower Glacier
Depot

South Barrier
Depot

Mid Barrier
Depot

Mt. Hooper
Depot

One Ton
Depot

0   5   10   15   20   25   30   35   40

Daily Minimum Temperature (°F)

30

20

10

0

-10

-20

-30

-40

-50

0   5   10   15   20   25   30   35   40

Days since passing 86° S

the presence of the Polheim tent and the Norwegian flag at their hard-won goal surely disheartened Scott and his companions, they nevertheless worked their way home at the planned rate of speed all the way back across the agony of the polar plateau, passing 84°S at a clip comparable to that achieved by the two earlier return parties. Nor does seaman Evans's declining health appear to have greatly slowed their travel, for he died near the end of this period of rapid progress.

At the base of the glacier, Lieutenant Evans had begun to experience some symptoms of scurvy. Within a few days, he was enduring great pain, and Lashly recorded the terrifying progress of the debilitating disease. Yet in the next two weeks, the lieutenant and his two companions managed to march at the planned rate of speed (again comparable to that of the first return party) for more than two hundred miles to reach One Ton Camp. They did so with one member of their party gravely ill, but in blissfully warm daily temperatures above 0°F. They frequently profited, as anticipated, from the help of the southerly wind in their sail, as on February 8, when seaman Lashly recorded that in weather "favourable and fine, we had a good breeze and set sail after lunch." After February 9 (thirty days after the party reached 86°S), specific temperatures were no longer recorded by the very ill Lieutenant Evans. He was carried on the sledge by his two valiant companions from about February 13 to February 18, and on the fifteenth Lashly noted "fine weather this morning." On February 19, Lashly wrote that "the temperature is dropping rapidly" while he and the now-incapacitated Evans anxiously waited in the tent, hoping for rescue by the dogs.[19] As the dogs carried the lieutenant back to the safety of Hut Point, the minimum temperatures recorded by the polar party behind them on the Barrier near 83°S began falling (near day 13, fig. 53).

From at least February 18 (day 14, fig. 53) through February 26, Scott's party enjoyed the pony meat that Lieutenant Evans's team had deliberately and stoically left behind for them.[20] This would have furnished the polar party with some badly needed vitamin C, as well as increased portions. But in spite of improved food and nutrition, it was at this point that Scott's party began to fall farther and farther behind the distances achieved by both of the earlier groups. The men in the first return party and those in Lieutenant Evans's struggling team both profited from minimum daily temperatures close to +10°F as they worked their way cross the Barrier north of 83°S—a region where Scott and his men experienced daily minimum temperatures never above −10°F and sometimes dropping below −40°F. As the temperatures plummeted, the daily distances achieved by Scott's party fell farther and farther behind those of the other two returning parties. By the time the sling thermometer broke on March 10 and brought an end to Bowers's record of temperatures, Scott and his three companions were lagging far behind the distances achieved by the scurvy-ravaged Evans and his team. Oates's frostbite began to be a topic of great concern on March 2, but Scott's party had already been progressing at a dangerously slow speed for many days, and Scott attributed their difficulties not to scurvy or lack of food but to the cold and to the associated sandpapery surfaces with which they grappled as day upon bitter day unfolded.

On March 11 Scott wrote: "Oates is very near the end, one feels. . . . He is a brave fine fellow and understands the situation, but he practically asked for advice. Nothing could be said but to urge him to march as long as he could." The incessant cold persisted, and by March 12, Oates had "hands as well as feet pretty well useless. . . . The surface remains awful, the cold intense and our physical condition running down." [21] After the thermometer broke on March 10, Bowers recorded barometer readings for two more days, but he made no further entries after March 12, 1912. [22] According to Scott's diary, the winds picked up on March 14, blowing cruelly in their faces as often as it helped them from behind. With his personal thermometer, Scott reported a temperature of −43°F, and he noted that "poor Oates got it again in the foot. . . . No idea there could be temperatures like this at this time of year with such winds. Truly awful outside the tent." [23]

A few days later, Oates asked to be left in his sleeping bag. Like Lieutenant Evans and his party, Scott, Wilson, and Bowers refused to leave their companion and "induced him to come on." But while Evans had dragged himself along in the relative ease afforded by above zero temperatures a month earlier, the severely frostbitten Oates now battled for his life in daily minimum temperatures of about −40°F. Nevertheless, "in spite of its awful nature for him he struggled on and we made a few miles." [24]

When he became too ill to march, Lieutenant Evans had been carried on the sledge, but Oates and his companions were facing an utterly different climate, which made such an effort far more difficult. Scott wrote that Oates "slept through the night, . . . hoping not to wake; but he woke in the morning. . . . It was blowing a blizzard. He said 'I am just going outside and may be some time.' He went out into the blizzard and we have not seen him since. . . . We knew that poor Oates was walking to his death but though we tried to dissuade him, we knew it was the act of a brave man and an English gentleman. We all hope to meet the end with a similar spirit, and assuredly the end is not far." When the blizzard cleared, the party marched on. They carried Oates's sleeping bag for several miles. But when they reached their next camp without finding their missing comrade, they decided that the heavy bag could be left behind to lighten their load, even though they kept the thirty-five pounds of geologic specimens they had collected "at Wilson's special request." [25] Wilson took the time to write a letter to Mrs. Oates, telling her that "the cold has been intense" and "you, he told me, are the only woman he has ever loved." [26]

March 18 brought yet another day of −35 °F minimum temperatures, and in the frigid air Scott suffered severe frostbite in his right foot. By the next day, with temperatures of −40 °F, Scott wrote that "there is no chance to nurse one's feet. . . . Amputation is the least I can hope for now, but will the trouble spread?" [27] The incessant deep freeze had now debilitated Scott, just as it had Oates scant days before.

Scott made only a few more diary entries. On March 21 he wrote that the party had gotten within eleven geographic miles (12.66 statute miles) of One Ton Camp but had "to lay up all yesterday in severe blizzard. . . . Today forlorn hope, Wilson and Bowers going to depot for fuel." The midnight sun was well below the horizon now, and each day dawned darker and shorter. For his diary entry of March 22 and 23, Scott wrote that the blizzard was as bad as before, and hence "Wilson and Bowers unable to start—tomorrow last chance. . . . Must be near the end. Have decided it shall be natural—we shall march for the depot with or without our effects and die in our tracks." [28]

In his last diary entry, on March 29, Scott emphasized that an incessant gale for the previous ten days had prevented them from leaving the tent as hoped. He wrote, "I do not think we can hope for any better things now. We shall stick it out to the end, but we are getting weaker of course, and the end cannot be far. It seems a pity, but I do not think I can write more. R. Scott. Last entry. For God's sake look after our people."[29]

In their dying days, all the men wrote farewell letters. Scott told Mrs. Wilson "how splendid [Wilson] was at the end—everlastingly cheerful and ready to sacrifice himself for others, never a word of blame to me for leading him into this mess." To Bowers's mother, Scott spoke of the little man as a gallant, noble gentleman, one whose "dauntless spirit ever shone brighter and he has remained cheerful, hopeful, and indomitable to the end. . . . To the end he has talked of you and his sisters." He asked his friend Sir J. M. Barrie to help his widow and son and asserted that "we are showing that Englishmen can still die with a bold spirit, fighting it out to the end. . . . I could never show you how much your friendship meant to me, for you had much to give and I nothing." Other letters were sent to his mother, his wife, and various friends and supporters.[30]

Wilson wrote to his "beloved wife" that "life has been a struggle for some weeks now on this return journey from the Pole—so much so that I have not been able to keep my diary going. . . . My love is as living for you as ever. . . . We will all meet after death, and death has no terrors."[31] He also expressed his love in his parting letter to his parents, and again he wrote of a happy life in the hereafter and of his abiding faith in God.[32] Wilson wrote to his good friend Reginald Smith and to Mrs. Smith on March 21 or 22: "I want to say how I have valued your friendship and your example." The naturalist also reflected upon his life's work, and because Smith was not only his friend but also his publisher, he added: "I should like to have seen the Grouse Book, but it is not allowed me."[33]

Bowers's thoughts also turned to his family in England. At the top of his last letter to his "own dearest mother" he wrote that the date was uncertain, about March 22: "As this may possibly be my last letter to you—I am sorry it is such a short scribble. I have written little since we left the Pole but it has not been for want of thinking of you and the dear girls [his sisters]. . . . We have had a terrible journey back. . . . When man's extremity is reached God's help may put things right. . . . It is splendid to pass however with such companions as I have. . . . I should so like to come through for your dear sake. . . . Much and dearest love to your dear self and May and Edie."[34]

Scott also left a "message to [the] public" in which he presented his summary of the trying events that had befallen his expedition. Like some of his other writings, it seems to reflect a defensive turn of mind, as if he were already dreading the way that history would record his actions. And perhaps that tone contributed to the way the record indeed evolved.

MESSAGE TO PUBLIC

The causes of the disaster are not due to faulty organization, but to misfortune in all risks which had to be undertaken.

1. The loss of pony transport in March 1911 obliged me to start later than I had intended, and obliged the limits of stuff transported to be narrowed.

2. The weather throughout the outward journey, and especially the long gale in 83°S, stopped us.

3. The soft snow in lower reaches of the glacier again reduced pace.

We fought these untoward events with a will and conquered, but it cut into our provision reserve.

Every detail of our food supplies, clothing, and depots made on the interior ice sheet and over that long stretch of 700 miles [geographic] to the Pole and back, worked out to perfection. The advance party would have returned to the glacier in fine form and with surplus of food, but for the astonishing failure of the man whom we had least expected to fail. Edgar Evans was thought the strongest man of the party.

The Beardmore glacier is not difficult in fine weather, but on our return we did not get a single completely fine day; this with a sick companion enormously increased our anxieties.

As I have said elsewhere we got into frightfully rough ice and Edgar Evans received a concussion of the brain—he died a natural death, but left us a shaken party with the season unduly advanced.

But all the facts above enumerated were as nothing to the surprise which awaited us on the Barrier. I maintain that our arrangements for returning were quite adequate, and that no one in the world would have expected the temperatures and surfaces which we encountered at this time of the year. On the summit in lat. 85°, 86° we had −20, −30 [F]. On the Barrier in lat. 82°, 10,000 feet lower, we had −30 [F]

in the day, −47 [F] at night pretty regularly, with continuous head
wind during our day marches. It is clear that these circumstances
come on very suddenly, and our wreck is certainly due to this sudden
advent of severe weather, which does not seem to have any satisfactory cause. I do not think human beings ever came through such a
month as we have come through, and we should have got through
in spite of the weather but for the sickening of a second companion,
Captain Oates, and a shortage of fuel in the depots for which I cannot account, and finally, but for the storm which has fallen on us
within 11 miles [12.66 statute miles] of the depot at which we hoped
to secure our final supplies. Surely misfortune could scarcely have
exceeded this last blow. We arrived within 11 miles of our old One
Ton Camp with fuel for one last meal and food for two days. For four
days we have been unable to leave the tent—the gale blowing about
us. We are weak, writing is difficult, but for my own sake I do not
regret this journey, which has shown that Englishmen can endure
hardships, help one another, and meet death with as great a fortitude
as ever in the past. We took risks, we knew we took them; things have
come out against us, and therefore we have no cause for complaint,
but bow to the will of Providence, determined still to do our best to
the last. But if we have been willing to give our lives to this enterprise,
which is for the honor of our country, I appeal to our countrymen to
see that those who depend on us are properly cared for.

Had we lived, I should have had a tale to tell of the hardihood,
endurance, and courage of my companions which would have stirred
the heart of every Englishman. These rough notes and our dead
bodies must tell the tale, but surely, surely, a great rich country like
ours will see that those who are dependent on us are properly provided for. R. Scott[35]

Thus Scott's final message reveals his humanity, his defeat, his concern
for the families who would be left behind, and a series of contradictions. Although he says that they would have gotten through in spite of the weather,
he also says that the wreck is certainly due to the sudden advent of severe
weather. He begins by presenting an orderly list of numbered problems, then

shifts to a rambling text. It must be remembered that the writer was nearing the end of a month of unbelievable pain and hardship and was surely suffering from exposure and hypothermia. Indeed, it is remarkable that the message has any lucidity given the circumstances. But Scott's writings thus ended in a manner consistent with his leadership—inspiring yet surprising, incisive yet confusing. A bewildered world would take many different approaches to understanding the leader, his companions, and their fate in the decades that followed.

ELEVEN

The Anguish of Helplessness

The visitor returned to McMurdo with his sprained ankle in a stretch bandage. The soreness in his foot made the plane ride back from the Pole even less comfortable than the outbound trip, and he squirmed and fidgeted in his seat throughout the three-hour journey. But since arriving at McMurdo he has rested, staying mainly in bed for four days. While he lay in a warm bunk, he read Scott's diary. Now he has finished the book, and the pain in his ankle has subsided. A good friend and scientific colleague is due to arrive on today's flight from New Zealand, and the visitor leaves the comfort of his room to greet her. The woman gets off the vehicle bearing passengers in from the snow airfield. It is warm, near zero degrees Fahrenheit, and they take off their gloves to shake hands.

They walk across the station to the cafeteria for dinner. With these warm temperatures, the snow beneath their feet is slippery. The visitor treads carefully, limping slightly to favor his injured ankle. As they begin their meal, the visitor tells his friend that he wonders what really happened to Scott and his men. Perhaps their final and most fatal enemy was largely the very cold weather the polar party reported in March 1912, just as Scott said.

His friend listens attentively, then asks whether Scott could have faked the numbers. As she casually spears a fried shrimp from her plate, she suggests with a cynical laugh that Scott may have lied to make the fickle conditions provided by nature seem worse than the grim reality of his many startling errors.

The visitor is dumbfounded. He shakes his head in disbelief. It has come to this. So deeply rooted is the legend of Scott as a bumbler that today's Antarctican even doubts his truthfulness. His friend is only expressing the widespread cynicism regarding the story of Scott. It will do no good to tell her that it was Bowers and not Scott who took the meteorological data, for she does not understand how exceptional a man Bowers was. As the legend has cast its dark pall over the leader, so too has it thoroughly blotted out the stories of his remarkable companions. Bumbling has become a curiously contagious disease.

But there is one thing his friend will understand, hard evidence that the visitor himself has only now considered. "Cherry-Garrard," he says. His friend stares at him, uncomprehending. "Cherry-Garrard was on the Barrier waiting for the friends who never came. And he had another thermometer."

As January 1912 progressed at the Cape Evans base camp, the photographer Ponting scanned the horizon using his Zeiss lenses to search for the *Terra Nova*. Her masts were spotted on January 17, but it was not until February 3 that the vessel drew close enough for Meares to take a dog team out to communicate with the ship and to retrieve the mail that would bring their first news of the outside world in a year. Among the letters was one for the meteorologist Simpson, informing him that a colleague's illness had left the Indian meteorological office shorthanded. Simpson therefore would board the ship to return to his post in Simla to assist. Meares also decided to depart with the vessel, leaving only the young Russian Dimitri to care for the dogs.[1]

After sailing out of McMurdo Sound on March 5, 1912, the ship's company tried desperately to reach the northern party. This group of six men had encountered Amundsen at the Bay of Whales just over a year before. Because of Amundsen's unexpected presence on the eastern part of the Barrier, the team had returned to Cape Evans, then begun a series of forays along the coast to the north instead. The northern party would provide new geologic data, an independent set of meteorological measurements at a site away from the main Cape Evans base, and geographical surveys of new regions. At this moment, they were awaiting relief by the vessel in the region near Terra

Nova Bay, about two hundred miles from Cape Evans. But after nearly being frozen into the pack and under threat of being "crushed in the pressure of the incoming ice," the ship's crew was "reluctantly compelled to give up further efforts to relieve the party. . . . Course was laid for New Zealand." The northern party was left marooned for an entire Antarctic winter. They passed the terrible season buffeted by particularly strong winds and enduring great hardships as they struggled to survive on penguin and seal meat.[2]

The rescue of the scurvy-ridden Lieutenant Evans from the Barrier had occurred on February 20, just as Dr. Atkinson and Dimitri were preparing to trek south with the dogs. The primary goal of this journey was to speed the return of the polar party, perhaps even enough to allow Captain Scott to catch the ship. Although the men at Cape Evans could not yet know whether their own captain, or Amundsen, or both had attained the Pole the previous summer, they all knew that being the first to report the news of their exploration could be as important as the achievement itself. If Scott had indeed reached the Pole, then it was imperative that he return to tell of it as rapidly as possible. But the rescue of the gravely ill Lieutenant Evans changed both the date of departure and the composition of the dog-driving team. Atkinson believed that Evans's condition was very grave and told Cherry-Garrard that the lieutenant would surely have perished if two more days—perhaps even one—had passed without rescue. The doctor continued to care for Evans until the patient was invalided on board the ship before its departure from McMurdo Sound on March 5.[3]

On February 23 Atkinson sent Dimitri to Cape Evans from Hut Point. He carried a message to the effect that either the Canadian Wright or Cherry-Garrard would have to take Atkinson's place with the dog-team party, so that the doctor could remain with his scurvy-ridden patient. Atkinson did not know at this point that Simpson was also preparing to depart because of the unexpected news the mail had brought from India, and that Wright was therefore assuming all responsibility for several scientific measurements, particularly the unbroken record of Cape Evans meteorological observations. And so the responsibility to go with Dimitri onto the Barrier fell to a man with no prior experience of dog driving or of navigation—Cherry-Garrard. He was told to take food for man and dog and to travel to One Ton Camp as fast as possible.[4]

Captain Scott had explicitly ordered that the dogs not be risked in this last journey of the season. Men had tried and failed to reach the Pole before. In the event that neither Amundsen nor Scott had succeeded in 1911–12, the dogs would have been a critical part of a second attempt at the Pole in the next year, a point that Scott made clear in a letter to his agent in New Zealand, Kinsey: "We must . . . get to the South Pole, if not on the first attempt then at the second but the enterprise must not be relinquished till the work is done."[5]

Although the dogs were a key part of the grand plan for exploration, the events that led to a change of expedition leadership in the second year were unanticipated. With unforeseen circumstances precipitating the departures of both Lieutenant Evans and Simpson, Dr. Atkinson was now forced to issue commands as senior naval officer.[6] He surely did so believing that these duties would be short-lived. Undoubtedly, Captain Scott would return from the Barrier in just a few days or weeks.

Cherry-Garrard left Hut Point for the Barrier with Dimitri, two dog teams, and their fully loaded sledges on February 26 at 2 A.M. They carried enough dog biscuits for twenty-four days, along with food for themselves for twenty-one days. Like all other sledging journeys, this one was an opportunity to obtain a meteorological record away from the base camp, so the two men also had one of the expedition's sling thermometers. Its name to the contrary, "One Ton" had been largely depleted by this time, and the men also took critical stores of food for the polar party. If Scott's team had traveled as fast as the first and second return parties did down the glacier and over the Barrier, they would have reached One Ton Camp about thirty days after passing 86°S, or around March 5. Because Scott's sledge group was always the fastest, Cherry-Garrard feared that the polar party might already be past the depot and hence on the march without their full rations of food and fuel.[7]

Cherry-Garrard owned a personal sextant, for such expensive instruments were easily within his financial means.[8] But although the tool was of the highest quality, he knew that his own expertise in using it was sorely lacking. To his private diary he confided his excitement and fear, writing on February 26, "Well I'm off on my own for the first time—first time navigation and first time dog driving with thick weather . . . so it's not an easy beginning."

Figure 54. Apsley Cherry-Garrard at his typewriter in the hut at Cape Evans. Photograph by H. Ponting. Scott Polar Research Institute, Cambridge.

He was now in charge of a trek rather than just a participant in it, and he was twenty-six years old. On February 28 the classics and modern history major lamented, "Give me anything to do but navigation." During the long winter months he had spent a substantial portion of time at his typewriter editing the *South Polar Times,* the expedition news magazine that later became a classic chronicle of their saga; he may now have regretted not doing more navigation exercises instead. Wright was a scientist and an experienced navigator, well practiced in the detailed mathematical calculations needed to turn sextant readings into position information. But the dual demands of science and exploration had once again vied for the available human resources, and Wright's work with the meteorological data at the Cape Evans base was deemed more important than the dog sledge trip. After all, the journey was never intended as a rescue mission but was expected only to expedite Scott's return. Lieutenant Evans later wrote that he believed that Scott himself would have chosen to keep the young physicist at the base camp, given the importance of his scientific responsibilities there. And so on February 29 an exasperated Cherry-Garrard again wrote in his private diary: "This navigation is very anxious work indeed."[9]

The dogs pulled well on the first day, covering thirty-four miles. But the sledgemeters were not working quite as they should, further adding to Cherry-Garrard's anxieties about finding his way. By the end of the day on February 29 they had covered ninety miles, and on the night of March 3, after a journey of less than a week, they reached One Ton, relieved to have arrived before the polar party. It was cold and Dimitri became concerned about the dogs, which were growing thin and losing their coats. The two men decided to increase the dogs' rations of biscuit.[10] Though probably necessary to safeguard the dogs' health, this decision reduced the time that could be spent on the Barrier, either waiting for the polar party to arrive or driving farther south to seek them.

Cherry-Garrard now had to consider what to do. Out on the Barrier were his two great friends, Bowers and Wilson, with whom he had endured the winter journey to Cape Crozier and whom he credited with saving his own life. He assumed that Captain Scott, Oates, and seaman Evans were with them, although as the sun emerged on the morning of March 4, Cherry-Garrard's first day at One Ton, seaman Evans had already been dead for more than two weeks. There was some wind at One Ton, and Cherry-Garrard feared that "the chance of seeing another party at any distance was nil." He also confided a crushing burden to his diary on March 2: "I am afraid if it gets very cold that I shall not be able to wear spectacles." He knew that cold conditions would render him virtually blind, as they had on the winter journey to Cape Crozier. As temperatures plunged, a pervasive fog would condense on his glasses from the moisture of his own skin and breath. Like today's bespectacled visitors to the Antarctic, he probably tried to breath very shallowly in a futile effort to avoid the condensation. But the problem is an inescapable one in still air at cold temperatures. On the winter journey he had been led by Bowers and Wilson, but now it was he leading the effort to find them. Much of the time, he was forced to rely on Dimitri to find the way.[11]

Rather than drive south and risk missing the polar party, he waited at the depot, hoping that they would appear on the white horizon outside the tent. As night fell on March 5, he recorded a temperature of −34 °F, though it had been warmer when the wind was blowing. Scott and the polar party were then near 81°S, about one hundred miles away, and they recorded a similar minimum temperature of −37.5 °F that day. Scott described their progress as a slow "plod on our weary way, cold and very miserable, although outwardly cheerful." Calm weather on March 8 brought evening temperatures down to −37 °F at One Ton, as documented by Cherry-Garrard, while on the Barrier at 80°45′S, Bowers recorded a temperature of −38.5 °F. That day Scott wrote, "God help us indeed. We are in a very bad way." [12] On the same day, Cherry-Garrard wrote in his diary, "It is a very cold wait—waiting & thinking. I was so sure I saw them coming last night I nearly started to walk to them." [13] But the polar party was still about eighty miles away from One Ton Camp, far out of sight even for a man with excellent vision. Although high mountains can often be seen with surprising clarity at a distance on clear days in Antarctica, visibility on the nearly flat Barrier surface is seldom much more than about ten miles. It is more often far less, especially when cold conditions produce ice crystals suspended in the air near the ground. Cherry-Garrard's image must have been another of the many mirages that dance across the snow—the product of temperature gradients, reflection, and, sometimes, human hope.

Cherry-Garrard had no way of knowing of the terrible hardships the polar party was now suffering, nor how close they were. Scott had said that he expected to be back by March 27, so perhaps the dog team had gone out much too early to meet them. There was plenty of food in the depots; indeed, the polar party was not suffering from lack of food at this time. Although Cherry-Garrard did not know it, they were, however, already short of the precious oil needed to warm their food and melt their water.[14]

As the dog biscuits ran out, Cherry-Garrard pondered the question of whether to go farther south to search for the polar party by killing some of the dogs to feed others. Although he didn't know it, the dogs could have reached the polar party in just two or three days of driving south. But that would have been strictly against his orders, and with no dog food left, the return would have been problematic at best. At this point, he "felt little anxiety for the Polar Party," a view shared by the more experienced Evans, who wrote that "there was never any anxiety felt for the Southern party until after March 10. They themselves never imagined they would reach Hut Point before that time. . . . It was not considered likely that the Southern party would fail." Cherry-

Garrard was now completely dependent on his companion, for "the glasses which I must wear are almost impossible, because of fogging." Dimitri had begun to feel ill from the cold shortly after arrival at One Ton, and by this point the young Russian reported difficulty in movement on his right side.[15]

Out of dog food, nearly blind at times, and therefore completely dependent on a sick companion, Cherry-Garrard took a temperature measurement at 8 A.M. on March 10 of −33.5°F. His friend Bowers recorded similarly chilling conditions of −35°F that morning, a little more than seventy miles away at 80°31′S. Cherry-Garrard packed up the sledges and turned north for home shortly thereafter, leaving the food he had brought for the polar party stowed at the depot.[16]

The hungry dogs were hard to control on the return journey, and Dimitri's condition seemed to be getting worse. The party encountered a blizzard on March 11, and a bewildered Cherry-Garrard wrote that "we did not know where we were going. . . . I think we were turning circles most of the time." They camped to wait for the wind to die out. As the weather cleared on the morning of March 13, the welcome sight of Ross Island came into view. Even without navigation, they could now follow easy landmarks home.[17]

Another blizzard stopped them on March 15, but the two men and their dogs finally reached Hut Point late in the afternoon of March 16, 1912.[18] Out on the Barrier to the south a few hours later, Oates left the tent never to return.

Atkinson was alarmed at the desperate state in which the dog sledge party returned to Hut Point. The dogs were "frostbitten, miserably thin. . . . In many cases their harnesses were iced up and frozen to them." He also wrote that Cherry-Garrard's condition caused serious alarm. The doctor took pains to note that "Cherry-Garrard under the circumstances and according to his instructions was in my judgment quite right in everything that he did. I am absolutely certain no other officer of the Expedition could have done better." Lieutenant Evans also emphasized that "Cherry-Garrard very properly remained at One Ton camp" rather than driving the dogs south to seek the polar party.[19] Orders were orders at the turn of the twentieth century, especially for a junior man such as young Cherry-Garrard.

Within a few days of the dog teams' return, Atkinson began to plan another journey to try to reach the polar party. He and Cherry-Garrard discussed whether to start on March 22 or March 27. The dogs were in no shape to be taken out again, and this trip, like so many others, would have to rely solely upon the strength of men. But Cherry-Garrard could not be part of this next effort. The doctor wrote that "three days after his return from the Barrier, Cherry-Garrard collapsed. . . . It was a very sad blow to him to realize that he was unable to help during this anxious time, and it was a hard measure to have to tell him that further sledging that year was impossible for him." [20] The doctor determined to go himself, with a single seaman as companion.

On the night of March 26 the men at Hut Point heard five or six knocks on the window. They sprang to their feet, sure that the polar party had returned. But no one was there, and they concluded that the unearthly sound must have been a dog's tail hitting the window. The next day, Atkinson and seaman Keohane left on the last brave attempt to reach the polar party. They went only as far as Corner Camp on the edge of the Barrier, where they depoted more provisions. Although they recorded relatively mild temperatures above $-15\,°F$, it was cold with just two men in a tent normally shared by four. Before turning back on March 30, Atkinson wrote, "At this date in my own mind I was morally certain that the party had perished." Atkinson and Keohane arrived back at Hut Point on April 1. A few days later Cherry-Garrard wrote: "We have got to face it now. The Pole Party will not in all probability ever · get back. And there is no more that we can do." [21]

The tireless doctor also made a last-ditch attempt to aid the northern party, leading a group of four men out onto the frozen sea on April 13. But when the ice before them broke up on April 20, they laid a depot of food in the hope that the others might eventually reach it, then returned to Hut Point. While this relief party struggled to reach their missing comrades, Cherry-Garrard was left alone at the *Discovery* hut for four days. Isolated and perhaps becoming despondent, Cherry-Garrard became so weak that he could only crawl on hands and knees around the cold, empty hut, trying to alleviate his pain with morphia.[22]

A few times in the next several weeks the men thought they spied a party arriving on the ice. But the image always proved to be a seal or a mirage. The sun sank below the horizon for the last time that season on April 23, not to reemerge until the following spring.[23] The enveloping darkness of another long Antarctic winter had begun.

Whether from physical damage brought on by the ravages of the trip on the Barrier or from the mental agonies of grief and guilt at the loss of his friends, Cherry-Garrard began a battle with illness in early 1912 that was to continue throughout much of his life. His lack of knowledge of navigation and his nearsightedness likely tormented him as he lived and relived the agonizing question of what else he could have done, or whether someone else could have done more.

Although he could not reach his beloved friends, his journey to One Ton Camp bore important fruit in the form of the meteorological measurements he recorded. He provided proof beyond reasonable doubt that temperatures had indeed been persistently below $-30\,°F$ while the polar party waged their desperate struggle to return. But the import of the scientific data recorded as he waited in vain on the Barrier was not fully revealed until many decades after Cherry-Garrard joined his friends in death (see Chapter 13).[24]

Just as Atkinson returned to Hut Point from the last attempt to reach the polar party on April 1, the *Terra Nova* arrived at Akaroa Harbor in New Zealand. Ponting expressed doubts whether "it is possible for anyone to appreciate the glorious beauty of leafy trees and pasture-clad hills, bathed in the warm rays of the sun, as could those who had just returned from a year's existence in the barren, blizzard-swept ice and lava wildernesses of the Antarctic."[25]

But the uplifting effect of the green landscape was brief, for the crew of the *Terra Nova* "all felt much disappointed" when they learned in New Zealand what the outside world had already known for weeks: Amundsen had beaten their captain to the Pole. Amundsen had returned to his base camp on January 25, 1912. He set sail on January 30 and arrived in Hobart, Tasmania, on March 7.[26] By March 8 the Manchester *Dispatch* and other newspapers had reported the outcome of the quest for the South Pole.

Before leaving New Zealand, Amundsen visited Lieutenant Evans, who was recovering from scurvy in Christchurch. Evans later wrote that "Captain Amundsen . . . expressed his wonder at our performance—and in his modest way he told me that he himself could never have man-hauled as Scott's men did."[27]

Evans returned to the United Kingdom to attend to the business affairs of the expedition, not knowing that Scott had perished on the Barrier. In

THE ANGUISH OF HELPLESSNESS

the summer of 1912 at Cardiff, King George V and Queen Mary summoned Evans on board the royal yacht. The king promoted him on the spot, making him the youngest commander then in the Royal Navy.[28] When interviewed a few weeks later by the *Daily Graphic*, Commander Evans said: "I expect that Scott reached the Pole two weeks after I left him. I imagine he probably returned to Hut Point about March 10, 1912, just too late to send back his final news by the Terra Nova. The organization of the southern journey was splendid, every detail having been thought out by Captain Scott." In November 1912, Evans returned to New Zealand to take command of the *Terra Nova* for the relief voyage back to Antarctica and to bring the remaining expedition members home, still not knowing that the members of the polar party would not be among them.

Blizzards kept the sea ice unstable in the vicinity of Hut Point throughout April 1912. Not until May 1 did Atkinson, Dimitri, and Cherry-Garrard finally leave the safety of the hut to trek across the uncertain ice back to Cape Evans.[29]

Two new men had joined for the expedition's last year as nine departed on the ship, and seven well-trained mules had been sent down by the Indian government as requested. Unlike the ponies that had preceded them, the mules were in excellent condition. They would bear heavy burdens in the sledging journey of the coming spring. Additional dogs were also brought. In spite of the hardships faced by the eleven continuing members of the expedition, or perhaps because of them, the company again enjoyed a winter characterized by "good fellowship."[30]

One bright spot in this second winter came from science. The Australian geologist Debenham found fossils of plants and marine animals in the rocks that had been brought back by the first return party from the Beardmore glacier. This news "gave great joy to the company," just as examination of similar rocks had been among Wilson's last delights on February 8.[31]

Still, the men were confronted by the sad outcome of the explorations of the expedition. Most believed that the polar party had probably met their end on the Beardmore glacier, tumbling into one of the huge crevasses that the other teams had so narrowly avoided. Lashly thought that they might have succumbed to scurvy.[32]

The men at Cape Evans now faced a terrible choice, between seeking the northern party or trying to find the remains of the polar party; there were not enough men to attempt both journeys. After dinner on midwinter's day of 1912, Dr. Atkinson called the members of the expedition together to discuss alternatives. He expressed his own view that they ought to seek the polar party, as "it was of great importance not to leave the record of the Expedition incomplete, with one of its most striking chapters a blank." If the polar party could not be found, it was doubtful that their fate would ever be known. Nor could it even be determined whether they had achieved their goal of reaching the Pole, for it would likely be many years, if ever, before another expedition would come close to that "awful place" at the bottom of the world. Debenham wrote, "We owe it to England, to the expedition, to the relatives, and to the memory of the men themselves to find out what has happened." [33]

The alternative was to try to cross the dangerously unstable ice and trek up the coast to seek the northern party. Some men felt that those might have been picked up already by the *Terra Nova* just before the vessel left for New Zealand in the previous season, while others pointed out that the risks on the ice would be doubled by a rescue party's traveling north and back. Furthermore, the ship would soon arrive and could rescue a coastal party more safely. [34]

A vote was taken, and although Atkinson wrote that "officers and men unanimously supported the decision to go south," others recorded that one man did abstain. Wright speculated that the abstaining vote was Cherry-Garrard's. If this was so, the latter never explicitly stated it. But Cherry-Garrard did describe the painful process of the vote, writing, "It is impossible to express and almost impossible to imagine how difficult it was to make this decision." And many weeks before, Cherry-Garrard and Atkinson had privately discussed the matter of what to do in the next spring as they were walking back to Cape Evans from Hut Point on May 1. At that time, Cherry-Garrard said that he preferred to seek the northern party because "it seemed to me unthinkable that we should leave live men to search for those who were dead." [35] Perhaps Cherry-Garrard was a man ahead of his time who approached the issue with a logical rather than romantically loyal bent. Or perhaps he dreaded the prospect of the knowledge that the search ultimately did reveal—that the polar party had not perished in a crevasse on the distant

Beardmore glacier but had succumbed only a few miles away from One Ton Camp while he had helplessly waited for their arrival.

On October 29, 1912, seven mules and eight men left Cape Evans to begin the search. Among them were Wright, Lashly, and seamen Keohane and Crean. A few days later, Dr. Atkinson, Cherry-Garrard, and Dimitri followed with two dog teams. Wright felt cold in his sleeping bag; upon inspecting it, he realized that it was riddled with more than thirty holes. Thus the men again suffered sleepless and frigid nights in icy sleeping bags, as they had on previous sledging journeys, and the mules ate the ropes of their tethers just as the ponies had done before them.[36]

The search party reached One Ton Camp on the morning of November 11. There they found that some of the food stores left by Cherry-Garrard and Dimitri the previous March were soaked in paraffin and therefore inedible, though there was no evidence of a hole or other flaw in the tin cans that contained the oil.[37] The mystery of the leaking oil cans was to take on greater importance when they learned of the polar party's shortage of fuel in their final desperate weeks.

It was Wright who spied something protruding from the snow surface as he marched across the Barrier the next day. At first he wasn't sure what the object was, and he left the mule party to walk a half-mile to investigate. When he reached the spot, he realized that he was seeing the very tip of a tent protruding from a mound of snow. Had there been just six more inches of drift that winter, the polar party's remains, their diaries, and photographs might never have been found.[38]

Seaman Keohane wrote: "We knew at least some of our comrades lay sleeping. After digging for some time we uncovered the tent and found only 3 of them in it so then we knew that trouble must have started early on the return march. The sledge was about four to five feet down."[39] Atkinson and Lashly were the first to enter the tent. Wilson and Bowers appeared to have died in their sleep. In contrast, Scott was partly out of his bag, with an arm thrown over Wilson. Dr. Atkinson emphasized in his official report that "certainly . . . they all died natural deaths." The tough old seaman Lashly emerged from the scene in tears.[40]

The search party removed the diaries, letters, and other gear from the tent.

They recovered the thirty-five pounds of geologic specimens that had been dragged to the very last from the sledge. Atkinson read aloud from the diaries to the men, who learned of the earlier deaths of seaman Evans and Oates.[41]

The search party did not remove the bodies, choosing instead to leave them there in "the most fitting tomb in the world." They removed the bamboos and allowed the tent to drape over their lifeless comrades. Then they built a large snow cairn above them and erected a cross out of two skis to place on top. They recited a burial service and placed a note on top of the cairn:

> This cross and cairn are erected over the bodies of Capt. Scott, C. V. O., R. N., Doctor E. A. Wilson, M. B., B. C., Cantab., and Lieutenant H. R. Bowers, Royal Indian Marine—a slight token to perpetuate their successful and gallant attempt to reach the Pole. This they did on January 17, 1912, after the Norwegian expedition had already done so. Inclement weather with lack of fuel was the cause of their death. Also to commemorate their two gallant comrades, Captain L. E. G. Oates of the Inniskilling Dragoons, who walked to his death in a blizzard to save his comrades about eighteen miles south of this position; also of Seaman Edgar Evans, who died at the foot of the Beardmore Glacier. The Lord gave and the Lord taketh away; blessed be the name of the Lord.

The note was signed by all members of the search party.[42]

They spent the night next to the tent, and Keohane wrote: "We had no sleep last night but thinking of our poor comrades laying in the snow grave a hundred yards away." Then they continued on their southward trek, trying to find Captain Oates's remains. They found his sleeping bag, which had been brought north by Scott, Wilson, and Bowers. They also found his personal bag containing his theodolite, socks, and fur boots. One of the boots had been cut fully open across the front, telling its own poignant tale of the terrible swelling and pain of the dragoon's feet. But when they drew close to the spot where he had left the tent, seaman Keohane realized that Oates himself had long since been deeply covered by snow and that "looking for a body here you may as well look for a needle in a hayfield." The search party

Figure 55. The snow cairn erected by the search party at the site of Scott's last camp. Photographer unknown. Scott Album, number 2934, Alexander Turnbull Library, Wellington, New Zealand.

constructed a snow cairn near the spot where Oates was believed to have died, and topped it with a cross and another note: "Hereabouts died a very gallant gentleman, Captain L. E. G. Oates of the Inniskilling Dragoons. In March 1912, returning from the Pole, he walked willingly to his death in a blizzard, to try and save his comrades, beset by hardships. This note is left by the Relief Expedition of 1912."[43]

As he turned north, the doctor was already contemplating what route to take to try to reach the northern party as soon as possible. But when the searchers reached Hut Point on November 25, they were met with the "best news that any men could wish for many, many a long weary day." The entire northern party had survived the winter and made their own way back to Hut Point. They arrived on November 6 at the hut, where they left a note before continuing on to Cape Evans. When he rejoined his fellows at the base camp,

Cherry-Garrard wrote: "It is the happiest day for nearly a year—almost the only happy one." [44]

Commander Evans brought the *Terra Nova* back to Cape Evans on January 18, 1913. He spotted a member of the northern party on the beach and "was overjoyed, for I feared more on [their] behalf than on the others [Scott's party]." He shouted to the man on shore, asking whether all were well, only to learn that the polar party had perished. Then, "slowly and with infinite sadness the flags were lowered from the mastheads and Scott's little *Terra Nova* stood bareheaded at the Gate of the Great Ice Barrier." [45]

A large wooden cross was constructed of Australian wood. It was engraved with the names of Scott, Wilson, Bowers, Oates, and Evans and placed at the top of Observation Hill, overlooking Hut Point. Commander Evans took formal charge of the expedition as the surviving senior officer, and on January 26, 1913, he and his men finally sailed away from the southern continent. As they "watched the familiar rocky snow-capped shores fast disappearing from view . . . some of us must have realized that these ice-girt rocks and mountains were not meant for human beings to associate their lives with." [46]

Evans endured one more personal tragedy before the expedition was over. His wife, Hilda, was reunited with him in New Zealand, only to contract peritonitis and die on board a passenger liner a few months later, during her return journey to England. [47]

As Evans turned away from the stark land in which "disaster overtook our expedition," he predicted, "It is doubtful if ever the great inland plateau will be re-visited, except perhaps by aeroplane." [48] Although he could not conceive that humans would deliberately seek to re-create the hardships that he and others had undergone for the sake of exploration and science, before the twentieth century drew to a close, latter-day adventurers had trekked from the coast to the Pole by dog sled and ski. As he perceptively surmised, airplanes eventually did come, and in about a half-century there was a manned station at the South Pole in which people lived and worked comfortably year-round at the bottom of the world.

TWELVE

In Search of Explanations

The visitor gazes past McMurdo Sound to the sculpted outline of White Island on the edge of the Barrier. It is cold today, about −35°F, and he waves his arms and stamps the ground in an effort to get warm. He has been outside moving small boxes full of scientific equipment for an hour. His last task of the day is to drag a big container of computer paper from the outdoor storage area into the lab. The two hundred–pound cardboard box is mounted on a wooden pallet, and he pulled it easily across the snow by himself two months ago on a warm Antarctic summer afternoon when the temperature hovered near plus ten degrees. But today the box remains motionless as the visitor heaves on the thick rope attached to its base. He braces himself and pulls even harder, but manages only a few inches of movement. The wooden slats have no glide at all on the frigid snow. He walks behind the box, listening to the loud squeak of his steps on the dry and intractable surface. He notices that the snow gleams where the sunlight glints on the razor-sharp edges of its crystal facets. Some frost was laid down last night, when it was even colder. Those delicate crystals are now behaving like sandpaper. The texture, the sound, and the look of the snow have all been transformed as the temperature has dropped.

From behind the box, the visitor pushes to the very limit of his strength and is rewarded by a gain of nearly six inches. He grunts with effort as he slowly moves the pallet a few inches at a time toward the door to the lab. It took only five minutes to put the box into storage two months ago, but today it takes half an hour of strenuous work to cover a distance of only twenty feet.

He feels a trickle of sweat run down his cheek, and he realizes that he must get inside and get dry before his face is frostbitten. He heaves against the box with greater urgency.

This is the hardest labor he has done in a long time, and his muscles will be sore tomorrow. As he crosses the last few inches before the door into the warm laboratory, he reflects on Scott's descriptions of the awesome challenge of man-hauling hundreds of pounds of supplies tied onto a wooden sledge across the Antarctic vastness on a similarly cold day in the last weeks of his march back from the Pole. Didn't he say that the surface was awful, the cold intense, the men at the limit of their endurance without a favorable wind from behind?

The visitor shakes his head at his own ignorant failure to truly grasp until today the enormity of the task that Scott and his men faced in the twilight of their lives, as they pulled their supplies across the Barrier in March of 1912.

News of Scott's death reached England on February 12, 1913. The reporting and editorials of the day reflect the grief that spread rapidly throughout a stunned nation. The *Times* of London announced: "News reached London last night that Captain Scott and four of his companions in the expedition which set out for the Antarctic on board the *Terra Nova* in 1910 have lost their lives. One has to go a long way back in the history of British exploring enterprise to find any disaster of like magnitude" (February 13). The *Daily Mail*'s account read: "For the great proof which they have given by their bearing in the closing hours of their lives that the metal of our race still rings true upon the touchstone of death Englishmen owe an everlasting debt to Captain Scott and his fellow heroes" (February 12). Oates's noble effort to increase his companions' odds of survival received special homage: "In all the pages of heroism which brighten the history of England, none is finer than the tale of the death of Captain Lawrence Edward Grace Oates, of the Inniskilling dragoons" (*Daily Mail*, February 12).

Popular magazine articles extolled the heroism and suffering of Scott and his men many times in the months and years to follow. One of these stressed "the supreme manliness of character that he exhibited throughout his life and in the moments of his lonely death."[1] A fund drive addressed Scott's dying request that dependents be provided for. Each of the families received support that exceeded their dead loved one's annual salaries. Seaman Evans's wife and three young children—Norman, Muriel, and Ralph, aged seven, five, and four—were not forgotten in this key financial matter (*Daily Mirror*, May 21, 1913). But Victorian class structure apparently did exclude Mrs. Evans from a reception involving wives and mothers of the deceased at Buckingham Palace.[2]

After the shocked grief of the first few years came decades of analysis and reanalysis. Adulation vied with condemnation, curiously commingled as a frustrated world struggled to form a picture of the personal qualities of Scott himself, his actions, and his motivations.[3] As the twentieth century drew to a close, Scott's legacy continued to alternate between courageous pioneer and incompetent mismanager, as biographical books and films presented conflicting portraits of the man, his interactions with others, and his successes and problems.[4]

Cherry-Garrard died in 1959. He therefore lived long enough to hear the caustic views of some of the critics, and even to bear their brunt concerning the issue of whether he might have saved the polar party by driving south with the dogs instead of waiting at One Ton Camp. He hardly needed others to raise this agonizing question, which had tormented him from the moment it became clear that Scott and the others were dead. The depths of his soul-searching led to his own account of the expedition, entitled *The Worst Journey in the World*, published in 1922, and a brief *Postscript to the Worst Journey*, self-published in 1951. In the *Postscript* he wrote: "It is difficult for those who have never been to the Antarctic to write about it." He also said: "We know more now than we did then."[5] As Cherry-Garrard suggested, in seeking to understand Scott, his men, and their fates, we turn here to two primary and fundamental sources: first, to the writings of those who were there, and second, to nearly a century of human experience and scientific understanding of Antarctica and exploration that has been gained since their deaths.

What did Scott himself contribute to his legacy? Scott's journals present deeply personal and lyrical impressions of the vast forbidding continent. He wrote of

> the eternal silence of the great white desert. Cloudy columns of snow drift advancing from the south, pale yellow wraiths, heralding the coming storm, blotting out one by one the sharp-cut lines of the land. The blizzard, Nature's protest—the crevasse, Nature's pitfall— that grim trap for the unwary—no hunter could conceal his snare so perfectly—the light rippled snow bridge gives no hint or sign of the hidden danger, its position unguessable till man or beast is floundering, clawing and struggling for foothold on the brink. The vast silence is broken only by the mellow sounds of the marching column.

But Scott's choices of phrase were sometimes more shocking than evocative. In a letter written to Sir Francis Bridgeman, under whom he had served in the navy, Scott said: "I want to tell you that I was not too old for this job. It was the younger men that went under first." After seaman Evans died, Scott acknowledged that his passing was "a help to the commissariat" in terms of food supplies, and in his message to the public, Scott wrote of the big seaman's collapse as "the astonishing failure of the man whom we had least expected to fail."[6]

Scott was sometimes prone to exaggeration. On December 2 and 3, 1911, he emphasized that Shackleton had experienced a month of fine weather between November 15 and December 15, omitting mention of the blizzard that kept that rival explorer and his men from advancing at all just a few days earlier, November 8–9, 1908. Scott lamented that "with us a fine day has been the exception so far" and that "our luck in weather is preposterous. . . . It makes me feel a little bitter to contrast such weather with that experienced by our predecessors."[7] Critics have been quick to point out that Scott's luck in the weather to this point appeared to be normal.[8] Scott's complaints during relatively kind and typical Antarctic conditions fueled widespread skepticism regarding his assessments of the weather, including in particular his description of the last frigid weeks on the Barrier. To those inclined to a positive view, his musings might be dismissed as the brooding worries of a sensitive man. But to those more negatively disposed, such statements could provide ample

Figure 56. Captain Scott in his den at the Cape Evans hut. Photograph by H. Ponting. Scott Album, number 11384, Alexander Turnbull Library, Wellington, New Zealand.

ammunition to condemn him as a whiner or worse. Scott's own writings thus raised questions about his decisions, actions, and protestations.

As the legend of Scott's gaffes grew, even the issue of whether he was largely esteemed or disliked by his men became subject to question.[9] Some men did report personality conflicts. In a letter to his mother dated October 24, 1911, Oates expressed anger and resentment, writing, "I dislike Scott intensely." Oates also reported disharmony between Meares and Scott, which may have precipitated Meares's departure on the ship the following February.[10] This discord may have indirectly led to Scott's death, for the experienced dog driver Meares, rather than Cherry-Garrard, would otherwise likely have gone to the Barrier with Dimitri. The Canadian Wright also expressed his fury at Scott over not being chosen to continue on the polar journey in December 1911, and his diary documents personal differences with Lieutenant Evans.[11] But it would be more remarkable if there were no such private declarations of frustration among a party alone in the Antarctic than if there were a few. There were also indications of conflict within Amundsen's team—problems so profound that they apparently affected the choice of who would take part in the journey to the Pole.[12] A doctor who walked to the Pole with one companion in 1993 described the anger and resentments that flew furiously and openly between the two as a problem that rivaled their physical challenges.[13] A group of three men skied "in the footsteps of Scott" from Ross Island to the South Pole in 1985. Although they walked Scott's path, by their own admission their interpersonal relations bore little resemblance to those of the Victorians they sought to emulate, becoming instead a "microcosm of human pettiness," in which intense conflicts arose.[14] In contrast, the overwhelming majority of Scott's men expressed a profound personal admiration for their leader, even a devotion far beyond that which would merely be seemly. As he waited for the pack ice to break up while the ship sailed south in December of 1910, Bowers, for example, found time to write a private letter to his mother in which he said: "Captain Scott who has to face all the anxiety and worry of things is splendid—he never shows it and is geniality itself always. You could not imagine a more congenial leader, or one that inspires more confidence."[15]

Like some of today's visitors to the Antarctic, Oates seemed to suffer more than others from the blackness of polar winter, telling his mother in a letter describing that dark season, "The winter here was wretched although we got on very well together. . . . You will not catch me doing another Antarctic winter if I can help it," and "Life here is so monotonous." Week after week of unending dark, like the cold, affects some people far more than others, and has been the source of more than one feud at an Antarctic station. The return of the sun certainly affected Oates's spirits, prompting him to tell his mother just a few weeks later, "We have quite a nice day for a change. . . . It was so nice and sunny out that I almost felt like staying another year." Even the taciturn Oates recognized that "when a man is having a hard time he says hard things about other people which he would regret afterwards."[16]

Some of the surviving members of the expedition offered both high praise and carefully considered criticism in the years after Scott's death. In 1926 Priestley, the geologist who had survived the ghastly winter faced by Scott's northern party, deemed the decision to take five men on to the Pole instead of the original four "a grave mistake" that he assigned a large role in their deaths. In criticizing this fateful act, however, he also wrote: "What Scott's motives were we can only guess: doubtless they were high." Priestley expanded on this view thirty-six years later, writing that the decision "illustrated . . . one of the more lovable, if one of the weaker, elements in Scott's character. He was very human in his loves and in his prejudices. At the last moment he had to choose three out of four good men and found this choice impossible to make."[17]

Lieutenant Evans had abandoned a planned expedition of his own to serve as Scott's second.[18] It has been suggested that his appointment to the *Terra Nova* expedition was aimed mainly at subsuming him as a possible rival.[19] But the putative rival who might have led his own assault on the Pole wrote, "No living man could have taken Scott's place effectively as leader of our expedition—there was none other like him. He was the Heart, Brain, and Master," a powerful statement of praise, particularly coming nearly a decade after Scott's death. Each reader of this statement must decide whether these are the genuine feelings of the remarkable man who barely escaped from the H of Hell. Some evidence of Evans's honesty is provided by other statements in which the lieutenant openly acknowledged that errors had indeed been made. In particular, as he reflected on his own role in the expedition and his near-fatal brush with scurvy, he expressed mild criticism of his treatment: "I had done too much on the outward journey, what with the effects of the spring sledge journey, too much had been asked of me." Cherry-Garrard independently voiced the same notion, remarking that "every emergency was met by calling for volunteers. . . . Volunteering was relied on not only for emergencies, but also for a good deal of everyday work that should have been organized as routine and the inevitable result was that the willing . . . were overworked. . . . Men were allowed to do too much, and were told afterwards that they had done too much; and that is not discipline."[20]

The prodigious demands on the expedition's company were in part a result of its diversity of goals in both science and exploration. As Cherry-Garrard wrote, "Wilson wanted to obtain the egg of the Emperor penguin: a horribly dangerous and inhumanly exhausting feat which is none the less impracticable because the three men who achieved it survived by a miracle." The same three men, Bowers, Wilson, and Cherry-Garrard, were called upon repeatedly—as key players in the depot journey, in the polar journey, and, in Cherry-Garrard's case, ultimately in the agonizing dog journey, a failed search to save the other two and their companions. As Cherry-Garrard said, "We took on the work of two or three expeditions."[21]

Scott's personal interests and talents provided a portion of the fuel for this damaging diversity of purpose. Shackleton believed that attainment of the Pole was Scott's "heart's desire, and the desire of his countrymen" (*The Standard*, November 29, 1909). But enthusiasm for science also ran strong in Scott. His intellect apparently won the deep respect of many if not all of *Terra Nova*'s scientific staff. One of them wrote of Scott as a man who "was, before everything, a scientist," and another credited Scott as "quicker to see the weak link in a chain of argument than any man I have ever met."[22] Scott's diaries are replete with absorption in the work and findings of the scientists. After Wilson's lecture on Antarctic flying birds, Scott mused over why petrels are often white in color. After Simpson's lecture on auroras, Scott pondered their movement and origin.[23] Scott was chosen to command the *Discovery* expedition by Clements Markham because of these very profound and unusual strengths. But exploration was nevertheless the primary goal, as well as being a far more potent magnet for funds than science alone could ever have been. Scott perforce had to fulfill many different and challenging roles, and he did so with the eyes of both his men and the world upon him.

Scott, Bowers, and Wilson were still carrying thirty-five pounds of geologic specimens when they died. Were these rocks indicative of scientific dedication or of fatally poor judgment by the leader? Cherry-Garrard pointed out that "the practical man of the world has plenty of criticism of the way things were done. . . . He is scandalized because . . . geological specimens were deliberately added to the weight of the sledge that was dragging the life out of the men who had to haul it; but he does not realize that it is the friction surfaces of the snow on the runners which mattered and not the dead weight, which in this case was almost negligible." The weight of the rocks was only a small fraction of the total the polar party had to drag behind them on every step: the tent, cooker, food, oil, sleeping bags, and other essential goods typically accounted for more that two hundred pounds.[24] More important, the writings as well as contemporary physical studies demonstrate that the difficulty or ease of sledge dragging is governed primarily not by the weight carried on the sledge but by the character of the snow, especially under cold, windless conditions with recent hoarfrost. The weight of the rocks would have taken on a different meaning in other, more normal environments. But Scott and his companions were traveling in one of the most extreme corners of the world, where thirty-five pounds of geological samples were a drop in a bucket controlled by friction.

And was the day spent collecting those rocks an act of poor judgment at a time when all possible speed should have been directed toward a homeward push that might have allowed them to reach One Ton Camp, or was it a compassionate attempt to allow the desperately ill seaman Evans to get the rest that might have renewed his strength? No one can know the answer for certain, because those who were present on that fateful day all perished, but again we find Lieutenant Evans in staunch support of the captain beyond the call of loyalty, stating that "Evans . . . was rested on the Beardmore glacier, Oates looking after him while the others made a halt for a geographical investigation." [25]

The scientific side of Scott spurred his interest in the technology of the motor sledges. The descendants of these new and innovative machines eventually proved their great worth in polar regions. One even saved the life of Adm. Richard Byrd. The admiral tried to winter alone on the Barrier in 1934 to obtain meteorological measurements. But he waged a battle with carbon monoxide poisoning, probably from his generator and stove. Ultimately, the admiral was saved from a choice between certain death by chemical or by cold only through his telegraph link to his main base and a daring overland mission in a vehicle like today's Snowcats.[26] But years of technological improvements were required before this dramatic rescue could occur, and Scott's early "motors" helped to lay some of the critical groundwork. Shackleton also took motorized vehicles, but it was with Scott's expedition that the step forward from ordinary round wheels to revolving tracks occurred, allowing the vehicles to negotiate such uneven terrain as sastrugi.[27] The engines of these early vehicles, however, proved to be no match for the extreme conditions, clanking past only about fifty of the nine hundred miles to the Pole from the Cape Evans base before breaking down from the cycle of overheating followed by exposure to intense cold.

The *Yorkshire Post* of March 15, 1910, indicated Scott's initial delight and hopes for the motors after testing them on snowy surfaces in Norway before the start of the *Terra Nova* expedition: "He was so satisfied with the behavior of the motor sledges that he anticipated ordering one or two more. He and his wife paid a visit to Fefor, a mountain plateau 2800 feet above the sea. . . . The motor sledge was tried on the ski running slopes with great success, drawing [1900 pounds] easily over soft snow." Furs and skins were procured on the same trip but received only brief mention (*Manchester Guardian*, March 15, 1910). Did Scott the scientist focus on these fascinating tests of the innovative motor sledges rather than on the all-essential furs and skins? In the following year, his men suffered through night after sleepless night in icy, clammy sleeping bags. Some would complain that the furs of the sleeping bags and boots seemed to lose their hair readily. While all reindeer fur sheds to some degree, Amundsen declared that excessive loss of hair is a symptom of poor selection of skins. Shackleton documented the same problem in his book published in 1909—a book studied by Scott. Shackleton wrote: "We selected skins for the sleeping bags, taking those of young reindeer, with short thick fur, less liable to come out under conditions of dampness than is the fur of the older deer." Shackleton also commented upon the considerable efforts necessary to acquire the very best finnesko, writing that "the special finnesko are made from the skin of the reindeer stag's legs, but they are not easily secured, for the reason that the native tribes, not unreasonably, desire to keep the best goods for themselves. I had a man sent to Lapland to barter for finnesko of the best kind, but he only succeeded in getting twelve pairs." [28]

The most weighty evidence that Scott had not paid sufficient attention to the critical matter of furs and sleeping bags is provided in a volume that describes the various types of goods and equipment of the *Terra Nova* expedition, where the following understated remark appears: "The finneskoe used by the Expedition were obtained from . . . Kristiania [Oslo]. . . . It would probably repay any future explorers to visit a Lapp village on the coast of Russia, a day's run from Vardoe in Norway, and obtain from the Lapps the finneskoe and sleeping bags for a projected expedition. Good finneskoe will last for a year on snow surface with good treatment, but bad ones will last only a month or less." The same document notes that "the best fur is the close thick fur of the winter coat of the reindeer. The hairs of the summer coat after wetting tend to come out in clumps, and such skins should be rejected." [29] Debenham's writings suggest that his furs were in a sorry state on

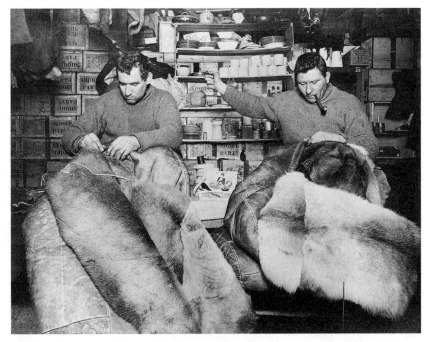

Figure 57. Seamen Crean, left, and Evans mending the sleeping bags. Photograph by H. Ponting. Scott Album, number 11338, Alexander Turnbull Library, Wellington, New Zealand.

February 18, 1911: "The sleeping bags are moulting badly and the hairs get into every nook and cranny." The overarching importance of the sleeping bags upon the men's rest on cold nights was poignantly expressed by Cherry-Garrard, who wrote that "there was nothing on earth that a man under such circumstances would not give for a good warm sleep. He would give everything he possessed: he would give . . . years of his life. One or two at any rate—perhaps five? Yes—I would give five." When Scott's party returned to the blessed warmth of the Barrier on February 10, 1912, at balmy temperatures near +10°F, for once they "had a splendid night's sleep, showing great change in all faces." [30] But nighttime temperatures soon plummeted, never to rise to such heights again in their journey, and faces likely fell along with them as the men trudged north with their icy sleeping bags through weeks of unremitting cold nights below −35°F. The motor sledges that had at least distracted if not occupied Scott's fertile scientific imagination on his supply trip to Norway stood broken and motionless, hundreds of miles away on the edge of the Barrier, as he and his men suffered their nightly agonies.

As he had the motor sledges, Scott the scientist also tested the use of dogs. The animals had proven to be of limited value on the *Discovery* expedition, at least in part because of spoiled dog food. Based upon his frustrations with the canines on that trek, Scott had little hope that they would be useful for more than shorter journeys as far as the edge of the Barrier in 1911–12. Yet with characteristic honesty, Scott remarked with surprise halfway up the glacier that "certainly dogs could have come up as far as this." Indeed, eleven of Amundsen's dogs completed the full circuit to the Pole and back, and one animal lived out his last days in retirement in Norway.[31] Scott's choice of ponies instead of dogs was based on personal experience—an experience and a viewpoint shared by Shackleton. Shackleton is reported by the *Evening Standard* to have said: "I cannot see how Amundsen can hope to reach the South Pole unless he has a large number of ponies on board. He may have dogs, but they are not very reliable" (*Evening Standard*, October 14, 1910). Like Scott, Shackleton chose to use ponies on his attempt to reach the South Pole in 1908–9. Shackleton failed to reach the Pole, at least in part because of that choice. But he went on from that expedition—the farthest south to date—to become one of the most widely admired heroes of world exploration. In contrast, the same choice made by Scott became a fundamental cornerstone in the legend of his mistakes. The legacies of both Scott and Shackleton are grounded not in the basic facts surrounding their use of ponies instead of dogs as the principal mode of transport, but from later deeds, their ultimate fates—not least, living in the case of Shackleton, dying in the case of Scott—and the emphasis adopted by historical analysts.

Some of Scott's tests were successful. He and his men carried out careful studies of the motion of glaciers, documenting their rates of flow.[32] The decision to place a minimum thermometer at One Ton Camp was a useful one, as it provided the first measurements of midwinter temperatures deep in the heart of the Barrier, relevant both for science and for exploration. Scott wisely stuck with the proven value of a fresh-meat diet to ward off scurvy even though many learned men of the day eschewed meat as a preventative, be-

Figure 58. The ill-fated motor sledge being unloaded from the *Terra Nova*, January 8, 1911. Photograph by H. Ponting. Scott Album, number 11259, Alexander Turnbull Library, Wellington, New Zealand.

lieving scurvy to be caused not by vitamin deficiency but by tainted foods or poor ventilation.

Perhaps those very scientific leanings lie at the root of Scott's tendency to choose paths that ought to work, instead of those with large enough margins for error to ensure success under the worst cases rather than the likely ones. Scott persistently faltered by cutting things too fine. The third motor sledge never had a prospect of a real test on the polar journey, for it sank while being unloaded from the ship. The mate, Campbell, was responsible for testing the ice, and he "found it rotten the whole way." The mate dutifully reported his tests of the uncertain ice to the captain, who in turn "gave orders, that the ponies should not cross the bad bit. . . . The motor sledge he thought could be pulled safely across owing to its big bearing surface." [33] The remains of that motor sledge still lie at the bottom of McMurdo Sound, and as it sank into the frigid water it sketched an unforgettably vivid paragraph in the legend of Scott the bumbler.

Of all the errors of fine margins, none was more tragic than that of the oil cans. Lashly was the first member of the *Terra Nova* expedition to note that the paraffin oil in the depots had been mysteriously depleted as he and Crean struggled to bring the scurvy-ridden Lieutenant Evans home. Leakage of stored oil was a problem that Scott had first encountered years earlier, on the *Discovery* expedition. In 1902–3 Scott attributed the problem to the cork stoppers then employed, and he therefore attacked this obvious weak point, using leather washers with screwed metal caps for his 1911 expedition. But there is no evidence that this solution was ever tested. If tests were performed, then they proved inadequate. Scott, Bowers, and Wilson discovered a grave deficit in the precious fluid essential for heating their food and melting snow for water as they slogged across the Barrier in the final weeks of their lives, even though the first and second return parties reported having taken less than their full shares. Cherry-Garrard later noticed that a wooden case containing eight such cans was buried in the snow for more than a year at the Cape Evans base. When dug up, three were full, three were empty, and two were partly full, showing that the cans had leaked in spite of their improved fixtures of leather and metal.[34] Just as Scott was surprised to see his third motor sledge sink below the sea ice, he seems to have been surprised that the cap and washers did not solve the problem of leakage from the oil cans.

Amundsen also carried oil in "the usual cans." But he noticed that they "proved too weak" and set one of his men to work soldering and resoldering to prevent loss. In the far northern reaches of the Arctic a few years earlier, Peary's man Henson labored similarly to reinforce the joints of the cans carried on the American journey toward the North Pole, for these polar explorers had also noticed the problem of leakage of their fuel cans. Henson described the work of soldering with hot molten metal in intense cold as a "job for a demon in Hades."[35]

Near the rock outcropping that Amundsen named Mount Betty for his housekeeper in Norway, a team of scientists studying glacier flow rates came upon one of Amundsen's depots buried in the snow more than fifty years later. The soldered oil can it held was still intact and full.[36]

Scott's struggles with leaking cans were not confined to those that held fuel, nor to those left in depots on the polar route. On the *Discovery* expedition, Wilson noticed that many cans of condensed milk were spoiled, at least in part due to leakage.[37] Five tin food cans from the Scott and Shackleton expeditions were examined in the 1950s. Some had rusted or leaked. But others, like Amundsen's oil can from the Mount Betty depot, were fully intact and still contained unspoiled quantities of such foods as baked beans and lunch tongue.[38]

Priestley, the geologist of Scott's northern party, suggested that the leakage in Scott's cans might have been due to changes in tin's metallic structure that can occur at temperatures below −40°F—in particular, a spontaneous chemical conversion from white tin to the more brittle form of gray tin.[39] But modern science shows that this intriguing speculation, while reasonable for its day, is unlikely to be the solution to the mystery of the leaky oil cans. Even after decades of exposure to those extremes of Antarctic winter temperatures, some of Scott's other cans remained intact. If a fundamental chemical change had occurred, it would likely have affected all the cans. Amundsen's added solder would also not have saved him from a characteristic of the metal itself. The answer lies in the nature of the materials used. The transformation from white to gray tin is a property only of the pure metal and is practically eliminated by even a trace of other elements.[40] While referred to as "tins," the cans and solder of Scott's day, like modern cans, contained significant amounts of other metals, including copper, nickel, and antimony. Only if there were great variability in the composition of the solder could a transformation to gray tin have occurred in some but not all cans. But this ought to have lent a powdery appearance to the metal, which was not reported either by Scott's party or by others who saw and handled the cans, including Lieutenant Evans's party as well as those who found the last tent. And the problem first arose not during the cold winter but well before, under mild conditions. The oil cans already found to be leaking by Lashly in late January had been stored on the Barrier only since November—at sea level during the height of summer. Those cans would have been subjected to relatively warm temperatures no colder than about −10°F, not to the extremes of winter conditions below −40°F.[41]

The leakage also cannot be attributed to evaporation in the warmth of the summer sun, for the deeply buried cans described by Cherry-Garrard displayed the same problem. Stress on the seams of the cans due to variable temperatures and/or rough transport seems a more likely explanation for the problem. Peary's man Henson believed the reason for the leakage of their cans was the severe jolting the supplies received in transportation, especially over rough ice—a fate that Scott's cans also suffered as the sledges lurched over high sastrugi, cracks, and other obstacles.[42] And this was a problem that could indeed have been combated by reinforcing the joined pieces, as Amundsen and Peary did. Amundsen wrote that "victory awaits him who has everything in order."[43] Amundsen chose a solution to the problem with a large margin of safety, while Scott selected a scientific one that ought to have worked but did not.

Scott confessed more than a decade before he died in the Antarctic that he had no predilection for polar exploration. But he did have a predilection for science, and he approached the myriad challenges of polar travel as many a scientist would: by estimating requirements based upon observations and experience rather than by guessing what might be needed in his worst imagination. He was an honest man who wrote frankly of his mistakes, a sensitive man who depicted the Antarctic with great literary skill. As he died, he eloquently described a failed experiment with the frustration of a scientist who discovers the source of his miscalculations too late.

It has been suggested that the main cause of the deaths of the polar party was lack of food. But Scott and his men had carefully and scientifically tested the rations that would be used on the polar journey. Cherry-Garrard, Bowers, and Wilson had been the human guinea pigs whose remarkable midwinter trip to Cape Crozier seemed to prove that their food supplies would engender only limited weight losses even under extreme conditions. What went wrong? Tragically, it was Scott's very care and logical approach to the problem that led to his miscalculations. The midwinter journey took place at sea level, but such factors as increased respiration rates commonly lead to weight loss at high elevation, a phenomenon that remains a subject for scientific study even today. Scott's standard summit ration is estimated to have provided about 4,500 calories per day, but the men probably required as much as 6,000 calories per day while man-hauling. Several of those who walked to the Pole in the "footsteps of Scott" expedition lost more than twenty pounds apiece on their journey, and they did not attempt to complete the round trip but were airlifted out.[44]

It may be imagined that perhaps the polar party of five had only the food meant for four—that is, that Scott did not adjust the rations that had been prepacked for two groups of four after deciding to take five in his party. But Lieutenant Evans wrote of "repacking the depot," and Scott lamented that preparation of the food for five was slower than cooking for four.[45] Clearly, then, more food was being cooked in Scott's tent after his group of five men parted company from the other three. And for the most tragic reasons, Scott's party had much more food per man per day than the standard in the most critical final phases of their trek. Only four men remained to eat the food meant for five after the death of seaman Evans, and only three after Oates's demise. Cyclists in the Tour de France require about seven thousand calories per day to maintain the frenetic pace of their sport, a record value that is believed to lie near the human ceiling of possible sustained metabolic rate. The body is not capable of absorbing food calories above this ceiling, and Scott's men probably required considerably fewer calories than this extreme.[46]

At the depot at 80°32', Lashly left nearly all of his team's pemmican behind, so that from this point on, Scott's party of four would have had the better part of the food supplies meant for eight. Lashly also left the bulk of the stored pony meat behind for the polar party. On March 7 Scott wrote: "We are only kept going by good food."[47] The party may have suffered from dehydration earlier in their trek (particularly in the dry, thin air of the plateau), but the deaths increased the water rations among the survivors. The fundamental problem at least at this point appears to have been not the limited availability of food or water but rather the sudden slowing of their pace across the Barrier. Excess supplies could do little but prolong the inevitable unless they could achieve better daily distances.

If the problem was not the amount of food, then perhaps it was the food itself—specifically, its vitamin content. Many historians have assumed that Scott and his men must have had scurvy, perhaps making them so weak that they simply could not achieve better distances than a few wretched miles per day in the last several weeks of their lives. While Wilson wrote graphically about other medical problems such as the cut on seaman Evans's hand, he never indicated any observation of symptoms of scurvy, even in his final letters to his loved ones. Dr. Atkinson, who led the search party and saw the bodies of his dead comrades, is quoted by Cherry-Garrard as being emphatic that there was no scurvy. Priestley stressed in 1926 that "Wilson was an expert; knew the symptoms of scurvy from personal experience; was a conscientious and scientific observer and does not suggest that visible signs of scurvy had appeared." But in 1962 the same man, himself an excellent scientific observer, wrote that when they reached the Barrier the party began "to suffer from vitamin deficiency."[48] Priestley's change of view and the widespread belief that Scott and his men must have been afflicted by scurvy may have been quite naturally affected by the rapid evolution of scientific understanding of that disease that occurred between the turn of the century and the mid-1930s.

Humans share the affliction of scurvy with monkeys and guinea pigs. Research on vitamin C accelerated after the early 1900s, when the use of guinea pigs as a convenient animal model for the human disease was discovered. Unidentified compounds "A" and "B" had earlier been shown to be essential for the human diet. By 1920, a series of experiments had shown that another accessory food factor, dubbed "C," was essential to the health of guinea pigs and human beings. In the early 1930s the mystery molecule $(C_6H_8O_6)$ was isolated and identified by a Hungarian chemist named Albert Szent-Györgi, who was to win the Nobel Prize for physiology and medicine in 1937 in honor of the work. In the same year, Prof. Norman Haworth of the University of Birmingham received the prize for chemistry for elucidating the detailed chemical structure and bonding of vitamin C, also called ascorbic acid.[49] Priestley served as chancellor of the University of Birmingham from 1938 to 1952. Thus some of the prize-winning research that helped solve the riddle of scurvy occurred within his own institution and would naturally have attracted his interest, as it did the world's. In science as in history, timing can be as important as content. The fact that vitamins were discovered and the precise cause of scurvy determined shortly after Scott's death may have played a role in the growing assumption not only by Priestley but by an entire generation that it must have been scurvy that killed Scott and his party.

But what is the specific evidence regarding scurvy in the polar party? The onset of scurvy varies from one individual to another and depends in part upon the body's reserves. Serious symptoms of scurvy have occurred in some test subjects after nineteen weeks on a vitamin C–free diet, and in others after thirty weeks.[50] Scott and his men took steps to combat the dreaded disease before starting their southern journey—in particular, consuming fresh seal meat, as did Shackleton on his expedition. Both the Scott and Shackleton expeditions also obtained some vitamins from their rations of dried milk, jam, and bottled fruits while at their base camps, allowing for about 15–20 mg of vitamin C per man per day, believed to be more than enough to prevent scurvy.[51] During their southern sledge journeys, however, the explorers' diets were far more limited, and their only significant source of vitamin C would have been the pony meat they consumed on the Barrier.

How long could the men hope to march on a southern journey before becoming first weakened and then incapacitated by the dreaded disease? On his southern journey of more than seventeen weeks, none of Shackleton's party displayed significant symptoms of scurvy.[52] Lashly, Crean, and Lieutenant Evans left the bulk of their pony meat behind for Scott's party, but even so Lashly remained strong enough to run alongside the dog sledge carrying Evans to safety in the seventeenth week of their trek. The ill lieutenant had been sledging for several weeks longer than his companions, and his initial symptoms of scurvy began after about twenty-one weeks on the sledging-trail diet. He was able to continue marching painfully but steadily for about three more weeks, achieving distances of more than ten miles per day. The polar party began to progress slowly near the beginning of March, after about seventeen weeks on the sledging trail, and they perished after twenty-one weeks. But for more than three weeks, on both the outbound and return legs of the journey, they would have been consuming some vitamin C in the form of pony meat. With notably more pony meat and comparable times spent sledging to those of Shackleton and to Lashly and Crean, it seems unlikely that all the members of the polar party would have succumbed to scurvy in early March.

What of other vitamin-deficiency diseases? Among the most notable of these is pellagra, a debilitating condition that, like scurvy, was thought in Scott's time to be contagious or perhaps the result of tainted foods. But we now know that pellagra results from a lack of the B vitamin niacin (nicotinic acid). Meat provides significant amounts of all of the B vitamins and is an especially effective source of niacin. Pellagra is a disease that modern science has demonstrated to be an affliction of those who subsist largely on cereals, especially corn. It is virtually unknown among cultures where large amounts of meat are frequent items on the menu. Meat products not only contain significant amounts of niacin, but they also furnish tryptophan, which is effectively converted to niacin within the human body.[53] Scott's diet both on and off the sledging trail was rich in the meat products that are known to prevent pellagra.

As Scott's legacy has evolved over the decades, so too have his companions been subject to derision, and it has been assumed that they all died mainly because they engaged in a series of stunningly foolish errors. Cherry-Garrard said that Scott was a complicated man, full of light and shade. But Cherry-Garrard also said, "As things got worse and worse so Birdie [Bowers] got better and better. So far as a human being can be simple Birdie was a perfectly simple man."[54] Perhaps the men were indeed quite different from their leader. As we seek to understand their struggle and the factors that killed not only Scott but also Wilson, Bowers, Oates, and seaman Evans, we may benefit from an understanding of the characters of these men as well as those of Cherry-Garrard, Lieutenant Evans, and others.

Although the ponies were in poor condition when purchased, with Oates's consummate skill at horse management, the animals succeeded in transporting the planned amount of material to the base of the glacier. Scott fully understood both his own failing and Oates's role in saving the situation, for on November 24, 1911, he wrote a letter to his wife from the Barrier admitting that the ponies were "not well selected[.] I knew this in New Zealand though I didn't tell you. . . . They are going well now and bidding fair to carry us through the first stage of the journey . . . entirely due to Oates."[55] Thus the excellence of one key and highly capable man made up for critical mistakes committed in the purchase of the ponies.

Of Bowers much has been said—of his courage in the gale, his physical strength and resistance to cold, his skill and endurance at navigation, and his devotion to duty. It has become part of the legend of Scott's failures that perhaps the polar party simply lost the will to live after suffering the indignity of being beaten to the Pole. But Scott and his companions made progress comparable to that achieved by the first return party and by Lieutenant Evans's team in the first several weeks after leaving the Pole. Their brisk pace of between fifteen and twenty-four miles per day from January 25 through February 6 does not suggest a dispirited party ready to die but rather one striving to live. And it seems difficult to reconcile Bowers's steadfast refusal to abandon

Figure 59. A uniformed Captain Scott and his wife, Kathleen, inspect the ponies in New Zealand. Photograph by Steffano Francis Webb. Steffano Webb Collection, number 31147, Alexander Turnbull Library, Wellington, New Zealand.

the ponies from a drifting ice floe in McMurdo Sound in February 1911 with a choice to deliberately lay down his life over an issue of historical priority in March of the next year.

Seaman Evans is sometimes remembered only for falling into the sea in a New Zealand harbor, perhaps because of drunkenness. This incident was indeed described by a participant in the expedition.[56] The big seaman reportedly dreamed of opening his own pub after returning home, but this desire was shared by others on "the lower deck" and is not necessarily indicative of an excessive proclivity for alcohol. A future as a proprietor of a pub was one of few avenues of reward for the ordinary seamen, who would never give lectures, write books, or otherwise enjoy the benefits of exploration that were reserved for the officers and scientists in a class-conscious Victorian society. Seaman Crean eventually did open a pub in his native Ireland, calling it The South Pole.[57] Seaman Evans's drinking habits are a matter for speculation, but his remarkable contributions to the expedition are well documented. Although failure to furnish ski boots and crampons ahead of time may be cited among Scott's apparent shortcomings of preparation, it was seaman Evans who made good the want. The big seaman meticulously constructed these critical items upon which the trip to the Pole and back heavily depended. Lieutenant Evans described seaman Evans as a "man of enormous strength . . . and to Evans we owed the splendid fitting of our travelling equipment, every detail of which came under his charge." [58] Although planning was flawed and limited advance preparations are a subject of legitimate criticism, seaman Evans's deft skill met the challenge of constructing essential sledging gear on the spot in the Antarctic.

Wilson's contributions to the expedition include not only his science and his paintings but also his personal qualities. It was he whom most of the men credited with creating an overall spirit of harmony and cooperation that largely prevailed in the *Terra Nova* expedition and that later polar adventurers have found difficult to recapture. Wilson was a self-contained man who inspired Cherry-Garrard to write: "He was beyond ambition and beyond fear. Such men do occur in history but they are very rare, and when they do happen they are among the great ones of our race. Glory? He knew it for a bubble: he had proved himself to himself." [59] Like Bowers, Wilson appears unlikely to have chosen to end his life because Amundsen had been first at the Pole.

Lieutenant Evans, Lashly, and Crean each contributed importantly and selflessly to many of the expedition's goals. The three of them survived their return journey from 87°35'S only through staunch support of one another. As a last gallant act, they also bravely left the polar party as well supplied with pony meat and sledging foods as possible, and at their own peril.

The words and actions that laid the groundwork for the legend of Scott as a bumbler were those of the captain, not those of his men. Indeed, the members of the expedition overcame many remarkable challenges, including some of their leader's shaping. From the moment Scott chose to use ponies rather than dogs, the outcome of any race with Amundsen could have been altered only if a natural catastrophe had befallen the Norwegians—a major calving of the coastline of the Bay of Whales, or a disastrous plunge into a crevasse. Although he was doomed to lose the race, Scott and his companions were not necessarily doomed to lose their lives as a result of the human errors that had been made. If Lieutenant Evans's band of three survived despite being shorthanded at the start and in the face of a terrible bout with scurvy, how could the polar party composed of the strongest men have failed, particularly when so much food and fresh meat had been carefully left for them? Cherry-Garrard and the others felt no anxiety as they waited for the captain to arrive in March, for they were confident that he and his team would survive. But as week after week ended with no sign of Scott on the ever-darker horizon, they realized that something must have gone terribly wrong.

THIRTEEN

A Chillingly Unusual Month

The visitor felt well and strong when he left the McMurdo cafeteria an hour ago after a generous breakfast of coffee, toast, and eggs. Now each step along the gently sloping snow road is slow and labored, as if he had not eaten for days. He has completed half the two-mile walk to the laboratory where his scientific equipment is kept, but he is beginning to wonder whether he can finish the trip. The jaunt that he has come to enjoy, even in temperatures as low as −20°F, has strangely changed this morning to an agonizing crawl. He wonders what the temperature is, for the air feels strangely frigid. There is a light breeze, too weak to warm the icy air but strong enough to make his cheeks feel numb in spite of his woolen balaclava and tightly zipped parka. The intense cold freezes his nostrils as he struggles to breathe. His legs are starting to feel like ice beneath his jeans, and he wishes he had put on heavier long underwear. Then he notices that the road seems oddly quiet. Normally at least a few vehicles pass him on their way to and from the snow airstrip on the Sound as he walks this way. But today he is alone, and the ice-covered landscape around him is silent. He is beginning to dread the solitude that he normally relishes, and to question with a growing sense of apprehension whether he ought to go on or turn back. Each step is slower than the one before, and his energy is fading fast. The painful march to shelter is about the same either way, and he is becoming uncertain of survival even though the distances involved are pathetically small compared, for example, to those that Scott and his men endured.

Just when he feels close to collapse, he hears the blessed clanking of a Snowcat's tracks behind him. He waves, even though the big vehicle is already turning purposefully in his direction. The driver stops and opens the passenger door. It is an effort, but he summons up the energy to put his foot on the metal track and climb into the shelter of the Snowcat's interior. It feels like heaven. In a harsh tone the driver asks what he is doing out here. Before he can respond, the other man tells him that the air temperature is −47°F today and the wind chill is −100°F. Like others at McMurdo he is required to stay put in his quarters until the weather improves. The driver is making a sweep of the area to check for the stragglers who, like him, have foolishly overlooked the warnings that were clearly posted in every building that morning. One must have been on the doors of the cafeteria as he left it, but he failed to see.

When they reach the end of the road without encountering any other careless strollers, the driver expertly swings the Cat around. The vehicle clanks its way back to the station, and the man pulls up outside the visitors' dormitory to drop him off. He is admonished one more time to check weather conditions carefully before he ventures out again, and then the Snowcat clanks away in a large cloud of exhaust.

A crowd has gathered in the dormitory lounge to wait out the weather with one of the many tapes from the station's video library. The film is a favorite on the ice, a well-acted account of the voyages of Scott and Amundsen based upon a popular and engaging book. As the visitor passes the lounge on his way to his room, he can clearly hear the television. The voice of a British actor pronounces: "A man who sits in his tent in the Antarctic and whines about the weather is unfit to lead."

Visitors to the Antarctic were few, and their time on the continent was largely ephemeral, until the late 1950s, when more and more permanently manned scientific stations were founded. Still the forbidding plain of the Barrier remained nearly untouched by any but the few explorers who had trodden its snowy ground at the turn of the twentieth century, and as decade after decade passed, the legend of Scott's mistakes flourished. But interest in the meteorology of the remote Antarctic also mounted. Scientific curiosity, along with the need for aviation safety of the growing enterprise of Antarctic research, resulted in the installation of a network of automated weather stations around the coldest continent on Earth beginning in the 1980s. The meteorological observations obtained for the sake of science as a party of men struggled for their very survival took on a new and startling meaning as they were compared to the data points routinely and impassively collected over the passing years by the machines. The scientific data showed that the three key weeks from February 27 to March 19, 1912, during which Scott's party fell farther and farther behind the daily distances that they had to achieve in order to survive, were far colder than normal.[1] The new information points not to errors made by men but toward the capriciousness of nature as the stunningly decisive blow to the survival of Scott, Bowers, Wilson, and Oates.

One of Scott's men, and only one, understood a great deal about the circumstances of Scott's death long before the automated weather station was invented. And his thorough study of the meteorological data was critical for later attempts to evaluate their accuracy. The meteorologist, George Simpson, left Antarctica in February 1912 to return to his post in India. It was not until late 1913 that he received all of the expedition's records of temperature and wind. But before he could complete and publish his study of their implications, World War I broke out and Simpson found himself "engaged on war work." His analysis of the Antarctic meteorological data could be done only in his spare time, and that in turn was limited in view of the "great issues then being fought out on the battlefields of Europe." He completed the first of three volumes describing his findings by mid-1916, but the war dragged on and publication was further delayed. Eventually Simpson decided to have his first book printed in Calcutta in 1919.[2]

Simpson pored over the expedition's meteorological records with care, devoting considerable attention to such key technical matters as instrument design, precision, and calibration.[3] In January 1914 he sent personal letters from India to each of the men who had been responsible for taking observations on sledging journeys—Cherry-Garrard, Dr. Atkinson, his Canadian assistant Wright, Lieutenant Evans, and others—noting the importance of referring "in detail to the methods employed" and asking such questions as whether the thermometer readings appeared to be stable, what precautions were taken to keep the instruments out of the sun while taking data, and other specifics. Perhaps the most poignant response to these queries came in early February 1914 from Cherry-Garrard, who wrote from his estate at Lamer that he was still feeling "a bit groggy from breakdown in March 1912." But he dutifully responded to Simpson's technical queries, indicating that after a few minutes of swinging the thermometer he found that his observations were absolutely steady as long as the instrument had been in the shade before data-taking began.[4] Evans's response came from a hotel in Berlin, for he had taken the place of the dead Captain Scott on a speaking tour in order to raise money to help pay the debts of the expedition; he informed Simpson that he had usually tried to keep the thermometer out of the sun by swinging it in the shadow of the tent.[5] In his book Simpson presented independent sets of data taken by three of his key observers in November 1911 when they were within a few miles of one another—those of the main southern party (with Bowers as observer), the dog party (with Meares as observer), and the motor party (with Lieutenant Evans as observer). The three separate temperature measurements agreed extremely well with one another, demonstrating good instrument precision.[6] But although the thermometers were mutually consistent to within a few degrees, they might all have been wrong in an absolute sense if poorly calibrated. Before departure for the Antarctic, Simpson had personally calibrated the instruments by comparisons to high-quality measurements at Kew Observatory in London, and he showed that this analysis suggested that both the mercury and the spirit thermometers were accurate to better than ±0.5°F.[7] The wooden-handled sling spirit thermometer used on the polar journey had been calibrated over the full temperature range from −77°F to +32°F before the expedition.[8] Although the specific thermometer carried by the polar party was broken, as documented by Bowers in the meteorological log book, Wright took other spirit thermometers back to England and retested their calibrations. He found changes of a few tenths of a degree or less in those instruments, and he wrote to Simpson in India describing those tests.[9]

On February 26, 1914, Simpson wrote to Wright, who was then back at his studies in Cambridge, that "judging from yours and the other replies the low temperatures were real," and the modern record supports Simpson's conclusions.[10] Summer is the halcyon season of warmth at the South Pole. Although conditions fluctuate greatly at the Pole in the darkness of polar winter, the radiant energy of the sun yields far more regular temperatures from year to year there during summer.[11] The average of the minimum daily values recorded at the Pole from January 13 to January 23 since 1986 are consistently quite near −23 °F (−22.6 ± 3.7 °F), as illustrated in figure 49 (page 215). Bowers's observation of an average minimum temperature of −23 °F near the South Pole on the same days of the year more than half a century before may stir the heart to sympathy for the bitter cold the polar party faced, and they surely bolster Simpson's view that his calibration was indeed accurate. There is more evidence of this type at a range of other temperatures, such as the good agreement between the measured average annual cycle of temperatures from summer to winter at Cape Evans in 1911–12 compared with many years of observations taken in the McMurdo Sound area since the 1980s (see fig. 22, page 110).

The weather was key to the plan for the polar journey. Priestley wrote:

> The journey was bound to develop into a struggle against time and temperatures, for Shackleton's experience, with similar transport, had shown that the distance out and back could only just be covered in that period of the year within the limits of which any long journey under the harsh conditions of manhauling must be confined. The employment of pony transport necessarily was the limiting factor as regards the date of starting, for ponies cannot survive cold weather. . . . At the other end of the "navigable" period comes the inevitable autumn seasonal drop of temperature.[12]

Scott and his men were well aware that it would be the men and not the ponies who would run the critical race against time as the summer faded on the return leg of the trip — a race they thought they could win whether or not they lost to Amundsen at the Pole.

Scott and his companions at the Pole understood the risks of the plan. As Bowers wrote to his sister, "We are not going forward like a lot of schoolboys

Figure 60. Dr. Simpson taking data near Cape Evans. Photograph by H. Ponting. Scott Album, number 30600, Alexander Turnbull Library, Wellington, New Zealand.

on a holiday picnic but rather as a party of men who know what they have got to face. I for one am sure that the journey will be no child's game but a hard one, as hard as any have ever been[,] and the Pole will not be gained without a terrible struggle. . . . If man can make for success we have the right stuff with us, but as I say when man has done all he can do he can only trust with God for the rest." [13] And of all Scott's men, it was Simpson who weighed and evaluated the meteorological challenges that the polar party would be likely to encounter.

Scott and his men did more than speculate about what to expect on the Barrier. They gathered direct evidence of its nature in the most critical month of their planned journey—for Lieutenant Evans had led a party of men onto the dreaded snow plain in March of the year before, as part of the depot journey. There he had documented temperatures about 20°F colder than Cape Evans, a key data point for Simpson to ponder. Simpson also considered the depot journey of February 1911, the winter journey to Cape Crozier in July 1911, and Lieutenant Evans's supply journey of September 1911. In each case Simpson carefully compared the temperatures recorded on the Barrier with those recorded simultaneously at Cape Evans, for by studying the differences between the two sets he would gain insights into the climate of the forbidding region that lay between them and the Pole. By November 1911 Simpson wrote: "There can be no doubt now that during the winter the Barrier is from 20° to 30° colder than it is here [Cape Evans], and therefore must be one of the coldest places in the world." [14] This assessment was a highly accurate estimate of the conditions that could ordinarily be expected on the Barrier. But Simpson could not have predicted that extraordinary weather would strike in March of 1912, at exactly the time when Scott's party had to make good progress in order to survive, and when they could least afford the added challenge of extreme conditions.

The daily minimum temperatures recorded by Scott's party from January 20, as they left the South Pole, to their last trek on the Barrier on March 19 can now be compared with the average daily minima recorded by the automated weather stations that monitor the region of their fateful path (fig. 61). The daily minima in the minus twenties that Scott's men encountered were normal for late January on the high plateau at the South Pole. And temperatures warmed dramatically as anticipated when Scott and his men descended the Beardmore glacier to reach sea level—just as noted by Shackleton in 1909, and by Lieutenant Evans's party a few weeks earlier. When they regained the Barrier, Scott's party enjoyed an initial period of normal or even slightly warmer than normal temperatures above −20°F; indeed, they had been counting on the warmth of sea level in the last stage of the journey. At

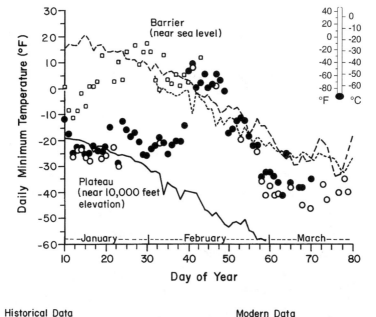

Figure 61. Daily minimum temperatures encountered by Scott's and Lieutenant Evans's parties in 1912, compared with modern observations at the South Pole, at 83°8′S (station 5 in map 2), and at 79°54′S (station 4; see map 2). Temperatures experienced by Evans's party were close to normal throughout their return journey. Scott's party encountered normal conditions for about the first fifty-five days of 1912, followed by a period of more than three weeks with daily minimum temperatures persistently 10–20°F colder than normal on the Barrier.

this point both the minimum temperatures and the daily distances recorded by Scott's party were similar to those reported by the other two returning parties (see fig. 53, page 239).[15]

In his last two diary entries near the end of February 1912, Wilson wrote of nightly temperature minima of −37°F. Although he did not know it, these days heralded the beginning of an unusual cold snap that was to deepen in the weeks to come, as Bowers, Oates, Scott, and he fought their desperate battle for survival. From the end of February until the last temperatures were recorded on March 19, Scott and his men struggled through three weeks when almost every daily minimum temperature was a bitter and debilitating 10–20 °F colder than what can now be shown to be typical based on many years of observations in this region (see fig. 61). Minimum temperatures day after grueling day were forty to fifty degrees colder than those that Lieutenant Evans had encountered on the Barrier just a month before. The temperatures had taken a sharp and unusual turn for the worse, and with them went Scott's chances for survival.

Oates's death demonstrates the crushing toll taken on the party by this unusual weather. Oates revealed his badly frostbitten feet to his companions on March 2, after five days of daily minimum temperatures that were 10–20 °F colder than average. Minimum temperatures soared to –20 °F on March 4, which Scott described as "an improvement which makes us much more comfortable." The modern record shows that this single day was the sole normal one enjoyed by the polar party from late February through mid-March (see day 63 in fig. 61). Scott wrote that he feared another cold snap, and that "Oates at least will weather such an event very poorly." The next day Scott's fears were realized when the minimum temperature plunged back below –35 °F, where it remained until the last measurement recorded on March 19, 1912—two days after Oates left the tent never to return.[16]

Before leaving on the polar trek, Oates had written to his mother that "the only dangerous part of the journey is the ascent of the glacier and you will have heard if we get up that safely. The coming back is not nearly so bad." [17] The meteorological data now show that he was right, in principle—coming back should not have been nearly so bad as it was.

On March 18, 1912, Scott wrote that he too had now been badly stricken by frostbite: "My right foot has gone, nearly all the toes." Until that point Scott had been "proud possessor of best feet," but he had put some curry powder in his pemmican and thereby contracted indigestion. He noted that he was distracted as a result and did not realize when his foot began to freeze. The next day again brought temperatures of –40 °F, well below what can now be shown to be typical, and Scott wrote that amputation would be his best hope for the future, because under these frigid conditions there was "no chance to nurse one's feet." [18]

Simpson studied the meteorological data taken during the tragic march across the Barrier at his home in the warmth of Simla, India, and he realized that fate had dealt the captain and his companions a remarkable blow. Even on the bitter winter journey to Cape Crozier, the average difference between temperatures measured at Cape Evans and those recorded by the party on the Barrier had been only about 20°F. Although Scott, Bowers, and Wilson were farther south than Cape Crozier during the last weeks of their lives, they were at sea level not in winter but in autumn, and only a few hundred miles away. But Simpson found that the temperatures recorded by the southern party in March 1912 were a frigid 38°F colder than Cape Evans had been at that time, a difference that he concluded simply could not be typical. He wrote that 1912 must have been "an abnormal year" and stressed that "it is quite impossible to believe that normally there is a difference of nearly 40 degrees in March between McMurdo Sound and the south of the Barrier."[19] The modern record reveals that these insights were entirely correct.

Simpson later wrote, "There can be no doubt that the weather played a predominating part in the disaster, and . . . was the immediate cause of the final catastrophe." He asserted that "the Barrier could be traversed many times without again encountering such low temperatures so early in the year."[20]

Cherry-Garrard quoted Simpson as saying that the polar party would probably have survived in nine years out of ten, but struck the unlucky tenth one.[21] The contemporary weather record can provide a partial test of the meteorologist's insights (fig. 62). A measure of the remarkable and unusual challenge that Scott and his men faced is provided by comparing the average of the daily minima for February 25–March 19 from 1912 to each year of data from three weather stations on the Barrier that lie near Scott's path at 77°54′S, 79°54′S and 83°8′S (the manned New Zealand base and automated weather stations 3 and 4 on map 2, page 15); missing data reflect occasional instrument failures. The automated measurements from these separate but nearby sites track one another well, supporting their precision and accuracy.

Scott and his men marched between about 82° and 80°, very close to the line between the two weather stations that have kept their lonely vigils at 83°8′S and 79°54′S for about fifteen years. The data from these two automated weather stations show that only one year in that record rivals the severity of the temperatures measured there in 1912 by Scott and his party,

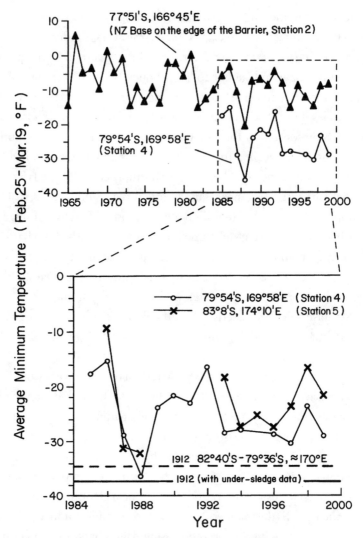

Figure 62. Average of daily minimum temperatures on the Barrier for the days from February 25 to March 19, comparing data from stations shown in map 2 with conditions endured by Scott's party in 1912. Temperatures comparable to those observed in 1912 for this period of more than three weeks were observed only in a single year (1988) in all data taken between 1985 and 1999 (bottom panel). Data from the New Zealand base on the edge of the Barrier date back to 1965 and show ups and downs very similar to those seen in the middle of the Barrier (top panel). The top panel therefore suggests that only one year in three and a half decades has been as cold as 1912, confirming that such conditions are extremely unusual.

when the average of the daily minimum temperatures in this region dipped below −34°F, more than 10°F colder than can now be shown to be typical for this region. The minimum temperatures at the manned New Zealand base on the northernmost edge of the Barrier are warmer than those at higher latitudes—reflecting the moderating climate of McMurdo Sound as recognized by Simpson—but the ups and downs in these data closely track those measured farther south in the middle of the Barrier. The year 1988 stands out as particularly cold in this extended record of more than thirty years, supporting the view that Scott and his men endured a highly unusual twist of fate. Many more years of data in the heart of the Barrier would be needed to obtain exact statistics, but the observations are broadly consistent with Simpson's conclusions that conditions are considerably milder than those endured by the polar party in at least nine out of ten years, probably even more frequently. The weather stations demonstrate that Scott and his party were fighting for their lives under rare conditions that were surely very much colder than normal.

Simpson had noticed a few individual cold days as he pored over the meteorological data gathered from the Barrier before the polar party's fateful march. A cold day or two, or even three or more in a row, was not striking in the climatological record. But he realized that the persistence of the cold temperatures observed in 1912 over a period of about three weeks was highly unusual.[22] The automated weather station at 79°54′S confirms this conclusion, showing that many individual cold days with minimum temperatures of −35°F to −40°F have been measured since routine observations began in 1985. But the data also show that in a normal year a few cold days are followed by a series of warm ones. Typically, the temperatures oscillate between −30°F and −10°F, just as Lieutenant Evans found when he sledged onto the Barrier the previous March. On average there are about five days between February 25 and March 19 with minimum temperatures warmer than −15°F in the modern record from 1985 to 1999. But as four desperate men struggled to reach the safety of their camp in 1912, there were none.

On the return leg of the journey, Scott and his party expected the wind to blow from the south as a blessed aid to progress, as it had for the two previous returning parties. But the coldest temperatures are associated with windless conditions, as Wilson, Bowers, and Cherry-Garrard had painfully experienced at Windless Bight during their journey to Cape Crozier in July

1911. The southerly wind that the polar party eagerly looked forward to simply ceased to blow as the unusually cold temperatures descended on the Barrier during March 1912. On March 6 Scott wrote that "we did a little better with help of wind yesterday," but this was an exception. On March 13 he lamented that there had been "not a breath of favorable wind for more than a week." [23]

But the worst effect of the weather was not the lack of wind or even the impact of the cold on their physical comfort but the suddenly intractable nature of the surface across which the desperate men struggled to ski and drag their sledge behind them. The surfaces under these nearly windless and frigid temperatures were covered with fresh hoarfrost, and the effort required to pull the sledge across the sandpapery cold snow for only six miles each day was "the limit of our endurance." Day after grueling day Scott wrote of "a really terrible surface—it has been like pulling over desert sand, not the least glide in the world. . . . Surface as bad as ever . . . on this surface we know we cannot equal half our old marches, and that for that effort we expend nearly double the energy. . . . Sledge dreadfully heavy." [24] Simpson and Priestley emphasized that the loose new snow crystals that formed as the temperatures fell acted as a brake on the sledge.[25] Normal winds would have swept the crystals away, leaving a smoother and more navigable surface. And as temperatures fell, the friction of the snow surface increased, just as it had on the high plateau a few weeks earlier, and just as it does in today's scientific studies of the physical properties of snow. The threshold of about −20°F, below which skis no longer produce a liquid lubricating layer, had once again been crossed, and as temperatures dropped the effort demanded from the men mounted.[26] In a more typical year, there would have been some days of cold discomfort, but there would also have been warmer days to nurse frostbitten feet and, most important, many days in which to make far better and easier progress toward home across an infinitely more tractable surface. One weather-related problem thus added disastrously to another, because the unusually cold temperatures went hand in hand with both the lack of southerly wind to fill the sail and the terribly difficult surfaces that brought their progress to a crawl when they could least afford it.

Cherry-Garrard spent years asking himself what might have been different. He wrote: "The whole business simply bristles with 'ifs': if Scott had taken dogs and succeeded in getting them up the Beardmore; if we had not

lost those ponies on the Depot Journey; . . . if I had disobeyed my instructions and gone from One Ton, killing dogs as necessary . . ."²⁷ But although
Cherry-Garrard did not know it, the simple circumstance of normal March
weather on the Barrier would very likely have produced a different outcome.
If the polar party had not met with the severe cold that Simpson credited
with their downfall, it seems likely that they would have achieved distances
of about fifteen miles per day on the Barrier, just as they had been managing until that point, and just as the first return party and Lieutenant
Evans's party both had achieved, in spite of the lieutenant's struggle with
scurvy (see fig. 53, page 239). At a rate of fifteen miles per day, the polar party
would have reached One Ton Camp on March 4—and Cherry-Garrard
would have been there waiting for a joyous reunion, having arrived with
Dimitri and twenty-two dogs the night before. They would have still been
there as late as March 10. And even if the polar party had arrived at One
Ton on March 11, just too late to rendezvous with Cherry-Garrard, they
would have had to achieve an average of only about six miles per day from
that point on in order to stagger to Corner Camp by March 30; there they
would have found help from Dr. Atkinson and seaman Keohane. They could
have waited out bad weather for half of those days and still reached the doctor by making twelve miles per day. In a milder and more normal year, with
greatly reduced chances of frostbite, helpful winds to whisk their burden
along, and a considerably kinder snow surface, surely their fates would have
been different.

Along with the technology that built the automated weather stations, man-
kind has changed the planet in myriad ways since Scott's time. The addition of greenhouse gases to the atmosphere has led to a new meteorological
phenomenon known as global warming, and the modern reader may wonder whether perhaps temperatures on the Barrier have been affected. The
Antarctic peninsula has recently warmed in some areas, with dramatic con-
sequences for its ice shelves.²⁸ But this is largely a localized change far removed from the region where Scott and his men walked. Temperatures have
been systematically measured since the 1950s at several Antarctic stations,
and most of these show very little warming, less than 2°F, from about 1950
to the 1990s.²⁹ And there are a few places in Antarctica where temperature
records have been compiled for decade upon decade all the way back to the

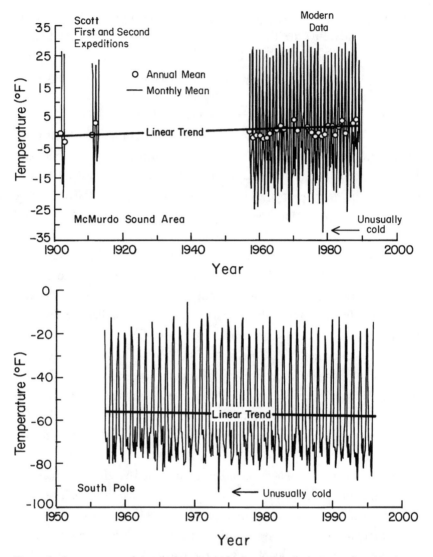

Figure 63. Long-term trends in temperatures at the South Pole (bottom panel) and in the McMurdo Sound area (top panel). The thin lines show data for each month over many years, so that excursions indicate unusual months. A few of these are pointed out to illustrate the variability that can occur in a particular month. The linear trends of both data sets are also plotted, showing that the average temperatures at both sites have been very stable over many decades. Temperatures of the 1980s and 1990s are only a few degrees warmer at McMurdo than they were during the Scott expeditions of the turn of the twentieth century. The South Pole (bottom panel) may have cooled slightly on average since the 1950s based upon this data set, but the small changes there are not statistically significant. Data courtesy of the University of Wisconsin archive (see Selected Bibliography for Internet site address).

turn of the twentieth century. These observations suggest long-term trends in annually averaged Antarctic temperatures of less than 4°F, probably closer to 2°F.[30] At the South Pole, average temperatures have actually grown slightly cooler rather than warmer since routine measurements began in the late 1950s. Data specifically from the McMurdo Sound area are consistent with those recorded by Simpson and others during Scott's first and second expeditions and also suggest a long-term warming of less than 2°F in the twentieth century (fig. 63)—a small fraction of the departures from average daily minimum temperatures that were endured by Scott and his men over a period of about three weeks. The long-term climate of the Antarctic therefore shows high stability when averaged over a year, but Scott's fate reflects the fact that short-term weather varies in the Antarctic, just as it does worldwide. Temperatures sometimes dip far below the average or rise well above it for a month or so at the South Pole or at McMurdo. Just as an early-winter cold snap can strike London or Washington, so too can temperatures vary in an individual period of several weeks in the Antarctic, and the modern record shows that such unlucky variability is what struck Scott's party on the Barrier in March 1912.

Simpson dug deeper, trying to find a reason for the unusual weather that he believed had killed Scott, Wilson, Bowers, and Oates. In March 1914 he wrote to a Mr. Hunt of the meteorological bureau of Australia, informing him that he was "just engaged on investigating a very interesting relationship between the pressure in the Antarctic and that of Australia and New Zealand. The relationship is remarkable during 1911–12 and I now wish to see if it held in 1902–3 when the Discovery was in the Antarctic. . . . Could you kindly let me have by return of post the monthly pressure departures from normal of Hobart [Australia]. . . . I am awfully sorry to give you so much trouble." Hunt responded enthusiastically that the request was no trouble but rather of great interest because he would be "delighted to hear of any success in showing correlations between the pressures in the Antarctic and those in Australia." He sent the requested data on April 8, 1914.[31]

Surface pressure is a parameter closely tied to the weather. Its effect is seen in the fronts of highs and lows that frequently dip across the continents of the world and are a familiar sight on modern television weather forecasts. Simpson published the results of his study of Antarctic pressure data only in his scientific book, where he remarked upon the curiously high correlation between the surface pressure measured at McMurdo Sound and that at locations as far away as New Zealand, Australia, and South America. He wrote of a "sea-saw of pressure between the Antarctic and the belt of anticyclones over the Southern Ocean." He also noticed that these linkages changed in a peculiarly nonrandom way—that is, multiple stations displayed the same behavior—between 1902–3 and 1911–12, and that the correlations became surprisingly strong in the northern part of Australia, farther removed than southern Australia from the Antarctic.[32] He thus presented evidence for a connection between Antarctic weather and the larger scale weather of the entire hemisphere, particularly that of northern Australia.

Simpson was beginning to see the patterns that we now believe reach across the globe to affect worldwide weather. One such connection is well known as El Niño, which modulates surface pressures strongly in northern Australia with an average periodicity of about four years, though it can be as short as two years or as long as seven. Indeed, the difference in surface pressure between Darwin, Australia, and Tahiti is the basis for the El Niño southern oscillation index or SOI.

The Indian Meteorological Office, where Simpson worked, was the birthplace of a great deal of the earliest understanding of El Niño. The man whose illness had prompted Simpson's early departure from Antarctica in February 1912, Gilbert Walker, later defined the term *southern oscillation* (SO) in surface pressure (later the El Niño Southern Oscillation, or ENSO) as he sought to understand the reasons for variability in the Indian monsoon, which plays a key role in that country's climate and agriculture.[33] Although the ENSO is the best-known global weather oscillation, Walker showed that similar oscillations occur elsewhere, like the NAO in the North Atlantic.[34] In general terms these weather patterns are linked to slow interactions between the Earth's atmosphere and oceans. Changes in the weather in some parts of the world can thereby reach across thousands of miles to influence conditions elsewhere.

The Antarctic weather record remains short even today, and it is difficult to be confident of a four-year oscillation when only a few decades of high-quality data are available. Much as Simpson did, however, scientists have begun to search for correlations in a variety of recent observations. A statistical study of temperatures at Antarctic stations has indeed suggested a modulation on an ENSO-like time scale of about four years, with minimum Antarctic surface temperatures tending to occur on the Barrier near the El Niño phase of the ENSO cycle.[35] It is at least intriguing and perhaps even poignant to note that March of 1912 was indeed in the El Niño phase of the cycle, and therefore consistent with such a connection — to a weather phenomenon that would begin to be understood only about a decade after Scott's death, a phenomenon upon which pioneering ground would be gained by Simpson's colleague Walker in India.[36]

Other recent scientific work supports the notion of a slowly varying oscillation in the environment of the mysterious continent at the bottom of the world. Observations point toward a link between ENSO and climatic variables including precipitation in west Antarctica.[37] And the Antarctic sea ice that stood in Scott's path as he sailed to begin his expedition has also been shown to display some variability on a time scale of about four years.[38] But there is an ocean flow pattern called the Antarctic circumpolar current that streams around Antarctica during all phases of the ENSO, and one study suggests that the observed four-year variability in atmospheric pressure may occur because this flow provides an oscillation with a similar beat.[39] It will not be possible to determine whether the oscillatory behavior observed in these weather-related variables is truly linked to ENSO until the physical mechanisms responsible for the correlations are fully proven. But it is increasingly clear that both the Antarctic continental weather and key processes in its oceans do fluctuate in roughly a four-year cycle, and Scott's party struck these variable rhythms in their most unfortunate cadence. Although they are probably unaware of it, current researchers are pursuing the directions suggested by Simpson, who wrote that "it is the duty of meteorologists to investigate these conditions, and to say whether similar conditions exist in this region year after year or whether in this as in so many other experiences Scott was the sport of fate."[40]

Although he did not have the benefit of late-twentieth-century data, Scott's writings showed his surprise at the severely cold conditions he encountered in late February and March, which he believed to be the primary reason that he and his companions lay dying on the Barrier. In his message to the public, he underscored that "our arrangements for returning were quite adequate, and that no one in the world would have expected the temperatures and surfaces which we encountered at this time of year. . . . Our wreck is certainly due to this sudden advent of severe weather, which does not seem to have any satisfactory cause." But he also wrote of other factors, like the illnesses of Captain Oates and seaman Evans and the loss of ponies in March of 1911 on the depot journey.[41] He wrote to Sir George Edgerton that "subsidiary reasons of our failure to return are due to the sickness of different members of the party, but the real thing that has stopped us is the awful weather and unexpected cold towards the end of the journey. There is no accounting for it, but the result has thrown out my calculations."[42] As the critics examined his writings, Scott's statements about the weather fueled confusion rather than adding clarity. The only one of Scott's men who could cut through the mixed messages to the reality of scientific fact was Simpson. But while Simpson's technical talents handily met the challenges of unraveling the science, the task of dissemination of those findings to the world ultimately proved to be too great for the meteorologist.

Simpson's three-volume treatise is replete with detail and unlikely to be understood in full by nontechnical readers. He presented his view of the weather's role in Scott's story in much simpler form at a scientific lecture given on May 17, 1923, at Oxford. The text of that lecture was published as a book in 1926 and summarized in a short article in *Nature*. But these documents appeared many years after the expedition, delayed by the Great War and by Simpson's other obligations, and were read mainly by a limited community of scientists. Cherry-Garrard's far more widely distributed and popularly oriented book was published in 1922 and emphasized starvation as the primary cause of the polar party's deaths. Wright doubted that the weather conditions were unusual, as did the geologist, Priestley.[43] Perhaps these men had come to fear Antarctic weather so deeply that they believed the severe weather must have been normal and not exceptional. But the data now provided by the automated weather stations add new and direct proof that Scott and his men perished after enduring highly unusual weather, during what may be dubbed one of the coldest "marches" yet recorded on the Great Barrier.

Figure 64. Dr. Simpson in his laboratory at the base at Cape Evans. Photograph by H. Ponting. Scott Polar Research Institute, Cambridge.

Simpson's insights about the key role of the weather were presented only in his books and his lecture, and after the 1920s he never again contributed in print to the debate about the expedition. Wright said that his colleague was called Sunny Jim because of his smile but noted that he had "a supreme contempt for everything but Meteorology."[44] One reason that Simpson scarcely entered into the public discussion of the expedition was probably this strong focus upon the science to which he was devoted. As the Norwegian ski-runner Gran described him, Simpson "slaves away, living in a separate world of science."[45] And as the years passed, Simpson changed in a way that swept him even further away from debates about the expedition of his youth. George Simpson began to lose his hearing after returning from the Antarctic, and colleagues who met him later in life found not a person of sunny disposition but a remote and distant man.[46] By the 1930s his increasing deafness hampered his participation in meetings and conferences. He devoted his attention to his responsibilities as director of the prestigious U. K. Meteorological Office and to personal research in which he addressed such issues as the physical processes that lead to ice ages.[47] And as his smile faded along with his hearing, he became less and less inclined to explain to others what he believed had happened to Scott, Bowers, Oates, and Wilson on the Barrier.

But there is one more piece of direct evidence that bears upon the mystery of the deaths of the polar party. The combined power of the automated weather stations and the records left by Scott's men provide clues to what happened in the last days in the tent in a way that even Simpson could not have foreseen.

FOURTEEN

The Winds of Chance and Choice

The unusual cold that the visitor encountered yesterday on his lonely walk toward the laboratory has been replaced by a blizzard of stunning fury. The wind slams hard against the walls of the dormitory, and the building shudders as gust after gust rocks the structure. The visitor stares into the hypnotic cloud of drift that has swirled outside his window for more than twenty hours. It is a vivid reminder of the vulnerable fragility of man and the power of Antarctic weather.

He pads down the hall in stocking feet to the small room where the emergency food supplies are kept. He is tired of the peanut butter and jelly sandwiches that staved off his hunger all day yesterday. The military K rations look even less appetizing. So he chooses a packet of cereal and a can of condensed milk. As he walks back to his room, he passes the television lounge, where a dozen residents are still focused on the film version of the sagas of Scott and Amundsen. It is a miniseries of considerable length, a popular way to pass the time during an Antarctic blizzard. The tragic drama unfolds slowly on the screen as the howling wind builds huge drifts outside. The visitor hesitates at the door to listen to the portrayal of the deaths of Scott, Wilson, and Bowers. The canvas of the tent snaps in a pounding blizzard as Bowers shouts "God save the King" in his final moments.

As he opens the door to his room, the visitor notices that the roar of the maelstrom outside the window has changed in intensity and pitch. The wind still sounds like a freight train, but one that has begun to recede slightly into the distance. He sets down the cereal and milk, stretches out on his bed, and picks up his copy of Scott's diary. He will wait awhile before eating. Maybe the storm will subside long enough to allow the station's residents to walk over to the cafeteria for more palatable food. It occurs to him that he has witnessed a dozen similar storms, and they have never lasted more than a few days.

An hour later he hears a voice in the hall calling "condition two, condition two," signaling that it is once again safe to walk around the station. He slips on his boots and parka and steps outside. It is hard to imagine that yesterday's temperature could have been so brutally low. The air is warm now, stirred to a balmy −5°F by the driving force of the wind. He has noticed that before, too. It would be hard to miss. The power of the wind always sweeps in strikingly warmer temperatures.

There are still a few narrow rivers of windblown snow running low across the ground like ghostly white snakes. But he can easily see the surrounding buildings now, and it is perfectly safe, even pleasant, to be outside. He pulls up his parka hood to ward off any gusts that should come his way and sets out toward the cafeteria. A hot lunch is already available there, and he fills his metal tray with food.

It is crowded in the dining room, but he finds an open seat next to the young navy lieutenant who has been the station's lead weather forecaster for two seasons. He is a tall man, with stooped shoulders and a smooth rolling gait. The visitor is reminded of the descriptions of Wilson. They joke over the convenient way that blizzards always seem to die down after a day or two, just at the precise moment when everyone is getting tired of emergency food.

Suddenly the visitor realizes the import of this simple fact. He asks the meteorologist whether there is any fundamental limit to how long a blizzard can last in the Antarctic. The man smiles and says that this is easy to demonstrate. He picks up his fork and begins to sculpt the mashed potatoes on his plate into a form. With a flourish, he pushes the white potatoes into a crude semblance of Antarctica, complete with a high plateau just off the center. Then he puts a large pat of butter onto the middle of the potato plateau. The butter melts and runs down an imaginary glacier. The meteorologist explains that intense Antarctic blizzards are fed by the cooling of surface air on the high plain in the interior. The cold dense air rushes down the contours of the continent because of the force of gravity, gathering speed and building up to the terrific intensity of a katabatic wind. It warms on the way down those steep slopes, too. But there's only so much cold air to start with, says the meteorologist, just as there's only so much butter on this mound of potatoes. Once that air has spilled down from the heights, building up another frigid reservoir takes time. And so the blizzard must cease. He puts another pat of butter on the "plateau," and then three more. Each melts slowly and runs down a different path to his plate. Only a few locations receive air from so many different parts of the interior that they can experience blizzards of more than a couple of days at a time, explains the meteorologist. He points to an area on the potato model with his fork, noting that a famous group of early Australian explorers wintered there in such a spot.

The visitor chews on a slice of juicy steak as he watches the last stream of butter flow down the slope of potato to ooze into a yellow circle on the flat plate. Then he asks the man about the region well away from the mountains, out in the middle of the Barrier. That's where Scott died in a blizzard that he said had blown hard and continuously for ten days straight. "Doesn't seem possible," says the meteorologist, with a look of puzzlement on his face. He shakes his head as he scoops up some butter and potato from the imaginary Pole with his fork, gouging out a depression right in the middle of the mock continent.

Scott's party continued marching across the Barrier in day after day of frigid temperatures during the weeks from February 27 through March 19, 1912. On March 20 their northward progress came to a halt only a few miles (12.66 statute, 11 geographic) away from One Ton Depot. Scott wrote that it was a blizzard that stopped them. They died on or shortly after March 29, the date of Scott's last diary entry. Only Scott's journal comments on the weather of those final days. In his final entry on March 29, he wrote, "Since the 21st we have had a continuous gale from W. S. W. and S. W," suggesting that the blizzard had raged for ten days straight. He ended his diary and his life with the entreaty, "For God's sake look after our people."[1]

Lack of visibility confined Scott and his men to their tents during previous blizzards on the polar trek. In a blinding state of drift, with no sun to check their compasses or theodolites, they faced the terror of becoming stranded far off the course where their vital depots of food and fuel were stored. There was little choice but to camp when both sun and horizon were replaced by unending sheets of driving white snow.

Scott's own northern party lived through two seasons of furious winds in the glacier outflow areas of Cape Adare and Terra Nova Bay (see map 2, page 15). These quickly became "the bane of our existence during winter."[2] Priestley, the geologist of the northern party, wrote to Simpson, "I have never experienced anything like the force of the wind we have had here," and he reported that "it is impossible to walk against the gusts sometimes even on a good holding ground, and I have frequently had to hold on, crouching low, and wait for a lull before it was possible to make way against the wind on my return to the hut. . . . As long as the anemometer lasted I took one minute observations for estimating the force of the wind, but it did not last long, and I was divided between a very unscientific relief at the cessation of the observations and a more scientific regret that the anemometer had not proved equal to its task."[3]

When anemometers were not available, the men judged the wind speed using the Beaufort scale of wind long employed by sailors. They simply estimated the force of the wind from visual observations. Sledging parties carried no anemometers, and the winds recorded on those journeys are based solely upon human judgment. Although the detailed accuracy of such measurements is surely subject to question, Simpson noted that the northern party members did not overestimate the wind but if anything underestimated its peak intensities compared with quantitative data taken by anemometers of good quality.[4]

The intense katabatic winds that ravage Antarctica are born as winter begins and frigid air builds up on the high plateau in the continental interior (see map 1, page 7). The cold dense air sinks down the contours of the mountains and valleys, gathering great speeds as it rushes down the steepest slopes and through narrow glacial inlets. As this massive drainage wind flows, it warms both by compression and by mixing. The river of wind that results is usually about 5–10°F warmer than the surrounding air by the time it runs out onto the flat plain of sea level.[5] Satellite imagery provides a vivid picture of this vast torrent of warm, windy air, as shown in figure 65.

The ferocious wind that spirited away the tent of the Cape Crozier party and threatened the survival of Wilson, Bowers, and Cherry-Garrard in July 1911 was a textbook example of a katabatic blizzard. It blew with hurricane-force at more than seventy miles per hour, but the trio survived the storm in large part because it subsided in less than forty-eight hours, when the reservoir of cold air was emptied.[6]

The most precipitous grades are found on the western side of the Barrier along the edge of the towering Transantarctic mountain range (see map 1). Here the plateau rises to an elevation of more than six thousand feet in only about sixty miles of horizontal distance, and these steeply pitched slopes are the sites of intense winds. Winds at the automated weather stations in the center of the Barrier, where Scott and his men perished, are considerably weaker than those on its western border, which inspire Antarctica's reputation.[7] Winds also flow down to the eastern side of the Barrier from the area now known as Marie Byrd Land. Once these variable winds reach the flat Barrier, they turn to the west until they encounter the obstacle of the Transantarctic Mountains on the western side. There they are largely diverted by the formidable topographic barricade to sweep the Barrier from south to north. As the wind flows north, it joins with the winds rushing down from the Beardmore, Nimrod, and Byrd glaciers.[8] These physical features produce the prevailing Barrier winds from the south and southwest, the following winds that Scott and his men expected as a relief to lighten the burden of their sledges on their return.

Before they pitched their tent that final time, Scott and his companions marched on many days with this welcome wind in their sail. On the afternoon of March 5, Scott described how a "slant of wind yesterday afternoon" converted a miserable morning march of 3.5 miles into more than 9.[9] Bowers's meteorological log shows that this beneficial wind ranged from 3 to 5 on the Beaufort scale (about eight to twenty-four miles per hour) and came out of the southwest and south-southwest—down the steep slopes of the Trans-

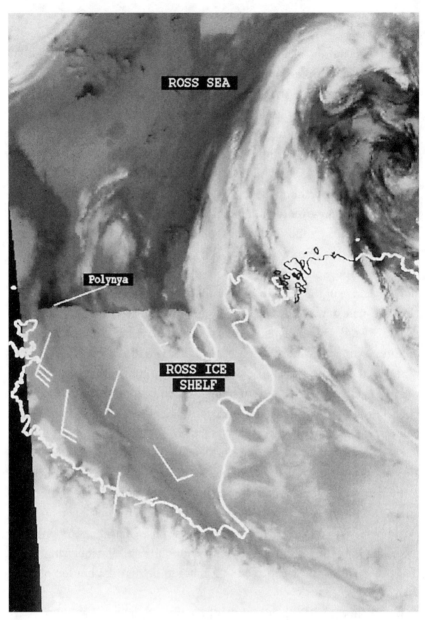

Figure 65. Advanced very high resolution radiometer (AVHRR) image of a katabatic windstorm in 1988. The dark band across the Barrier shows the region where strong winds flow from the mountains to the Ross Sea. Outflow can even be seen at the bases of several of the glaciers on the western side of the Barrier. Wind barbs show the flow measured at the same time by automated weather stations on the ground (where the angle shows the direction of flow and the number of lines indicates its speed). A polynya has been created just north of the ice shelf by the warm wind. Image courtesy of David Bromwich, Ohio State University.

antarctic Mountains. On March 2 the men marched in a wind from the southwest in force 5–6 on the Beaufort scale (about nineteen to thirty miles per hour) and managed to achieve ten miles with its aid.[10] On January 25 they marched in force 7, with "light enough to see the old track." They covered fourteen miles on that day and nearly eighteen on the next, surely grateful for the "good stiff breeze." [11]

How strong a wind stopped Scott's party from marching? When the southerly wind crept up to about 8 on the Beaufort scale (roughly forty miles per hour), failing visibility forced them to camp. On January 21 they "awoke to a stiff blizzard" of force 8. Bowers wrote in his diary on this day that "the wind would have been of great assistance to us but the drift was so thick that steering a course would have been next to impossible." [12] On January 24 the men began their trek in a wind of force 6 from the southwest, but stopped to camp when it intensified to force 8.

The automated weather station at 79°54′S, 169°58′E has stood lonely guard since 1985 over the region close to the site of the camp where Scott, Bowers, and Wilson perished. The data from that station show that the kind of winds that stymied the polar party—peak speeds faster than about force 7 on the Beaufort scale, perhaps a bit less if the snow was powdery—are neither frequent nor persistent at the place where Scott, Wilson, and Bowers camped in 1912, as figure 66 shows. Blizzards there are linked to drainage down the Byrd glacier and come from the southwest. But the Byrd glacier is more than sixty miles away from the site, and its winds have lost much of their power when they reach the area of the last camp.

One of the longest and strongest March gales that has buffeted the automated weather station near One Ton Camp occurred on March 17–20, 1993 (fig. 67). This storm had peak winds above thirty miles per hour for less than three days, and more often the breeze flowed at a modest and helpful twenty miles per hour, about 5 on the Beaufort scale. The wind raised the temperature dramatically—from −40°F on March 16 to above zero by the time the wind slackened on the twentieth, leaving the region blessed with light southerly breezes and temperatures averaging near −10°F for the next four days. Although the wind immediately raised the temperature by mixing in warm air, the cooling process after it died was much slower, as is typical of such storms. Days like those after this blizzard would surely have been wonder-

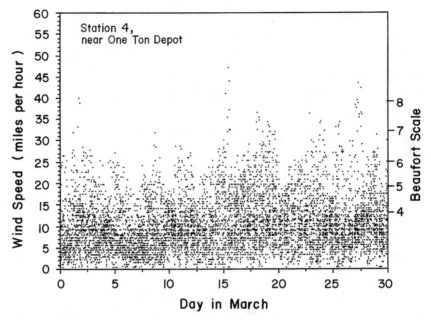

Figure 66. Hourly winds at station 4 (see map 2) for March of all the years between 1985 and 1999. Winds are frequently below force 5 on the Beaufort scale in this location. Winds very seldom rise above 6 or 7, and only for a very few days.

ful times for rapid progress across the Barrier if they had occurred in 1912 — easy times in which to progress under full sail, with well-lubricated runners gliding on warm snow under the sledge, and an indescribable improvement in personal comfort. Under such conditions, achieving the paltry distance of 12.66 statute miles to reach the vital cache of supplies that were stored at One Ton Camp would have been almost effortless. Whether or not the blizzard had ended, the temperature at the last camp must have been above −10°F after a few days of blizzard winds. Surely a strong man would try to go on in such conditions, even if the wind were still gusting at times.

There have been many March storms measured by the weather station in this region since 1984, but there has not been a single one of more than four days' duration at a strength above 6 on the Beaufort scale in the entire automated record. More often, the strongest winds blow for only a couple of days, as expected from the basic nature of the katabatic wind and its links to a finite reservoir of air on the cold plateau. The insightful Bowers once com-

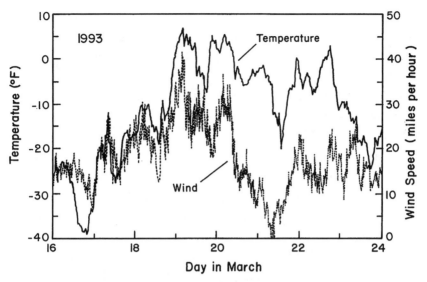

Figure 67. Winds and temperatures observed at the automated weather station near One Ton Camp (station 4; see map 2) on March 16–24, 1993. The blizzard raised the temperature quickly from −40°F to above zero as warm air blew in on March 16–20, as it has during many other similar blizzards observed there. The high winds (near 6 on the Beaufort scale) lasted less than four days in 1993, one of the longest gales recorded there to date.

mented to his diary that typical blizzards seemed to last for a "regulation two days," and the automated record supports his view.[13]

If the wind truly raged for ten days straight outside the last camp at a force above 6, then the blizzard of March 1912 was therefore one of unprecedented duration and intensity, not only never equaled but never even approached in modern data. But the contemporary record covers only about fifteen years, and this information alone does not prove that a ten-day blizzard did not strike the polar party in 1912. It shows only that such a blizzard would be highly unusual, far more so even than the very cold temperatures that occurred earlier in the polar party's awful return trek.

For those unusual and debilitating temperature data discussed in chapter 13, multiple records tell a consistent tale. It was Bowers and not Scott who kept the meteorological log, recording his daily observations of the nearly incessant cold from late February until the sling thermometer broke on March 10. Wilson's private diary entries for February 26 and 27 confirm the temperatures recorded on those days, while Cherry-Garrard's desperate vigil at One Ton Camp on March 4–10 provides sad proof that Bowers's temperature data were precise beyond reasonable doubt. For March 14–19, we have only Scott's diary to describe the exact weather encountered by the polar party during the last desperate days of the cold snap—including March 17, when Oates performed his heroic sacrifice. But support for those cold conditions is provided in Simpson's measurements of unusually cold days at Cape Evans at the same time.[14] And in a last letter to his mother written around March 22, Bowers told her that they had "terribly low temperatures on the Barrier." [15] The observations from the automated weather stations show that the prolonged cold conditions reported in 1912, while very unusual, are not unprecedented.

For the remarkably long blizzard that followed, we have little beyond Scott's own reports. On March 29 Scott wrote, "Every day we have been ready to start for our depot 11 [geographic] miles away, but outside the door of the tent it remains a scene of whirling drift," implying incessant strong wind since the storm began ten days earlier.[16] Based on this information alone, we might conclude that a March "blizzard of the century" was the last episode of uncommon weather that assailed the polar party, a final twist of the most capricious and devastating bad luck. But other data demonstrate that this cannot be so. One last time, the meteorological observations recorded by one of Scott's remarkable men, taken together with new information provided by modern machines, give fresh insights into the circumstances that befell the polar party. These data clarify some aspects of the mystery of what happened in the last days on the Barrier. The full answer is a human question beyond the powers of science to answer.

Dr. Atkinson and seaman Keohane made a desperate sledging trip to Corner Camp (78°3′S, 168°59′E) in late March to try to reach Scott's party. Atkinson recorded temperatures with another of Simpson's sling thermometers, and he estimated the wind speed three times per day for March 27–April 1, 1912, at the northern edge of the Barrier.

When Wilson had gotten his first good look at the Barrier, where he was one day to end his life, he described it as "miles and miles and miles of smooth ice plain—not a pimple on it in sight, but just waves, the whole surface looking absurdly like the sea with the sun on it." [17] The katabatic wind flows uninterrupted across that endless snow plain all the way from the base of the Beardmore glacier to the spot where Atkinson and Keohane waited in vain for the polar party. That site was given the name Corner Camp because it was here that the sledging parties could turn due south to march straight across the Great Barrier after maneuvering past the bluffs and islands that shield McMurdo Sound from the southerly wind.

The storms that strike the region of One Ton Camp often join with air flowing out of other glaciers to the north (see map 4, page 28, and maps 1 and 2) and intensify by the time they approach Corner Camp Depot (see map 5, page 87). In fifteen years of modern meteorological data, every storm with winds of several days' duration stronger than about twenty miles per hour (6 on the Beaufort scale) at the site near One Ton Camp has been mirrored by a matching gale in the region once called Corner Camp. The two locations are inextricably linked by the basic physics of fluid flow: the southerly wind from the Barrier has no option but to continue on its course until it passes Corner Camp and encounters the obstacles of terrain in the McMurdo Sound region, like the rushing waters of a flood. Figure 68 shows data from a typical March blizzard, demonstrating the way that the winds vary in lockstep at the two sites during a storm. Each day of strong winds at station 3 is matched by a comparable gale at station 4. When intense winds pound the middle of the Barrier, gusts above force 6 on the Beaufort scale are even observed at Williams Field, the site that serves as McMurdo station's snow runway, at the northernmost edge of the Barrier—the point past which Atkinson and Keohane marched as they started their search journey in 1912. Although the winds at all these sites on the smooth expanse of the western Barrier are tightly linked, the same kind of comparison cannot be made for sheltered locations on Ross Island (for example, Cape Evans or Hut Point).

It was relatively warm as Atkinson and Keohane neared Corner Camp, just as it should have been after a major katabatic storm. The coldest nightly temperature the two men recorded was −17°F, and daytime weather was as warm as a balmy −0.5°F. But the storm on the Barrier was over. As the two men marched, they encountered not a swirling mass of roaring white but a quietly empty plain of snow on which the crunch of their steps would have been the loudest sound. Winds were light on March 27–29, 1912, as Atkinson

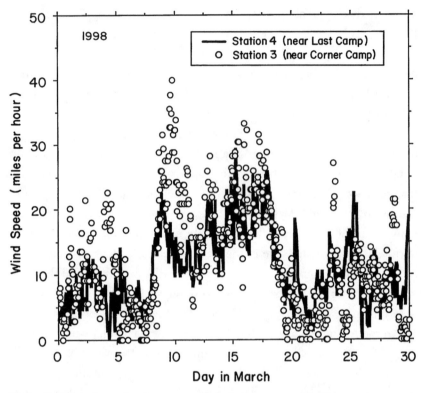

Figure 68. Winds observed at the automated weather station near Last Camp and near Corner Camp (stations 4 and 3, respectively; see map 2) in March 1998. Note that the winds at the two locations closely track each other. The similarities shown have been observed in every strong March blizzard measured on the Barrier in the automated record (since 1984).

and Keohane progressed to and reached Corner Camp, always hoping to see a party of men emerge on the horizon. For each day, their estimates of the wind never exceeded Beaufort force 4, less than twenty miles per hour.[18]

In short, there was not the slightest trace of a blizzard at Corner Camp on these key days in March 1912. If conditions were relatively warm with light breezes near Corner Camp, then it is a virtual certainty that there could not have been a continuous and intense blizzard raging at the lonely tent close to One Ton Camp, about one hundred miles away and directly upwind.

Atkinson depoted yet another week's provisions for four men at Corner Camp but turned back for the *Discovery* hut certain in his own mind that the polar party must be dead.[19] In such weather, they ought to have reached him unless something else was preventing them from marching. And the weather stations now confirm that he, too, was right.

Atkinson's weather log thus proves that there was no blizzard on or after March 27. It is highly likely that the storm subsided or became intermittent enough to allow a healthy party to march even earlier than this, based on the contemporary record of typical storms in the area of the last camp.

Why didn't Scott, Bowers, and Wilson go on? If it was not the savagery of an Antarctic blizzard that kept them in the tent, then what was it?

Like Oates before him, Scott had been stricken by frostbite in his foot on one of the last intensely cold days that preceded the blizzard. He wrote that he could only hope for amputation, and on March 21 he said that it would be Wilson and Bowers alone who would try to make the journey to One Ton Depot. Strangely, in a later entry for two days, March 22–23, he wrote that "we shall march for the depot with or without our effects and die in our tracks," suggesting that at this point the plan had changed to one in which all three would go on together no matter what. Scott also wrote to his wife, telling her that he and his companions would "fight to the last for that depot" whenever the storm abated.[20] But they never left.

Wilson wrote an undated letter to his friend Reginald Smith, telling him that "this looks like a finish to our undertaking for we are out of food and oil, and not able to move now for 3 days on account of the blizzard. We have had a long struggle against intense cold on very short fuel, and it has done us up. We shall make a forlorn-hope effort to reach the next depot to-morrow."[21] Thus Wilson's letter further attests to the cold snap and confirms the first three days of the blizzard, a duration consistent with the longest storms yet documented in this region. This was an unlucky "blizzard of a decade" or so, a further stroke of bad luck in the weather. But what happened next?

The party was running very short of food and oil, so perhaps they were simply too weak to continue. On March 19, just before the blizzard struck, Scott wrote that they had two days' food but barely a day's fuel.[22] They were probably thirsty by March 22. But Bowers at least still deemed himself fit enough to continue at this point. He wrote a letter to his "own dearest mother" on a day that he guessed was March 22. He told her that he and Wilson were about to attempt to reach the depot and return, making a march of

Figure 69. Captain Scott on skis. Photograph by H. Ponting. Scott Polar Research Institute, Cambridge.

twenty-two geographic miles. Just as he had when he described his efforts to save the ponies on the return from the depot journey, he told his mother that with her intimate understanding of his personality she would surely "know that I have struggled to the end." He also said that "each depot has been a harder struggle to reach but I am still strong and hope to reach this one."[23] At this point, the indomitable Bowers appeared both confident of his continued strength and fiercely determined to leave the tent as soon as the wind permitted. It is possible that even Bowers could not have reached the depot and returned in just one day, and the team had only one tent. But Bowers and Wilson had been faced with the threat of marching without a tent before, when the wind stole theirs during the winter journey to Cape Crozier. Wilson then thought it would be possible to dig a nightly hole in the Barrier and cover his head with a floorcloth, and the same strategy could have been employed now.[24]

Wilson penned a letter to his wife in which he said that "Today may be the last effort. Birdie [Bowers] and I are going to try and reach the Depot 11 miles north of us and return to this tent where Captain Scott is lying with a frozen foot."[25]

Wilson also wrote to his parents, most likely a few days later. In this key letter bearing no date, the doctor made no mention of scurvy and no longer indicated any plan to try to reach the depot. Nor did he say that a storm was still blowing outside the tent. Surely he would have done so if that had been the case, for it seems likely that the loyal Wilson would very much have wished to avoid the implication that Scott was the sole member of the party whose health now impeded their progress. And in his letter to his parents, Wilson added an important new detail: he explicitly said not only that Scott was frostbitten but that his condition was so bad he could scarcely walk.[26]

To his nearest and dearest family, the doctor's last letters suggest that the factor now stopping the polar party was medical rather than meteorological: the injured Captain Scott could not continue. If his foot did not improve, then the three men were confronted not with a twelve- or twenty-four-mile problem of securing food and fuel that would allow all of them to go on. Instead they would be faced with the agonizing truth that only two of them were well enough to negotiate not just the few miles to One Ton Camp but more important the rest of the 170 mile stretch of barren snow plain that still lay between the polar party and the safety of Cape Evans.

Even so, it is curious that Bowers didn't try to reach the depot, to succeed or die in the struggle as he had pledged to do. Keohane's diary suggests why neither Bowers nor Wilson attempted the round trip to the depot to bring supplies back. Keohane wrote, "We had the wind behind us with the sail set the pulling was very heavy we could not have moved the sledge without the sail." [27] Figure 68 shows that after a blizzard, winds generally continue to blow, albeit much more lightly. The flood subsides, but a stream continues. The prevailing direction of those breezes is southerly, like the blizzards. A round trip from the last camp to the depot therefore would have required not just an easy outbound journey with the sail but also an excruciating trek back with the wind in the sledger's face. Although he told his mother he would try no matter what, even Bowers may have come to the crushing realization that the weather made such a Herculean effort impossible. The cold had ended, the Barrier was warm and a breeze was lightly blowing. But the magic carpet of the wind blew only one way, and that way was north. This may explain why the plan apparently changed around March 23 from a scenario in which one or two would go for supplies and return to a design in which all three simply had to go together. Perhaps they attempted to leave, only to find that Scott was too injured to move, as Lieutenant Evans had been about a month before. Perhaps they were too weak to carry their injured leader on the sledge after weeks on the trail—three of those in a deep freeze of unimaginable agony. Crean went on alone thirty-five miles to find help when Lieutenant Evans's party was faced with a similar decision. But this time help was much too far away.

Scott wrote a final letter to his friend and agent in New Zealand, Kinsey, thanking him for his service to the expedition and noting that the blizzard had held them up for four days. He later scrawled the words "now 9" in the margin of the letter, presumably the day before his last diary entry. He stressed that "nothing but the most exceptional hard luck at the end would have caused us to fail to return." [28] It was Scott who had insisted upon the distribution of thirty opium tablets to each man on March 11, so that each would have "the means of ending our troubles." But he had to "practically order" his best friend Dr. Wilson to release the tablets, perhaps because the religious Wilson opposed the idea of suicide—and Bowers's writings show that he shared Wilson's religious devotion.[29] Scott told his wife that in the end he and his companions decided not to kill themselves.[30]

Although Scott wrote many farewell letters, there was one correspondent who had received many earlier reports but to whom no parting letter was now addressed. To Clements Markham, the man who had chosen him as a polar explorer for his youth and scientific bent, the man who eschewed the need for experience, Scott sent only a message via his wife, asking her to tell him: "I thought much of him and never regretted his putting me in command of the Discovery."[31]

The legend of Scott's tragic errors of leadership goes so far as to suggest that he expressly decided not to continue, not because of the misery of his frostbitten foot but out of shame at losing the race to the Pole or as a desperate means of bolstering his legacy. An extreme footnote in the legend suggests that he convinced or perhaps even ordered the others to remain with him.[32] But perhaps it was instead Wilson and Bowers who made the decision neither to try to go on nor to let Scott take the opium. Perhaps Wilson and Bowers could not face risking a repetition of the terrible scene they had witnessed just a few days earlier, when they allowed Oates to leave the tent, knowing that he was doing so for the sake of their survival. Perhaps they waited, hoping that the captain's condition would improve or that he would soon die a natural death. Perhaps they simply waited too long.

Wilson added several undated notes to his wife in his final days. In these he spoke of his love for both her and his God: "I shall simply fall asleep and wake with Christ. . . . Don't be unhappy, Darling, all is for the best. We are playing a good part in a great scheme arranged by God himself and all is well."[33] Bowers wrote no more letters after the one to his mother on March 22, but he appeared to be well enough to scrawl a note on the back of one of Scott's letters at the very end of his life, a sentence apparently reflecting Bowers's assiduousness to the end as master of stores: he stressed that Dr. Wilson's letter to his wife could be found in the instrument box.[34] All three men were presumably still alive on March 29, when Scott made his final diary entry, for he wrote that "we shall stick it out to the end, but we are getting weaker."[35] Although Scott continued writing, neither Bowers nor Wilson chose to say anything more about why they remained in the tent in the last full week of

Figure 70. Clements Markham, left, Kathleen Scott, and Captain Scott, on board the *Terra Nova*. Photographer unknown. Scott Polar Research Institute, Cambridge.

their lives, and this may be the most telling point of all. Bowers, who had written to his beloved mother and sisters at every opportunity, sending letters back from the Beardmore glacier with Cherry-Garrard and from 87°35′ with Lieutenant Evans's party, never explained why he didn't try to march as he had said he would. If the reason was only a very unusual blizzard, that would seem to be easy to state and helpful for his family and the world to know.

It is conceivable that Scott and his companions lost all track of time—that it was really only the 26th or earlier when Scott wrote that it was the 29th. But by this time the sun was setting daily, and it seems improbable that they could have failed to note so many cycles of light and dark.

Oates had cut open his sleeping bag to keep his foot frozen during the period of extreme cold—for frostbite hurts only as flesh thaws. In the much warmer conditions of the blizzard, Scott's frozen foot probably did thaw, resulting in agonizing pain and perhaps even delirium. It seems likely that the badly injured Scott would not have been the one to go outside to check on the weather. If so, then he could have estimated the wind only by its sound. Interestingly, Scott described the winds after March 23 not as a blizzard but rather as a gale. To a naval officer of his day, wind of 7 on the Beaufort scale corresponded to "moderate gale." Scott may thus have been trying to describe winds of significantly less than blizzard strength—and weaker winds are not always correlated between the regions of One Ton and Corner Camps. But if his companions could not carry him and told him it was not possible for them to leave, then it might as well have been blowing a hurricane.

That Bowers was a person of great physical strength and even greater personal commitment seems apparent. That Wilson was a man of strong religious devotion, and an even stronger devotion to duty also seems manifest in his diaries. Key passages in both Bowers's and Wilson's writings point toward the great importance they each attached to connections with others. Nearly a decade earlier, in June 1902, Scott asked Wilson to accompany him on the south polar trek of the *Discovery* expedition. Wilson recorded in his diary that he responded with concern "that if either of the two broke down on a three months' sledge journey it would mean that neither would get back."[36] The doctor's statement demonstrates that the notion of abandoning a sick companion was to him simply unthinkable. Bowers, too, had made his devotion to the expedition and to its leader manifestly clear. In a letter to his

Figure 71. From left, Wilson, Lashly, Bowers, and Gran. Photograph by H. Ponting, Scott Polar Research Institute, Cambridge.

mother written just before beginning the polar trek, he wrote, "I am Captain Scott's man and shall stick by him right through."[37] The weather station data, taken together with Dr. Atkinson's 1912 observations, suggest that this may be exactly what Bowers and Wilson ultimately chose to do.

Like Oates, Scott was bitten by the unusually cold temperatures that struck before the blizzard ever began, leaving his right foot so badly frostbitten that he could not hope to traverse the long expanse between One Ton Camp and Cape Evans. Both Scott and Oates therefore died as a direct result of the exceptionally frigid weather that prevailed on the Barrier from late February to March 19. Wilson and Bowers met their deaths with the injured Scott, but the scientific constraints of modern meteorology as shown here suggest that their deaths may have been a matter of choice rather than chance. Whether such a choice was made, and whether it reflected their own dedication or an order by a desperate Scott vainly attempting to save legacies rather than lives is a question not for science but for the human heart.

The closing paragraph of Scott's message to the public begins, "Had we lived, I should have had a tale to tell of the hardihood, endurance, and courage of my companions which would have stirred the heart of every Englishman. These rough notes and our dead bodies must tell the tale."[38] Along with their notes and bodies, Bowers's meteorological log book documenting their battle with debilitating and unusual cold was found buried on the sledge, deep under the snow at the site of the last camp. Another weather log was dutifully kept by Dr. Atkinson in the last days of March as he searched for companions who never arrived, in spite of light southerly winds and relatively mild temperatures. A few scant miles from the footprints these men left in the snow in 1912, machines were put in place almost three quarters of a century later to gather new data that would ultimately shed fresh light on their struggle, the strength of their characters, and the reasons for their deaths.

The Worst Weather in the World

The visitor picks up his Walkman radio and tucks it into his shirt pocket so that the device will be kept warm by his body. Then he puts on the earphones and adjusts the frequency dial to bring in the KICE radio announcer. The radio reaches only those within a few miles of McMurdo, and it is more of a hobby for the enthusiasts who operate the transmitting station than a serious attempt at communication. But for the small audience within its range, it is often entertaining and occasionally even informative.

He pulls on his parka and boots and opens the door to the dormitory. He squints as the cold wind bites at his face, and within seconds he can feel a crust of hard ice forming at the edge of his right eye. But he puts his head down to ward off the wind and marches resolutely off toward the *Discovery* hut.

There are probably many residents tuned to KICE this evening, and the announcer's voice carries a lilt of excitement. He has news of an interesting and unusual nature, for there has been a development in this season's remarkable saga of exploration. The KICE announcer is beginning to relate the story, a top story of the hour not only here on radio Antarctica but also for media around the world.

Three men left Ross Island nine weeks ago to attempt the first completely unsupported journey all the way to the Pole and back. All of them were accomplished outdoorsmen and athletes, skilled skiers and mountaineers who had achieved such badges of extreme physical prowess as a traverse of Greenland and more than one ascent of Everest. They were sponsored not by donations from schoolchildren but by a private corporation whose satellites encircle the world, uniting it in a global web of instant communication. They were equipped with the finest modern equipment—the most effective skis, the very best lightweight clothing and boots, and the most advanced polar sleds of aerodynamic design. And they made use of highly sophisticated parasails to draw themselves efficiently along on the wind, a novel and logical advance on previous efforts.

Everyone at McMurdo thought that they would make it—with such credentials and thoroughly contemporary gear, how could they possibly fail? Daily positions and written reports of progress were posted electronically on the Internet for the world to examine in near–real time. On good days, when a generous wind filled their parasails, they easily made eighteen miles. The people of McMurdo nodded their approval at this thoroughly modern technological feat. Fast, sleek, and effective—and unlike even dogs, their wind-driven transport required absolutely no food. It appeared that the grand challenge of Antarctica would at last be tamed by men in superb physical shape and possessed of great ingenuity, experience, and skill.

But in spite of all this, the web site reports that the trio is now in trouble. They are on the plateau, not yet even at the Pole. It has been cold, sometimes below −30°F. The surfaces have been rough and intractable. And there has been a series of blizzards that have confined them to their tent. All of the meteorological information has been placed on the Internet, and yesterday the visitor was examining some of the data taken just hours before.

The visitor climbs over a large snowdrift in front of the hut. The door is locked at this hour, but he can walk the periphery on the verandah. It is quiet here tonight, and he is alone with the wind, the frozen ice of the Sound before him, and the mummified seal. He isn't sure why he has come here to listen to the radio news about the fate of these modern explorers. Perhaps it has something to do with the seal. He now knows that Scott's men did indeed eat seals and penguins, for he has read about it in more than one of their books and diaries. It challenged his preconceived beliefs, so he wasn't convinced at first, but so many of the men independently remarked on it that there can no longer be any doubt.

He pulls the Walkman up closer to his heart. It is silent here, so quiet that the squawk of the radio suddenly seems terribly loud. He adjusts the volume knob awkwardly with his gloved hand.

The announcer hesitates, then says that the update has finally arrived. The three men have given up the plan of a round trip. They were pinned down by bad weather, ran short of food, and have fallen farther and farther behind the schedule that is required for safety. So they picked up the satellite phone provided by their sponsors and called for assistance. An airplane will be on the way as soon as the weather clears, and everyone knows that an Antarctic blizzard cannot last more than a few days. They will shortly be eating well again, and soon thereafter they will fly home from the Pole instead of walking.

"There's no mystery or shame in being beaten by Antarctic weather. That's happened to us all at one time or another," says the announcer. "Check out the details—it's all on the web." Then he concludes the news, and his voice is replaced by music.

The visitor tries to look through the window into the hut. But it's dark inside and all he can make out are shadows. Then he turns his gaze south across the Sound, watching the late evening sun glint on the frozen surface. Everyone knows that the weather here is the worst in the world. It is unstoppably savage, an overpowering colossus that the strongest of humans have not yet conquered and perhaps never will. It is, after all, Antarctica. There is no other place on Earth quite like it.

The Men of the Mission

The shore parties of the *Terra Nova* Expedition for 1910–12 (does not include ship's party or those who joined only for 1912–13).

Main Party, at Cape Evans in the Winter of 1911

Robert Falcon Scott ("The owner"): Captain, R. N., and expedition leader

Edward R. G. R. Evans ("Teddy"): Lieutenant, R. N., and second-in-command

Edward Adrian Wilson ("Uncle Bill"): Chief of scientific staff, also a medical doctor

Henry R. Bowers ("Birdie"): Lieutenant, Royal India Marine, in charge of stores

Lawrence E. G. Oates ("Titus" or "Soldier"): Captain, Royal Inniskilling Dragoons, in charge of ponies

Edgar Evans ("Taff"): Petty Officer, R. N., key seaman for all manual work on equipment

Apsley Cherry-Garrard ("Cherry"): Assistant zoologist

George C. Simpson ("Sunny Jim"): Meteorologist

Edward L. Atkinson ("Atch"): Surgeon, R. N., parasitologist

William Lashly ("Lash"): Petty Officer, R. N., chief stoker

Thomas Crean: Petty Officer, R. N.

Herbert G. Ponting ("Ponco"): Camera artist

Charles S. Wright ("Silas"): Physicist (Canadian)

Frank Debenham ("Deb"): Geologist (Australian)
T. Griffith Taylor ("Griff"): Geologist (Australian)
Cecil H. Meares: In charge of dogs
Bernard C. Day: Motor sledge engineer
Frederick J. Hooper: Steward, R. N.
Tryggve Gran ("Trigger"): Ski expert (Norwegian)
Patrick Keohane: Petty Officer, R. N.
Edward W. Nelson ("Marie"): Biologist
Robert Forde: Petty Officer, R. N.
Thomas Clissold: Cook, R. N.
Anton Omelchenko: Groom (Russian)
Dimitri Gerof: Dog driver (Russian)

The Northern Party

Victor L. Campbell ("The wicked mate"): Lieutenant, R. N.
George P. Abbott: Petty Officer, R. N.
Frank V. Browning: Petty Officer, R. N.
Harry Dickason: Able seaman, R. N.
George M. Levick ("Toffer"): Surgeon, R. N.
Raymond E. Priestley ("Ray"): Geologist

A Timeline of Interconnected Lives

1845 A British expedition headed by Sir John Franklin attempts to find the Northwest Passage across the Arctic. They become trapped in the ice and all of them eventually die, many of scurvy in spite of consumption of lime concentrate. The episode casts prominent doubts on the value of limes and lemons as a preventative for the disease.

1850 A young British midshipman named Clements Markham serves on a relief ship on an unsuccessful mission to rescue the Franklin party. He never participates in another such expedition himself, but he returns to England with a passion for polar exploration that greatly influences the futures of other men.

1893–96 The Norwegian explorer Fridtjof Nansen sails to the Arctic on board his specially designed polar ship, the *Fram*, leaving the vessel with a single companion to make a sledging journey to 86°14′N, setting a celebrated farthest-north record.

1898 Roald Amundsen of Norway and Frederick Cook of the United States become shipmates on board a Belgian vessel exploring the Antarctic. They are among the first men to experience Antarctic winter, as the ship becomes trapped in the ice for more than a year but eventually breaks free.

1903 British explorers Robert Falcon Scott, Edward Adrian Wilson, and Ernest Shackleton establish a record for farthest south, 82°17′S. The patron of their expedition is Markham, who personally selects Scott as its leader.

1904–6 Amundsen becomes the first to traverse the Northwest Passage, achieving the epic goal that vanquished many others, among them Franklin. Hearing the story of the Franklin expedition as a boy had helped inspire Amundsen's polar explorations.

1909 Frederick Cook claims to have reached the North Pole, together with two Inuit companions, in the previous year (April 1908). Shortly after Cook's announcement, Robert E. Peary claims to have reached the North Pole in April 1909, along with his black assistant Matthew Henson and four Inuits. A long and acrimonious battle for priority begins between Peary and Cook. Debates regarding whether either or both truly attained the North Pole were to continue to the end of the century. But the claims are strong enough that Amundsen feels compelled to change his own intent to lead a new expedition aimed at the North Pole to one directed southward. He keeps his plan to go south a secret until he and his crew are well on the way to the Antarctic in the great Norwegian vessel *Fram*, which he borrows from Nansen.

1909 Ernest Shackleton and three companions achieve a new farthest-south record of 88°23', stopping less than one hundred miles from the South Pole. A few months later, Scott announces that he will lead a new expedition with the goal of attaining the South Pole for Britain.

1910 Scott departs from England for Antarctica. While en route in Australia he receives a telegram from Amundsen stating that he too is headed south.

February 1911 After leaving the captain and most of the crew at Cape Evans on McMurdo Sound, Scott's men sail along the Ross Ice Shelf. They are surprised to encounter Amundsen's *Fram* at the Bay of Whales, and the two ships' crews breakfast and lunch together.

December 1911 Amundsen is the first to reach the South Pole, together with four Norwegian companions.

January 1912 Scott and four British teammates arrive at the South Pole, where they find Amundsen's tent, flag, and a note from him.

March 1912 Amundsen sails into Hobart, Tasmania, and announces his expedition's successful bid for the South Pole.

February and March 1912 Scott and his companions die during their return from the polar trek.

1914–16 Ernest Shackleton leads an expedition aimed at the first crossing of Antarctica from one side to the other. But before that journey can even begin, his ship, the *Endurance*, is trapped and slowly breaks up in the ice, changing his expedition of exploration into one of survival. Eventually he and five companions cross the south Atlantic in a lifeboat to reach help at a remote whaling station on South Georgia Island. They then bring help back to Elephant Island to rescue other expedition members left there.

1921–22 Shackleton begins another Antarctic expedition. He dies en route of heart failure and is buried on the island that had proved to be his salvation in 1916, South Georgia.

1926 Admiral Richard E. Byrd of the United States announces that he has flown an airplane over the North Pole. As in the cases of his countrymen Cook and Peary, debate ensues as to whether Byrd truly achieved his goal. Three days after Byrd's flight, Amundsen is among the members of an expedition that flies over the North Pole in a dirigible piloted by Umberto Nobile of Italy. One of his Antarctic companions, Oscar Wisting, is with him, and depending on the legitimacy of the American claims in the north, the two Norwegians may have been among the first men to see not only the South Pole but also the North Pole.

1928 Nobile is involved in a new aerial expedition to explore the Arctic but is lost in a plane crash. Amundsen is among those who search for him. Nobile is eventually rescued by others, but Amundsen's search plane crashes in the Arctic, and he dies in the north polar wastelands that inspired his life.

NOTES

Preface

1. Gwynn, *Captain Scott*; Seaver, *Scott of the Antarctic*; Huxley, *Scott of the Antarctic*.
2. Hayes, *Antarctica*, 200; Thomson, *Scott's Men*.
3. Huntford, *Scott and Amundsen*. See also Huntford, *Last Place on Earth*; T. Griffiths, *Judgement Over the Dead: The Screenplay of The Last Place on Earth* (London: Verso/New Left, 1986).
4. F. Spufford, *I May Be Some Time: Ice and the English Imagination* (New York: St. Martin's, 1997); Preston, *A First Rate Tragedy*; Baughman, *Pilgrims on the Ice*; Yelverton, *Antarctica Unveiled*.

1 Into the Pack

1. Scott, *Voyage of the "Discovery,"* 16.
2. Ibid., 17–20.
3. Total raised: ibid., 20–23.
4. Markham, *Antarctic Obsession*, 20; see detailed discussions in Baughman, *Pilgrims on the Ice* and Yelverton, *Antarctica Unveiled*.
5. Seaver, *Scott of the Antarctic*, 5.
6. Scott, *Voyage of the "Discovery,"* 24.
7. Markham, *Antarctic Obsession*, 2–5.
8. Scott, *Voyage of the "Discovery,"* 24.
9. Ibid., 601, 27.
10. Cherry-Garrard, *Worst Journey*, 204.
11. Letter from R. F. Scott to Reginald Smith, November 18, 1910, quoted by G. Seaver in Foreword to Cherry-Garrard, *Worst Journey*, lxi.
12. Cherry-Garrard, *Worst Journey*, 204.
13. Scott, *Voyage of the "Discovery,"* 170.

14. Ibid., 29–31.
15. Cherry-Garrard, *Worst Journey*, xxi.
16. Scott, *Voyage of the "Discovery,"* 25.
17. Ibid., 31, 35, 65.
18. L. C. Bernacchi, *Saga of the "Discovery"* (London: Blackie, 1938), 23.
19. Scott, *Voyage of the "Discovery,"* 39–40.
20. Ibid., 58.
21. Cherry-Garrard, *Worst Journey*, 210.
22. Simpson, *British Antarctic Expedition*, vol. 1, viii.
23. Scott, *Voyage of the "Discovery,"* 96.
24. Markham, *Antarctic Obsession*, 43.
25. Scott, *Voyage of the "Discovery,"* 122.
26. Ibid., 128.
27. Wilson, *Diary of the Discovery Expedition*, 111.
28. Ibid., 135, 147, 151.
29. Ibid., 160–62.

2 Of Dogs and Men

1. Scott, *Voyage of the "Discovery,"* 172; quotation, 167.
2. Ibid., 177.
3. Ibid., 179–80.
4. Ibid., 194–95.
5. Ibid., 200.
6. Amundsen, *South Pole*, vol. 1, 180.
7. Scott, *Voyage of the "Discovery,"* 432.
8. Scott, *Voyage of the "Discovery,"* 341.
9. R. Amundsen, Amundsen and the dogs, in *Antarctic Adventurers*, J. W. Roche, ed. (Somerset: Hulton Educational, 1959), 91.
10. Scott, *Voyage of the "Discovery,"* 342–43.
11. Ibid., 359.
12. Wilson, *Diary of the Discovery Expedition*, 289.
13. Cherry-Garrard, *Worst Journey*, 250.
14. Scott, *Voyage of the "Discovery,"* 357.
15. M. K. Bakkevig and R. Nielsen, Optimal combination of garments in work clothing for cold and wet environments, *Arctic Medical Research* 53 (1994), 311–13.
16. R. Fiennes, Foreword to D. Mawson, *The Home of the Blizzard* (New York: St. Martin's, 1998), xi.
17. Scott, *Voyage of the "Discovery,"* 352.
18. Ibid., 330.
19. Scott, *Scott's Last Expedition*, vol. 1, 423.
20. Wilson, *Diary of the Discovery Expedition*, 192.
21. Scott, *Voyage of the "Discovery,"* 406.

22. Seaver, *Edward Wilson of the Antarctic*, 27, 32–56.
23. Wilson begins to keep journal: ibid., 7.
24. Wilson, *Diary of the Discovery Expedition*, 214.
25. Seaver, *Edward Wilson of the Antarctic*, 77–78.
26. Scott, *Voyage of the "Discovery,"* 398, 404.
27. Huntford, *Last Place on Earth*, 164–65.
28. Scott, *Voyage of the "Discovery,"* 398–99, 401–2.
29. Ibid., 409–10.
30. Ibid., 417–30.
31. Scott, *Scott's Last Expedition*, vol 1, 597.
32. Scott, *Voyage of the "Discovery,"* 433–34.
33. Wilson, *Diary of the Discovery Expedition*, 222.
34. Scott, *Voyage of the "Discovery,"* 447–49.
35. Wilson, *Diary of the Discovery Expedition*, 221.
36. Scott, *Voyage of the "Discovery,"* 450.
37. Ibid., 454.
38. Wilson, *Diary of the Discovery Expedition*, 221.
39. Scott, *Voyage of the "Discovery,"* 452.
40. Wilson, *Diary of the Discovery Expedition*, 228.
41. Ibid., 228–29.
42. Cherry-Garrard, *Worst Journey*, 123.
43. Scott, *Voyage of the "Discovery,"* 457–60; Wilson, *Diary of the Discovery Expedition*, 228.
44. Scott, *Voyage of the "Discovery,"* 469.
45. E. R. G. R. Evans (Lord Mountevans), Rise and shine in the Antarctic, in Roche, *Antarctic Adventurers*, 25–26.
46. Wilson, *Diary of the Discovery Expedition*, 231.
47. Scott, *Voyage of the "Discovery,"* 473–81; Wilson, *Diary of the Discovery Expedition*, 235.
48. Scott, *Voyage of the "Discovery,"* 482–83.
49. S. C. Colbeck, The kinetic friction of snow, *Journal of Glaciology* 34 (1988), 78–86; Lind and Sanders, *Physics of Skiing*, 171–79.
50. Cherry-Garrard, *Worst Journey*, 114.
51. Colbeck, The kinetic friction of snow; Lind and Sanders, *Physics of Skiing*.
52. Huntford, *Last Place on Earth*, 290.
53. Scott, *Voyage of the "Discovery,"* 485; Wilson, *Diary of the Discovery Expedition*, 238.
54. Seaver, *Edward Wilson of the Antarctic*, 78.
55. Scott, *Voyage of the "Discovery,"* 491; Wilson, *Diary of the Discovery Expedition*, 237.
56. Wilson, *Diary of the Discovery Expedition*, 239.
57. Scott, *Voyage of the "Discovery,"* 487–503.

58. Ibid., 529–41.
59. Ibid., 545–61.
60. Ibid., 567; Wilson, *Diary of the Discovery Expedition*, 288–98.
61. E. A. Wilson, On some Antarctic birds, *Proceedings IVth International Ornithological Congress* (1905), 231–34.
62. Scott, *Voyage of the "Discovery,"* 573.
63. Ibid., 576–77.
64. Ibid., 584, 587.
65. Ibid., 597.
66. Ibid., 600–601, 603.
67. Ibid., 609.
68. Ibid., 614–15.
69. Ibid., 617.
70. Ibid., 629.
71. For more complete accounts of the *Discovery* expedition, see Baughman, *Pilgrims on the Ice* and Yelverton, *Antarctica Unveiled*.
72. Scott, *Voyage of the "Discovery,* 485.
73. Cherry-Garrard, *Worst Journey*, lix.
74. E. Shackleton, *South: A Memoir of the Endurance Voyage* (New York: Carroll and Graf, rpt. 1998), 371.

3 The Return
1. Scott, *Voyage of the "Discovery,"* 639.
2. Ibid., 640–42; L. C. Bernacchi, *Saga of the "Discovery"* (London: Blackie, 1938), 87.
3. Scott, *Voyage of the "Discovery,"* 643–45.
4. Ibid., 651–59.
5. Ibid., 664–78.
6. Ibid., 681–82.
7. Ibid., 709.
8. Markham, *Antarctic Obsession*, 125–47.
9. J. W. Gregory, The work of the National Antarctic Expedition, *Nature* 73 (1906), 297–300; see also Markham, *Antarctic Obsession*, 133–51.
10. Seaver, *Scott of the Antarctic*, 76–83.
11. Ibid., 84–92; Huxley, *Scott of the Antarctic*, 172.
12. Seaver, *Edward Wilson of the Antarctic*, 107–8.
13. Ibid., 113.
14. Ibid., 127–31.
15. Wilson, *Diary of the Discovery Expedition*, 140.
16. Seaver, *Edward Wilson of the Antarctic*, 128.
17. Ibid., 130–31.
18. Shackleton, *Heart of the Antarctic*, 43–56.

19. Ibid., 185–86, 210, 226.
20. Huxley, *Scott of the Antarctic*, 181.
21. H. King, Introduction to *South Pole Odyssey, Selections from the Antarctic Diaries of Edward Wilson* (Dorset: Blandford, 1982), 17–18.
22. R. F. Scott, "Men versus Motors," typescript, Archives, Scott Polar Research Institute Collection.
23. R. M. Bryce, *Cook and Peary: The Polar Controversy Resolved* (Mechanicsburg, Pa.: Stackpole, 1997), 344–75, 516–48, 969–78.
24. Ibid., 189–92.
25. Huntford, *Last Place on Earth*, 96–112.
26. F. Nansen, Introduction to Amundsen, *South Pole*, vol. 1, xxix.
27. Huxley, *Scott of the Antarctic*, 182.
28. G. Hattersley-Smith, Foreword to Gran, *Norwegian with Scott*, 12.
29. Scott, *Scott's Last Expedition*, vol. 1, 609, 622–23.
30. Evans, *South with Scott*, 21.
31. Wilson, *Diary of the Terra Nova Expedition*, 249–57; Huxley, *Scott of the Antarctic*, 186–87.
32. Pound, *Evans of the Broke*, 3–9.
33. Cherry-Garrard, *Worst Journey*, 4.
34. Evans, *South with Scott*.
35. A. Savours, *The Voyages of the Discovery: The Illustrated History of Scott's Ship* (London: Virgin, 1992), 108–33.
36. Evans, *South with Scott*, 17.
37. Ibid., 25.
38. Seaver, *Birdie Bowers of the Antarctic*, 1–49.
39. Ibid., 146.
40. Evans, *South with Scott*, 20–21.
41. Ponting, *Great White South*, 160–61.
42. Scott, *Scott's Last Expedition*, vol. 1, 410.
43. Evans, *South with Scott*, 13.
44. Wilson, *Diary of the Discovery Expedition*, 275.
45. Seaver, *Edward Wilson of the Antarctic*, 134.
46. Wilson, *Diary of the Terra Nova Expedition*, 249–57.
47. Simpson, *Meteorology*, vol. 1, iii.
48. D. E. Pedgley, Pen portraits of Presidents—Sir George Clarke Simpson, KCB, FRS, *Weather* 50 (1995), 347–49.
49. G. Seaver, Foreword to Cherry-Garrard, *Worst Journey*, lv–lvi.
50. Ibid., lvii–lix.
51. H. King, Introduction to Wilson, *Diary of the Terra Nova Expedition*, xvii.
52. Seaver, Foreword to Cherry-Garrard, *Worst Journey*, lix–lx, lxi, lxxv.
53. Ibid., lxxxiv.
54. Cherry-Garrard, *Worst Journey*, liii.

55. Evans, *South with Scott*, 85.
56. Limb and Cordingley, *Captain Oates*, 33.
57. Wilson, *Diary of the Terra Nova Expedition*, 74.
58. Evans, *South with Scott*, 108.
59. S. Bergan, *Cross Country Skiing* (Indianapolis: Masters, 1996), 66–68, 91–115.
60. Debenham, *In the Antarctic*, 31–32.
61. Wilson, *Diary of the Terra Nova Expedition*, 82–83.
62. Evans, *South with Scott*, 40–41.
63. Huxley, *Scott of the Antarctic*, 203–4.
64. Evans, *South with Scott*, 22.
65. Huxley, *Scott of the Antarctic*, 192.
66. H. R. Bowers, Letter to E. Bowers, June 7, 1910, Archives, Scott Polar Research Institute, Cambridge.
67. Wilson, *Diary of the Terra Nova Expedition*, 16, 33.
68. Ibid., 16.
69. Cherry-Garrard, *Worst Journey*, 27.
70. Evans, *South with Scott*, 35.
71. Wilson, *Diary of the Terra Nova Expedition*, 45.
72. Ibid., 26.
73. Seaver, *Edward Wilson of the Antarctic*, 121.
74. H. R. Bowers, Letter to his mother, August 23, 1910, Archives, Scott Polar Research Institute, Cambridge.
75. Evans, *South with Scott*, 36.
76. Wilson, *Diary of the Terra Nova Expedition*, 52–54.
77. Evans, *South with Scott*, 63–64; Cherry-Garrard, *Worst Journey*, 40–41.
78. Evans, *South with Scott*, 40.
79. Wilson, *Diary of the Terra Nova Expedition*, 57.
80. Evans, *South with Scott*, 45–46.
81. Wilson, *Diary of the Terra Nova Expedition*, 64.
82. Ibid.
83. Evans, *South with Scott*, 46–47.
84. Scott, *Scott's Last Expedition*, vol. 1, 16.
85. Evans, *South with Scott*, 47.
86. Cherry-Garrard, *Worst Journey*, 50.
87. Ibid., 51.
88. Wilson, *Diary of the Terra Nova Expedition*, 66.
89. Cherry-Garrard, *Worst Journey*, 51–52.
90. Evans, *South with Scott*, 49.
91. Cherry-Garrard, *Worst Journey*, 51, 53–54; Evans, *South with Scott*, 46.
92. Wright, *Silas*, 45; Evans, *South with Scott*, 48–49.
93. Evans, *South with Scott*, 48–51.
94. Cherry-Garrard, *Worst Journey*, 55.

95. Scott, *Scott's Last Expedition*, vol. 1, 14.
96. Wilson, *Diary of the Terra Nova Expedition*, 74.
97. Evans, *South with Scott*, 54.
98. Cherry-Garrard, *Worst Journey*, 62.
99. Scott, *Scott's Last Expedition*, vol. 1, 25.
100. Wilson, *Diary of the Terra Nova Expedition*, 92.

4 The Safety of Supplies

1. Scott, *Scott's Last Expedition*, vol. 1, 80.
2. Ponting, *Great White South*, 49–50.
3. Evans, *South with Scott*, 56–58.
4. Ibid., 53–61.
5. Amundsen, *South Pole*, vol. 1, 164–66.
6. Shackleton, *Heart of the Antarctic*, 39–42.
7. See C. F. Ropelewski, Spatial and temporal variations in Antarctic sea ice (1973–82), *Journal of Climate and Applied Meteorology*, 22 (1983), 470–73; C. Parkinson, Spatial patterns in the length of the sea ice season in the Southern Ocean, 1979–1986, *Journal of Geophysical Research*, 99 (1994), 16327–39; D. G. Martinson, Evolution of the southern ocean water mixed layer and sea ice: Open ocean deepwater formation and ventilation, *Journal of Geophysical Research*, 95 (1990), 11641–54.
8. Evans, *South with Scott*, 56–57.
9. H. R. Bowers, Letter to his sister Edie, December 18, 1910, Archives, Scott Polar Research Institute, Cambridge.
10. Evans, *South with Scott*, 65.
11. Wilson, *Diary of the Terra Nova Expedition*, 91.
12. Evans, *South with Scott*, 65.
13. Ibid., 66, 68–69.
14. Scott, *Scott's Last Expedition*, vol. 1, 89.
15. Evans, *South with Scott*, 62–63.
16. Amundsen, *South Pole*, vol. 1, 206–58.
17. Wilson, *Diary of the Terra Nova Expedition*, 93.
18. Cherry-Garrard, *Worst Journey*, 87.
19. Evans, *South with Scott*, 70.
20. Wilson, *Diary of the Terra Nova Expedition*, 93.
21. Scott, *Scott's Last Expedition*, vol. 1, 103.
22. Cherry-Garrard, *Worst Journey*, 89–90.
23. Evans, *South with Scott*, 70.
24. Scott, *Scott's Last Expedition*, vol. 1, 95.
25. Evans, *South with Scott*, 71–72; Cherry-Garrard, *Worst Journey*, 93–94; Wilson, *Diary of the Terra Nova Expedition*, 93.
26. Evans, *South with Scott*, 72, preface.

27. Wilson, *Diary of the Terra Nova Expedition*, 96.
28. Taylor, *With Scott*, 99–100.
29. Scott, *Scott's Last Expedition*, vol. 1, 106.
30. Evans, *South with Scott*, 72–76.
31. Ibid., 88; Cherry-Garrard, *Worst Journey*, 94.
32. Cherry-Garrard, *Worst Journey*, 95, 96–98.
33. Evans, *South with Scott*, 75.
34. R. F. Scott, Letter to Joseph James Kinsey, January 22, 1911, MS-Papers-0022-6, Alexander Turnbull Library, NLNZ.
35. R. F. Scott, Letter to Maj. Gen. Douglas Haig, January 22, 1911, MS-Papers-0022-6, Alexander Turnbull Library, NLNZ.
36. Evans, *South with Scott*, 77–83.
37. Scott, *Scott's Last Expedition*, vol. 1, 141–43.
38. Cherry-Garrard, *Worst Journey*, 107.
39. Evans, *South with Scott*, 86–87.
40. E. Shackleton, *South: A Memoir of the Endurance Voyage* (New York: Carroll and Graf, rpt. 1998), 371–72.
41. Cherry-Garrard, *Worst Journey*, 112–14.
42. Scott, *Scott's Last Expedition*, vol. 1, 145–49.
43. Gran, *Norwegian with Scott*, 50.
44. Scott, *Scott's Last Expedition*, vol. 1, 150–51.
45. G. C. Simpson, quoted in Seaver, *Birdie Bowers of the Antarctic*, 199.
46. Scott, *Scott's Last Expedition*, vol. 1, 150, 155.
47. Ibid., 152.
48. Ibid., 151, 156–57.
49. Wilson, *Diary of the Terra Nova Expedition*, 102.
50. Scott, *Scott's Last Expedition*, vol. 1, 161.
51. Cherry-Garrard, *Worst Journey*, 116.
52. Wilson, *Diary of the Terra Nova Expedition*, 102.
53. Cherry-Garrard, *Worst Journey*, 116.
54. Scott, *Scott's Last Expedition*, vol. 1, 162.
55. L. E. Oates, Letter to his mother, January 31, 1911, Archives, Scott Polar Research Institute, Cambridge.
56. Scott, *Scott's Last Expedition*, vol. 1, 171–72, 163.
57. Ibid., 169.
58. Ibid.
59. Wilson, *Diary of the Terra Nova Expedition*, 103.
60. Ibid., 104.
61. Cherry-Garrard, *Worst Journey*, 183.
62. Scott, *Scott's Last Expedition*, vol. 1, 4–5.
63. Limb and Cordingley, *Captain Oates*, 123.
64. Cherry-Garrard, *Worst Journey*, 184.

65. Scott, *Scott's Last Expedition*, vol. 1, 173.
66. Cherry-Garrard, *Worst Journey*, 119.
67. Scott, *Scott's Last Expedition*, vol. 1, 174–75.
68. Ibid.
69. S. D. Livingstone, R. W. Nolan, and A. A. Keefe, Effect of a 91-day polar ski expedition on cold acclimitization, in *Circumpolar Health 90: Proceedings of the 8th International Congress on Circumpolar Health, Whitehorse, Yukon, May 20–25, 1990* (Winnipeg: University of Manitoba Press, 1991), 486–88.
70. Wilson, *Diary of the Terra Nova Expedition*, 105–6.
71. Cherry-Garrard, *Worst Journey*, 130.
72. Scott, *Scott's Last Expedition*, vol. 1, 185–86, 5, 37.
73. Evans, *South with Scott*, 94–95.
74. Shackleton, *Heart of the Antarctic*, 45–52.
75. J. G. Hayes, *The Conquest of the South Pole* (New York: Macmillan, 1933), 114.
76. Cherry-Garrard, *Worst Journey*, 134–38.
77. Scott, *Scott's Last Expedition*, vol. 1, 187–88.
78. Wilson, *Diary of the Terra Nova Expedition*, 107.
79. Amundsen, *South Pole*, vol. 1, 49.
80. J. H. Zumberge, The remains of Camp Michigan, *Antarctic Journal of the United States*, 9 (1974), 84–87.
81. *Los Angeles Times*, November 6, 1987.
82. Wilson, *Diary of the Terra Nova Expedition*, 108.
83. Scott, *Scott's Last Expedition*, vol. 1, 191–92.
84. Wilson, *Diary of the Terra Nova Expedition*, 108–109.
85. Ibid., 110–12.
86. Scott, *Scott's Last Expedition*, vol. 1, 191–92.
87. H. R. Bowers, Personal journal sent to his mother, transcript in Scott Polar Research Institute, Cambridge; also quoted in Cherry-Garrard, *Worst Journey*, 141–44.
88. Cherry-Garrard, *Worst Journey*, 160.
89. Ibid., 158–60.
90. Ibid., 144–48.
91. Bowers journal; also quoted by Cherry-Garrard, *Worst Journey*, 148.
92. Cherry-Garrard, *Worst Journey*, 124, 150–52.
93. H. R. Bowers, Letter to his mother quoted in Seaver, *Birdie Bowers of the Antarctic*, 159.
94. Cherry-Garrard, *Worst Journey*, 152–57, 163, 149.
95. Wilson, *Diary of the Terra Nova Expedition*, 109.
96. Evans, *South with Scott*, 93, 148.
97. L. E. Oates, Letter to his mother, October 24, 1911, Archives, Scott Polar Research Institute, Cambridge.
98. Scott, *Scott's Last Expedition*, vol. 1, 192.

5 The Start of a "Coreless" Winter

1. Cherry-Garrard, *Worst Journey*, 161.
2. Gran, *Norwegian with Scott*, 72.
3. Cherry-Garrard, *Worst Journey*, 164–69.
4. Evans, *South with Scott*, 103.
5. Wilson, *Diary of the Terra Nova Expedition*, 116.
6. A. Cherry-Garrard, in Seaver, *Edward Wilson of the Antarctic*, xvi.
7. Wilson, *Diary of the Terra Nova Expedition*, 116.
8. Taylor, *With Scott*, 260.
9. Cherry-Garrard, *Worst Journey*, 164–67.
10. Ibid., 160, 164.
11. Wilson, *Diary of the Terra Nova Expedition*, 119.
12. Evans, *South with Scott*, 106–7.
13. Ibid., 108.
14. Cherry-Garrard, *Worst Journey*, 248.
15. H. R. Bowers, Personal journal for December 21 and 25, 1911, transcript in Archives, Scott Polar Research Institute, Cambridge.
16. Amundsen, *South Pole*, vol. 1, 232–48; Wilson, *Diary of the Terra Nova Expedition*, 118.
17. J. v. Hann, Die meteorologischen Ergebnisse der englischen antarktischen Expedition, 1901–4, *Meteorologische Zeitschrift*, 26 (1909), 289–301.
18. Huxley, *Scott of the Antarctic*, 176; Yelverton, *Antarctica Unveiled*, 410–12.
19. Simpson, *Meteorology*, vol. 1, iii, 16, 79.
20. Ibid., 15–21.
21. C. R. Stearns, L. M. Keller, G. A. Weidener, and M. Sievers, Monthly mean climatic data for Antarctic automated weather stations, *Antarctic Reseach Series*, 61 (1993), 1–21.
22. Simpson, *Meteorology*, vol. 1, 85–89.
23. Scott, *Scott's Last Expedition*, vol. 1, 300.
24. Evans, *South with Scott*, 180.
25. Scott, *Scott's Last Expedition*, vol. 1, 176.
26. Simpson, *Meteorology*, vol. 1, vii.
27. Ibid., 85–94.
28. Cherry-Garrard, *Worst Journey*, 170.
29. Simpson, *Meteorology*, vol. 1, 92–93.
30. M. L. Savage and C. R. Stearns, Climate in the vicinity of Ross Island, Antarctica, *Antarctic Journal of the United States*, 20 (1985), 1–9; W. P. O'Connor, D. H. Bromwich, and J. F. Carrasco, Cyclonically forced barrier winds along the Transantarctic mountains near Ross Island, *Monthly Weather Review*, 122 (1994), 137–50.
31. Simpson, *Meteorology*, vol. 1, 52–73.
32. Evans, *South with Scott*, 108–9.

33. Cherry-Garrard, *Worst Journey*, 260, 302.

34. Simpson, *Meteorology*, vol. 1, 17–19.

35. Shackleton, *Heart of the Antarctic*, 221–24.

36. Wilson, *Diary of the Terra Nova Expedition*, 118.

37. Scott, *Scott's Last Expedition*, vol. 1, 220–22.

38. Cherry-Garrard, *Worst Journey*, 175–76.

39. Ponting, *Great White South*, 108.

40. Cherry-Garrard, *Worst Journey*, 176.

41. Evans, *South with Scott*, 113–14.

42. Cherry-Garrard, *Worst Journey*, 173–82.

43. Evans, *South with Scott*, 128–29, 132.

44. Ibid., 115–16; Cherry-Garrard, *Worst Journey*, 230.

45. Cherry-Garrard, *Worst Journey*, 207–8.

46. Scott, *Scott's Last Expedition*, vol. 1, 295.

47. Cherry-Garrard, *Worst Journey*, 222.

48. Limb and Cordingley, *Captain Oates*, 15–19; Ponting, *Great White South*, 129.

49. Debenham, *Quiet Land*, 126.

50. Scott, *Scott's Last Expedition*, vol. 1, 231–39.

51. L. E. Oates, Letter to his mother, October 24, 1911, Archives, Scott Polar Research Institute, Cambridge.

52. Evans, *South with Scott*, 121.

53. Cherry-Garrard, *Worst Journey*, 184, 177.

54. Scott, *Scott's Last Expedition*, vol. 1, 240–45.

55. Cherry-Garrard, *Worst Journey*, 179–202.

56. Ibid., 198.

57. Debenham, *Quiet Land*, 106. Low temperature: G. C. Simpson, *Meteorology*, vol. 3, 5.

58. Cherry-Garrard, *Worst Journey*, 198.

59. Evans, *South with Scott*, 124–25.

60. Cherry-Garrard, *Worst Journey*, 217–19; Scott, *Scott's Last Expedition*, vol. 1, 377.

61. Scott, *Scott's Last Expedition*, vol. 1, 384.

62. K. J. Carpenter, *The History of Scurvy and Vitamin C* (Cambridge: Cambridge University Press, 1986), 5–7, 233–37, 133–57.

63. Cherry-Garrard, *Worst Journey*, 221.

64. Carpenter, *History of Scurvy*, 232.

65. R. V. Southcott and N. J. Chesterfield, Vitamin A content of the livers of huskies and some seals from Antarctic and subantarctic regions, *Medical Journal of Australia*, 1 (1971), 311–13, 226.

66. Carpenter, *History of Scurvy*, 232.

67. Cherry-Garrard, *Worst Journey*, 167.

68. Taylor, *With Scott*, 192.

69. Ponting, *Great White South*, 131.

70. Carpenter, *History of Scurvy*, 231–32.
71. G. C. Simpson, Text of a lecture given in Simla, India, in 1914, Collection of Simpson letters and papers, Archives, U.K. Meteorological Office, Bracknell, England.
72. Cherry-Garrard, *Worst Journey*, 218.
73. Scott, *Scott's Last Expedition*, vol. 1, 266.
74. Shackleton, *Heart of the Antarctic*, 13–15, 144.
75. Ibid., 100, 150, 174.
76. D. Martyn, *Climates of the World* (Amsterdam: Elsevier, 1992), 152, 162.
77. Shackleton, *Heart of the Antarctic*, 100.
78. Ibid., 100–101.
79. Debenham, *Quiet Land*, 102–3.
80. Ibid., 109.
81. Cherry-Garrard, *Worst Journey*, 222.
82. Scott, *Scott's Last Expedition*, vol. 1, 453, 632–33.
83. Cherry-Garrard, *Worst Journey*, 117, 183.
84. Evans, *South with Scott*, 121, 148.
85. Cherry-Garrard, *Worst Journey*, 184.
86. Evans, *South with Scott*, 62.
87. Debenham, *Quiet Land*, 103.
88. Wright, *Silas*, 7.

6 For the Love of Science
1. Evans, *South with Scott*, 132.
2. Wilson, *Diary of the Terra Nova Expedition*, 135.
3. Ponting, *Great White South*, 141.
4. Evans, *South with Scott*, 135–36.
5. Amundsen, *South Pole*, vol. 1, 265, 335–43, 272–76.
6. Ibid., 269–70, 332–33.
7. Cherry-Garrard, *Worst Journey*, 239.
8. Wilson, *Diary of the Terra Nova Expedition*, 141–42.
9. Cherry-Garrard, *Worst Journey*, 240, 254.
10. Evans, *South with Scott*, 138.
11. Wilson, *Diary of the Terra Nova Expedition*, 136.
12. Cherry-Garrard, *Worst Journey*, 238.
13. Scott, *Scott's Last Expedition*, vol. 1, 333.
14. Wilson, *Diary of the Terra Nova Expedition*, 142–49.
15. Ibid., 141, 142.
16. Cherry-Garrard, *Worst Journey*, 242.
17. Ibid., 264, 247.
18. Ibid., 244–46.
19. Wilson, *Diary of the Terra Nova Expedition*, 143.

20. Cherry-Garrard, *Worst Journey*, 239.

21. Ibid., 250.

22. Wilson, *Diary of the Terra Nova Expedition*, 144.

23. Cherry-Garrard, *Worst Journey*, 252.

24. Simpson, *Meteorology*, vol. 3, 52 and 607.

25. Debenham, *Quiet Land*, 113–14.

26. Evans, *South with Scott*, 145.

27. Scott, *Scott's Last Expedition*, vol. 1, 347.

28. Cherry-Garrard, *Worst Journey*, 252.

29. Wilson, *Diary of the Terra Nova Expedition*, 144.

30. Cherry-Garrard, *Worst Journey*, 253–54, 244.

31. Ibid., 251.

32. Evans, *South with Scott*, 139.

33. Debenham, *Quiet Land*, 115.

34. Cherry-Garrard, *Worst Journey*, 255.

35. Wilson, *Diary of the Terra Nova Expedition*, 147.

36. Cherry-Garrard, *Worst Journey*, 261.

37. Ibid., 264–65; Wilson, *Diary of the Terra Nova Expedition*, 149.

38. Wilson, *Diary of the Terra Nova Expedition*, 129–31.

39. Cherry-Garrard, *Worst Journey*, 265.

40. Ibid., 266–67.

41. Wilson, *Diary of the Terra Nova Expedition*, 151–52.

42. Cherry-Garrard, *Worst Journey*, 270.

43. Ibid., 271–74.

44. Wilson, *Diary of the Terra Nova Expedition*, 154–55.

45. Cherry-Garrard, *Worst Journey*, 277–78.

46. Wilson, *Diary of the Terra Nova Expedition*, 155.

47. Cherry-Garrard, *Worst Journey*, 278.

48. Wilson, *Diary of the Terra Nova Expedition*, 155.

49. Cherry-Garrard, *Worst Journey*, 281.

50. Simpson, *Meteorology*, vol. 3, 612.

51. Wilson, *Diary of the Terra Nova Expedition*, 155.

52. Cherry-Garrard, *Worst Journey*, 282.

53. Wilson, *Diary of the Terra Nova Expedition*, 155.

54. Ibid., 156; Cherry-Garrard, *Worst Journey*, 281–82.

55. Cherry-Garrard, *Worst Journey*, 238.

56. Ibid., 282–83.

57. Ibid., 283.

58. Simpson, *Meteorology*, vol. 3, 612.

59. Wilson, *Diary of the Terra Nova Expedition*, 156–57; Cherry-Garrard, *Worst Journey*, 284.

60. Cherry-Garrard, *Worst Journey*, 284.

61. Ibid., 285.

62. Cherry-Garrard, *Worst Journey*, 286–87. July 24 temperature: Simpson, *Meteorology*, vol. 3, 612.

63. Wilson, *Diary of the Terra Nova Expedition*, 156–57; Cherry-Garrard, *Worst Journey*, 285.

64. Wilson, *Diary of the Terra Nova Expedition*, 157; Cherry-Garrard, *Worst Journey*, 288–90.

65. Wilson, *Diary of the Terra Nova Expedition*, 157–58; Cherry-Garrard, *Worst Journey*, 290.

66. Cherry-Garrard, *Worst Journey*, 291.

67. Wilson, *Diary of the Terra Nova Expedition*, 158.

68. Cherry-Garrard, *Worst Journey*, 292.

69. Ibid., 291–92.

70. Wilson, *Diary of the Terra Nova Expedition*, 158–60; Cherry-Garrard, *Worst Journey*, 296–98.

71. Cherry-Garrard, *Worst Journey*, 300–301.

72. Wilson, *Diary of the Terra Nova Expedition*, 160.

73. Cherry-Garrard, *Worst Journey*, 303–4, 251.

74. Evans, *South with Scott*, 141–42.

75. Cherry-Garrard, *Worst Journey*, 312.

76. Debenham, *In the Antarctic*, 31.

77. Cherry-Garrard, *Worst Journey*, 312.

78. Scott, *Scott's Last Expedition*, vol. 1, 362.

79. G. C. Simpson, Text of a lecture given in Simla, India, in 1914, Collection of Simpson letters and papers, Archives, U.K. Meteorological Office, Bracknell, England.

80. Cherry-Garrard, *Worst Journey*, 304–10.

81. Scott, *Scott's Last Expedition*, vol. 1, 367–69.

82. Thomson, *Scott's Men*, 235–41; Huntford, *Last Place on Earth*, 373.

83. Scott, *Scott's Last Expedition*, vol. 1, 367.

84. Simpson, *Meteorology*, vol. 3, 52, 612–13.

85. Ibid., vol. 1, 110–12.

86. W. P. O'Connor and D. H. Bromwich, Surface airflow around Wingless Bight, Ross Island, Antarctica, *Quarterly Journal of the Royal Meteorological Society*, 114 (1988), 917–38; Z. Liu and D. H. Bromwich, Acoustic remote sensing of planetary boundary layer dynamics near Ross Island, Antarctica, *Journal of Applied Meteorology*, 32 (1993), 1867–82.

87. Simpson, *Meteorology*, vol. 1, 270–77.

88. D. Bromwich, Satellite analyses of Antarctic katabatic wind behavior, *Bulletin of the American Meteorological Society*, 70 (1989), 738–49; W. M. Connolley, The Antarctic temperature inversion, *International Journal of Climatology*, 16 (1996), 1333–42.

89. Gran, *Norwegian with Scott,* 114.
90. Amundsen, *South Pole,* vol. 1, 367.
91. Ibid., 79–80.
92. E. R. G. R. Evans, Outfit and preparation, in *Scott's Last Expedition,* vol. 2, *Being the Journals of Captain R. F. Scott, R. N., C. V. O,* 5th ed. (London: Smith, Elder, 1914), 495.
93. A. Cherry-Garrard, The winter journey to Cape Crozier, in *Scott's Last Expedition,* vol. 2, 14.
94. Debenham, *Quiet Land,* 50.
95. Cherry-Garrard, *Worst Journey,* 289.
96. Evans, *South with Scott,* 176.

7 In the Footsteps of Shackleton

1. Evans, *South with Scott,* 150–51.
2. Taylor, *With Scott,* 294.
3. Debenham, *In the Antarctic,* 27.
4. E. R. G. R. Evans, Spring depot journey, in *Scott's Last Expedition,* vol. 2, 292; Evans, *South with Scott,* 153–54.
5. Evans, *South with Scott,* 154–55.
6. Amundsen, *South Pole,* vol. 1, 383; Simpson, *Meteorology,* vol. 3, 614.
7. Evans, *South with Scott,* 157.
8. Evans, *South with Scott,* 162–64.
9. Amundsen, *South Pole,* vol. 1, 384–87.
10. Ibid., 387–90.
11. Huntford, *Last Place on Earth,* 381–84.
12. Amundsen, *South Pole,* vol. 1, 82–85, 369.
13. Scott, *Scott's Last Expedition,* vol. 1, 338.
14. Debenham, *Quiet Land,* 46.
15. Scott, *Scott's Last Expedition,* vol. 1, 535.
16. Debenham, *Quiet Land,* 46.
17. Debenham, *In the Antarctic,* 30.
18. Scott, *Scott's Last Expedition,* vol. 1, 534–35.
19. Simpson, *Meteorology,* vol. 1, 31.
20. Simpson, *Meteorology,* vol. 1, 81; Scott, *Scott's Last Expedition,* vol. 1, 417–30.
21. Scott, *Scott's Last Expedition,* vol. 1, 429.
22. Ibid., 417–18.
23. Ponting, *Great White South,* 7, 166.
24. Scott, *Scott's Last Expedition,* vol. 1, 422.
25. Ponting, *Great White South,* 167–68.
26. Seaver, *Birdie Bowers of the Antarctic,* 225.
27. Evans, *South with Scott,* 179–82.
28. Amundsen, *South Pole,* vol. 2, 1–2.

29. Evans, *South with Scott*, 166.

30. Ibid., 187–88, 172–74, 178.

31. R. F. Scott, Letter to Joseph James Kinsey, October 28, 1911. MS-Papers-0022-6. Alexander Turnbull Library, NLNZ.

32. Evans, *South with Scott*, 191–96.

33. Scott, *Scott's Last Expedition*, vol. 1, 440–41.

34. Evans, *South with Scott*, 199.

35. Simpson, *Meteorology*, vol. 3, 644–45.

36. Cherry-Garrard, *Worst Journey*, 322.

37. Evans, *South with Scott*, 197.

38. Simpson, Meteorology, vol. 1, 112.

39. Ibid., vol. 3, 646.

40. Evans, *South with Scott*, 197–202.

41. Wilson, *Diary of the Terra Nova Expedition*, 191.

42. Gran, *Norwegian with Scott*, 130.

43. Wright, *Silas*, 185.

44. Wilson, *Diary of the Terra Nova Expedition*, 195.

45. Taylor, *With Scott*, 325.

46. Cherry-Garrard, *Worst Journey*, 333.

47. Simpson, *Meteorology*, vol. 3, 618–21.

48. Ibid., 618.

49. Scott, *Scott's Last Expedition*, vol. 1, 456–57.

50. Ibid., 460–63.

51. Wright, *Silas*, 193.

52. Wilson, *Diary of the Terra Nova Expedition*, 207, 197.

53. Ibid., 199–200.

54. Simpson, *Meteorology*, vol. 3, 7.

55. Wilson, *Diary of the Terra Nova Expedition*, 200.

56. Scott, *Scott's Last Expedition*, vol. 1, 467; Cherry-Garrard, *Worst Journey*, 343.

57. Cherry-Garrard, *Worst Journey*, 344.

58. Wright, *Silas*, 206.

59. Scott, *Scott's Last Expedition*, vol. 1, 477–79; Cherry-Garrard, *Worst Journey*, 352.

60. Carpenter, *History of Scurvy and Vitamin C*, 232.

61. Seaver, *Birdie Bowers of the Antarctic*, 234, 236.

62. Scott, *Scott's Last Expedition*, vol. 1, 482–83.

63. Ibid., 482–86.

64. Simpson, *Meteorology*, vol. 3, 625.

65. Evans, *South with Scott*, 211.

66. Cherry-Garrard, *Worst Journey*, 357–58.

67. Evans, *South with Scott*, 212.

68. Wilson, *Diary of the Terra Nova Expedition*, 212.

69. Evans, *South with Scott*, 213.

70. Scott, *Scott's Last Expedition*, vol. 1, 489.

71. Cherry-Garrard, *Worst Journey*, 359–60.

72. Simpson, *Meteorology*, vol. 3, 624–25.

73. W. Schwerdtfeger, *Weather and Climate of the Antarctic* (Amsterdam: Elsevier, 1984), 156.

74. D. Bromwich, Snowfall in high southern latitudes, *Reviews of Geophysics*, 26 (1988), 149–68; W. Rudloff, *World Climates* (Stuttgart: Wissenschaftliche Verlagsgesellschaft, 1981), 481.

75. Bromwich, Snowfall in high southern latitudes; Rudloff, *World Climates*, 330–38.

76. Rudloff, *World Climates*, 122.

77. Amundsen, *South Pole*, vol. 2, 109, 110–14.

78. Huntford, *Last Place on Earth*, 429–31.

79. Wilson, *Diary of the Terra Nova Expedition*, 202.

80. Cherry-Garrard, *Worst Journey*, 362–63.

81. Ibid., 361–64.

82. Shackleton, *Heart of the Antarctic*, 186–91.

83. Scott, *Scott's Last Expedition*, vol. 1, 487.

84. Ibid., 485.

8 Beyond the H of Hell

1. Evans, *South with Scott*, 217–18.

2. Scott, *Scott's Last Expedition*, vol. 1, 508, 495–96.

3. Cherry-Garrard, *Worst Journey*, 364.

4. Evans, *South with Scott*, 219.

5. Scott, *Scott's Last Expedition*, vol. 1, 498.

6. Simpson, *Meteorology*, vol. 3, 659–60.

7. Cherry-Garrard, *Worst Journey*, 394–97.

8. Wilson, *Diary of the Terra Nova Expedition*, 216.

9. Evans, *South with Scott*, 220.

10. Scott, *Scott's Last Expedition*, vol. 1, 495–512.

11. Cherry-Garrard, *Worst Journey*, 367.

12. Wilson, *Diary of the Terra Nova Expedition*, 215, 216, 218.

13. Evans, *South with Scott*, 221.

14. Cherry-Garrard, *Worst Journey*, 370.

15. Evans, *South with Scott*, 221, 222.

16. Scott, *Scott's Last Expedition*, vol. 1, 508.

17. M. A. Henson, *A Black Explorer at the North Pole* (Lincoln: University of Nebraska Press, rpt. 1989; first pub. 1912), 119.

18. Scott, *Scott's Last Expedition*, vol. 1, 510.

19. Committee on Military Nutrition Research, *Nutritional Needs in Cold and in High-Altitude Environments* (Washington: National Academy Press, 1996), 30–32.

20. Scott, *Scott's Last Expedition*, vol. 1, 495–501.

21. Ibid., 502.
22. Cherry-Garrard, *Worst Journey*, 370.
23. H. R. Bowers, Letter to E. Bowers from head of the Beardmore glacier, December 21, 1911, Archives, Scott Polar Research Institute, Cambridge.
24. Scott, *Scott's Last Expedition*, vol. 1, 508–11.
25. Evans, *South with Scott*, 224.
26. Scott, *Scott's Last Expedition*, vol. 1, 511.
27. Cherry-Garrard, *Worst Journey*, 395.
28. Scott, *Scott's Last Expedition*, vol. 1, 511.
29. Wright, *Silas*, 220–22.
30. Evans, *South with Scott*, 224.
31. Wright, *Silas*, 234.
32. Cherry-Garrard, *Worst Journey*, 378.
33. Cherry-Garrard, *Worst Journey*, 380.
34. Wilson, *Diary of the Terra Nova Expedition*, 219.
35. Cherry-Garrard, *Worst Journey*, 381.
36. Wilson, *Diary of the Terra Nova Expedition*, 219.
37. Seaver, *Birdie Bowers of the Antarctic*, 244.
38. H. R. Bowers, Letter to E. Bowers from head of the Beardmore glacier, December 21, 1911, Archives, Scott Polar Research Institute, Cambridge.
39. Evans, *South with Scott*, 226.
40. Scott, *Scott's Last Expedition*, vol. 1, 514–16; Evans, *South with Scott*, 226; Wilson, *Diary of the Terra Nova Expedition*, 219.
41. R. E. Priestley, Mountain climbing and Antarctic exploration, *Oxford and Cambridge Mountaineering* (1924), 1–8.
42. Scott, *Scott's Last Expedition*, vol. 1, 517.
43. Wilson, *Diary of the Terra Nova Expedition*, 219.
44. Simpson, *Meteorology*, vol. 3, 628.
45. Evans, *South with Scott*, 229.
46. Lashly, *Diary*, 2–3.
47. Evans, *South with Scott*, 230.
48. Cherry-Garrard, *Worst Journey*, 386.
49. Scott, *Scott's Last Expedition*, vol. 1, 521.
50. Evans, *South with Scott*, 231.
51. Scott, *Scott's Last Expedition*, vol. 1, 521; temperature: Simpson, *Meteorology*, vol. 3, 628.
52. Scott, *Scott's Last Expedition*, vol. 1, 522–23.
53. Evans, *South with Scott*, 232.
54. Wilson, *Diary of the Terra Nova Expedition*, 220–21.
55. Scott, *Scott's Last Expedition*, vol. 1, 525.
56. Ibid., 506, 532.

57. Ibid., 525–26.
58. Ibid., 527–28.
59. Evans, *South with Scott*, 234.
60. Cherry-Garrard, *Worst Journey*, 532.
61. Wilson, *Diary of the Terra Nova Expedition*, 229.
62. Evans, *South with Scott*, 234–35.
63. Lashly, *Diary*, 4–5.
64. Cherry-Garrard, *Worst Journey*, 393.
65. Evans, *South with Scott*, 236.
66. Cherry-Garrard, *Worst Journey*, 512.
67. L. E. Oates, letter to his mother, January 3, 1912, Archives, Scott Polar Research Institute, Cambridge.
68. Scott, *Scott's Last Expedition*, vol. 1, 529.
69. Admiral Lord Mountevans, *Man Against the Desolate Antarctic* (New York: Funk, 1951), 50.
70. Evans, *South with Scott*, 235.
71. Mountevans, *Desolate Antarctic*, 55–56.
72. Scott, *Scott's Last Expedition*, vol. 1, 529.
73. Shackleton, *Heart of the Antarctic*, 50, 197–221.
74. Evans, *South with Scott*, 236, 240.
75. Lashly, *Diary*, 6–7.
76. Edward Broke Evans, personal communication, June 18, 2000; Pound, *Evans of the Broke*, 152.
77. Evans, *South with Scott*, 237–40.
78. Ibid., 239–41.
79. Simpson, *Meteorology*, vol. 3, 667. Quotations: Lashly, *Diary*, 11–12.
80. Evans, *South with Scott*, 241–42.
81. Simpson, *Meteorology*, vol. 3, 666–67.
82. Evans, *South with Scott*, 243–45.
83. Lashly, *Diary*, 13.
84. Evans, *South with Scott*, 242–51.
85. Ibid., 243, 248.
86. Lashly, *Diary*, 13.
87. Evans, *South with Scott*, 251.
88. Contrast with interpretation in Huntford, *Last Place on Earth*, 484–85.
89. Lashly, *Diary*, 14–17.
90. Ibid., 18.
91. Ibid., 19.
92. K. J. Carpenter, *The History of Scurvy and Vitamin C* (Cambridge: Cambridge University Press, 1986), 202–4.
93. Lashly, *Diary*, 18.

94. Evans, *South with Scott*, 235.
95. Simpson, *Meteorology*, vol. 3, 668–69.
96. Lashly, *Diary*, 19–20.
97. T. Parish and D. H. Bromwich, The surface windfield over the Antarctic ice sheets, *Nature*, 328 (1987), 51–54.
98. H. R. Bowers, Letter to his mother, January 3, 1912, Archives, Scott Polar Research Institute, Cambridge.
99. Lashly, *Diary*, 19–21, 21–23.
100. Evans, *South with Scott*, 253.
101. Lashly, *Diary*, 23–25.
102. Ibid., 25–27.
103. Ibid., 25–26.
104. Meteorological log of the second return party, Archives, U.K. Meteorological Office, Bracknell, England.
105. Lashly, *Diary*, 28–29.
106. Ibid., 29.
107. Evans, *South with Scott*, 253.
108. Lashly, *Diary*, 31.
109. Ibid., 31–32.
110. Evans, *South with Scott*, 253–54.
111. Lashly, *Diary*, 32.
112. Ibid., 32–33.
113. Evans, *South with Scott*, 255.
114. Cherry-Garrard, *Worst Journey*, 420–28.
115. Lashly, *Diary*, 33–36.
116. Carpenter, *History of Scurvy*, 224.
117. Lashly, *Diary*, 36–37.

9 **This Awful Place**
1. Amundsen, *South Pole*, vol. 2, 119–20.
2. Ibid., 121–22.
3. Ibid., 125–26.
4. Ibid., 127–32; A. Alexander, in appendix to *Amundsen, South Pole*, vol. 2, 401–3.
5. A. R. Hinks, The observations of Amundsen and Scott at the South Pole, *Geographical Journal* 102 (1944), 160–80.
6. Amundsen, *South Pole*, vol. 2, 132–35.
7. H. Mohn, *Roald Amundsen's Antarctic Expedition Scientific Results, Meteorology* (Kristiania: Kommission Hos Jacob Dybwad, 1915), 60–68.
8. Amundsen, *South Pole*, vol. 2, 135–74.
9. Seaver, *Edward Wilson of the Antarctic*, 205.
10. L. E. Oates, Letter to his mother, January 3, 1912, Archives, Scott Polar Research

Institute, Cambridge; reproduced in Limb and Cordingley, *Captain Oates*, 192–94.

11. H. R. Bowers, Letter to his mother, January 3, 1912, Archives, Scott Polar Research Institute, Cambridge.

12. Wilson, *Diary of the Terra Nova Expedition*, 229.

13. Scott, *Scott's Last Expedition*, vol. 1, 530–31.

14. Cherry-Garrard, *Worst Journey*, 513.

15. Scott, *Scott's Last Expedition*, vol. 1, 531.

16. Ibid., 532.

17. Wilson, *Diary of the Terra Nova Expedition*, 230.

18. Scott, *Scott's Last Expedition*, vol. 1, 534–36.

19. Ibid., 531–32, 536.

20. Wilson, *Diary of the Terra Nova Expedition*, 230; Scott, *Scott's Last Expedition*, vol. 1, 531–32, 537.

21. F. Debenham, *Report on the Maps and Surveys, British (Terra Nova) Antarctic Expedition, 1910–1913* (London: Harrison, 1923), 25.

22. Scott, *Scott's Last Expedition*, vol. 1, 537–40; Wilson, *Diary of the Terra Nova Expedition*, 230–31.

23. Scott, *Scott's Last Expedition*, vol. 1, 541–42, 636.

24. Amundsen, *South Pole*, vol. 2, 118; Scott, *Scott's Last Expedition*, vol. 1, 540.

25. Scott, *Scott's Last Expedition*, vol. 1, 542.

26. Debenham, *In the Antarctic*, 32.

27. Expedition-era mug volume was measured by R. Headland and S. Solomon at Scott Polar Research Institute, Cambridge, June 23, 2000.

28. Committee on Military Nutrition Research, *Nutritional Needs in Cold and in High-Altitude Environments* (Washington: National Academy Press, 1996), 297, 370–71, 468.

29. E. R. G. R. Evans (Lord Mountevans), Rise and shine in the Antarctic, in *Antarctic Adventurers*, J. W. Roche, ed. (Somerset: Hulton Educational, 1959), 20.

30. Scott, *Scott's Last Expedition*, vol. 1, 543.

31. Ibid., 543.

32. Wilson, *Diary of the Terra Nova Expedition*, 231.

33. Scott, *Scott's Last Expedition*, vol. 1, 544–45; Wilson, *Diary of the Terra Nova Expedition*, 232.

34. Quoted in Limb and Cordingley, *Captain Oates*, 196.

35. Scott, *Scott's Last Expedition*, vol. 1, 545.

36. Mohn, *Amundsen's Antarctic Expedition*, 50.

37. Simpson, *Meteorology*, vol. 3, 633.

38. Hinks, Observations.

39. Scott, *Scott's Last Expedition*, vol. 1, 546.

40. Evans, *South with Scott*, 260–61.

41. Simpson, *Meteorology*, vol. 3, 632–34.
42. H. R. Bowers, Letter to May Bowers, January 18, 1912, Archives, Scott Polar Research Institute, Cambridge.
43. Cherry-Garrard, *Worst Journey*, 525.
44. Limb and Cordingley, *Captain Oates*, 185.
45. Cherry-Garrard, *Worst Journey*, 526–27.
46. Ibid., 527.
47. Scott, *Scott's Last Expedition*, vol. 1, 551.
48. Wilson, *Diary of the Terra Nova Expedition*, 237.
49. Cherry-Garrard, *Worst Journey*, 528.
50. Committee on Military Nutrition Research, *Nutritional Needs*, 19–23, 181–214.
51. Cherry-Garrard, *Worst Journey*, 544.
52. Calorie requirement based upon figures given in Committee on Military Nutrition Research, *Nutritional Needs*, 200.
53. Ibid., 357–87.
54. Committee on Military Nutrition Research, *Nutritional Needs*, 85, 310–11; Houston, *Going Higher* (Seattle: The Mountaineers, 1998), 162–63.
55. M. Stroud, Scott: 75 years on, *British Medical Journal*, 293 (1986), 1652–53.
56. Scott, *Scott's Last Expedition*, vol. 1, 556.
57. Admiral Lord Mountevans, *Man Against the Desolate Antarctic* (New York: Funk, 1951), 98.
58. Seaver, *Birdie Bowers of the Antarctic*, 250.
59. Simpson, *Meteorology*, vol. 3, 634–36.
60. Cherry-Garrard, *Worst Journey*, 527; Scott, *Scott's Last Expedition*, vol. 1, 550.
61. M. A. Henson, *A Black Explorer at the North Pole* (Lincoln: University of Nebraska Press, rpt. 1989; first pub. 1912), 117.
62. Scott, *Scott's Last Expedition*, vol. 1, 547.
63. Amundsen, *South Pole*, vol. 1, 383.
64. Scott, *Scott's Last Expedition*, vol. 1, 552–56.
65. Cherry-Garrard, *Worst Journey*, 529–33; Evans, *South with Scott*, 267.
66. Simpson, *Meteorology*, vol. 3, 634–38.
67. Scott, *Scott's Last Expedition*, vol. 1, 557.
68. Wilson, *Diary of the Terra Nova Expedition*, 239.
69. Scott, *Scott's Last Expedition*, vol. 1, 558–59, 634.
70. Scott, *Voyage of the "Discovery,"* 621.
71. Scott, *Scott's Last Expedition*, vol. 1, 560.
72. Wilson, *Diary of the Terra Nova Expedition*, 240.
73. Ibid., 241; Scott, *Scott's Last Expedition*, vol. 1, 562.
74. Scott, *Scott's Last Expedition*, vol. 1, 562.
75. Wilson, *Diary of the Terra Nova Expedition*, 241.
76. Scott, *Scott's Last Expedition*, vol. 1, 564.
77. Wilson, *Diary of the Terra Nova Expedition*, 241.

78. Scott, *Scott's Last Expedition*, vol. 1, 565.
79. Evans, *South with Scott*, 268.
80. Scott, *Scott's Last Expedition*, vol. 1, 566–69.
81. Ibid., 570–71.
82. Wilson, *Diary of the Terra Nova Expedition*, 243.
83. Scott, *Scott's Last Expedition*, vol. 1, 572–73.
84. Cherry-Garrard, *Worst Journey*, 544.
85. A. F. Rogers, The death of Petty Officer Evans, *Practitioner*, 212 (1974), 570–80.
86. Scott, *Scott's Last Expedition*, vol. 1, 573; Rogers, Death of Evans.
87. Rogers, Death of Evans; see also Carpenter, *History of Scurvy*, 155.
88. Debenham, *Quiet Land*, 88.
89. H. R. Bowers, Letter to E. Bowers, October 27, 1911, Archives, Scott Polar Research Institute, Cambridge.
90. Shackleton, *Heart of the Antarctic*, 203–4.
91. Houston, *Going Higher*, 88, 110–14.
92. J. Lynch, personal communication, National Science Foundation, Washington, D.C., 1999.
93. Houston, *Going Higher*, 88, 107–11.
94. Cherry-Garrard, *Worst Journey*, 544–45.

10 Sunset on the Barrier

1. Wilson, *Diary of the Terra Nova Expedition*, 243; Scott, *Scott's Last Expedition*, vol. 1, 574–75.
2. Simpson, *Meteorology*, vol. 3, 639.
3. Scott, *Scott's Last Expedition*, vol. 1, 576.
4. Quotation: Wilson, *Diary of the Terra Nova Expedition*, 245.
5. Scott, *Scott's Last Expedition*, vol. 1, 577.
6. Ibid., 578–79; Wilson, *Diary of the Terra Nova Expedition*, 245.
7. Wilson, *Diary of the Terra Nova Expedition*, 245; Cherry-Garrard, Introduction to Seaver, *Edward Wilson of the Antarctic*, xxi.
8. Scott, *Scott's Last Expedition*, vol. 1, 580–83.
9. Simpson, *Meteorology*, vol. 3, 641.
10. Scott, *Scott's Last Expedition*, vol. 1, 583–84.
11. Ibid., 584–85.
12. Simpson, *Meteorology*, vol. 3, 641.
13. Scott, *Scott's Last Expedition*, vol. 1, 585–86.
14. Ibid., 586–87.
15. Simpson, *Meteorology*, vol. 3, 641–42; Scott, *Scott's Last Expedition*, vol. 1, 587–88, 634.
16. Scott, *Scott's Last Expedition*, vol. 1, 588.
17. Ibid.
18. Simpson, *Meteorology*, vol. 3, 640–42.

19. W. Lashly, *The Diary of W. Lashly* (Reading: University of Reading Fine Art Department, 1939), 26–30.
20. Wilson, *Diary of the Terra Nova Expedition*, 243–45; Scott, *Scott's Last Expedition*, vol. 1, 574.
21. Scott, *Scott's Last Expedition*, vol. 1, 589–90.
22. Simpson, *Meteorology*, vol. 3, 642.
23. Scott, *Scott's Last Expedition*, vol. 1, 591.
24. Ibid., 591–92.
25. Ibid., 592–93.
26. E. A. Wilson, Letter to Caroline Oates, Archives, Scott Polar Research Institute, Cambridge.
27. Scott, *Scott's Last Expedition*, vol. 1, 593–94.
28. Ibid., 594.
29. Ibid., 594–95.
30. Ibid., 597–99.
31. Seaver, *Edward Wilson of the Antarctic*, 217.
32. Wilson, *Diary of the Terra Nova Expedition*, 247.
33. Seaver, *Edward Wilson of the Antarctic*, 217.
34. Seaver, *Birdie Bowers of the Antarctic*, 262.
35. Scott, *Scott's Last Expedition*, vol. 1, 605–7.

11 The Anguish of Helplessness

1. Ponting, *Great White South*, 261–63; Wright, *Silas*, 247–51.
2. Ponting, *Great White South*, 266; R. E. Priestley, *Antarctic Adventure: Scott's Northern Party* (Carlton, Victoria: Melbourne University Press, rpt. 1974).
3. Wright, *Silas*, 252; Cherry-Garrard, *Worst Journey*, 429.
4. Wright, *Silas*, 252–53.
5. Cherry-Garrard, *Worst Journey*, 430; R. F. Scott, Letter to Joseph James Kinsey, October 26, 1909. MS-Papers-0022-6. Alexander Turnbull Library, NLNZ.
6. Cherry-Garrard, *Worst Journey*, 429–30, 441–42.
7. Ibid., 430–31.
8. This sextant is in the collection of artifacts at the Scott Polar Research Institute, Cambridge.
9. A. Cherry-Garrard, Diary of the dog journey to One Ton Camp, Archives, Scott Polar Research Institute, Cambridge; Cherry-Garrard, *Worst Journey*, 431; Evans, *South with Scott*, 274.
10. Cherry-Garrard, *Worst Journey*, 431–33.
11. Cherry-Garrard, Diary of the dog journey; see also Cherry-Garrard, *Worst Journey*, 431.
12. Cherry-Garrard, *Worst Journey*, 430–34; Simpson, *Meteorology*, vol. 3, 641–42; 676; Scott, *Scott's Last Expedition*, vol. 1, 586–88; 632.
13. Cherry-Garrard, Diary.

14. Cherry-Garrard, *Worst Journey*, 434.
15. Cherry-Garrard, *Worst Journey*, 434–35; Evans, *South with Scott*, 274.
16. Simpson, *Meteorology*, vol. 3, 642, 677; Cherry-Garrard, *Worst Journey*, 435.
17. E. L. Atkinson, The attempt to meet the polar party, in *Scott's Last Expedition*, vol. 2, 304.
18. Ibid., 305–6.
19. Ibid., 306; Evans, *South with Scott*, 275.
20. Cherry-Garrard, *Worst Journey*, 438–39; Atkinson, The attempt to meet the polar party, in *Scott's Last Expedition*, vol. 2, 307–8.
21. Atkinson, Attempt, 309; Cherry-Garrard, *Worst Journey*, 440–41.
22. Evans, *South with Scott*, 278–79; Cherry-Garrard, *Worst Journey*, 444–45.
23. Cherry-Garrard, *Worst Journey*, 442, 448.
24. Cherry-Garrard, *Worst Journey*, preface, 441–45, 565.
25. Ponting, *Great White South*, 268.
26. Ibid.; Amundsen, *South Pole*, vol. 2, 173, 176, 201–3.
27. Admiral Lord Mountevans, *Man Against the Desolate Antarctic* (New York: Funk, 1951), 99; Evans, *South with Scott*, 273.
28. A. M. Johnson, *Scott of the Antarctic and Cardiff* (Cardiff: Captain Scott Society, 1995), 44–45; R. Pound, *Evans of the Broke* (London: Oxford University Press, 1963), 121; personal communication, Edward Broke Evans, October 20, 2000.
29. Cherry-Garrard, *Worst Journey*, 446–50.
30. Ibid., 451–53, 57.
31. Evans, *South with Scott*, 280; Wilson, *Diary of the Terra Nova Expedition*, 241.
32. Cherry-Garrard, *Worst Journey*, 457.
33. Debenham, *Quiet Land*, 149.
34. Ibid.; Wright, *Silas*, 274; Gran, *Norwegian with Scott*, 202.
35. Atkinson, The second winter, in *Scott's Last Expedition*, vol. 2, 328; Wright, *Silas*, 275; Cherry-Garrard, *Worst Journey*, 449–50, 458.
36. Wright, *Silas*, 339.
37. Cherry-Garrard, *Worst Journey*, 495; Atkinson, Finding, 345.
38. Wright, *Silas*, 346.
39. P. Keohane, Original diary of the Terra Nova expedition, Archives, Scott Polar Research Institute, Cambridge.
40. T. Gran, quoted in *Under Scott's Command*, A. R. Ellis, ed. (New York: Taplinger, 1969), 152; E. L. Atkinson, Account of events concerning the southern party, in Joseph James Kinsey, Papers. MS-Papers-0022-4. Alexander Turnbull Library, NLNZ.
41. Cherry-Garrard, *Worst Journey*, 498.
42. Ibid.; Atkinson, Finding, 346–48.
43. Atkinson, Finding, 347–48; Cherry-Garrard, *Worst Journey*, 501–2; Keohane, Diary, Archives, Scott Polar Research Institute, Cambridge.
44. Atkinson, Finding, 348–49; Cherry-Garrard, *Worst Journey*, 510.

45. Evans, *South with Scott*, 313–14.
46. Ibid., 317.
47. Johnson, *Scott of the Antarctic and Cardiff*, 47.
48. Evans, *South with Scott*, 317.

12 In Search of Explanations

1. H. Leach, The heart of things, *Chambers Journal* 4, no. 161 (1914), 49–53.
2. Pound, *Evans of the Broke*, 128.
3. See, for example, Hayes, *Antarctica*; Gwynn, *Captain Scott*; Seaver, *Scott of the Antarctic*; Huxley, *Scott of the Antarctic*.
4. See, for example, Huntford, *Last Place on Earth*; T. Griffiths, *Judgement Over the Dead: The Screenplay of The Last Place on Earth* (London: Verso/New Left, 1986); Thomson, *Scott's Men*; F. Spufford, *I May Be Some Time: Ice and the English Imagination* (New York: St. Martin's, 1997); Preston, *First Rate Tragedy*.
5. G. Seaver, Foreword to Cherry-Garrard, *Worst Journey*, lxxxv; Hayes, *Antarctica*, 204–5; A. Cherry-Garrard, *Postscript to the Worst Journey in the World* (self-published, 1951; copy in Archives, Scott Polar Research Institute, Cambridge), 579, 582.
6. Scott, *Scott's Last Expedition*, vol. 1, 153–54, 575, 601, 605.
7. Scott, *Scott's Last Expedition*, vol. 1, 482–83; Shackleton, *Heart of the Antarctic*, 155–57.
8. Hayes, *Antarctica*, 392–93.
9. Thomson, *Scott's Men*, and Huntford, *Last Place on Earth*.
10. L. E. Oates, Letters to his mother, winter quarters, dated October 24 and 28, 1911, but containing material describing the winter, Archives, Scott Polar Research Institute, Cambridge; see also Limb and Cordingley, *Captain Oates*, 169.
11. Wright, *Silas*, 206, 209, 221.
12. Huntford, *Last Place on Earth*, 382–84.
13. M. Stroud, *Shadows on the Wasteland* (Woodstock: Overlook, 1996), 99–110, 144, 163–64, 176–78.
14. R. Mear and R. Swan, *A Walk to the Pole: To the Heart of Antarctica in the Footsteps of Scott* (New York: Crown, 1987), 112, 117, 119, 124, 202.
15. H. R. Bowers, Letter to his mother, December 25, 1910, Archives, Scott Polar Research Institute, Cambridge.
16. L. E. Oates, Letters to his mother, one dated October 24, 1911, but containing material describing the winter, and another October 28, 1911, Archives, Scott Polar Research Institute, Cambridge.
17. R. E. Priestley, The Scott tragedy, *Geographical Journal* 68 (1926), 340–43; R. E. Priestley, Scott's northern party, *Geographical Journal* 128 (1962), 129–42.
18. A. M. Johnson, *Scott of the Antarctic and Cardiff* (Cardiff: Captain Scott Society, 1995), 52.

19. Thomson, *Scott's Men*, 140.
20. Evans, *South with Scott*, 252, 259; Cherry-Garrard, *Worst Journey*, 566.
21. Cherry-Garrard, *Worst Journey*, 564.
22. R. E. Priestley, *Antarctic Adventure: Scott's Northern Party* (Carlton, Victoria: Melbourne University Press, rpt. 1974), 25; Taylor, *With Scott*, 248.
23. Scott, *Scott's Last Expedition*, vol. 1, 254–55, 258.
24. Cherry-Garrard, *Worst Journey*, 565; Debenham, *In the Antarctic*, 32.
25. E. R. G. R. Evans, The British Antarctic Expedition, 1910–13, *Geographical Journal*, 42 (1913), 10–28.
26. R. E. Byrd, *Alone* (New York: Kodansha, facsimile ed., 1995, first pub., 1938).
27. A. G. E. Jones, Scott's transport, in *Polar Portraits: Collected Papers* (Whitby: Caedmon, 1992), 278–79.
28. Shackleton, *Heart of the Antarctic*, 8; Debenham, *Quiet Land*, 52; Amundsen, *South Pole*, vol. 1, 79–80.
29. H. G. Lyons, *British (Terra Nova) Antarctic Expedition, 1910–1913: Miscellaneous Data* (London: Harrison, 1924), 35–36.
30. Debenham, *Quiet Land*, 78; Cherry-Garrard, *Worst Journey*, 291; Scott, *Scott's Last Expedition*, vol. 1, 566.
31. Scott, *Scott's Last Expedition*, vol. 1, 506; H. Hanssen, Sledge dogs on Amundsen's south polar journey, *Polar Record*, 2, no. 13 (1937), 57–59.
32. Scott, *Scott's Last Expedition*, vol. 1, 408–10.
33. Ponting, *Great White South*, 76; V. E. Campbell, *The Wicked Mate: The Antarctic Diary of Victor Campbell* (Norfolk: Bluntisham, 1988), 36.
34. Cherry-Garrard, *Worst Journey*, 569–70.
35. Amundsen, *South Pole*, vol. 2, 19; Henson, *A Black Explorer at the North Pole*, 54.
36. C. Swithinbank, To the valley glaciers that feed the Ross Ice Shelf, *Geographical Journal*, 130 (1964), 45–46.
37. Wilson, *Diary of the Discovery Expedition*, 287.
38. Internal report, "Tinplate from Historic Cans," International Tin Research Institute, Paul Harris, personal communication, January 2000; see also *Tin and Its Uses* 39 (1957), 6–7; and 41 (1959), 12.
39. Priestley, Scott tragedy.
40. B. T. K. Barry and C. J. Thwaites, *Tin and Its Alloys and Compounds* (Chichester: Ellis Horwood, 1983), 12–16.
41. Priestley, Scott tragedy.
42. Henson, *Black Explorer*, 54.
43. Amundsen, *South Pole*, vol. 1, 370.
44. Cherry-Garrard, *Worst Journey*, 571–76; M. Stroud, Physiological Report, in Mear and Swan, *A Walk to the Pole*, 285–91; A. F. Rogers, The death of Petty Officer Evans, *Practitioner*, 212 (1974), 570–80.
45. Evans, *South with Scott*, 241; Scott, *Scott's Last Expedition*, vol. 1, 531.

46. C. C. Peterson, K. A. Nagy, and J. Diamond, Sustained metabolic scope, *Proceedings of the National Academy of Sciences* 87 (1990), 2324–28; K. A. Hammond and J. Diamond, Maximal sustained energy budgets in humans and animals, *Nature* 386 (1997), 457–62.

47. W. Lashly, *The Diary of W. Lashly* (Reading: University of Reading Fine Art Department, 1938), 24; Scott, *Scott's Last Expedition*, vol. 1, 587.

48. A. Cherry-Garrard, Foreword to Seaver, *Edward Wilson of the Antarctic*, xxi; Priestley, Scott tragedy; Priestley, Scott's northern party.

49. K. J. Carpenter, *The History of Scurvy and Vitamin C* (Cambridge: Cambridge University Press, 1986), 173–97.

50. Ibid., 200–203.

51. E. J. C. Kendall, Scurvy during some British polar expeditions, *Polar Record* 7 (1955), 467–85; A. Hoygaard and H. Rasmussen, Vitamin C sources in Eskimo food, *Nature* 143 (1939), 943.

52. Kendall, Scurvy during some British polar expeditions.

53. S. Davidson, A. P. Meiklejohn, and R. Passmore, *Human Nutrition and Dietetics* (Baltimore: Williams and Wilkins, 1959), 314–16, 448–53; J. S. Garrow and W. P. T. James, *Human Nutrition and Dietetics* (Edinburgh: Churchill Livingstone, 1993), 254–56; 310–11; R. J. Jarrett, *Nutrition and Disease* (Baltimore: University Park Press, 1979), 110–13; compare with interpretation given in Huntford, *Last Place on Earth*, 476, 545.

54. Cherry-Garrard, *Worst Journey*, 205–6; Cherry-Garrard, *Postscript to Worst Journey*, 594.

55. Gwynn, *Captain Scott*, 211.

56. Mear and Swan, *A Walk to the Pole*, 46.

57. J. L. Hallock, Profile: Thomas Crean, *Polar Record* 22 (1985), 665–78.

58. Evans, British Antarctic Expedition.

59. Cherry-Garrard, *Postscript to the Worst Journey in the World*, 604.

13 A Chillingly Unusual Month

1. S. Solomon and C. Stearns, On the role of the weather in the deaths of R. F. Scott and his companions, *Proceedings of the National Academy of Sciences*, 96 (1999), 13012–16.

2. Simpson, *Meteorology*, vol. 1.

3. Simpson, *Meteorology*, vol. 1, 15–21.

4. G. C. Simpson, Collection of Simpson letters and papers, Archives, U. K. Meteorological Office, Bracknell, England.

5. Pound, *Evans of the Broke*, 130; Simpson, Letters and papers.

6. Simpson, *Meteorology*, vol. 1, 19–21.

7. Ibid., 16–17.

8. Meteorological log book of the polar party, Archives, Scott Polar Research Institute, Cambridge.

9. C. S. Wright and G. C. Simpson, Correspondence, Archives, U. K. Meteorological Office, Bracknell, England.

10. Quotation: Simpson, Letters and papers.

11. S. G. Warren, Antarctica, in *Encyclopedia of Climate and Weather* (Oxford: Oxford University Press, 1996), 32–39.

12. R. E. Priestley, The Scott tragedy, *Geographical Journal* 68 (1926), 340–43.

13. H. R. Bowers, Letter to E. Bowers, October 27, 1911, Archives, Scott Polar Research Institute, Cambridge.

14. G. C. Simpson, Diary, November 26, 1911, Archives, Scott Polar Research Institute, Cambridge.

15. Shackleton's meteorological log transcript can be found in Archives, Scott Polar Research Institute, Cambridge; one data point from Scott's trek on March 6, 1912, was omitted from Simpson, *Meteorology*, vol. 3, but was included here based on the original log book in the Scott Polar Research Institute, Cambridge, archives.

16. Scott, *Scott's Last Expedition*, vol. 1, 585.

17. L. E. Oates, Letter to his mother, October 28, 1911, Archives, Scott Polar Research Institute, Cambridge.

18. Scott, *Scott's Last Expedition*, vol. 1, 593–94.

19. Simpson, *Meteorology*, vol. 1, 22–32.

20. Simpson, *Scott's Polar Journey and the Weather*, 23–30; see also *Nature*, 111 (1923), 758–59.

21. Cherry-Garrard, *Worst Journey*, 594.

22. Simpson, *Meteorology*, vol. 1, 22–32.

23. Scott, *Scott's Last Expedition*, vol. 1, 586–90.

24. Ibid., 575, 584, 588, 590, 594.

25. Simpson, *Scott's Polar Journey*, 26–27; Priestley, The Scott tragedy.

26. Lind and Sanders, *Physics of Skiing*, 169–79; S. C. Colbeck, The kinetic friction of snow, *Journal of Glaciology* 34 (1988), 78–86.

27. Cherry-Garrard, *Worst Journey*, 565.

28. D. G. Vaughan and C. S. M. Doake, Recent atmospheric warming and retreat of ice shelves on the Antarctic Peninsula, *Nature* 379 (1996), 328–30; J. C. King, Recent climate variability in the vicinity of the Antarctic Peninsula, *International Journal of Climatology* 14 (1994), 357–69.

29. P. D. Jones, Recent variations in mean temperature and the diurnal temperature range in the Antarctic, *Geophysical Research Letters* 22 (1995), 1345–48; J. Sansom, Antarctic surface temperature time series, *Journal of Climate* 2 (1989), 1164–72.

30. P. D. Jones, Antarctic temperatures over the present century: A study of the early expeditionary record, *Journal of Climate* 3 (1990), 1193–1203.

31. Simpson, Letters and papers.

32. Simpson, *Meteorology*, vol. 1, 201–5.

33. G. T. Walker, Correlation in seasonal variations of weather, *Memoirs of the India*

Meteorological Department 24, part 4 (1923), 75–131, and part 9 (1924), 275–332; see the review in R. Allan, J. Lindesay, and D. Parker, *El Niño Southern Oscillation and Climate Variability* (Collingwood, Australia: CSIRO, 1996), 3–25.

34. G. T. Walker and E. W. Bliss, World Weather IV, *Memoirs of the Royal Meteorological Society* 3 (1930), 81–95.

35. S. R. Smith and C. R. Stearns, Antarctic pressure and temperature anomalies surrounding the minimum in the Southern Oscillation Index, *Journal of Geophysical Research* 98 (1993), 13071–83.

36. X. G. Zhang and T. M. Casey, Long-term variations in the Southern Oscillation and relationships with Australian rainfall, *Australian Meteorological Magazine* 40 (1992), 211–25.

37. D. H. Bromwich and A. N. Rogers, The El Niño Southern Oscillation modulation of West Antarctic precipitation, *Antarctic Research Series* 77 (2001), 91–103; E. Isaksson, Climate records from shallow firn cores, Dronning Maud Land, Antarctica, Ph.D. diss., Stockholm University, 1994; see also the review in J. C. King and J. Turner, *Antarctic Meteorology and Climatology* (Cambridge: Cambridge University Press, 1997), 359–69.

38. P. Gloersen, Modulation of hemispheric sea-ice cover by ENSO events, *Nature* 373 (1993), 503–6; W. B. White and R. Peterson, An Antarctic circumpolar wave in surface pressure, wind, temperature, and sea ice extent, *Nature*, 380 (1996), 699–702.

39. W. Cai, P. G. Baines, and H. B. Gordon, Southern mid- to high-latitude variability, a zonal wavenumber-3 pattern, and the Antarctic circumpolar wave in the CSIRO coupled model, *Journal of Climate* 12 (1999), 3087–3104.

40. Simpson, *Scott's Polar Journey*, 28.

41. Scott, *Scott's Last Expedition*, vol. 1, 605–7.

42. R. F. Scott, Last letter to Sir George Edgerton, Archives, Scott Polar Research Institute, Cambridge.

43. Wright, *Silas*, 372–75; Priestley, The Scott tragedy.

44. Wright, *Silas*, 28.

45. Gran, *Norwegian with Scott*, 88.

46. D. E. Pedgley, Pen portraits of presidents—Sir George Clarke Simpson, KCB, FRS, *Weather* 50 (1995), 349.

47. E. Gold, George Clarke Simpson, *Biographical Memoirs of the Fellows of the Royal Society* 11 (1965), 157–75.

14 The Winds of Chance and Choice

1. Scott, *Scott's Last Expedition*, vol. 1, 595.

2. Priestley, *Antarctic Adventure: Scott's Northern Party*, 216.

3. Simpson, *Meteorology*, vol. 1, 129.

4. Ibid., 128–31.

5. T. R. Parish and D. H. Bromwich, The surface windfield over the Antarctic ice sheets, *Nature* 328 (1987), 51–54.
6. Simpson, *Meteorology*, vol. 3, 612.
7. C. R. Stearns and G. A. Weidner, Climatic differences in Antarctica from automated weather stations, *Third Conference on Polar Meteorology and Oceanography*, American Meteorological Society, Boston (1992), 111–14.
8. W. Schwerdtfeger, *Weather and Climate of the Antarctic* (Amsterdam: Elsevier, 1984), 94–96; C. J. Breckenridge et al., Katabatic winds along the Transantarctic Mountains, *Antarctic Research Series* 61 (1993), 69–92.
9. Scott, *Scott's Last Expedition*, vol. 1, 585.
10. Simpson, *Meteorology*, vol. 3, 634–42.
11. Scott, *Scott's Last Expedition*, vol. 1, 551–53, 635.
12. Ibid.; H. R. Bowers, Diary entry for January 21, 1912, Archives, Scott Polar Research Institute, Cambridge.
13. Bowers, Diary entry, January 21, 1912.
14. Simpson, *Meteorology*, vol. 3, 15.
15. H. R. Bowers, Last letter to his mother, Archives, Scott Polar Research Institute, Cambridge; also reproduced in Seaver, *Birdie Bowers of the Antarctic*, 262.
16. Scott, *Scott's Last Expedition*, vol. 1, 595.
17. Wilson, *Diary of the Discovery Expedition*, 105.
18. Simpson, *Meteorology*, vol. 3, 678.
19. E. L. Atkinson, Last efforts before the winter, in *Scott's Last Expedition*, vol. 2, 309.
20. Scott, *Scott's Last Expedition*, vol. 1, 594; Gwynn, *Captain Scott*, 222.
21. Seaver, *Edward Wilson of the Antarctic*, 216–17.
22. Scott, *Scott's Last Expedition*, vol. 1, 594.
23. Seaver, *Birdie Bowers of the Antarctic*, 262.
24. Wilson, *Diary of the Terra Nova Expedition*, 157.
25. Seaver, *Birdie Bowers of the Antarctic*, 217.
26. Wilson, *Diary of the Terra Nova Expedition*, 246–47.
27. P. Keohane, Original diary of the Terra Nova expedition, Archives, Scott Polar Research Institute, Cambridge.
28. R. F. Scott, Undated letter to Joseph James Kinsey. MS-Papers-0022-66. Alexander Turnbull Library, NLNZ; see also Scott, *Scott's Last Expedition*, vol. 1, 602.
29. Scott, *Scott's Last Expedition*, vol. 1, 590.
30. Gwynn, *Captain Scott*, 222.
31. Scott, *Scott's Last Expedition*, vol. 1, 604.
32. Huntford, *Last Place on Earth*, 506–9.
33. E. A. Wilson, Last letters to Oriana Wilson, transcripts in Archives, Scott Polar Research Institute, Cambridge.
34. Huntford, *Last Place on Earth*, 528.

35. Scott, *Scott's Last Expedition*, vol. 1, 595.

36. Wilson, *Diary of the Discovery Expedition*, 150.

37. H. R. Bowers, Original letter to his mother from winter quarters, November 1, 1911, Archives, Scott Polar Research Institute, Cambridge; see also Seaver, *Birdie Bowers of the Antarctic*, 227.

38. Scott, *Scott's Last Expedition*, vol. 1, 607.

GLOSSARY

Accuracy Quality of being true and correct. Not to be confused with PRECISION in scientific data.

Anemometer Instrument to measure the speed of the wind.

Balaclava Cloth head and neck covering, usually of wool, with one large hole exposing the eyes and upper nose.

Barrier Now known as the Ross Ice Shelf. Large inland sea, covered in snow and ice, with an average height above sea level of about 200 feet (see maps 1, page 7, and 4, page 28).

Calving Breaking or splintering of ice, typically glaciers or ice shelves, to produce a detached iceberg or floe.

Crevasse Fissure in ice or snow. Can be as deep as hundreds of yards or more on the Beardmore glacier.

Elevation (of sun) Angle between the sun and the horizon.

Fahrenheit (°F) Temperature scale employed by Scott's expeditions, still the common scale in the United States. Another scale used in most other parts of the world is the Celsius or Centigrade scale (°C). Water freezes at 32°F, which is 0°C. °F = 1.8 × °C + 32. For the reader's ease in examining temperature data in this book, the following table may be helpful:

Temperatures	°F	°C	°F	°C
	30	−1	−30	−34
	15	−9	−45	−43
	0	−18	−60	−51
	−15	−26		

369

Finnesko Boots made entirely of soft fur. Often lined with sennegrass, an Arctic plant that absorbs moisture well.

Fodder Food for livestock. Scott's fodder was mainly made from wheat, cut green and pressed.

Hoosh Stew, usually made from PEMMICAN and melted snow; a primary food on the sledging trail.

Hypsometer An instrument used to determine pressure, based upon measurement of the temperature at which water boils.

Icefall Similar to a waterfall, but frozen. A steep fall or flow of ice, sometimes from great heights.

Icefoot Fringe of ice at shoreline, common in Antarctica.

Jamesway Canvas structure supported by wood and lined with rubber. Has a curved roof and is mounted on a wooden platform. Sometimes used to house today's participants in the United States Antarctic program.

Katabatic Type of wind in which air flows down a slope.

Lower deck Collective noun used to describe enlisted men in the navy, who are generally housed on the lower deck of the ship.

Man-hauling The pulling of supplies by men, usually on a wooden sledge fitted with a canvas harness.

Miles (geographic) Also called nautical miles. Unit of distance equal to 1/60th of a degree of latitude, 15 percent longer than the common (statute) mile.

Miles (statute) Unit of distance on land equal to 5,280 feet or 1,760 yards.

Paraffin Hydrocarbon fuel, kerosene.

Pemmican Mixture of precooked dried meat and lard used as a mainstay of the diet on the polar sledging trail (see HOOSH).

Picket To fasten or tether an animal to a stake or post.

Polynya Area of open water in an otherwise ice-covered sea, often caused by the strong flow of warm winds.

Precision The extent to which multiple measurements of the same quantity agree with one another. Low precision generally indicates that the scatter in data is instrumental rather than real; high precision implies instrument consistency. Compare ACCURACY.

Primus Innovative camp stove designed by Fridtjof Nansen, generally of aluminum. An outer ring was used to melt snow for tea or cocoa, while an inner pot was used to melt snow to be mixed with PEMMICAN to produce HOOSH.

Refraction (of light) Bending of rays due to temperature variations within the atmosphere. Refraction affects the ACCURACY of measurement of position using a THEODOLITE or SEXTANT sight of the sun or other object.

Rotten ice Ice that appears solid but is not.

Runners Long strips of wood or metal-covered wood upon which sledges ride.

Sastrugi Furrows, often as deep as several feet, caused by the action of the wind on snow.

Sea ice Layer of ice on the surface of the sea that breaks up at least annually.

Sextant Astronomical device used to measure elevation of sun, moon, stars, or planets to determine latitude and longitude. Usually hand-held.

Skua Aggressive bird common to coastal areas of Antarctica, similar in appearance to a seagull.

Sledge Sled with wooden runners, typically ten to twelve feet long, used to transport supplies in polar regions.

Sledgemeter Wheel used to measure distance traveled by SLEDGE.

Snow bridge Snow that has filled the gap in a CREVASSE. Often strong enough to support weight, allowing passage across the gap.

Theodolite Precision astronomical instrument used to measure ELEVATION and horizontal angles of sun, moon, stars, or planets to determine latitude and longitude. Usually mounted on a tripod.

Upper deck Collective noun used to describe officers and scientists on Scott's expedition.

Personal Accounts

Amundsen, R. *The South Pole: An Account of the Norwegian Antarctic Expedition in the Fram, 1910–1912.* London: John Murray, 1912; rpt. London: Hurst, 1996.

Cherry-Garrard, A. *The Worst Journey in the World.* London: Constable, 1922; rpt. New York: Carroll and Graf, 1997.

Debenham, F. *In the Antarctic: Stories of Scott's Last Expedition.* London: John Murray, 1952.

———. *The Quiet Land: The Antarctic Diaries of Frank Debenham,* J. D. Back, ed. Norfolk: Bluntisham, 1992.

Evans, E. R. G. R. *South with Scott.* London: Collins, 1921.

Gran, T. *The Norwegian with Scott.* London: Her Majesty's Stationery Office, 1984.

Lashly, W. *The Diary of W. Lashly.* Reading: Fine Art Department, 1939.

Markham, C. *Antarctic Obsession: A Personal Narrative of the Origins of the British National Antarctic Expedition, 1901–1904.* Norfolk: Bluntisham, 1986.

Ponting, H. G. *The Great White South,* 7th ed. London: Duckworth, 1921.

Scott, R. F. *Scott's Last Expedition: Being the Journals of Captain R. F. Scott, R. N., C. V. O.,* 5th ed. 2 vols. London: Smith, Elder, 1914.

———. *The Voyage of the "Discovery."* London: John Murray, 1905; rpt. 1929.

Shackleton, E. H. *The Heart of the Antarctic: Being the Story of the British*

Antarctic Expedition, 1907–1909. London: William Heinemann, 1909; new popular ed., 1932.

Taylor, G. *With Scott: The Silver Lining*. London: Smith, Elder, 1916; rpt. Norfolk: Bluntisham, 1997.

Wilson, E. A. *Diary of the Discovery Expedition to the Antarctic, 1901–1904*. Poole: Blandford, 1975.

———. *Diary of the Terra Nova Expedition to the Antarctic, 1910–1912*. Poole: Blandford, 1972.

Wright, C. *Silas: The Antarctic Diaries and Memoir of Charles S. Wright*. Columbus: Ohio State University Press, 1993.

Biographies

Gwynn, S. *Captain Scott*. London: John Lane, 1929.

Huxley, E. *Scott of the Antarctic*. New York: Atheneum, 1978.

Limb, S., and P. Cordingley. *Captain Oates: Soldier and Explorer*. London: Leo Cooper, 1982; rev. ed. 1995.

Pound, R. *Evans of the Broke: A Biography of Admiral Lord Mountevans*. London: Oxford University Press, 1963.

Seaver, G. *Birdie Bowers of the Antarctic*. London: John Murray, rpt. 1951.

———. *Edward Wilson of the Antarctic*. London: John Murray, rpt. 1963.

———. *Scott of the Antarctic: A Study in Character*. London: John Murray, 1940.

Historical Analyses of the *Terra Nova* and *Discovery* Expeditions

Baughman, T. H. *Pilgrims on the Ice*. Lincoln: University of Nebraska Press, 1999.

Hayes, J. G. *Antarctica: A Treatise on the Southern Continent*. London: Richards, 1928.

Huntford, R. *The Last Place on Earth*. New York: Atheneum, 1986.

———. *Scott and Amundsen*. London: Pan, 1979.

Preston, D. *A First Rate Tragedy: Robert Falcon Scott and the Race to the South Pole*. Boston: Houghton Mifflin, 1998.

Thomson, D. *Scott's Men*. London: Allen Lane, 1977.

Yelverton, D. *Antarctica Unveiled: Scott's First Expedition and the Quest for the Unknown Continent*. Boulder: University Press of Colorado, 2000.

Science and Medicine

Carpenter, K. J. *The History of Scurvy and Vitamin C.* Cambridge: Cambridge University Press, 1986.

Committee on Military Nutrition Research. *Nutritional Needs in Cold and in High-Altitude Environments.* Washington, D.C.: National Academy Press, 1996.

Lind, D., and S. P. Sanders. *The Physics of Skiing: Skiing at the Triple Point.* Woodbury, N.Y.: American Institute of Physics, 1997.

Schwerdtfeger, W. *Weather and Climate of the Antarctic.* Amsterdam: Elsevier, 1984.

Simpson, G. C. *British Antarctic Expedition, 1910–1913, Meteorology,* vol. 1, *Discussion.* Calcutta: Thacker, Spink, 1919.

———. *British Antarctic Expedition, 1910–1913, Meteorology,* vol. 3, *Tables.* London: Harrison and Sons, 1923.

———. *Scott's Polar Journey and the Weather.* Oxford: Clarendon, 1926.

Internet Resources

Locations as of June 2000; see www.coldestmarch.com for updates.

Antarctic automatic weather stations and other climatic data (http://uwamrc. ssec.wisc.edu/aws/awsproj.html).

OMB Sea Ice Analysis History Page (http://polar.wwb.noaa.gov/seaice/ Historical.html).

Satellite imagery of Antarctica (http://TerraWeb.wr.usgs.gov/TRS/projects/ Antarctica/AVHRR.html).

INDEX

Boldface type indicates photographs, illustrations, and maps.